A Charlton Standard Catalogue

Royal Doulton Animals

Fourth Edition

By
Jean Dale

Introduction
by
Louise Irvine

W. K. Cross
Publisher

The Charlton Press

Toronto, Ontario • Palm Harbor, Florida

Library and Archives Canada Cataloguing in Publication

Royal Doulton animals : a Charlton standard catalogue

Biennial.
4th ed.-
Continues: Charlton standard catalogue of Royal Doulton animals.
ISSN 1714-0005
ISBN 0-88968-295-X (4th edition)

1. Royal Doulton figurines--Catalogs. 2. Porcelain animals--Catalogs.

NK4660.C502   738.8'2'02942   C2004-907165-3

**Printed in Canada
in the Province of Ontario**

The Charlton Press

Visit us at www.charltonpress.com

EDITORIAL

Author / Editor	Jean Dale
Editorial Assistant	Susan Cross
Graphic Technician	Davina Rowan

ACKNOWLEDGEMENTS

The Charlton Press wishes to thank those who have helped and assisted with the fourth edition of "The Charlton Standard Catalogue of Royal Doulton Animals."

SPECIAL THANKS

The publisher would like to thank: **Louise Irvine** for writing the introduction to this publication. Louise is an independent writer and lecturer on Royal Doulton's history and products and is not connected with the pricing of this catalogue.

Our thanks go to the staff of Royal Doulton, who have helped with additional technical information and images; especially **Sarah Williams**, Senior Product Manager, **Chetna Luthar**, Production Manager (U.K.); **Marion Proctor**, Marketing Manager, **Tricia Clemens**, Public Relations Manager, **Paula Bell**, Products Manager (Canada); **Janet Drift**, Director Retail Sales and **Joseph Schmidt**, Associate Product Manager (U.S.A.).

CONTRIBUTORS TO THE FOURTH EDITION

The Publisher would like to thank the following individuals or companies who graciously supplied photographs or allowed us access to their collections for photographic purposes. We offer sincere thanks to:

John Fornaszewski, Granite City, Illinois; **Ed Pascoe**, Pascoe and Co., Coral Gables, Florida; **Arron Rimpley and Gregg Whittecar**, Whitley Collection, North Miami, Florida; **Joseph Schenberg**, St. Louis, Missouri;

A SPECIAL NOTE TO COLLECTORS

We welcome and appreciate any comments or suggestions in regard to "The Charlton Standard Catalogue of Royal Doulton Animals." If any errors or omissions come to your attention, please do not hesitate to write to us, or if you would like to participate in pricing or supply previously unavailable data or information, please contact Jean Dale at (416) 488-1418, or e-mail us at **chpress@charltonpress.com**.

DISCLAIMER

While every care has been taken to ensure accuracy in the compilation of the data in this catalogue, the publisher cannot accept responsibility for typographical errors.

The Charlton Press

Editorial Office
P. O. Box 820, Station Willowdale B
North York, Ontario M2K 2R1
Telephone (416) 488 1418 Fax: (416) 488-4656
Telephone (800) 442-6042 Fax: (800) 442-1542
E-mail: chpress@charltonpress.com www.charltonpress.com

PRICING, OLD, NEW AND THE INTERNET

Over the past thirty years we gathered pricing information from auctions, dealer submissions, direct mail catalogues and newsletters and all contributed prices on one of two levels, wholesale or retail. We at the Charlton Press, consider auctions basically a dealer affair, with price lists, naturally retail. To equate both prices we needed to adjust the auction results upward by a margin of 30% to 40%, thus allowing for dealer markups before comparing and then looking for a consensus on a retail price.

The marketplace has changed, the Internet on-line auctions are growing at such a rate that all other pricing sources we used are being completely overwhelmed by the sheer volume of items being offered for sale.

At a moment in time on November 15th, 2004, under the category 'Royal Doulton Animals" over 1,000 individual items were posted for sale on e-Bay. Assuming this is an average day, then for the week 7,000 items are offered, and for the year nearly 364,000 will be offered for sale. The "Economist," a weekly news magazine, put on-line auctions with over 100,000,000 registered users.

The impact the Internet will have on collectables has yet to be appreciated by collectors and dealers alike. All the old avenues such as fairs, shows, dealer stores, retail outlets, direct mail houses and auction rooms are being forced to change due to the extreme pressure of this new marketing force. Margins have come under pressure, wholesale and retail prices are starting to blend, and competition for the collectors' budget will intensify. However, through it all one point remains, a price guide is just that, a guide, and the final say is between the buyer and the seller.

HOW TO USE THIS CATALOGUE

THE PURPOSE

As with other catalogues in Charlton's Royal Doulton reference and pricing library, this publication has been designed to serve two specific purposes. First, to furnish the Royal Doulton enthusiast with accurate listings containing vital information and photographs to aid in the building of a rewarding collection. Secondly, this publication provides Royal Doulton collectors and dealers with current market prices for Royal Doulton Animals. Jugs are covered in "The Charlton Standard Catalogue of Royal Doulton Jug," and figures are covered in "The Charlton Standard Catalogue of Royal Doulton Figurines."

STYLE AND VARIATIONS

On the pages that follow, Royal Doulton animals are listed, illustrated and described in HN number order.

STYLES: When two or more animals have the same name but different physical modelling characteristics, they are listed as Style One, Style Two, and so on. Such animals will also have a different HN number.

VARIATIONS: Slight design alterations in a mould for any reason is considered a variation. In variations the HN number assigned will not change. Colourways (change in colouring) are also termed variations.

STATISTICS

D Number:	D numbers are the design numbers assigned to items manufactured by Royal Doulton. This number carries throughout the early part of animal production.
HN Number:	The animals with HN numbers flow from HN 7 to HN 4706
Height:	Stated in inches and centimetres
Issue Date:	Dates of production
Colourway:	Colours of the animal figure
Backstamp:	Maker's marks
Pricing:	Market pricing in three currencies, U.K. Pounds, U.S. dollars, and Canadian dollars.
Images:	Although the publisher has made every attempt to obtain and photograph all animals and their varieties, several pieces, naturally, have not come into the publisher's view and thus original images are not available. In this case, if an image of another colourway is available, that image will be used for shape recognition purposes.

TABLE OF CONTENTS

INTRODUCTION
by Louise Irvine

THE HISTORY OF ROYAL DOULTON ANIMALS

The Doulton company was founded in 1815 and the first animal models were produced at their factory in Lambeth, London during the 1880s. New models were introduced occasionally until the Lambeth factory closed in 1956.

In the early 1900s, at Royal Doulton's factory in Burslem, Stoke-on-Trent, Charles Noke modelled several animal models to be decorated with flambé glazes. Noke, who became the company's Art Director, also modelled some animals dressed as humans for Doulton's famous HN collection which was launched in 1913. The 'HN' numbering system refers to Harry Nixon, who was in charge of the new figure painting department.

Over the years, a number of in-house and freelance sculptors have contributed to the animals collection and modelling styles have varied from highly realistic with textured fur and feathers, as in the DA collection of the 1980s, to contemporary stylized, as in the Images of Nature and Fire collections. Miniature animals were produced for the K series in the 1930s.

BUILDING A COLLECTION

Since 1908, more than 1,000 animals have been introduced to the HN, DA, RDA, BA and K series and these are now avidly collected in many parts of the world, Most collectors specialise in one category or another as it would be virtually impossible to acquire them all. Fox collectors can have a field day chasing more than a dozen models in various sizes, whilst elephant collectors can look out for at least ten types in lots of different sizes, colours and glazes, including flambé and Chinese Jade. No doubt there are other collectors pursuing rabbits, monkeys or pigs but some of the most popular collecting categories are discussed in detail below.

MAKING ROYAL DOULTON ANIMALS

Many different creative processes are involved in the production of Royal Doulton animals but essentially they all start the same way with an image in the designer's mind. If the model is to represent a specific breed then the artist will visit the stable, kennel or farm to study the animal in detail. Many photographs will be taken for reference and sometimes sketches will be made of important details. Having decided on the most appropriate pose, the modeller will set to work in clay, recreating the personality of his subject, as well as the precise details of its bone structure, muscles and finally the texture of its skin, fur or feathers. Even if the sculpture is destined for the stylised Images of Nature collection, the artist must study the animal in action to capture the essence of its character and abstract the leading lines of the design.

When the original clay sculpture has been completed and approved, the block maker will divide the model into appropriate sections in order to make the master mould. A few prototype pieces will be cast from this mould to produce colour trials and, once these have been approved by the marketing, design and production teams, together with the animal's owner, working moulds will be made of plaster of Paris.

Over the years both earthenware and bone china have been used to make animals at Royal Doulton's factories in Stoke-on-Trent. Bone china is a traditionally British body, with a high proportion of bone ash, which creates the much admired translucency when the body is fired to a high temperature.

Earthenware is fired at a lower temperature than china and remains porous. Earthenware is usually painted under the glaze and bone china on top, creating different decorative effects. In the early 1900s, the same models were often offered in both bodies. From the early 1970s until 2002 earthenware models were made at the John Beswick factory which had a long tradition in animal production. Bone china models were made at the Royal Doulton factory in Burslem until 2004.

Different ingredients and firing techniques are used to produce the two ceramic bodies but the casting process is the same. Liquid clay, known as slip, is poured into the plaster of Paris moulds and, once the body has set to the required thickness, the excess slip is poured out. The pieces are carefully removed from the mould as the clay is still very fragile at this stage and the various parts are jointed together using slip as an adhesive. The seams are then gently sponged away by a process known as fettling and the piece is ready for its first firing, during which the water is driven off and it shrinks to its 'biscuit' state.

Earthenware animal models are decorated at this stage by a combination of spraying and hand painting. For instance, a horse model will have its coat sprayed to the required colour and then all the details, such as head, mane, tail, hooves, etc. will be painted by hand. The Connoisseur collection obviously has a high proportion of hand painting to recreate the animal's distinctive markings, for example the leopard's spots in 'The Watering Hole' DA39 and the variegated plumage on the 'Barn Owl' DA1. Once the painted decoration has dried, some animals are finished with a matt glaze to best capture their natural appearance. Others are coated with a high gloss glaze, creating a typical ceramic look when fired. In some cases the same models are offered with a choice of glaze effects.

Bone china animals are dipped or sprayed with liquid glaze and then fired again before decoration. In the past these would then have been hand painted by specialists in on-glaze colours. However, most of the bone china figures produced today are for the Burslem Artwares collection and they are finished in flambé glazes.

A complex process is used to create the flambé effect and the precise recipe is still a closely guarded secret. The unglazed pieces are taken to the flambé studios in their biscuit state and the features are painted in touches of blue, which will eventually shine through the flambé glaze. The flame effect on larger pieces is achieved by arranging thin strands of hemp over the piece to act as a template and then spraying on various colours. The hemp is removed leaving a unique veined effect and the piece then undergoes the various flambé glaze and firing procedures. In the final stage the kiln is deprived of oxygen which results in the fiery red finish.

CURRENT AND DISCONTINUED ANIMALS

Animals which are produced at the Royal Doulton factories today are referred to as 'current' and most of the range can be purchased in specialist china shops or from mail order companies. Royal Doulton publishes catalogues of their general range and these are obtainable from their Headquarters in England or their distribution companies around the world. Occasionally models have been commissioned exclusively for independent organisations and distribution of these varies. Doulton-Direct, the direct mail division of Royal Doulton, publishes an annual catalogue for their customers which often features animal offers. The Royal

Doulton International Collectors Club usually publishes details of these private commissions in their quarterly magazine 'Gallery' and they may have, on occasion, offered animal models exclusively to their members. They also provide information on new introductions to the general range and the pieces being withdrawn to make way for the new models.

Once a piece has been withdrawn from production, it is referred to as 'discontinued' or 'retired' and it enters the secondary market. Many dealers around the world carry discontinued Royal Doulton animals as part of their general stock but some specialise in the field more than others. They regularly exhibit at antique fairs, some of which are exclusively for Royal Doulton products, and many run mail order services. Specialist animal dealers will often help collectors find specific models but it is still fun to scour general antique fairs and flea markets in case there are animals to be found. Auction rooms and estate sales sometimes feature Royal Doulton animals and successful purchases can be made if there is the time to view the lots, armed with techniques for spotting restorations and a good knowledge of prices.

Collecting Dogs

Dogs are by far the most collectable animals in the Royal Doulton range. Appealing puppies cocking their ears, playing with bones or rolling on their backs were amongst the first models and it would appear that Art Director Charles Noke was more concerned with the character of the dog than its pedigree. This has led to some confusion in identifying the various breeds represented in the early years, for example HN 127 has often been listed as a Pekinese but Noke's notebook describes it as a Blenheim Spaniel, in other words a liver and white coloured Cavalier King Charles. The conformation of this breed has altered over the years and in the early 1900s it had a flatter muzzle like the Pekinese hence the confusion. Another puzzle is HN 231 which some dog experts say looks most like an English St. Bernard and others a foxhound. To confuse matters even more the pattern books describe it variously as a setter and a bloodhound. Whatever the breeds, these early models are hard to find and would be welcomed in most dog collections.

The most desirable Royal Doulton breed is undoubtedly the bulldog, which has been portrayed in many different guises. During the First World War, the breed symbolised the dogged determination of the British people and is now regarded as the country's national animal. Bulldogs, patriotically draped with the Union Jack, were introduced at the end of the 1914-18 war and they were reintroduced during World War Two in three sizes, D5913A, B and C. Cartoons of the period picked up the breed's resemblance to Winston Churchill and Charles Noke responded with new versions of the Union Jack bulldog smoking a cigar and wearing a derby hat or Trinity cap in the manner of the great war leader. The popularity of the great British bulldog has ensured its widespread use in advertising and there are several rare Royal Doulton models promoting various brands of drinks. Bar accessories, such as ashpots and match holders, were modelled in the form of bulldog's heads and sometimes complete miniature dogs are posed on top of bowls or pintrays. Keen canine collectors often seek out all the different types of dog derivatives which were produced in the 1920s and 30s. Various breeds were adapted to decorate tobacco jars, ashtrays, bookends, calendars, pen holders, wall plaques, and brooches and they are all hard to find today.

Terriers seem to have been the most popular type of dogs with Doulton artists in the mid 1920s and from HN 900 onwards they produced a succession of Fox Terriers, Scottish Terriers, Sealyhams and Airedales in standing or seated poses. Most were offered in a choice of colourings and, although they might not have the same amount of detail as the later Championship series, they are still very collectable and it is quite a challenge to complete the series as most had disappeared from the range by 1946. The rarest terrier of all is the white 'West Highland Terrier' HN 1048 which seems to have been produced for one year only in 1931. It is very similar to the 'Cairn Terrier' HN 1104 in the Championship series but the head is at a different angle and the ears are smaller.

New standards were set for Royal Doulton dog sculptures when the celebrated animal artist Frederick Daws became involved in the collection. He strove for complete accuracy in his representations of named champions and he liaised with the breeders on precise details of conformation. Most of his portraits are in show poses but occasionally he modelled the same dog sitting or lying, although these were not promoted with the champion names. The first show dog to join the range was 'Lucky Star of Ware' HN 1000, a blue roan Cocker Spaniel, which was twice overall champion at Crufts in 1930 and 1931. Later models feature the name 'Lucky Pride of Ware' - perhaps the owner had reservations about the change of colouring to plain black. Another name change occurred with the Rough Haired Terrier 'Crackley Starter' HN 1007 who is also known as 'Crackley Hunter.'

When Frederick Daws retired, other artists contributed to the series. Peggy Davies modelled the Doberman Pinscher 'Rancho Dobe's Storm' HN 2645 and the French Poodle HN 2631, which was originally going to be offered in a plain white decoration in three different sizes HN 2625-7, but in the end only one model was introduced. Perhaps Peggy was responsible for the Chow champion 'T'Sioh of Kin-Shan' HN 2628-30 but judging from the scarcity of this model it is doubtful if it actually went into production. The last championship dog in this series was the black labrador 'Bumblekite of Mansergh' HN 2667 modelled by John Bromley in 1967.

After a gap of some years, dogs became an important part of the Royal Doulton range again in the 1980s. Many breeds originally modelled for the Beswick backstamp were transferred to the DA series in 1989, and the design team at the Beswick studios regularly introduced new subjects, including a charming series of dogs and their puppies. In 1993, Graham Tongue revived the idea of modelling famous dogs with his portrait of 'Mick the Miller' DA 214, the famous 1930s racing greyhound, which was the first ever limited edition dog in the collection

Collecting Cats

Feline fanciers are well served in the Royal Doulton collection with around 40 cat models to find in various colours and glaze effects. The earliest is model number 9 which was issued in flambé in 1908 and was also offered for a while in naturalistic colours as HN 109. Collectors can choose from miscellaneous moggies or pedigree Persians (HN 999) and Siamese (HN 2655). There are playful cats about to pounce on unsuspecting mice (HN 203) as well as studies of these popular pets in an equally familiar pose, catnapping on the best seat of the house (HN 210). The antics of a kitten inspired one of the most popular series ever (HN 2579 - 84) and the artist, Peggy Davies, recalled that her model threatened to cause havoc in the studio, weaving in and out of Charles Noke's precious flambé vases. Fortunately he was an animal lover and welcomed the kitten's invasion.

Two of the cats in the HN collection were inspired by famous cartoon characters; 'Kateroo,' the creation of David Souter, who appeared in the Sydney Bulletin and little 'Ooloo' from George Studdy's comic strips of the 1920s, who is perhaps better known to collectors as 'Lucky' from the miniature K series. Other miniature cats, less than one inch tall, were included in the HN collection but these are very hard to find today. At the other end of the scale, Alan Maslankowski modelled a large stylised cat, 11 ½ inches tall, for the flambé range in 1977 and he has produced models for the DA series, the haughty 'Cat (Walking)' DA 148 and 'Cat (Stalking)' DA 149. 'The Cat with Bandaged Paw' DA 195, which was introduced by Martyn Alcock in 1992, takes a new sentimental approach and tugs at the heartstrings of all cat lovers. The detailed, realistic approach in the DA series contrasts greatly with the modern streamlined sculptures 'Shadowplay' HN 3526 and 'Playtime' HN 3544 in the Images range and ensures that Royal Doulton's interpretations of cats are as varied as the animals themselves.

Collecting Horses

Royal Doulton was the name of the first horse portrayed in the HN collection. Owned by the Roulston Brothers of New Zealand, this successful racehorse was modelled in action by a French freelance artist G. D'Illiers and launched as 'The Winner' HN 1407 in 1930. Sadly, it is now virtually impossible to find. More accessible is the portrait of another famous racehorse 'Merely a Minor' HN 2530, which was modelled by Frederick Daws, who is better known for his championship dogs.

Most of the early horse models were the work of the distinguished sculptor William Chance, who was responsible for the exceptional model of the royal steeplechaser 'Monaveen.' He also paid tribute to the gentle giants of the horse world in 'Pride of the Shires' HN 2563 and 'Chestnut Mare' HN 2565, portraying them with and without their foals. Some of his first studies also included riders who were later removed to produce independent horses, for example the mount in 'Farmer's Boy' HN 2520 became 'Dapple Grey' HN 2578.

Occasionally stylised horse models have been included in the HN collection, for example Raoh Schorr's 'Prancing Horse' HN 1167 and 'The Gift of Life' HN 3524 from the Images series. There have also been legendary horses such as 'Pegasus' HN 3547 and the 'Unicorn' HN 3549 modelled by Alan Maslankowski.

The range of Royal Doulton horses was expanded when models were transferred from the Beswick range in 1989. Horses had long been the speciality of the John Beswick factory and modellers such as Arthur Gredington and Albert Hallam were renowned in the industry for their portraits of famous racehorses. 'Arkle' DA15 and 'Nijinski' DA16 are just two examples of their work now in the DA series. When Albert Hallam retired, Graham Tongue became head modeller at the Beswick Studio and continued the tradition with portraits of 'Red Rum' DA18 and 'Troy' DA37 amongst others. In more recent years he modelled Britain's favourite racehorse 'Desert Orchid' DA134.

As well as all his famous models, Graham endeavoured to capture the essential qualities of horses in general with his evocative 'Spirit' range, contrasting subjects such as the powerful 'Spirit of the Earth' DA61 with the playful 'Young Spirit' DA70. His young successors contributed to all these established collections, for example Warren Platt portrayed 'Mr. Frisk' DA190 and Amanda Hughes-Lubeck modelled several Spirit horses as well as 'My First Horse' DA193B, an ideal purchase to start a collection.

Collecting Birds and Butterflies

Birds have always formed an important part of the Royal Doulton collection, beginning with Charles Noke's models of fledglings for the flambé glaze in 1908. A flock of feathered friends followed in the first few years of the HN collection and by 1920 the list included cockerels, pigeons, pelicans, guinea fowl, eagles, kingfishers, budgies, ducks and penguins, not forgetting all the miscellaneous

chicks. Some are realistically rendered like the 'Cockatoo' HN 185, which was modelled by Leslie Harradine, whilst in Noke's hands others assume human characteristics, like 'Granny Owl' HN 187 and the 'Toucan in Tails' HN 208. The comic approach continued during the 1920s with a series of tiny character toucans and penguins but generally a naturalistic style of modelling prevailed over the years.

During the war years two series of birds (HN 2540-2556 and HN 2611-2619) were made specially for export to the USA but these were short lived and are hard to find today. The same applies to the miniature models of birds which, for some reason, were added to both the HN and the K series in the early 1940s. Some of the K birds are so rare that they have eluded discovery in time for this publication.

In 1952 several large bird models were added to the Prestige range and in the 1970s Robert Jefferson produced some magnificent limited edition sculptures of birds specifically for the US market. A few years later, in 1979, the Lem Ward series of decoy ducks was also produced with American collectors in mind. Ward's carvings of wildfowl counterfeits are very sought after in the USA and Design Manager Harry Sales was asked to interpret the wooden originals in a matt glazed ceramic body.

For a brief period, between 1979 and 1982, the birds produced at the Royal Adderley factory, now one of the companies in the Royal Doulton group, were given Royal Doulton backstamps. There are 50 models in this range and they are quite different in style, body and texture from the earlier Royal Doulton birds.

Birds have regularly provided inspiration for the stylised Images of Nature collection and some have been produced in both white bone china and fiery flambé. In contrast, the team at the John Beswick studio, aimed to recreate the feel of the bird's feathers and were regular visitors to aviaries and falconry displays as well as avid bird watchers. From 1989 until the Beswick factory closed in 2002, they introduced a variety of familiar garden birds to the DA range as well as endangered species such as kestrels and owls.

Bird collectors can also find lots of different derivatives from the 1930s. Ashtrays and bowls often have birds perched on top and flower holders were frequently adorned with birds. Some of these were designed to be placed in the floating flower bowls which were fashionable at the time. Models of butterflies on rocks were made for the same purpose and there are also clip-on varieties for attaching to the side of the bowls. During the Second World War a collection of six different species of butterflies alighting in foliage was introduced but, like the birds of the period, they came and went and are consequently very hard to find today.

Collecting Prestige, Limited Editions and Special Commissions

Art Director Charles Noke specialised in large, ambitious sculptures of wild animals. Massive fighting elephants are depicted with their trunks aggressively outstretched, as in HN 1120, whilst others are shown in repose, HN 1121. Big cats, including lions, tigers and leopards, stalk their prey or crouch ready to pounce from rocks. Most of these impressive studies were first introduced to the HN collection during the 1920s and 1930s but, in 1952, a few of them were given new HN numbers and a new prestige status. 'Tiger on Rock' HN 2639, 'Leopard on Rock' HN 2638, 'Lion on Rock' HN 2641 and 'Fighter Elephant' HN 2640 could also be purchased on a special order basis until 1989 and were the most expensive models in the range.

Raoh Schorr's large fox model HN 2634 was also re-classified as a prestige piece in 1952, together with the large 'Peruvian Penguin' HN 2633 and the 'Drake' HN 2635. Peggy Davies modelled 'Indian Runner Drake' HN 2636 especially for the new prestige range and a large study of a polar bear and cub was offered in naturalistic colouring as HN 2637 instead of its earlier flambé finish. With the exception of the fox, these prestige pieces had all been discontinued by the early 1970s.

In 1974 freelance artist Robert Jefferson was commissioned to model Royal Doulton's first limited edition animal sculptures. His studies of animals and birds in their habitats were observed in minute detail and finely executed in matt porcelain to enhance the different textures of fur and feathers. The artistic and technical virtuosity of Jefferson's work is much appreciated by collectors today but examples are hard to find as most were only made in editions of 75-250, exclusively for the US market.

In the 1980s and 90s, Graham Tongue was responsible for most of the prestige and limited edition models in the Royal Doulton range. Many of his studies of prize bulls and famous race horses were originally produced for the Beswick Connoisseur range but in 1989 they were given Royal Doulton backstamps and DA numbers. Connoisseur sculptures are generally mounted on polished wooden bases with metal name plaques to reinforce their prestige status.

In 1989 several prestige sculptures of wild animals and birds were launched to raise funds for the World Wide Fund for Nature and a percentage of sales from 'The Majestic Stag' DA32 and 'The Watering Hole' DA39, amongst others, went to help save endangered species and stop environmental destruction. Lawleys by Post, the mail order division of Royal Doulton, continued this gesture with the limited edition 'Kestrel' DA144, which was commissioned exclusively for their customers in 1991. Since that date they have added several limited editions and prestige pieces to their catalogue.

On occasion, Royal Doulton have been approached by independent companies to produce an animal model for promotional or commemorative purposes, for example a turkey has been made for the well-known poultry company Bernard Matthews and a limited edition paperweight, in the form of a partridge, was produced for the 'Financial Times.' Because of the limited distribution of these pieces to staff and customers of the organisations concerned, they are often difficult to find in the market-place. This is also the case with the older advertising pieces such as the liqueur containers made for Ervan Bols in the 1930s and National Distillers in the 1950s.

Collecting Miniatures

Tiny collectables have always had a special appeal and animals are no exception. They have the advantage of not taking up too much space and a wide range of animal species can be accommodated in a single cabinet. Lots of little models, including frogs, mice and fledglings, were produced in the early 1900s for the flambé glaze and some were later coloured naturalistically for the HN collection. These models are generally less than 2 ½ inches tall but even small pieces, around one inch in height, were introduced during the 1920s. Collectors can have fun looking for all the tiny character birds, which are comic interpretations of owls, puffins, penguins and toucans. There are 11 different models to find in the first series, some in alternative colour schemes (HN 256-66 and 290-93) but unfortunately only a few were located in time for this publication. Also very rare are the six character toucans in the second series (HN 913-918), the character pigs (HN 892-7) and the young elephants (HN 949-952).

Some of the designs resemble Japanese netsuke, in particular the tiny curled up kittens (HN 820-825) and puppies (HN 834-839) which nestle comfortably in the palm of your hand. Some slightly larger seated and standing puppies followed and the star of this group is undoubtedly Bonzo. The creation of George Studdy, this popular cartoon dog, appeared in comic strips, films, advertisements and postcards during the 1920s. Bonzo collectables became all the rage and in 1923 Doulton offered five different models of the famous character in several different colourways plus a very rare Chinese Jade version (HN 804, 808-15, 826). His feline friend Ooloo was sold in five different colours (HN 818, 819, 827-29) and later joined the K series as 'Lucky,' K12, continuing in production until 1977.

The new K numbering system for miniatures was launched in 1931 and applied to 12 little dogs, less than three inches tall, and 'Lucky' the cat. Six more dogs joined the series in 1940 along with three hares, six penguins and 11 other types of birds. These birds are the hardest of all to find as they were withdrawn within a few years of issue. Three of the K dogs are more elusive than the others as they were withdrawn in 1959 compared to 1977 for the rest. K dogs were frequently mounted on calendars, ashtrays and pen trays and they were sometimes offered in conjunction with figures, for example the 'Old Balloon Seller' with the K1 bulldog on a wooden stand was sold as HN 1791

More miniature birds were introduced in 1941 but for some reason they were given HN numbers rather than K ones. To add to the confusion the 'Drake Mallard' is numbered HN 2572 whilst his mate the 'Duck' is K26. Subsequent miniatures were also numbered in the HN series. In the late 1940s and 50s, Peggy Davies modelled some collections of baby animals, including kittens, piglets and lambs. The kittens, in particular, proved very popular and stayed in the range until 1985 together with a collection of little puppies. Sadly there have been no new miniature animals in recent years but, given Royal Doulton's successful revival of tiny character jugs and figures, there would surely be an enthusiastic reception for tiny animals too.

Collecting Animals in Flambé and other Experimental Glazes

The fiery red flambé glaze was inspired by Oriental ceramics and was perfected by Royal Doulton, after many years of experimentation, in 1904. The precise recipe has always been a closely guarded secret but essentially the glaze consists of copper and iron oxides which fire to a glorious red colour when the kiln is deprived of oxygen.

Within a few years of the launch, Charles Noke was applying this lustrous glaze to little animal models and it continues to be used for new designs today. Some of the earliest models, including the cat, the foxes, the ducks and the penguin, were in continuous production for more than 80 years.

The flambé models that were illustrated in the early catalogues and publicity photographs turn up most frequently in the market place and must have been produced in some quantities, for example the 'Cuddling Apes' (52) the 'Guinea Fowl' (69) and the 'Leaping Salmon' (666). Many other animals were decorated with the flambé glaze purely as an experiment and there may be only one or two in existence. Charles Noke was constantly trying out new ideas and some designs turned out to be more suitable for the effect than others.

As well as the monochrome flambé glaze, Noke also developed lots of mottled and veined variations, including Sung and Chang. In most cases, these effects were too capricious to be used on a regular basis but spectacular Sung and Chang animals do come on to the market from time to time. Many of these special pieces bear the monograms of Charles Noke and his assistants Harry Nixon and Fred Moore. Chinese Jade was another of Noke's special effects, perfected in 1920, and he modelled a range of stylised animals especially for this tactile, soft green glaze, including some fish (625 and 632), an elephant (633) and a pair of cockatoos

(630). Production of this unpredictable glaze was very short lived so examples are hard to find. Also for a brief period between the wars, animals were decorated with Noke's Titanian glaze, which ranges from a pale, smoky blue to a deep midnight hue but again only a few examples of each would ever have been produced. Occasionally models appear with a dark blue veining on a white ground, which is the second stage in the flambé decoration so, although interesting, these are actually unfinished pieces.

In the course of his glaze experimentation, Noke produced various bright yellow, orange, and red glazes and a greenish brown which was intended to simulate bronze. These effects turn up on animal models from time to time but they will be isolated examples. During the late 1950s and 60s, the new Art Director, Jo Ledger, also produced some interesting flambé glaze effects, including a mottled blue and green colour which he called Mandarin. Some of the animals in his Chatcull range can be found with this finish but they did not go into commercial production.

After a gap of many years, three large models went into the general flambé range in 1973, the 'Owl' (2249), the 'Rhinoceros' (615), and the 'Dragon' (2085). The 'Cat' (2269) which joined them a few years later, continued in production until 1997. The Royal Doulton International Collectors Club helped promote interest in flambé again when they launched their exclusive 'Dog of Fo' in 1982 and their exotic flambé 'Dragon.' In recent years, new subjects have periodically joined the dramatic Images of Fire and Burslem Artwares collections.

CARE AND REPAIR

Careful handling and cleaning of Royal Doulton animal models will ensure that a collection can be enjoyed for many years to come. Tails, ears and other protruding features are particularly prone to damage when transporting, displaying and cleaning the collection. The Championship Dogs, in particular, have very vulnerable tails as they were modelled to portray the show stance as accurately as possible. When purchasing dogs like the 'Dalmatian' HN 1111, always check for restoration to the tail and seek the dealer's opinion. A reputable dealer will stand by any guarantees he gives regarding restorations.

Take care not to damage the animal models during cleaning by following these basic procedures. When dusting 'in situ,' a soft cosmetic brush or photographic lens brush is useful for getting into tight corners. Make sure the animals do not knock against each other causing chips or imperceptible cracks in the glaze which could open up at a later date. When necessary, models should be sponged with lukewarm water, using a mild liquid detergent, and then sponged again with clean water to rinse. It is important that water does not get inside the animal so block up the holes in the bottom before washing. Allow the piece to dry naturally and then, if the piece is glazed, buff gently with a soft cloth.

If the worst happens and a piece gets broken, seek the help and advice of a professional restorer. A skilled practitioner can repair chipped, cracked and shattered models so that the original damage is invisible to all but the most experienced eye.

With the right approach, Royal Doulton animals are much easier to take care of than real pets as they do not need to be walked, fed or house-trained so make the most of them.

INSURING YOUR FIGURES

As with any other of your valuables, making certain your figures are protected is a very important concern. It is paramount that you display or store any porcelain items in a secure place - preferable one safely away from traffic in the home.

Your figures are most often covered under your basic homeowner's policy and there are generally three kinds of such policies - standard, broad and comprehensive. Each has its own specific deductible and terms.

Under a general policy, your figurines are considered 'contents' and are covered for all of the perils covered under the contractual terms of your policy (fire, theft, water damage and so on).

However, since figurines are extremely delicate, breakage is treated differently by most insurance companies. There is usually an extra premium attached to insure figures against accidental breakage or the carelessness of the owner. This is sometimes referred to as a 'fine arts' rider.

You are advised to contact your insurance professional to get all the answers.

In order to help you protect yourself, it is critical that you take inventory of your figures and have colour photographs taken of all your pieces. This is the surest method of clearly itemizing, for the police and your insurance company, the pieces lost or destroyed. It is also the easiest way to establish their replacement value in the event of such a tragedy.

ROYAL DOULTON YEAR CYPHERS

1998 Umbrella   1999 Top Hat   2000 Fob Watch   2001 Waistcoat   2002 Boot   2003 Gloves   2004 Bottle Oven   2005 Henry Doulton

ROYAL DOULTON

INTERNATIONAL COLLECTORS CLUB

Founded in 1980, the Royal Doulton International Collectors Club provides an information service on all aspects of the company's products, past and present. A club magazine, "Gallery," is published four times a year with information on new products and current events that will keep the collector up-to-date on the happenings in the world of Royal Doulton. Upon joining the club, each new member will receive a free gift and invitations to special events, and exclusive offers throughout the year. To join the Royal Doulton Collectors Club, please contact the club directly by writing to the address opposite or calling the appropriate number.

International Collectors Club
Sir Henry Doulton House
Forge Lane, Etruria
Stoke-on-Trent, Staffordshire
ST1 5NN, England
Telephone:
  U.K.: 8702 412696
  Overseas: +44 (0) 1782 404045
  On-line at www.doulton-direct.co.uk
  E-mail: icc@royal-doulton.com

WEBSITE AND E-MAIL ADDRESSES

Websites:
  www.royal-doulton.com
  www.doulton-direct.com.au
  www.royal-doulton-brides.com

E-mail:
  Consumer Enquiries: enquiries@royal-doulton.com
  Museum Curator: heritage@royal-doulton.com
  Doulton-Direct: direct@royal-doulton.com

DOULTON CHAPTERS

Detroit Chapter
Ronald Griffin, President
629 Lynne Avenue
Ypsilanti, MI 48198-3829

Edmonton Chapter
Mildred's Collectibles
6813 104 Street
Edmonton, AB Canada

New England Chapter
Lee Piper, President
Meredith Nelson, Vice President
Michael Lynch, Secretary
Scott Reichenberg, Treasurer
E-mail doingantiq@aol.com

Northern California Chapter
Edward L. Khachadourian, President
P. O. Box 214, Moraga, CA 94556-0214
Tel.: (925) 376-2221
Fax: (925) 376-3581
E-mail: khach@pacbell.net

Northwest, Bob Haynes, Chapter
Alan Matthew, President
15202 93rd Place N.E.
Bothell, WA 98011
Tel.: (425) 488-9604

Rochester Chapter
Judith L. Trost, President
103 Garfield Street, Rochester NY 14611
Tel.: (716) 436-3321

Ohio Chapter
Dave Harris
15 Lucy Lane
Northfield, OH 44067-1821
Tel.: (330) 467-4532

Western Pennsylvania Chapter
John Re, President
9589 Parkedge Drive
Allison Park, PA 15101
Tel.: (412) 366-0201
Fax: (412) 366-2558

THE DOULTON MARKETS
Land Auctions

AUSTRALIA

Goodman's

  7 Anderson Street
  Double Bay, Sydney, 2028, N.S.W. Australia
  Tel.: +61 (0) 2 9327 7311; Fax: +61 (0) 2 9327 2917
  Enquiries: Suzanne Brett
  www.goodmans.com.au
  E-mail: info@goodmans.com.au

Sotheby's

  118-122 Queen Street, Woollahra
  Sydney, 2025, N.S.W., Australia
  Tel.: +61 (0) 2 9362 1000; Fax: +61 (0) 2 9362 1100

CANADA

Empire Auctions

  Montreal
  5500 Paré Street, Montreal, Quebec H4P 2M1
  Tel.: (514) 737-6586; Fax: (514) 342-1352
  Enquiries: Isadore Rubinfeld
  E-mail: montreal@empireauctions.com

  Ottawa
  1380 Cyrville Road, Gloucester, Ontario
  Tel.: (613) 748-5343; Fax: (613) 748-0354
  Enquiries: Elliot Melamed
  E-mail: ottawa@empireauctions.com

  Toronto
  165 Tycos Drive
  Toronto, Ontario, M6B 1W6
  Tel.: (416) 784-4261; Fax: (416) 784-4262
  Enquiries: Michael Rogozinsky
  www.empireauctions.com
  E-mail: toronto@empireauctions.com

Maynard's Industries Ltd.

Arts / Antiques
415 West 2nd Avenue, Vancouver, BC, V5Y 1E3
Tel.: (604) 876-1311; Fax: (604) 876-1323
www.maynards.com
E-mail: antiques@maynards.com

Ritchie's
Montreal
1980 Rue Sherbrooke
Suite 100, Montreal, Quebec
Tel.: (514) 934-1864; Fax: (514) 934-1860

Toronto
288 King Street East, Toronto, Ontario, M5A 1K4
Tel.: (416) 364-1864; Fax: (416) 364-0704
Enquiries: Caroline Kaiser
www.ritchies.com
E-mail: auction@ritchies.com

Waddington's
Brighton
101 Applewood Drive
Brighton, Ontario, K0K 1H0
Tel.: (613) 475-6223
Fax: (613) 475-6224
Enquiries: David Simmons
www.waddingtonsauctions.ca/brighton

Toronto
111 Bathurst Street, Toronto, Ontario M5V 2R1
Tel.: (416) 504-9100; Fax: (416) 504-0033
Enquiries: Bill Kime
www.waddingtonsauctions.com
E-mail: info@waddingtonsauctions.com

UNITED KINGDOM

Bonhams
Bond Street
101 New Bond Street, London, W15 1SR, England

Chelsea
65-69 Lots Road, Chelsea, London, SW10 0RN
England

Knightsbridge
Montpelier Street, Knightsbridge, London, SW7 1HH
Enquiries: Tel.: +44 (0) 20 7393 3900
www.bonhams.com
E-mail: info@bonhams.com

Christies
London
8 King Street, London, SW1 England
Tel.: +44 (0) 20 7839 9060; Fax: +44 (0) 20 7839 1611

South Kensington
85 Old Brompton Road, London, SW7 3LD, England
Tel.: +44 (0) 20 7581 7611; Fax: +44 (0) 20 7321 3321
Enquiries: Tel.: +44 (0) 20 7321 3237
www.christies.com
E-mail: info@christies.com

Potteries Specialist Auctions
271 Waterloo Road, Cobridge, Stoke-on-Trent
Staffordshire, ST6 3HR, England
Tel.: +44 (0) 1782 286622
Fax: +44 (0) 1782 201518
Enquiries: Martyn Bullock
www.potteriesauctions.com
E-mail: enquiries@potteriesauctions.com

Sotheby's
London
34-35 New Bond Street, London, W1A 2AA, England
Tel.: +44 (0) 20 7293 5000; Fax: +44 (0) 20 7293 5989

Olympia
Hammersmith Road, London W14 8UX, England
Tel.: +44 (0) 20 7293 5555; Fax: +44 (0) 20 7293 6939

Sussex
Summers Place, Billinghurst, Sussex,
RH14 9AF, England
Tel.: +44 (0) 1403 833500; Fax: +44 (0) 1403 833699
www.sothebys.com
E-mail: info@sothebys.com

Louis Taylor
Britannia House,
10 Town Road, Hanley
Stoke-on-Trent, Staffordshire, England
Tel.: +44 (0) 1782 214111; Fax: +44 (0) 1782 215283
Enquires: Clive Hillier

Thomsom Roddick & Mecalf
60 Whitesands
Dumfries, DG1 2RS
Scotland
Tel.: +44 (0) 1387 279879; Fax: +44 (0) 1387 266236
Enquiries: C. R. Graham-Campbell

Peter Wilson Auctioneers

Victoria Gallery, Market Street
Nantwich, Cheshire, CW5 5DG, England
Tel.: +44 (0) 1270 610508; Fax: +44 (0) 1270 610508
Enquiries: Peter Wilson

UNITED STATES

Christie's East
219 East 67th Street, New York, NY 10012
Tel.: +1 212 606 0400
Enquires: Timothy Luke
www.christies.com

William Doyle Galleries
175 East 87th Street, New York, NY 10128
Tel.: +1 212 427 2730
Fax: +1 212 369 0892

Sotheby's Arcade Auctions
1334 York Avenue, New York, NY 10021
Tel.: +1 212 606 7000
Enquiries: Andrew Cheney
www.sothebys.com

VIRTUAL AUCTIONS

Amazon.com ® Auctions
Main site: www.amazon.com
Plus 4 International sites

AOL.com Auctions ®
Main site: www.aol.com
Links to - E-bay.com
- U-bid.com

E-BAY ® **The World's On-Line Market Place** ™
Main site: www.ebay.com
Plus 20 International sites

YAHOO! Auctions ®
Main site: www.yahoo.com
Plus 15 International auction sites.

FAIRS, MARKETS AND SHOWS

AUSTRALIA

Royal Doulton and Antique Collectable Fair
Marina Hall, Civic Centre,
Hurstville, Sydney

UNITED KINGDOM

20th Century Fairs
266 Glossop Road, Sheffield S10 2HS, England
Usually in May or June.
For information on times and dates:
Tel.: +44 (0) 114 275 0333; Fax: +44 (0) 114 275 4443

DMG Antiques Fairs Ltd.
Newark, the largest in the UK with usually six fairs
annually. For information on times and dates for
this and many other fairs contact:
DMG
Newark, P. O. Box 100, Newark,
Nottinghamshire, NG2 1DJ
Tel.: +44 (0) 1636 702326; Fax: +44 (0) 1636 707923
www.antiquesdirectory.co.uk

U.K. Fairs
Doulton and Beswick Fair for Collectors
River Park Leisure Centre, Winchester
Usually held in October. For information on times
and dates contact:
Enquiries U.K. Fairs; Tel.: +44 (0) 20 8500 3505
www.portia.co.uk
E-mail: ukfairs@portia.co.uk

LONDON MARKETS

Alfie's Antique Market
13-25 Church Street, London; Tuesday to Saturday

Camden Passage Market
London, Wednesday and Saturday

New Caledonia Market
Bermondsey Square, London; Friday morning

Portobello Road Market
Portobello Road, London; Saturday

UNITED STATES

Atlantique City
Atlantic City Convention Centre
One Miss America Way
Atlantic City, NJ 08401
Tel.: (609) 449-2000; Fax: (609) 449-2090
info@accenter.com

International Gift and Collectible Expo
Donald E. Stephens Convention Centre
Rosemont, Illinois

For information on the above two shows contact:
Krause Publications
700 East State Street, Iola, WI 54990-9990
Tel.: (877) 746-9757; Fax: (715) 445-4389
www.collectibleshow.com
E-mail: iceshow@krause.com

Doulton Convention and Sale International
West Palm Beach, Florida, U.S.A.
Usually February. For information on times
and dates:
Pascoe & Company
575 S.W. 22nd Ave., Miami, Florida 33135
Tel.: (305) 643-2550; Fax: (305) 643-2123
www.pascoeandcompany.com
E-mail: sales@pascoeandcompany.com

Royal Doulton Convention & Sale
Cleveland, Ohio
Usually August. For information on times and dates:
Colonial House Productions
182 Front Street, Berea, Ohio 44308
Tel.: (440) 826-4169; Fax: (440) 826-0839
www.Colonial-House-Collectibles.com
E-mail: yworrey@aol.com

FURTHER READING

Animal, Figures and Character Jugs

Character Jug Collectors Handbook, by Kevin Pearson
Charlton Standard Catalogue of Beswick Animals by Callows and Sweets
Charlton Standard Catalogue of Royal Doulton Figurines, by Jean Dale
Charlton Standard Catalogue of Royal Doulton Jugs, by Jean Dale
Collecting Character and Toby Jugs by Jocelyn Lukins
Collecting Doulton Animals by Jocelyn Lukins
Doulton Figure Collectors Handbook, by Kevin Pearson
Doulton Flambé Animals by Jocelyn Lukins
Royal Doulton Figures by Desmond Eyles, Louise Irvine and Valerie Baynton

Storybook Figures

Beatrix Potter Figures and Giftware, edited by Louise Irvine
Beswick Price Guide, by Harvey May
Bunnykins Collectors Book, by Louise Irvine
Cartoon Classics and other Character Figures, by Louise Irvine
Charlton Standard Catalogue of Royal Doulton Beswick Storybook Figurines, by Jean Dale
Charlton Standard Catalogue of Royal Doulton Bunnykins, by Jean Dale and Louise Irvine
Royal Doulton Bunnykins Figures, by Louise Irvine

General

Charlton Standard Catalogue of Beswick Pottery, by Diane and John Callow
Discovering Royal Doulton, by Michael Doulton
Doulton Burslem Advertising Wares, by Jocelyn Lukins
Doulton Burslem Wares, by Desmond Eyles
Doulton for the Collector, by Jocelyn Lukins
Doulton Kingsware Flasks, by Jocelyn Lukins
Doulton Lambeth Advertising Wares, by Jocelyn Lukins
Doulton Lambeth Wares, by Desmond Eyles
Doulton Story, by Paul Atterbury and Louise Irvine
George Tinworth, by Peter Rose
Hannah Barlow, by Peter Rose
John Beswick: A World of Imagination. Catalogue reprint (1950-1996)
Limited Edition Loving Cups and Jugs, by Louise Irvine and Richard Dennis
Phillips Collectors Guide, by Catherine Braithwaite
Royal Doulton by Julie McKeown
Royal Doulton, by Jennifer Queree
Royal Doulton Series Wares, by Louise Irvine (Vols. 1-5)
Sir Henry Doulton Biography, by Edmund Gosse

Magazines and Newsletters

Beswick Quarterly (Beswick Newsletter) Contact Laura J. Rock-Smith: 10 Holmes Court, Sayville, N.Y. 11782-2408, U.S.A. Tel./Fax (631) 589-9027
Collecting Doulton Magazine, Contact Barry Hill, Collecting Doulton, P. O. Box 310, Richmond Surrey TW10 7FU, England
Rabbitting On (Bunnykins Newsletter) Contact Leah Selig: 2 Harper Street, Merrylands 2160, New South Wales, Australia. Tel/Fax: 61 2 9637 2410 (International), 02 637 2410 (Australia)

JOHN BROAD

STONEWARE

Cockerel

Model No.:	Unknown
Designer:	John Broad
Height:	10 ¼", 26.0 cm
Colour:	Coloured Doultonware
Issued:	c.1900

Description	U.S. $	Can. $	U.K. £
Cockerel		Very Rare	

Photograph not
available
at press time

Kangaroo

Model No.:	X7621
Designer:	John Broad
Height:	6 ½", 16.5 cm
Colour:	Brown and green
Issued:	1912

Description	U.S. $	Can. $	U.K. £
Kangaroo		Very Rare	

Kangaroo Matchholder

Model No.:	X7056
Designer:	John Broad
Height:	Unknown
Colour:	Unknown
Issued:	1912

Description	U.S. $	Can. $	U.K. £
Kangaroo matchholder		Very Rare	

LESLIE HARRADINE

STONEWARE

Cockatoos (pair)
Model No.: H35
Designer: Leslie Harradine
Height: 6", 15.0 cm
Colour: Blue and grey Doultonware
Issued: 1912

Description	U.S. $	Can. $	U.K. £
Cockatoos (pair)	1,000.00	1,200.00	500.00

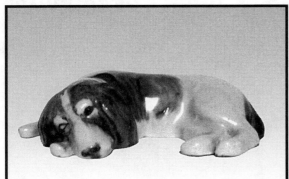

Dog Asleep
Model No.: X7732
Designer: Leslie Harradine
Length: 2 ¾", 7.0 cm
Colour: White and brown
Issued: 1912

Description	U.S. $	Can. $	U.K. £
Dog asleep		Very Rare	

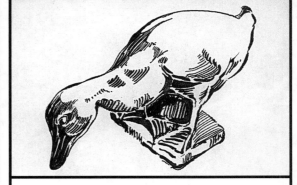

Duck Doorstop
Model No.: H33
Designer: Leslie Harradine
Height: Unknown
Colour: Unknown
Issued: c.1912

Description	U.S. $	Can. $	U.K. £
Duck doorstop		Extremely Rare	

Ducklings (pair)

Model No.:	X7731, H5
Designer:	Leslie Harradine
Height:	4 ½", 11.9 cm
Colour:	White and black
Issued:	1912

Description	U.S. $	Can. $	U.K. £
Ducklings (pair)	750.00	900.00	400.00

Monkey with Arms Folded

Model No.:	Unknown
Designer:	Leslie Harradine
Height:	8", 20.3 cm
Colour:	Brown
Issued:	c.1912

Description	U.S. $	Can. $	U.K. £
Monkey, arms folded	2,200.00	2,500.00	1,000.00

Note: A larger version of this design has also been recorded.

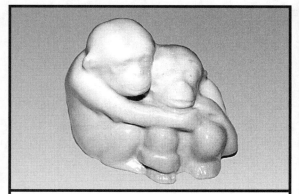

Monkeys Cuddling

Model No.:	Unknown
Designer:	Leslie Harradine
Height:	3", 7.6 cm
Colour:	Cream (slip cast)
Issued:	1912

Description	U.S. $	Can. $	U.K. £
Monkeys cuddling	450.00	550.00	250.00

Note: This model is similar to the Burslem monkey group HN254.

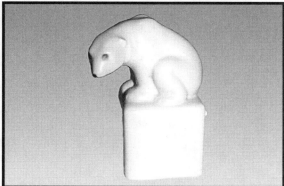

Polar Bear on Block of Ice

Model No.:	X7731
Designer:	Leslie Harradine
Height:	4", 10.1 cm
Colour:	White
Issued:	1912

Description	U.S. $	Can. $	U.K. £
Polar bear on block of ice	450.00	550.00	250.00

Note: See HN119, model 67 for a continuation of this model.

Polar Bears on Ice Floe (pair)

Model No.:	H58
Designer:	Leslie Harradine
Height:	8", 20.1 cm
Colour:	White
Issued:	c.1912

Description	U.S. $	Can. $	U.K. £
Polar Bears on ice floe	2,500.00	3,000.00	1,350.00

Rhinoceros

Model No.:	Unknown
Designer:	Leslie Harradine
Height:	6 ½", 16.5 cm
Colour:	Brown and blue
Issued:	c.1912

Description	U.S. $	Can. $	U.K. £
Rhinoceros		Extremely Rare	

MARK MARSHALL

STONEWARE

Bear Family

Model No.:	Unknown
Designer:	Mark Marshall
Height:	3", 7.5 cm
Colour:	Brown
Issued:	c.1905

Description	U.S. $	Can. $	U.K. £
Bear family	4,500.00	5,500.00	2,500.00

Chicken Bowl

Model No.:	896
Designer:	Mark Marshall
Height:	11 ½", 29.0 cm
Colour:	Light and dark green/white/
	reddish-brown/black
Issued:	Unknown

Description	U.S. $	Can. $	U.K. £
Chicken bowl	5,000.00	6,000.00	2,700.00

Creature Smiling

Model No.:	Unknown
Designer:	Mark Marshall
Height:	3 ½", 8.9 cm
Colour:	Blue and brown
Issued:	c.1902

Description	U.S. $	Can. $	U.K. £
Creature smiling	2,500.00	3,000.00	1,350.00

Fabulous Fish (Jug)

Model No.:	125
Designer:	Mark Marshall
Height:	9", 23.0 cm
Colour:	Browns/pinks/white/cream
Issued:	c.1885

Description	U.S. $	Can. $	U.K. £
Fabulous fish	5,500.00	6,500.00	3,000.00

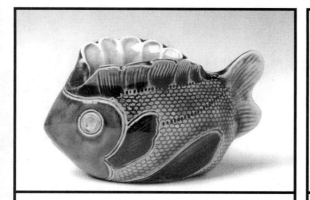

Fish Bowl

Model No.:	Unknown
Designer:	Mark Marshall
Height:	2 ½", 5.5 cm
Colour:	1. Blue/white/green/brown
	2. Browns and pale blue
Issued:	Unknown

Description	U.S. $	Can. $	U.K. £
1. Blue	3,000.00	3,500.00	1,600.00
2. Brown	3,000.00	3,500.00	1,600.00

Grotesque

Model No.:	Unknown
Designer:	Mark Marshall
Height:	3 ½", 8.9 cm
Colour:	Unknown
Issued:	c.1902

Description	U.S. $	Can. $	U.K. £
Grotesque	1,000.00	1,200.00	500.00

Grotesque - Bird

Model No.:	Unknown
Designer:	Mark Marshall
Height:	3", 7.6 cm
Colour:	Blue or brown
Issued:	c.1902

Colourways	U.S. $	Can. $	U.K. £
1. Blue	1,000.00	1,200.00	500.00
2. Brown	1,000.00	1,200.00	500.00

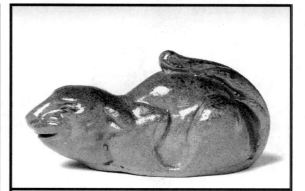

Grotesque - Cheshire Cat
(from Alice in Wonderland)

Model No.:	X6986
Designer:	Mark Marshall
Height:	3 ¾" x 1 ¾", 8.2 x 4.4 cm
Colour:	Blue, brown or green
Issued:	c.1902

Colourways	U.S. $	Can. $	U.K. £
1. Blue	700.00	850.00	375.00
2. Brown	700.00	850.00	375.00
3. Green	700.00	850.00	375.00

Grotesque - Duck

Model No.:	Unknown		
Designer:	Mark Marshall		
Height:	2 ¾", 7.0 cm		
Colour:	Blue or green		
Issued:	c.1902		

Colourways	U.S. $	Can. $	U.K. £
1. Blue	650.00	775.00	350.00
2. Green	650.00	775.00	350.00

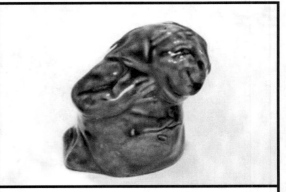

Grotesque - Mock Turtle
(from Alice in Wonderland**)**

Model No.:	X6987		
Designer:	Mark Marshall		
Height:	2 ½", 5.7 cm		
Colour:	Blue or green		
Issued:	c.1902		

Colourways	U.S. $	Can. $	U.K. £
1. Blue	700.00	850.00	375.00
2. Green	700.00	850.00	375.00

Grotesque - Rabbit

Model No.:	Unknown		
Designer:	Mark Marshall		
Height:	2", 5.0 cm		
Colour:	Green rabbit on brown base		
Issued:	c.1922		

Description	U.S. $	Can. $	U.K. £
Rabbit	1,000.00	1,200.00	500.00

Grotesque - Snake

Model No.:	Unknown		
Designer:	Mark Marshall		
Height:	Unknown		
Colour:	Green and brown		
Issued:	c.1902		

Description	U.S. $	Can. $	U.K. £
Snake	700.00	850.00	375.00

Grotesque - Toad

Model No.:	Unknown		
Designer:	Mark Marshall		
Height:	Unknown		
Colour:	Unknown		
Issued:	c.1902		

Description	U.S. $	Can. $	U.K. £
Toad	700.00	850.00	375.00

Lizard

Model No.:	X6988		
Designer:	Mark Marshall		
Length:	4 ½", 27.9 cm		
Colour:	Brown or blue		
Issued:	1904		

Description	U.S. $	Can. $	U.K. £
Lizard	1,500.00	1,800.00	800.00

Lizard on Rock

Model No.:	Unknown		
Designer:	Mark Marshall		
Height:	5", 12.7 cm		
Colour:	Brown and black		
Issued:	c.1905		

Description	U.S. $	Can. $	U.K. £
Lizard on rock	3,000.00	3,500.00	1,500.00

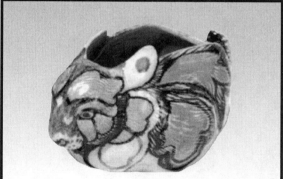

Rabbit Vase

Model No.:	381		
Designer:	Mark Marshall		
Length:	8", 20.5 cm		
Colour:	Blue, green, cream, purple and black		
Issued:	c.1880		

Description	U.S. $	Can. $	U.K. £
Rabbit vase	5,500.00	6,500.00	2,950.00

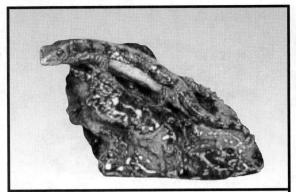

Salamander on Rock

Model No.:	Unknown
Designer:	Mark Marshall
Height:	3 ½", 8.5 cm
Colour:	Browns, purple and black
Issued:	Unknown

Description	U.S. $	Can. $	U.K. £
Salamander	4,000.00	4,750.00	2,200.00

Seahorse

Model No.:	Unknown
Designer:	Mark Marshall
Height:	6", 15.0 cm
Colour:	Green or white glazed Carraraware
Issued:	c.1910

Colourways	U.S. $	Can. $	U.K. £
1. Green	1,000.00	1,200.00	550.00
2. White	1,000.00	1,200.00	550.00

'The Waning of the Honeymoon' Rabbit Vase

Model No.:	Unknown
Designer:	Mark Marshall
Height:	4 ¾", 12.1 cm
Colour:	1. Blue Stoneware
	2. Brown Siliconware
	3. Coloured Doultonware
Issued:	1880

Description	U.S. $	Can. $	U.K. £
1. Blue stoneware	4,000.00	4,750.00	2,200.00
2. Brown Siliconware	4,000.00	4,750.00	2,200.00
3. Coloured Doultonware	4,000.00	4,750.00	2,200.00

'The Yawn Rabbit'

Model No.:	Unknown
Designer:	Mark Marshall
Height:	Unknown
Colour:	Brown
Issued:	c.1880

Description	U.S. $	Can. $	U.K. £
The Yawn rabbit		Very Rare	

HARRY SIMEON

STONEWARE

Character Bird

Model No.:	X8598
Designer:	Harry Simeon
Height:	3 ¾", 9.5 cm
Colour:	Blue, green, purple and yellow
Issued:	1926

Description	U.S. $	Can. $	U.K. £
Character bird	550.00	650.00	300.00

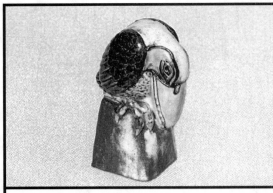

Character Bird Looking Down

Model No.:	X8597
Designer:	Harry Simeon
Height:	3 ¾", 9.5 cm
Colour:	Brown, white and blue
Issued:	1926

Description	U.S. $	Can. $	U.K. £
Bird looking down	650.00	775.00	350.00

Photograph not
available
at press time

Cormorant

Model No.:	X7622
Designer:	Harry Simeon
Height:	Unknown
Colour:	Unknown
Issued:	1912

Description	U.S. $	Can. $	U.K. £
Cormorant		Extremely Rare	

Duck

Model No.:	X8604
Designer:	Harry Simeon
Height:	5", 12.7 cm
Colour:	Beige, brown and blue
Issued:	1926

Description	U.S. $	Can. $	U.K. £
Duck	2,000.00	2,250.00	1,000.00

Ibex

Model No.:	X8605		
Designer:	Harry Simeon		
Height:	5", 12.7 cm		
Colour:	Green and brown		
Issued:	1926		

Description	U.S. $	Can. $	U.K. £
Ibex	1,100.00	1,300.00	600.00

Monkey and Young Bookend

Model No.:	X8768		
Designer:	Harry Simeon		
Height:	6 ½", 16.5 cm		
Colour:	Brown		
Issued:	1928		

Description	U.S. $	Can. $	U.K. £
Bookend		Extremely Rare	

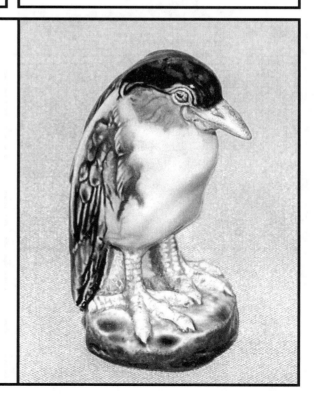

Night Heron

Model No.:	X8606		
Designer:	Harry Simeon		
Height:	5 ¾", 14.6 cm		
Colour:	White, blue and brown		
Issued:	1926		

Description	U.S. $	Can. $	U.K. £
Night heron	700.00	850.00	375.00

Note: Night Heron used for tray see page 20.

Harry Simeon Stoneware Bibelots

Bird on Stump (Heron)
Model No.:   X8596
Designer: Harry Simeon
Height: 7", 17.8 cm
Colour: Gilt enamelled
Issued: 1926

Description	U.S. $	Can. $	U.K. £
Bird on stump (heron)	1,200.00	1,450.00	600.00

Photograph not
available
at press time

Bird Tray
Model No.:   X8617
Designer: Harry Simeon
Height: Unknown
Colour: Unknown
Issued: 1926

Description	U.S. $	Can. $	U.K. £
Bird tray		Very Rare	

Bird (With Beak Open) Tray
Model No.:   X8740
Designer: Harry Simeon
Height: 3", 7.6 cm
Colour: Brown, green, white and blue
Issued: 1928

Description	U.S. $	Can. $	U.K. £
Bird/beak open	1,000.00	1,200.00	500.00

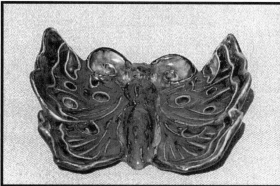

Bird (With Outstretched Wings) Tray

Model No.:	X8728		
Designer:	Harry Simeon		
Diameter:	5 ¾", 14.6 cm		
Colour:	Blue, green and brown		
Issued:	1928		

Description	U.S. $	Can. $	U.K. £
Bird/outstretched wings	750.00	900.00	400.00

Butterfly Tray

Model No.:	X7107		
Designer:	Harry Simeon		
Diameter:	5", 12.7 cm		
Colour:	Blue, green and brown		
Issued:	c.1925		

Description	U.S. $	Can. $	U.K. £
Butterfly tray	1,000.00	1,200.00	500.00

Character Bird On Boat Tray (Kookaburra On Boat)

Model No.:	X8685		
Designer:	Harry Simeon		
Height:	4 ¼", 10.8 cm		
Colour:	Blue, brown, green and white		
Issued:	1927		

Description	U.S. $	Can. $	U.K. £
Bird on boat tray	800.00	950.00	425.00

Note: This model is similar to X8598, X8614 and X8686.

Character Bird On Shell Tray

Model No.:	X8686		
Designer:	Harry Simeon		
Height:	4 ¼", 10.8 cm		
Colour:	Blue, brown, green and purple		
Issued:	1927		

Description	U.S. $	Can. $	U.K. £
Bird on shell tray	800.00	950.00	425.00

Note: This model is similar to X8598, X8614 and X8685.

Photograph not
available
at press time

Character Bird On Tray

Model No.:	X8614
Designer:	Harry Simeon
Height:	4 ¼", 10.8 cm
Colour:	Blue, green and white
Issued:	1926

Description	U.S. $	Can. $	U.K. £
Bird on tray	800.00	950.00	425.00

Note: This model is similar to X8598, X8685 and X8686.

Dragonfly Tray

Model No.:	X8713
Designer:	Harry Simeon
Diameter:	6", 15.0 cm
Colour:	Blue, green and white
Issued:	1928

Description	U.S. $	Can. $	U.K. £
Dragonfly tray	700.00	850.00	375.00

Note: A similar design was made for Wright's Coal Tar Soap c.1920.

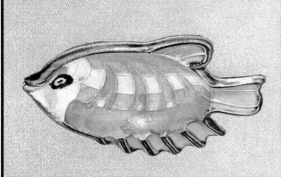

Duck Tray

Model No.:	Unknown
Designer:	Harry Simeon
Height:	6 ½", 16.5 cm
Colour:	Blue, green, pink and brown
Issued:	1928

Description	U.S. $	Can. $	U.K. £
Duck tray	600.00	725.00	325.00

Fish Tray

Model No.:	X8906
Designer:	Harry Simeon
Height:	6", 15.0 cm
Colour:	Blue, green, white and brown
Issued:	1934

Description	U.S. $	Can. $	U.K. £
Fish tray	600.00	725.00	325.00

Photograph not
available
at press time

Fish Tray (Plaice)

Model No.:	X8705		
Designer:	Harry Simeon		
Height:	Unknown		
Colour:	Unknown		
Issued:	1928		

Description	U.S. $	Can. $	U.K. £
Fish tray		Extremely Rare	

Koala Tray

Model No.:	X8902		
Designer:	Harry Simeon		
Height:	4", 10.1 cm		
Colour:	Blue, brown and green		
Issued:	1934		

Description	U.S. $	Can. $	U.K. £
Koala tray	1,000.00	1,200.00	500.00

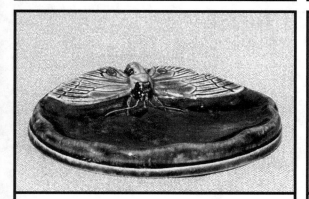

Moth Tray

Model No.:	X8730		
Designer:	Harry Simeon		
Height:	5 ¾", 14.6 cm		
Colour:	Blue, green, brown and purple		
Issued:	1928		

Description	U.S. $	Can. $	U.K. £
Moth tray	750.00	900.00	400.00

Mouse Ring Stand

Model No.:	X8673		
Designer:	Harry Simeon		
Height:	4", 10.1 cm		
Colour:	Blue and brown		
Issued:	1927		

Description	U.S. $	Can. $	U.K. £
Mouse ring stand	1,000.00	1,200.00	500.00

Mouse Tray

Model No.:	X8669			
Designer:	Harry Simeon			
Height:	1. Large − 3 ½", 8.9 cm			
	2. Small − 2 ¾", 7.0 cm			
Colour:	Brown			
Issued:	1927			

Description	U.S. $	Can. $	U.K. £
1. Large	1,000.00	1,200.00	500.00
2. Small	1,000.00	1,200.00	500.00

Night Heron Tray

Model No.:	X8948
Designer:	Harry Simeon
Height:	1. Large − 7", 15.5 cm
	2. Small − 4", 10.1 cm
Colour:	Blue, brown, green and white
Issued:	1934

Description	U.S. $	Can. $	U.K. £
1. Large	1,000.00	1,200.00	500.00
2. Small	900.00	1,075.00	475.00

Owl Tray

Model No.:	X8667
Designer:	Vera Huggins
Diameter:	1. Large − 3 ½", 8.9 cm
	2. Small − 2 ¾", 7.0 cm
Colour:	Brown and beige
Issued:	1926

Description	U.S. $	Can. $	U.K. £
1. Large	1,200.00	1,450.00	650.00
2. Small	1,000.00	1,200.00	500.00

Pelican On Octagonal Tray
Model No.:   X8978
Designer: Harry Simeon
Height: 5 ¾", 14.6 cm
Colour: Blue, brown and white
Issued: 1934

Description	U.S. $	Can. $	U.K. £
Pelican /octagonal tray	1,500.00	1,800.00	800.00

Pelican On Round Tray
Model No.:   X8900
Designer: Harry Simeon
Height: 3 ¾", 9.5 cm
Colour: Blue, brown, green and white
Issued: 1934

Description	U.S. $	Can. $	U.K. £
Pelican /round tray	1,250.00	1,500.00	700.00

Pigeon Tray
Model No.:   X8979
Designer: Harry Simeon
Height: 4 ¼", 10.8 cm
Colour: Blue, brown and white
Issued: 1934

Description	U.S. $	Can. $	U.K. £
Pigeon tray	1,500.00	1,800.00	800.00

Polar Bear Tray

Model No.:   X8715
Designer: Harry Simeon
Height: 4 ¾", 12.1 cm
Colour: White, blue and green
Issued: 1928

Description	U.S. $	Can. $	U.K. £
Polar bear tray	1,200.00	1,450.00	650.00

Rabbit Tray

Model No.:   X8756
Designer: Harry Simeon
Height: 3 ¼", 8.3 cm
Colour: Blue, brown, white and green
Issued: 1928

Description	U.S. $	Can. $	U.K. £
1. Brown rabbit	1,200.00	1,450.00	650.00
2. White rabbit	1,200.00	1,450.00	650.00

Photograph not
available
at press time

Seal tray

Model No.:   Not recorded
Designer: Harry Simeon
Height: 3", 7.6 cm
Colour: Silver lustre and blue
Issued: c.1925

Description	U.S. $	Can. $	U.K. £
Seal tray	900.00	1,075.00	500.00

Note: This ashtray was made for McMullen's Silver Seal Port.

Swan Tray

Model No.:   X8668
Designer: Harry Simeon
Height: Unknown
Colour: Unknown
Issued: 1927

Description	U.S. $	Can. $	U.K. £
Swan tray		Very Rare	

GEORGE TINWORTH

STONEWARE

Fables
Frog and Monkey Groups
Frog and Mice Groups
Mice Groups
Mouse Musicians

Fables

The Cat And The Sparrow

Model No.:   Unknown
Designer: George Tinworth
Height: 3 ½", 8.9 cm
Colour: Brown and green
Issued: c.1882

Description	U.S. $	Can. $	U.K. £
Cat/sparrow	6,000.00	7,250.00	3,250.00

The Eagle And The Fox With Vase

Model No.:   Unknown
Designer: George Tinworth
Height: 6", 15.0 cm
Colour: Brown and green
Issued: c.1882

Description	U.S. $	Can. $	U.K. £
Eagle/fox with vase	7,500.00	9,000.00	4,000.00

The Fox Inviting The Stork To Dinner

Model No.:   Unknown
Designer: George Tinworth
Height: 4", 10.1 cm
Colour: Blue, brown and green
Issued: c.1882

Description	U.S. $	Can. $	U.K. £
Fox/stork	6,000.00	7,250.00	3,250.00

The Monkey That Would Be King

Model No.:   Unknown
Designer: George Tinworth
Height: 4", 10.1 cm
Colour: Brown and blue
Issued: c.1882

Description	U.S. $	Can. $	U.K. £
Monkey	6,000.00	7,250.00	3,250.00

Monkey, Cats And Cheese

Model No.: Unknown
Designer: George Tinworth
Height: 6", 15.0 cm
Colour: Brown and blue
Issued: 1882

Description	U.S. $	Can. $	U.K. £
Monkey/cats/cheese	7,000.00	8,500.00	3,750.00

The Ox And The Frogs

Model No.: Unknown
Designer: George Tinworth
Height: 3", 7.6 cm
Length: 7 ¼", 18.4 cm
Colour: Brown and green
Issued: 1881

Description	U.S. $	Can. $	U.K. £
Ox/frogs	8,000.00	9,500.00	4,400.00

The Vain Jackdaw With Vase

Model No.: Unknown
Designer: George Tinworth
Height: 6", 15.0 cm
Colour: Blue, green and brown
Issued: c.1882

Description	U.S. $	Can. $	U.K. £
Vain jackdaw	7,000.00	8,500.00	3,750.00

Frog and Monkey Groups

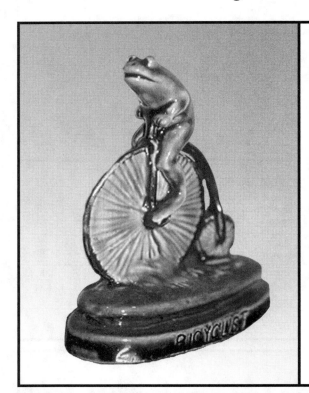

Bicyclist
Model No.: X929
Designer: George Tinworth
Height: 4 ½", 11.9 cm
Colour: Green, brown and yellow
Issued: c.1885

Description	U.S. $	Can. $	U.K. £
Bicyclist	7,000.00	8,500.00	3,750.00

Canoeist
Model No.: Unknown
Designer: George Tinworth
Height: 4, 10.1 cm
Colour: Blue and brown
Issued: c.1885

Description	U.S. $	Can. $	U.K. £
1. Blue boat	4,000.00	4,750.00	2,250.00
2. Brown boat	4,000.00	4,750.00	2,250.00

Cricketer
Model No.: Unknown
Designer: George Tinworth
Height: 4 ¾", 12.1 cm
Colour: Blue and brown
Issued: c.1885

Description	U.S. $	Can. $	U.K. £
Cricketer	5,000.00	6,000.00	2,750.00

Football

Model No.:	Unknown
Designer:	George Tinworth
Height:	5", 12.7 cm
Colour:	Blue and brown
Issued:	c.1885
Varieties:	Also called 'Football Scrimmage'

Description	U.S. $	Can. $	U.K. £
Football	7,500.00	9,000.00	4,000.00

Frogs With Vase

Model No.:	Unknown
Designer:	George Tinworth
Height:	4 ½", 11.9 cm
Colour:	Blue and brown
Issued:	c.1890

Description	U.S. $	Can. $	U.K. £
Frogs with vase	4,000.00	4,750.00	2,200.00

Jack In The Green

Model No.:	Unknown
Designer:	George Tinworth
Height:	5 ¼", 13.3 cm
Colour:	Brown and green
Issued:	c.1885

Description	U.S. $	Can. $	U.K. £
Jack in the green	7,500.00	9,000.00	4,000.00

The Public Library's Act

Model No.:	Unknown
Designer:	George Tinworth
Height:	5 ¼", 13.3 cm
Colour:	Brown and blue
Issued:	1888

Description	U.S. $	Can. $	U.K. £
Public library's act	6,000.00	7,250.00	3,300.00

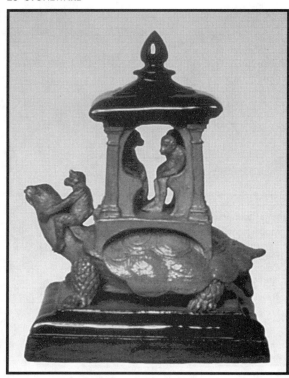

Safe Travelling
(Monkeys Riding A Tortoise)

Model No.:	Unknown
Designer:	George Tinworth
Height:	6 ¾", 17.2 cm
Colour:	Brown and blue
Issued:	c.1885
Varieties:	Also called 'Slow but Sure'

Description	U.S. $	Can. $	U.K. £
Safe travelling	12,500.00	15,000.00	6,750.00

Note: This piece is also known with front monkey wearing a hat.

United Family
(Monkeys Grooming Each Other)

Model No.:	Unknown
Designer:	George Tinworth
Height:	5", 12.7 cm
Colour:	1. Carraraware
	2. Green
Issued:	c.1892
Varieties:	Also called 'Busy,' 'Contentment'

Description	U.S. $	Can. $	U.K. £
1. Carraraware	3,000.00	3,600.00	1,650.00
2. Green stoneware	5,000.00	6,000.00	2,750.00

Frog And Mice Groups

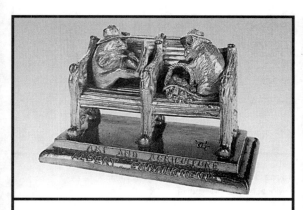

Art and Agriculture

Model No.:	Unknown
Designer:	George Tinworth
Length:	7", 17.8 cm
Colour:	Brown
Issued:	c.1885

Description	U.S. $	Can. $	U.K. £
Art/agriculture	12,500.00	15,000.00	6,500.00

The Combat

Model No.:	Unknown
Designer:	George Tinworth
Height:	3 ¾", 9.5 cm
Colour:	Blue and brown
Issued:	c.1885

Description	U.S. $	Can. $	U.K. £
Combat	6,000.00	7,250.00	3,300.00

Crossing The Channel

Model No.:	Unknown
Designer:	George Tinworth
Height:	5", 12.7 cm
Colour:	Blue and brown
Issued:	c.1885

Description	U.S. $	Can. $	U.K. £
Crossing the channel	6,000.00	7,250.00	3,300.00

The Frog Is Trying To Persuade The Mouse Across The Stream

Model No.:	Unknown
Designer:	George Tinworth
Height:	3", 7.6 cm
Colour:	Blue, green and brown
Issued:	c.1888

Description	U.S. $	Can. $	U.K. £
Across the stream	5,500.00	6,500.00	3,000.00

Photograph not
available
at press time

Photograph not
available
at press time

Frogs Carrying Mouse in Sedan Chair

Model No.:	Unknown
Designer:	George Tinworth
Height:	Unknown
Colour:	Unknown
Issued:	1888

Description	U.S. $	Can. $	U.K. £
Carrying sedan chair	9,000.00	11,000.00	5,000.00

Note: Companion piece to 'Frogs Returning Drunk with Sedan Chair.'

Frogs Returning Drunk with Sedan Chair

Model No.:	Unknown
Designer:	George Tinworth
Height:	Unknown
Colour:	Unknown
Issued:	1888

Description	U.S. $	Can. $	U.K. £
Drunk with sedan chair	9,000.00	11,000.00	5,000.00

Note: Companion piece to 'Frogs Carrying Mouse in Sedan Chair.'

Going to the Derby

Model No.:	Unknown
Designer:	George Tinworth
Height:	4", 10.1 cm
Colour:	Brown and blue
Issued:	1886

Colourways	U.S. $	Can. $	U.K. £
1. White frogs/mouse	6,500.00	7,750.00	3,500.00
2. Blue frogs/brown mouse	6,500.00	7,750.00	3,500.00

Note: Companion piece to 'Lost and Serves them Right.'

Lost and Serves them Right

Model No.:	Unknown
Designer:	George Tinworth
Height:	4", 10.1 cm
Colour:	Brown and blue
Issued:	1886

Colourways	U.S. $	Can. $	U.K. £
1. White frogs/mouse	6,500.00	7,750.00	3,500.00
2. Blue frogs/brown mouse	6,500.00	7,750.00	3,500.00

Note: Companion piece to 'Going to the Derby.'

Music and Literature

Model No.:	Unknown
Designer:	George Tinworth
Height:	5 ¼", 13.3 cm
Colour:	Brown
Issued:	c.1885
Varieties:	Also called 'The Albert Embankment'

Description	U.S. $	Can. $	U.K. £
Music and literature	12,500.00	15,000.00	6,500.00

The Race

Model No.:	Unknown
Designer:	George Tinworth
Height:	5 ¼", 13.3 cm
Colour:	White, brown and green
Issued:	c.1885

Description	U.S. $	Can. $	U.K. £
The Race	10,000.00	12,000.00	5,500.00

Steeplechase

Model No.:	Unknown
Designer:	George Tinworth
Height:	4 ½", 11.9 cm
Colour:	White, brown and green
Issued:	c.1888
Varieties:	Also called 'Hunting'

Description	U.S. $	Can. $	U.K. £
Steeplechase	9,000.00	11,000.00	5,000.00

Tug of War

Model No.:	Unknown
Designer:	George Tinworth
Height:	3 ¾" 9.5 cm
Colour:	White, blue and brown
Issued:	c.1885

Description	U.S. $	Can. $	U.K. £
Tug of war	8,000.00	9,500.00	4,250.00

Mice Groups

Apple Stall Menu Holder

Model No.:	Unknown
Designer:	George Tinworth
Height:	3 ¾", 9.5 cm
Colour:	Green and brown
Issued:	c.1885

Description	U.S. $	Can. $	U.K. £
Apple stall	5,000.00	6,000.00	2,750.00

Barber

Model No.:	X1212 - Unknown
	X1108 - Menu holder
Designer:	George Tinworth
Height:	3 ¼", 8.3 cm
Colour:	White, brown and blue
Issued:	1886

Description	U.S. $	Can. $	U.K. £
Barber	5,000.00	6,000.00	2,750.00

Chess Set

This set originally consisted of 32 pieces but now the pieces are usually found individually. For illustration of complete chess set see page 46.

Model No.:	Unknown
Designer:	George Tinworth
Height:	2 ½" - 3", 6.4 cm - 7.6 cm
Colour:	1. White with red or black details
	2. Brown
Issued:	c.1900

Description	U.S. $	Can. $	U.K. £
1. Major chessmen	1,500.00	1,800.00	825.00
2. Pawns	800.00	950.00	425.00

Note: A Chess Set (32 pieces) plus a Jacques carved wooden box sold by Sotheby's for $12,000.00 USF. Harriman Judd Collection, Part One, January 2001.

Cockneys at Brighton

Model No.:	Unknown
Designer:	George Tinworth
Height:	4", 10.1 cm
Colour:	White or brown, green and blue
Issued:	1886

Colourways	U.S. $	Can. $	U.K. £
1. White mice	7,500.00	9,000.00	4,000.00
2. Brown mice	7,500.00	9,000.00	4,000.00

Conjurers

Model No.:	X944
Designer:	George Tinworth
Height:	3 ¼", 8.3 cm
Colour:	White, blue and brown
Issued:	1885

Description	U.S. $	Can. $	U.K. £
Conjurers	5,000.00	6,000.00	2,750.00

Note: This model was also made in bone china.

Currant Bun

Model No.:	X64
Designer:	George Tinworth
Height:	2 ¾", 7.0 cm
Colour:	White or brown mouse on brown current bun
Issued:	1884

Colourways	U.S. $	Can. $	U.K. £
1. Brown mouse	2,000.00	2,500.00	1,000.00
2. White mouse	2,000.00	2,500.00	1,000.00

Drunkards

Model No.:	Unknown
Designer:	George Tinworth
Height:	3 ¼", 8.3 cm
Colour:	White and brown
Issued:	1888

Description	U.S. $	Can. $	U.K. £
Drunkards	7,000.00	8,500.00	3,750.00

Electricity

Model No.:	X1111 - Menu holder
	X1208 - Vase
Designer:	George Tinworth
Height:	5 ¼", 13.3 cm
Colour:	Brown and blue
Issued:	c.1885

Description	U.S. $	Can. $	U.K. £
1. Menu holder	4,500.00	5,500.00	2,500.00
2. Vase	4,500.00	5,500.00	2,500.00

Note: Vase variety illustrated.

Gunpowder Treason

Model No.:	Unknown - Menu holder
Designer:	George Tinworth
Height:	4 ¼", 10.8 cm
Colour:	Brown and blue
Issued:	c.1885

Description	U.S. $	Can. $	U.K. £
Gunpowder	6,000.00	7,250.00	3,250.00

**Hide and Seek Napkin Holder
(Mouse and Frog)**

Model No.:	Unknown
Designer:	George Tinworth
Height:	5 ½", 14.0 cm
Colour:	Blue and brown
Issued:	1881

Description	U.S. $	Can. $	U.K. £
Hide/seek (mouse/frog)	9,000.00	11,000.00	5,000.00

**Hide and Seek Napkin Holder
(Two Mice)**

Model No.:	Unknown
Designer:	George Tinworth
Height:	5 ½", 14.0 cm
Colour:	Blue and brown
Issued:	1881

Description	U.S. $	Can. $	U.K. £
Hide/seek (two mice)	9,000.00	11,000.00	5,000.00

Note: Also known with the two mice on the base of the model.

Home Comforts With Vase

Model No.:	Unknown
Designer:	George Tinworth
Height:	4 ½", 11.9 cm
Colour:	Blue and green
Issued:	c.1885

Description	U.S. $	Can. $	U.K. £
Home comforts	3,500.00	4,250.00	2,000.00

Note: Companion piece to 'Homeless with Vase.'

Homeless With Vase

Model No.:	Unknown
Designer:	George Tinworth
Height:	4", 10.1 cm
Colour:	Blue and green
Issued:	c.1885

Description	U.S. $	Can. $	U.K. £
Homeless with vase	3,500.00	4,250.00	2,000.00

Note: Companion piece to 'Home Comforts with Vase.'

Photograph not
available
at press time

Mice Eating Plum Pudding

Model No.:	Unknown
Designer:	George Tinworth
Height:	Unknown
Colour:	Unknown
Issued:	1888

Description	U.S. $	Can. $	U.K. £
Mice/plum pudding	6,500.00	7,750.00	3,500.00

Mice Pocket Watch Holder

Model No.:	Unknown
Designer:	George Tinworth
Height:	4 ½", 11.9 cm
Colour:	White, brown and green
Issued:	c.1885

Description	U.S. $	Can. $	U.K. £
Pocket watch holder	6,500.00	7,750.00	3,500.00

The Modeller

Model No.:	Unknown - Menu holder
Designer:	George Tinworth
Height:	4 ½", 11.9 cm
Colour:	White, brown and blue
Issued:	c.1885
Varieties:	Also called 'Sculptor'

Description	U.S. $	Can. $	U.K. £
The Modeller	5,500.00	6,500.00	3,000.00

Mouse Asleep Vase

Model No.:	Unknown
Designer:	George Tinworth
Height:	3 ¾", 9.5 cm
Colour:	Blue, green and brown
Issued:	c.1885

Description	U.S. $	Can. $	U.K. £
Mouse asleep vase	3,500.00	4,250.00	2,000.00

Mouse Smoking Tobacco Jar

Model No.:	Unknown
Designer:	George Tinworth
Height:	7 ¼", 18.4 cm
Colour:	Green, blue and brown
Issued:	c.1885

Description	U.S. $	Can. $	U.K. £
Tobacco jar	2,800.00	3,350.00	1,500.00

Painting

Model No.:	X1213
	X1113 - Menu holder
Designer:	George Tinworth
Height:	3 ½", 8.9 cm
Colour:	Blue; white or brown mice
Issued:	1886

Colourways	U.S. $	Can. $	U.K. £
1. White mice	5,000.00	6,000.00	2,750.00
2. Brown mice	5,000.00	6,000.00	2,750.00

Photography

Model No.:	Unknown
Designer:	George Tinworth
Height:	4 ½", 11.9 cm
Colour:	Blue; white or brown mice
Issued:	c.1885

Colourways	U.S. $	Can. $	U.K. £
1. White mice	5,500.00	6,500.00	3,000.00
2. Brown mice	5,500.00	6,500.00	3,000.00

The Pillars of Wealth and Poverty Between

Model No.:	Unknown
Designer:	George Tinworth
Height:	4 ½", 11.9 cm
Colour:	Brown and blue
Issued:	c.1885

Description	U.S. $	Can. $	U.K. £
Wealth and poverty	4,000.00	4750.00	2,200.00

Playgoers

Model No.:	Unknown
Designer:	George Tinworth
Height:	5 ¼", 13.3 cm
Colour:	Blue, green; white or brown mice
Issued:	1886

Colourways	U.S. $	Can. $	U.K. £
1. White mice	9,000.00	11,000.00	5,000.00
2. Brown mice	9,000.00	11,000.00	5,000.00

Photograph not
available
at press time

Potter

Model No.:	X1210		
	X1110 - Menu holder		
Designer:	George Tinworth		
Height:	3 ¾", 9.5 cm		
Colour:	Blue and brown		
Issued:	c.1885		

Description	U.S. $	Can. $	U.K. £
Potter	5,000.00	6,000.00	2,750.00

Quack Doctor

Model No.:	Unknown - Menu holder
Designer:	George Tinworth
Height:	4", 10.1 cm
Colour:	Brown; white or brown mice
Issued:	c.1885

Colourways	U.S. $	Can. $	U.K. £
1. White mice	5,500.00	6,500.00	3,000.00
2. Brown mice	5,500.00	6,500.00	3,000.00

School Board

Model No.:	Unknown - Menu holder
Designer:	George Tinworth
Height:	3 ½", 8.9
Colour:	Blue, green; white or brown mice
Issued:	c.1885

Colourways	U.S. $	Can. $	U.K. £
1. White mice	5,000.00	6,000.00	2,750.00
2. Brown mice	5,000.00	6,000.00	2,750.00

Tea Time Scandal

Model No.:	Unknown
Designer:	George Tinworth
Height:	3 ½", 8.9 cm
Colour:	Green and brown
Issued:	1888

Description	U.S. $	Can. $	U.K. £
Tea time scandal	8,000.00	9,500.00	4,250.00

Waits

Model No.:	Unknown
Designer:	George Tinworth
Height:	5 ¼", 13.3 cm
Colour:	Green and blue; white or brown mice
Issued:	c.1885
Varieties:	Also called Christmas Waits

Colourways	U.S. $	Can. $	U.K. £
1. White mice	7,500.00	9,000.00	4,000.00
2. Brown mice	7,500.00	9,000.00	4,000.00

Note: Companion piece to 'Waits Water.'

Waits Water

Model No.:	Unknown
Designer:	George Tinworth
Height:	5 ¼", 13.3 cm
Colour:	Blue; white or brown mice
Issued:	c.1885

Colourways	U.S. $	Can. $	U.K. £
1. White mice	7,500.00	9,000.00	4,000.00
2. Brown mice	7,500.00	9,000.00	4,000.00

Note: Companion piece to 'Waits.'

Wheelbarrow With Vase

Model No.:	Unknown
Designer:	George Tinworth
Height:	3 ¾", 9.5 cm
Colour:	Blue and green; white or brown mouse
Issued:	c.1885

Colourways	U.S. $	Can. $	U.K. £
1. White mouse	5,000.00	6,000.00	2,750.00
2. Brown mouse	5,000.00	6,000.00	2,750.00
3. Brown mouse with silver rim vase	5,000.00	6,000.00	2,750.00

Note: Also known in gilded Siliconeware.

The Wheelwright

Model No.:	X1107 - Menu Holder
Designer:	George Tinworth
Height:	3 ½", 8.9 cm
Colour:	Brown and green
Issued:	1886

Description	U.S. $	Can. $	U.K. £
Wheelwright	5,000.00	6,000.00	2,750.00

Mouse Musicians

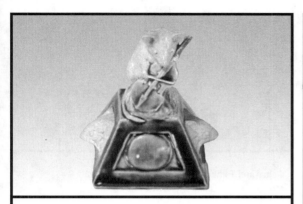

Bass Viol

Model No.:	X1207
Designer:	George Tinworth
Height:	Unknown
Colour:	White, blue and brown
Issued:	c.1884

Description	U.S. $	Can. $	U.K. £
Bass Viol	3,000.00	3,600.00	1,600.00

Cornet and Double Bass

Model No.:	Unknown - Menu holder
Designer:	George Tinworth
Height:	3 ½", 8.9 cm
Colour:	Brown and green
Issued:	c.1885

Description	U.S. $	Can. $	U.K. £
Cornet/double bass	5,000.00	6,000.00	2,750.00

Cornet Player

Model No.:	X1214 - Unknown
	X947 - Menu holder
Designer:	George Tinworth
Height:	3 ¼", 8.3 cm
Colour:	Brown and blue
Issued:	1886

Description	U.S. $	Can. $	U.K. £
1. Round base	3,500.00	4,250.00	2,000.00
2. Square base	3,500.00	4,250.00	2,000.00
3. Menu holder	3,500.00	4,250.00	2,000.00

Double Bass and Fiddle

Model No.:	X948 - Menu holder
	Unknown - Vase
Designer:	George Tinworth
Height:	5 ¼", 13.3 cm
Colour:	Green
Issued:	c.1884
Varieties:	Also made with a vase

Description	U.S. $	Can. $	U.K. £
Double bass/fiddle	4,500.00	5,500.00	2,500.00

Note: This piece was also made in bone china.

Flute Player

Model No.:	Unknown - see below
Designer:	George Tinworth
Height:	4 ¼", 10.8 cm
Colour:	Brown
Issued:	1884

Description	U.S. $	Can. $	U.K. £
1. Round base	3,000.00	3,600.00	1,600.00
2. Square base	3,000.00	3,600.00	1,600.00

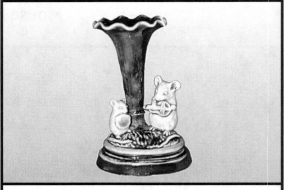

Guitar and Tambourine

Model No.:	Unknown - Vase
Designer:	George Tinworth
Height:	5 ¼", 13.3 cm
Colour:	Green, brown and white
Issued:	c.1884

Description	U.S. $	Can. $	U.K. £
Guitar/tambourine	4,500.00	5,500.00	2,500.00

Harp and Concertina

Model No.:	Unknown - Menu holder
Designer:	George Tinworth
Height:	4", 10.1 cm
Colour:	Blue, green and brown
Issued:	c.1884

Description	U.S. $	Can. $	U.K. £
Harp/concertina	5,000.00	6,000.00	2,750.00

Harp and Cornet

Model No.:	X1112 - Menu holder
	Unknown - Vase
Designer:	George Tinworth
Height:	5 ¼", 13.3 cm
Colour:	Green and brown
Issued:	c.1884

Description	U.S. $	Can. $	U.K. £
Harp/cornet	4,500.00	5,500.00	2,500.00

Harp and Piano

Model No.:	Unknown - Menu holder		
Designer:	George Tinworth		
Height:	3 ½", 8.9 cm		
Colour:	White and brown		
Issued:	1886		

Description	U.S. $	Can. $	U.K. £
Harp/piano	6,000.00	7,250.00	3,300.00

Harp and Violoncello

Model No.:	X1211 - Unknown		
	X1109 - Menu holder		
Designer:	George Tinworth		
Height:	3 ¾", 9.5 cm		
Colour:	White, blue and green		
Issued:	1885		

Description	U.S. $	Can. $	U.K. £
Harp/violoncello	5,000.00	6,000.00	2,750.00

Photograph not
available
at press time

Italian Music

Model No.:	X946		
Designer:	George Tinworth		
Height:	Unknown		
Colour:	Unknown		
Issued:	Unknown		

Description	U.S. $	Can. $	U.K. £
Italian music	6,000.00	7,250.00	3,300.00

Mouse Musician Tobacco Jar

Model No.:	Unknown		
Designer:	George Tinworth		
Height:	6 ½", 16.5 cm		
Colour:	White and brown		
Issued:	c.1885		

Description	U.S. $	Can. $	U.K. £
Tobacco Jar	5,500.00	6,500.00	3,000.00

Niggers

Model No.:	Unknown		
Designer:	George Tinworth		
Height:	3 ¾", 9.5 cm		
Colour:	Brown and blue		
Issued:	c.1885		

Description	U.S. $	Can. $	U.K. £
Niggers	7,500.00	9,000.00	4,000.00

Organ Grinder and Triangle

Model No.:	X945 - Menu holder		
	X1209 - Vase		
Designer:	George Tinworth		
Height:	3 ¼", 8.3 cm		
Colour:	Grey, blue and brown		
Issued:	1885		

Description	U.S. $	Can. $	U.K. £
1. Menu holder	4,500.00	5,500.00	2,500.00
2. Vase	4,500.00	5,500.00	2,500.00

Pianist, Horn Player and Singer

Model No.:	Unknown		
Designer:	George Tinworth		
Height:	3 ¼", 8.3 cm		
Colour:	White, brown and green		
Issued:	c.1884		
Varieties:	Also called 'A Little Of It Is All Very Well'		

Description	U.S. $	Can. $	U.K. £
Pianist/horn/singer	6,500.00	7,750.00	3,600.00

Photograph not
available
at press time

The Piano Player

Model No.:	Unknown		
Designer:	George Tinworth		
Height:	4", 10.1 cm		
Colour:	Unknown		
Issued:	c.1884		

Description	U.S. $	Can. $	U.K. £
Piano player	5,500.00	6,500.00	3,000.00

Sousaphone

Model No.:	Unknown
Designer:	George Tinworth
Height:	3 ½", 8.9 cm
Colour:	White, blue and brown
Issued:	1884
Varieties:	Also called 'French Horn'

Description	U.S. $	Can. $	U.K. £
1. Round base	3,000.00	3,600.00	1,600.00
2. Square base	3,000.00	3,600.00	1,600.00

Tuba Player

Model No.:	Unknown
Designer:	George Tinworth
Height:	3 ½", 8.9 cm
Colour:	White, brown and blue
Issued:	1886

Description	U.S. $	Can. $	U.K. £
Round base	3,500.00	6,250.00	1,900.00

Tuba and Trumpet

Model No.:	X1214 - Menu holder
Designer:	George Tinworth
Height:	3 ¾", 9.5 cm
Colour:	1. White and brown
	2. Brown
Issued:	c.1884
Varieties:	Also called 'The Cornet Blowers'

Description	U.S. $	Can. $	U.K. £
1. White mice	5,000.00	6,000.00	2,750.00
2. Brown mice	5,000.00	6,000.00	2,750.00

Note: This model was also made in bone china.

Violin

Model No.:	Unknown
Designer:	George Tinworth
Height:	3 ½", 8.9 cm
Colour:	Brown and blue, white mouse
Issued:	c.1884

Description	U.S. $	Can. $	U.K. £
1. Round base	3,000.00	3,600.00	1,600.00
2. Square base	3,000.00	3,600.00	1,600.00

Mice — 32-piece chess set
16-red and white pieces plus
16-black and white pieces.
circa 1900.

GARDEN ORNAMENTS

Beast

Model No.:	Unknown
Designer:	Mark Marshall
Height:	16 ½", 42.0 cm
Colour:	Brown
Issued:	c.1900

Description	U.S. $	Can. $	U.K. £
Beast	1,500.00	1,800.00	825.00

Cat

Model No.:	R21
Designer:	Unknown
Height:	16", 40.6 cm
Colour:	Terracotta
Issued:	c.1930

Description	U.S. $	Can. $	U.K. £
Cat	2,500.00	3,000.00	1,375.00

Drake

Model No.:	Unknown
Designer:	Richard Garbe
Height:	7", 17.8 cm
Length:	10 ½", 26.7 cm
Colour:	Green or white glaze
Issued:	c.1935

Colourways	U.S. $	Can. $	U.K. £
1. Green	1,500.00	1,800.00	825.00
2. White	1,500.00	1,800.00	825.00

Duck

Model No.:	R24
Designer:	Unknown
Height:	15", 38.1 cm
Colour:	Terracotta
Issued:	c.1930

Description	U.S. $	Can. $	U.K. £
Duck	1,500.00	1,800.00	825.00

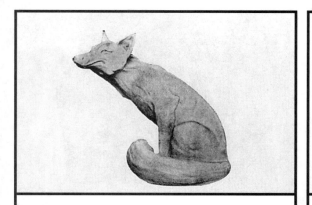

Fox

Model No.:	R16
Designer:	Harry Simeon
Height:	16", 40.6 cm
Colour:	Terracotta
Issued:	c.1930

Description	U.S. $	Can. $	U.K. £
Fox	1,500.00	1,800.00	825.00

Frog

Model No.:	R37
Designer:	Unknown
Length:	8", 20.3 cm
Colour:	Terracotta
Issued:	c.1920

Description	U.S. $	Can. $	U.K. £
Frog	1,000.00	1,200.00	550.00

Goat

Model No.:	R20
Designer:	Francis Pope
Height:	21", 53.3 cm
Colour:	Terracotta
Issued:	c.1930

Description	U.S. $	Can. $	U.K. £
Goat	1,500.00	1,800.00	825.00

Hare

Model No.:	R25
Designer:	Unknown
Height:	11" x 24", 27.9 x 61.0 cm
Colour:	Terracotta
Issued:	c.1930

Description	U.S. $	Can. $	U.K. £
Hare	2,500.00	3,000.00	1,350.00

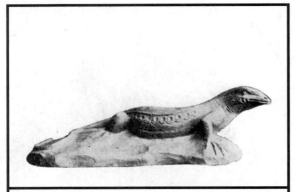

Lizard (Style One)

Model No.:	R31
Designer:	Unknown
Length:	16", 40.6 cm
Colour:	Terracotta
Issued:	c.1930

Description	U.S. $	Can. $	U.K. £
Lizard, style one	1,250.00	1,500.00	700.00

Lizard (Style Two)

Model No.:	Unknown
Designer:	Harry Simeon
Height:	Unknown
Colour:	Terracotta
Issued:	c.1930

Description	U.S. $	Can. $	U.K. £
Lizard, style two	1,250.00	1,500.00	700.00

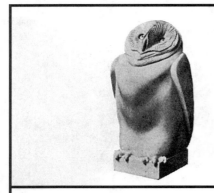

Owl (Style One)

Model No.:	R29
Designer:	Unknown
Height:	14", 35.6 cm
Colour:	Terracotta
Issued:	c.1930

Description	U.S. $	Can. $	U.K. £
Owl, style one	2,500.00	3,000.00	1,350.00

Owl (Style Two)

Model No.:	Unknown
Designer:	Francis Pope
Height:	17 ½", 44.5 cm
Colour:	Terracotta
Issued:	c.1930

Description	U.S. $	Can. $	U.K. £
Owl, style two	2,500.00	3,000.00	1,350.00

Pelican

Model No.:	R19
Designer:	Mark Marshall
Height:	14", 35.6 cm
Colour:	1. Brown
	2. Terracotta
Issued:	c.1930

Colourways	U.S. $	Can. $	U.K. £
1. Brown stoneware	1,500.00	1,800.00	825.00
2. Terracotta	1,500.00	1,800.00	825.00

Penguin

Model No.:	R23
Designer:	Unknown
Height:	17", 43.1 cm
Colour:	Terracotta
Issued:	c.1930

Description	U.S. $	Can. $	U.K. £
Penguin	2,500.00	3,000.00	1,350.00

Rabbit

Model No.:	R17
Designer:	Harry Simeon
Height:	18", 45.8 cm
Colour:	Terracotta
Issued:	c.1930

Description	U.S. $	Can. $	U.K. £
Rabbit	3,000.00	3,600.00	1,650.00

Rabbit and Young

Model No.:	R22
Designer:	Harry Simeon
Size:	7 ½" x 14", 19.0 x 35.6 cm
Colour:	Terracotta
Issued:	c.1930

Description	U.S. $	Can. $	U.K. £
Rabbit and young	2,500.00	3,000.00	1,350.00

Sealion Statue

Model No.:	Unknown
Designer:	Richard Garbe
Height:	8", 20.3 cm
Colour:	Dark brown
Issued:	c.1935

Description	U.S. $	Can. $	U.K. £
Sealion statue	1,500.00	1,800.00	825.00

Squirrel

Model No.:	R36
Designer:	Harry Simeon
Height:	13", 33.0 cm
Colour:	Terracotta
Issued:	c.1930

Description	U.S. $	Can. $	U.K. £
Squirrel	1,500.00	1,800.00	825.00

PRACTICAL ANIMALS

Baboon Cruet Set

Model No.:	Unknown		
Designer:	Harry Simeon		
Height:	Unknown		
Colour:	Siliconware, silver rim		
Issued:	c.1900		

Description	U.S. $	Can. $	U.K. £
Mustard	1,500.00	1,800.00	825.00
Pepper	1,500.00	1,800.00	825.00
Open salt	1,500.00	1,800.00	825.00
Complete Set	4,500.00	5,500.00	2,500.00

Note: Open salt illustrated.

Bear with Honey Pot

Model No.:	Unknown		
Designer:	Unknown		
Height:	4 ¼", 10.8 cm		
Colour:	Brown and beige		
Issued:	c.1910		

Description	U.S. $	Can. $	U.K. £
Bear/honey pot	1,000.00	1,200.00	550.00

Bears Cruet Set

Model No.:	Unknown		
Designer:	Harry Simeon		
Height:	3", 7.6 cm		
Colour:	Brown Siliconware, silver rim		
Issued:	c.1900		

Description	U.S. $	Can. $	U.K. £
Mustard	1,250.00	1,500.00	675.00
Pepper	1,250.00	1,500.00	675.00
Open salt	1,250.00	1,500.00	675.00
Complete Set	3,750.00	4,500.00	2,000.00

Cat Collecting Box for RSPCA

Model No.:	Unknown		
Designer:	Unknown		
Height:	8 ½", 21.6 cm		
Colour:	Light blue and dark blue		
Issued:	c.1900		

Description	U.S. $	Can. $	U.K. £
Cat box	2,000.00	2,500.00	1,100.00

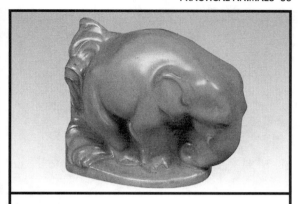

Dog Collecting Box for RSPCA

Model No.:	Unknown	
Designer:	Unknown	
Height:	7 ½", 19.1 cm	
Colour:	Blue; brown or white dog	
Issued:	c.1900	

Description	U.S. $	Can. $	U.K. £
1. White	2,000.00	2,500.00	1,100.00
2. Brown	2,000.00	2,500.00	1,100.00

Elephant Bookends (Pair)

Model No.:	Unknown	
Designer:	Gilbert Bayes	
Height:	6 ¼", 13.5 cm	
Colour:	Green glaze	
Issued:	c.1935	

Description	U.S. $	Can. $	U.K. £
Bookends (pair)	1,500.00	1,800.00	825.00

Photograph not
available
at press time

Frog Flowerstand

Model No.:	X8716
Designer:	Unknown
Height:	Unknown
Colour:	Unknown
Issued:	1933

Description	U.S. $	Can. $	U.K. £
Frog flowerstand		Extremely Rare	

Frog with Open Mouth

Model No.:	X8901
Designer:	Vera Huggins
Height:	3 ¾", 9.5 cm
Colour:	Blue
Issued:	1933

Description	U.S. $	Can. $	U.K. £
Frog with open mouth		Rare	

Marmoset Cruet Set

Model No.:	Unknown
Designer:	Unknown
Height:	2 ¾", 7.0 cm
Colour:	Siliconware
Issued:	c.1900

Description	U.S. $	Can. $	U.K. £
Mustard	1,500.00	1,800.00	825.00
Pepper	1,500.00	1,800.00	825.00
Open salt	1,500.00	1,800.00	825.00
Complete Set	4,500.00	5,500.00	2,500.00

Note: Mustard pot illustrated.

Owl Matchholder

Model No.:	Unknown
Designer:	Unknown
Height:	3 ¼", 8.3 cm
Colour:	Black Siliconware with silver beak
Issued:	c.1895

Description	U.S. $	Can. $	U.K. £
Matchholder	1,000.00	1,200.00	550.00

Note: Other sizes are known.

Owl Sugar Dredger

Model No.:	X8692
Designer:	Unknown
Height:	4 ¾", 12.1 cm
Colour:	Blue
Issued:	c.1910

Description	U.S. $	Can. $	U.K. £
Sugar dredger	900.00	1,100.00	500.00

Owl Tobacco Jar

Model No.:	Unknown
Designer:	Possibly John Broad
Height:	7 ½", 19.1 cm
Colour:	1. Brown and blue Siliconware
	2. Coloured Doultonware
Issued:	c.1910

Colourways	U.S. $	Can. $	U.K. £
1. Brown/blue	2,000.00	2,500.00	1,100.00
2. Coloured	2,000.00	2,500.00	1,100.00

Owls (pair) Bookend

Model No.:	X8767		
Designer:	Vera Huggins		
Height:	6", 15.0 cm		
Colour:	Brown, beige and green		
Issued:	c.1925		

Description	U.S. $	Can. $	U.K. £
Bookend	1,350.00	1,650.00	750.00

Polar Bear Bookends

Model No.:	Unknown		
Designer:	F. G. R. Roth		
Height:	8 ¾" x 8 ¼", 22.2 x 21.0 cm		
Colour:	White, light brown shading, green base		
Issued:	c.1930		

Description	U.S. $	Can. $	U.K. £
Bookends (Pair)	3,500.00	4,500.00	2,000.00

Photograph not
available
at press time

Polar Bear Sitting

Model No.:	Unknown		
Designer:	Leslie Harradine		
Height:	6 ¾", 17.2 cm		
Colour:	White Carraraware		
Issued:	c.1910		

Description	U.S. $	Can. $	U.K. £
Polar bear	800.00	950.00	425.00

Polar Bears on Bowl

Model No.:	Unknown		
Designer:	Vera Huggins		
Height:	5", 12.7 cm		
Colour:	Cream stoneware		
Issued:	c.1930		

Description	U.S. $	Can. $	U.K. £
Polar bears on bowl		Extremely Rare	

Note: This model was used to promote Doulton's Carraraware, a white glazed building material.

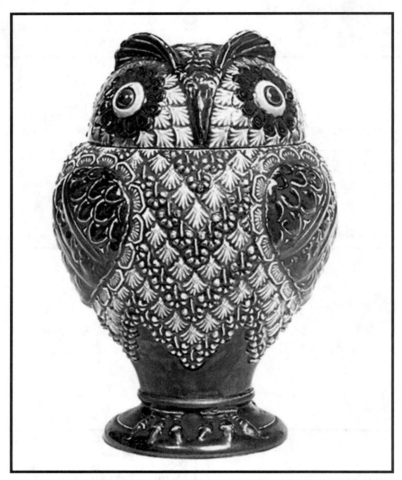

Brown and blue Siliconeware Owl Tobacco Jar
c.1910

MISCELLANEOUS

Cat

Designer:	Unknown
Height:	6 ½", 16.5 cm
Colour:	White Carraraware
Issued:	c.1910

Description	U.S. $	Can. $	U.K. £
Cat	1,250.00	2,250.00	700.00

Note: This model was made to promote Doulton's Carraraware, a white glazed building material.

Cat

Designer:	Agnete Hoy
Height:	10 ½", 26.7 cm
Colour:	See below
Issued:	1955

Colourways	U.S. $	Can. $	U.K. £
1. Black/blue	7,000.00	8,500.00	4,000.00
2. Black/white	7,000.00	8,500.00	4,000.00
3. Blue stripes	7,000.00	8,500.00	4,000.00
4. Brown stripes	7,000.00	8,500.00	4,000.00

Note: It is believed only 12 of these models, each in a different colourways were made.

Rabbit

Model No.:	Unknown
Designer:	Unknown
Height:	2 ¾", 7.0 cm
Colour:	1. Green
	2. Light brown
Issued:	c.1922

Colourways	U.S. $	Can. $	U.K. £
1. Green	500.00	600.00	250.00
2. Light brown	500.00	600.00	250.00

Squirrel

Model No.:	X8802
Designer:	Unknown
Height:	6 ½", 16.5 cm
Colour:	1. Brown
	2. Green
Issued:	c.1930

Colourways	U.S. $	Can. $	U.K. £
1. Brown	850.00	1,000.00	475.00
2. Green	850.00	1,000.00	475.00

HN SERIES

HN 7
Pedlar Wolf

Model No.:	76			
Designer:	Charles Noke			
Height:	5 ½", 14.0 cm			
Colour:	See below			
Issued:	1. 1913-1938			
	2. c.1913-1938			

Description	U.S. $	Can. $	U.K. £
1. Black wolf/blue cloak	Extremely Rare		
2. Flambé	Extremely Rare		

HN 100
Fox In Hunting Dress

Model No.:	151
Designer:	Charles Noke
Height:	6", 15.2 cm
Colour:	Brown fox wearing hunting pink riding coat, white shirt and cravat, gold stud
Issued:	1913-1942

Description	U.S. $	Can. $	U.K. £
Fox in hunting dress	2,200.00	2,700.00	1,200.00

Note: Also known with a green jacket.

HN 101
Rabbit In Morning Dress

Model No.:	152
Designer:	Charles Noke
Height:	6 ½", 16.5 cm
Colour:	Red coat, white trousers, black and white checkered cravat
Issued:	1913-by 1938
Varieties:	Also called "Hare In White Coat" HN 102

Description	U.S. $	Can. $	U.K. £
Rabbit in morning dress	Extremely Rare		

HN 102
Hare In White Coat

Model No.:	152
Designer:	Charles Noke
Height:	6 ½", 16.5 cm
Colour:	White coat
Issued:	1913-by 1938
Varieties:	Also called "Rabbit In Morning Dress" HN 101

Description	U.S. $	Can. $	U.K. £
Hare in white coat	Extremely Rare		

HN 103
Penguins

Model No.:	103		
Height:	6", 15.2 cm		
Colour:	See below		
Issued:	1913-by 1946		
Varieties:	HN 133		

Colourways	U.S. $	Can. $	U.K. £
1. Grey/white/black	1,000.00	1,200.00	550.00
2. Flambé	1,500.00	1,800.00	825.00
3. Blue	1,200.00	1,450.00	650.00

HN 104
Penguin
Style One

Model No.:	85		
Height:	4 ½", 11.4 cm		
Colour:	See below		
Issued:	1913-by 1946		
Varieties:	HN 134		

Colourways	U.S. $	Can. $	U.K. £
1. Black/white (earthenware)	800.00	950.00	425.00
2. Flambé	1,200.00	1,450.00	650.00
3. Chinese Jade	2,500.00	3,000.00	1,375.00

HN 105
Collie, Seated - brown

Model No.:	47		
Height:	7 ½", 19.1 cm		
Colour:	See below		
Issued:	1. 1912-by 1946; 2. and 3. c.1912		
Varieties:	HN 106, 112		

Colourways	U.S. $	Can. $	U.K. £
1. Brown/black/white	1,000.00	1,200.00	550.00
2. Black (gloss)	1,000.00	1,200.00	550.00
3. Red (matt)	1,000.00	1,200.00	550.00
4. Flambé	1,600.00	2,000.00	875.00
5. Sung	2,500.00	3,000.00	1,375.00

HN 106
Collie, Seated - blue (earthenware)

Model No.:	47		
Height:	7 ½", 19.1 cm		
Colour:	See below		
Issued:	1. 1912-by 1946; 2. and 3. c.1912		
Varieties:	HN 105, 112		

Colourways	U.S. $	Can. $	U.K. £
1. Blue-grey (earthenware)	1,000.00	1,200.00	550.00
2. Black (gloss)	1,000.00	1,200.00	550.00
3. Red (matt)	1,000.00	1,200.00	550.00
4. Flambé	1,600.00	2,000.00	875.00
5. Sung	2,500.00	3,000.00	1,375.00

HN 107
Hare
Crouching - Style One

Model No.:	119
Size:	2" x 4 ½", 5.1 x 11.4 cm
Colour:	See below
Issued:	1913-by 1946
Varieties:	HN 126, 142, 273, 803

Colourways	U.S. $	Can. $	U.K. £
1. Brown (earthenware)	650.00	800.00	350.00
2. Flambé	850.00	1,000.00	450.00
3. Sung	1,250.00	1,500.00	700.00

HN 108
Lop-eared Rabbit

Model No.:	113
Height:	4", 10.1 cm
Colour:	See below
Issued:	1. 1913-by 1946
	2. Unknown
Varieties:	HN 151, 276

Colourways	U.S. $	Can. $	U.K. £
1. White	750.00	900.00	425.00
2. Flambé (illustrated)		Very Rare	

HN 109
Cat
Seated - Style One

Model No.:	9
Designer:	Charles Noke
Height:	4 ½", 11.4 cm
Colour:	See below
Issued:	1. 1912-by 1946 2. 1920-1996
Varieties:	HN 120, 967

Colourways	U.S. $	Can. $	U.K. £
1. White/black (earthenware)	1,000.00	1,200.00	550.00
2. Flambé	200.00	250.00	110.00
3. Sung		Extremely Rare	

HN 110
Titanian Bowl Decorated with a Butterfly

Model No.:	Unknown
Height:	3", 7.6 cm
Colour:	Lid of bowl decorated in turquoise with brown and orange butterfly (china)
Issued:	1912

Description	U.S. $	Can. $	U.K. £
Titanian bowl		Extremely Rare	

HN 111
Cockerel
Crowing

Model No.:   25
Height: 3 ¼", 8.3 cm
Colour: See below
Issued: 1. 1912-1936
               2. c.1912-1936

Colourways	U.S. $	Can. $	U.K. £
1. White/black/red	1,000.00	1,200.00	550.00
2. Flambé		Rare	

HN 112
Collie, Seated - Blue (china)

Model No.:   47
Height: 7 ½", 19.1 cm
Colour: See below
Issued: 1. 1912-by 1946;   2. and 3.   c.1912
Varieties: HN 105, 106

Colourways	U.S. $	Can. $	U.K. £
1. Blue-grey (china)	1,000.00	1,200.00	550.00
2. Black (gloss)	1,000.00	1,200.00	550.00
3. Red (matt)	1,000.00	1,200.00	550.00
4. Flambé	1,600.00	2,000.00	875.00
5. Sung	2,500.00	3,000.00	1,375.00

HN 113
Emperor Penguin

Model No.:   84
Designer: Unknown
Height: 6", 15.2 cm
Colour: See below
Issued: 1. 1913-by 1946
               2. 1913-1996
Varieties: HN 296

Colourways	U.S. $	Can. $	U.K. £
1. Black/white/grey	1,000.00	1,200.00	550.00
2. Flambé (illustrated)	300.00	375.00	150.00

HN 114
Mallard Drake
Standing - Malachite head

Model No.:   137
Height: 5 ½", 14.0 cm
Size: Medium
Colour: See below
Issued: 1. 1913-by 1946
               2. 1913-1996
Varieties: HN 115, 116, 956, 1191, 2555, 2647

Colourways	U.S. $	Can. $	U.K. £
1. Malachite/green/white	450.00	550.00	250.00
2. Flambé	300.00	375.00	150.00

HN 115
Mallard Drake
Standing - Blue head

Model No.:	137
Height:	5 ½", 14.0 cm
Size:	Medium
Colour:	See below
Issued:	1. 1913-by 1946
	2. 1913-1996
Varieties:	HN 114, 116, 956, 1191, 2555, 2647

Colourways	U.S. $	Can. $	U.K. £
1. Blue/green/white	450.00	550.00	250.00
2. Flambé	300.00	375.00	150.00

HN 116
Mallard Duck
Standing - Green head

Model No.:	137
Height:	5 ½", 14.0 cm
Size:	Medium
Colour:	See below
Issued:	1. 1913-by 1946
	2. 1913-1996
Varieties:	HN 114, 115, 956, 1191, 2555, 2647

Colourways	U.S. $	Can. $	U.K. £
1. Green/white	450.00	550.00	250.00
2. Flambé	300.00	375.00	150.00

HN 117
Foxes, Curled - Style One

Model No.:	6
Height:	3 ½", 8.9 cm
Colour:	See below
Issued:	1. 1912-by 1946
	2, 3, and 4. c.1912
Varieties:	HN 179

Colourways	U.S. $	Can. $	U.K. £
1. Grey/light brown	1,500.00	1,800.00	800.00
2. Flambé	1,000.00	1,200.00	550.00
3. Holbien	600.00	725.00	325.00
4. Sung	2,000.00	2,500.00	1,100.00

HN 118
Monkey
Seated, arms folded

Model No.:	53
Height:	3", 7.6 cm
Colour:	See below
Issued:	1912-by 1946
Varieties:	HN 253
Derivative:	On alabaster base

Colourways	U.S. $	Can. $	U.K. £
1. Grey (china)	600.00	725.00	325.00
2. Flambé	700.00	850.00	375.00
3. Titanian		Very Rare	

CHESS SET
A REISSUE OF AN EARLY SET BY GEORGE TINWORTH

The Frog Chessmen (White)

The Mice Chessmen (Black)

Rook, Knight, Bishop, Queen, King, Bishop, Knight, Rook
Pawn, Pawn

GEORGE TINWORTH MODELS

Waits

The Pillars of Wealth and Poverty Between

United Family
(Monkeys grooming each other)

The Ox And The Frogs

Going to the Derby

Lost and Serves them Right

GEORGE TINWORTH MODELS

The Public Library's Act

The Monkey That Would Be King

Jack in the Green

Bicyclist

**Safe Travelling
(Monkeys Riding A Tortoise)**

Football

BIRDS

HN 169
Barn Owl, Style One

HN 150
Duck, Head stretched forward

HN 877
Cockatoo on Rock

HN 229
Duck, Head stretched forward

HN 973
Character Duck, Style Three

HN 195
Gannet

BIRDS

HN 164
Rooster, Style One

HN 2615
Cardinal, Style Three

HN 163
Budgerigar on Tree Stump

HN 136
Swallow on Rock

HN 2554
Cardinal, Style Two

WILD ANIMALS

HN 1082
Tiger, Stalking, Style Two

HN 990
Tiger, Stalking, Style One

HN 2639
Tiger on a Rock, Style Five

HN 919
Leopard

WILD ANIMALS

HN 2659
Brown Bear, Style Two

HN 2592
Hare, Crouching, Style Three

HN 140
Ape

HN 147C-1
Fox, Seated, Style One

HN 138
Squirrel

HN 2641
Lion on Rock, Style Two

HN 219
Rabbits

HORSES

HN 2530
"Merely a Minor"

HN 2571
"Merely a Minor"

HN 2564
Pride of The Shires

HN 2532
"The Gude Grey Mare"

HN 119
Polar Bear on Cube

Model No.:	67
Designer:	Leslie Harradine
Height:	4", 10.1 cm
Colour:	See below
Issued:	1. 1912-1936
	2. c.1936

Colourways	U.S. $	Can. $	U.K. £
1. Grey/yellow/green	600.00	725.00	330.00
2. Flambé	1,500.00	1,800.00	830.00

HN 120
Cat, Seated - Style One

Model No.:	9
Designer:	Charles Noke
Height:	4 ½", 11.4 cm
Colour:	See below
Issued:	1. 1912-by 1946
	2. and 3. 1920-1996
Varieties:	HN 109, 967

Colourways	U.S. $	Can. $	U.K. £
1. White/black (china)	1,200.00	1,500.00	670.00
2. Flambé	200.00	250.00	110.00
3. Sung	Extremely Rare		

HN 121
Polar Bear, Seated

Model No.:	39
Height:	3 ¾", 9.5 cm
Colour:	See below
Issued:	1. 1912-1936
	2. 3 and 4. c.1912-1936
Derivative:	Polar bear on dish, Model 40 (flambé)

Colourways	U.S. $	Can. $	U.K. £
1. White (china)	900.00	1,100.00	500.00
2. Flambé	1,250.00	1,500.00	675.00
3. Sung	2,000.00	2,500.00	1,100.00
4. Titanian	2,000.00	2,500.00	1,100.00

HN 122
Fantail Pigeons

Model No.:	46
Height:	4", 10.1 cm
Colour:	See below
Issued:	1. 1912-1936
	2. c.1912-by 1946

Colourways	U.S. $	Can. $	U.K. £
1. Grey-blue/black	800.00	975.00	400.00
2. Flambé	1,500.00	1,800.00	800.00
3. Chinese Jade	4,500.00	5,500.00	2,500.00

HN 123
Pelican
Beak Up

Model No.:	109
Height:	4", 10.1 cm
Colour:	See below
Issued:	1. 1913-1936
	2. c.1913-1936

Colourways	U.S. $	Can. $	U.K. £
1. White/black/orange	1,000.00	1,200.00	550.00
2. Flambé	1,500.00	1,800.00	825.00
3. Kingsware	1,000.00	1,200.00	550.00

HN 124
Cockerel, Crouching - cream

Model No.:	30
Height:	3 ¼", 8.3 cm
Colour:	See below
Issued:	1. 1912-1936
	2. c.1912
Varieties:	HN 178, 180, 267
Derivative:	Cockerel bowl with hollow centre and sterling silver rim (flambé)

Colourways	U.S. $	Can. $	U.K. £
1. Cream/black/red	350.00	425.00	200.00
2. Flambé	600.00	725.00	325.00

HN 125
Guinea Fowl

Model No.:	69
Size:	3 ¼" x 5 ¼", 8.3 x13.3 cm
Colour:	See below
Issued:	1. 1912-by 1946
	2. 1912-1967

Colourways	U.S. $	Can. $	U.K. £
1. Grey-pink/red-brown	600.00	725.00	325.00
2. Flambé	750.00	900.00	400.00

HN 126
Hare
Crouching - Style One

Model No.:	119
Size:	2" x 4 ½", 5.1 x 11.4 cm
Colour:	See below
Issued:	1913-by 1946
Varieties:	HN 107, 142, 273, 803

Colourways	U.S. $	Can. $	U.K. £
1. Brown (china)	650.00	800.00	350.00
2. Flambé	850.00	1,000.00	450.00
3. Sung	1,250.00	1,500.00	700.00

HN 127
Cavalier King Charles Spaniel
Style One

Model No.:	82
Designer:	Charles Noke
Height:	3 ½", 8.9 cm
Colour:	See below
Issued:	1. 1912-1936
	2. and 3. 1920-1936

Colourways	U.S. $	Can. $	U.K. £
1. Natural colours	850.00	1,000.00	475.00
2. Chinese Jade	2,500.00	3,000.00	1,350.00
3. Flambé	1,000.00	1,200.00	550.00

HN 128
Puppy
Seated

Model No.:	116
Height:	4", 10.1 cm
Colour:	See below
Issued:	1. 1913-by 1946
	2 and 3. c.1913
Derivative:	Flambé puppy on onyx pin tray

Colourways	U.S. $	Can. $	U.K. £
1. Natural colours (china)	800.00	975.00	450.00
2. Flambé	900.00	1,100.00	500.00
3. Sung	1,800.00	2,300.00	1,000.00

HN 129
Bulldog, Seated - Style Four

Model No.:	1. Natural 135
	2. Flambé 135A
Height:	6", 15.2 cm
Colour:	See below
Issued:	1. 1913-by 1946
	2. c.1913
Varieties:	HN 948

Colourways	U.S. $	Can. $	U.K. £
1. White/black	5,000.00	6,000.00	2,750.00
2. Flambé	3,000.00	3,600.00	1,700.00
3. Sung	5,000.00	6,000.00	2,750.00

HN 130
Fox, Seated - Style Three

Model No.:	102
Designer:	Charles Noke
Height:	1. 8 ½", 21.6 cm
	2. 9 ¼", 23.5 cm
Size:	Large
Colour:	See below
Issued:	1. 1913-by 1946
	2. 1913-1962

Colourways	U.S. $	Can. $	U.K. £
1. Brown	1,100.00	1,350.00	625.00
2. Flambé	1,100.00	1,350.00	625.00

HN 131
Kingfisher on Rock
Style One

Model No.:	44
Height:	4", 10.1 cm
Colour:	See below
Issued:	1. 1913-1936
	2. c.1913-by 1946
Varieties:	HN 152

Colourways	U.S. $	Can. $	U.K. £
1. Malachite/blue/green	300.00	375.00	150.00
2. Flambe	750.00	900.00	400.00

HN 132
Drake on Rock

Model No.:	138
Height:	3 ½", 8.9 cm
Colour:	See below
Issued:	1. 1913-1936
	2. c.1913-1936
Derivative:	Chinese Jade pin tray

Colourways	U.S. $	Can. $	U.K. £
1. Turquoise/white/ brown/pearl rock	350.00	425.00	175.00
2. Flambé	750.00	900.00	400.00

Note: Also known with a brown rock.

HN 133
Penguins

Model No.:	103
Height:	6", 15.2 cm
Colour:	See below
Issued:	1913-by 1946
Varieties:	HN 103

Colourways	U.S. $	Can. $	U.K. £
1. Black/white/brown	1,000.00	1,200.00	550.00
2. Blue	1,500.00	1,800.00	825.00
3. Flambé	1,200.00	1,450.00	650.00

HN 134
Penguin
Style One

Model No.:	85
Designer:	Unknown
Height:	4 ½", 11.4 cm
Colour:	See below
Issued:	1913-by 1946
Varieties:	HN 104

Colourways	U.S. $	Can. $	U.K. £
1. Black/white (china)	800.00	950.00	425.00
2. Flambé	1,200.00	1,450.00	650.00
3. Chinese Jade	2,500.00	3,000.00	1,375.00

HN 135
Raven

Model No.:	43
Size:	3" x 5 ¼", 7.6 x 13.3 cm
Colour:	See below
Issued:	1. 1913-1936
	2. c.1912

Colourways	U.S. $	Can. $	U.K. £
1. Blue/green/purple	Extremely Rare		
2. Flambé (illustrated)	2,000.00	2,500.00	1,000.00

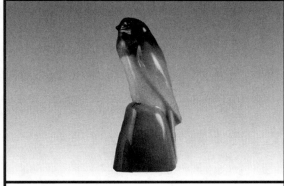

HN 136
Swallow on Rock

Model No.:	196
Height:	4 ½", 11.4 cm
Colour:	Blue feathers, brown head, red, grey and white breast, beige rock
Issued:	1917-1936
Varieties:	HN 149; Also called 'Blue Bird on Rock' HN 269

Description	U.S. $	Can. $	U.K. £
Blue swallow	375.00	450.00	200.00

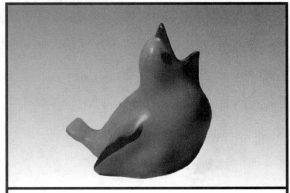

HN 137A
Fledgling
Style Four

Model No.:	99
Height:	2", 5.1 cm
Colour:	See below
Issued:	1. and 2. 1917-1936
	3. c.1912-by 1946

Colourways	U.S. $	Can. $	U.K. £
1. Blue/black	200.00	250.00	100.00
2. Yellow/black	200.00	250.00	100.00
3. Flambé	400.00	475.00	225.00

HN 137B
Fledgling
Style Two

Model No.:	1238	
Height:	Natural	1 ¼", 3.2 cm
	Flambé	2", 5.1 cm
Colour:	See below	
Issued:	1. and 2. 1917-1936	
	3. c.1908	

Colourways	U.S. $	Can. $	U.K. £
1. Blue/black	200.00	250.00	100.00
2. Yellow/black	200.00	250.00	100.00
3. Flambé	400.00	475.00	225.00

HN 138
Squirrel

Model No.:	115
Height:	2 ¼", 5.7 cm
Colour:	See below
Issued:	1. 1917-by 1946
	2. c.1912-by 1946
Varieties:	HN 1093A on fluted ashtray
	HN 1093B on plain ashtray

Colourways	U.S. $	Can. $	U.K. £
1. Brown	500.00	600.00	275.00
2. Flambé	1,500.00	1,800.00	850.00

HN 139
Eagle on Rock

Model No.:	145
Height:	9", 22.9 cm
Colour:	See below
Issued:	1. 1917-1936
	2. c.1913-1936

Colourways	U.S. $	Can. $	U.K. £
1. Brown/orange/yellow/ blue	Extremely Rare		
2. Pale brown (illustrated)	1,200.00	1,450.00	650.00
3. Titanian	2,000.00	2,500.00	1,100.00

HN 140
Ape

Model No.:	147
Height:	6", 15.2 cm
Colour:	Brown with orange highlights
Issued:	1917-1936

Description	U.S. $	Can. $	U.K. £
Ape	2,500.00	3,000.00	1,400.00

HN 141
Rhinoceros
Standing

Model No.:	107
Size:	3" x 6 ½", 7.6 x 16.5 cm
Colour:	See below
Issued:	1. 1917-by 1946
	2. c.1912

Colourways	U.S. $	Can. $	U.K. £
1. Grey/black/white	1,500.00	1,800.00	850.00
2. Flambé	2,000.00	2,500.00	1,100.00

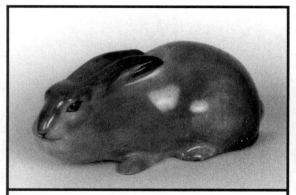

HN 142
Hare, Crouching - Style One

Model No.:	119
Height:	2", 5.1 cm
Colour:	See below
Issued:	1. 1917-by 1946
	2. and 3. 1913-by 1946
Varieties:	HN 107, 126, 273, 803

Colourways	U.S. $	Can. $	U.K. £
1. Brown (china)	650.00	800.00	350.00
2. Flambé	850.00	1,000.00	450.00
3. Sung	1,250.00	1,500.00	700.00

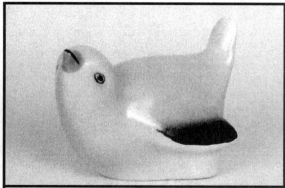

HN 143
Fledgling
Style Three

Model No.:	98
Height:	2", 5.1 cm
Colour:	See below
Issued:	1. and 2. 1917-by 1946
	3. c.1912

Colourways	U.S. $	Can. $	U.K. £
1. Blue/yellow	200.00	250.00	100.00
2. Yellow	200.00	250.00	100.00
3. Flambé	400.00	475.00	225.00

HN 144
Robin , Style One

Model No.:	104
Height:	2", 5.1 cm
Colour:	See below
Issued:	1. 1917-by 1946
	2. c.1913-by 1946
Varieties:	Also called 'Wren' Style One, HN 277;
	HN 1089A on fluted ashtray,
	HN 1089B on plain ashtray

Colourways	U.S. $	Can. $	U.K. £
1. Dark brown/red	400.00	475.00	200.00
2. Flambé	750.00	900.00	400.00

HN 145A
Fledgling
Style One

Model No.:	1236
Height:	Natural 1 ½", 3.8 cm
	Flambé 2 ½", 5.1 cm
Colour:	See below
Issued:	1. and 2. 1917-1936
	3. c.1908-by 1946

Colourways	U..S. $	Can. $	U.K. £
1. Blue/yellow/black	200.00	250.00	100.00
2. Yellow/black	200.00	250.00	100.00
3. Flambé	400.00	475.00	225.00

HN 145B
Fledgling on Rock
Style One

Model No.:	139
Height:	3 ¾", 9.5 cm
Colour:	1. Dark blue feathers, yellow breast, dark blue rock
	2. Green-turquoise feathers, yellow breast, beige rock
	3. White feathers, cream rock, overall pearl glaze
	4. Yellow feathers, black wing tips, yellow rock
	5. Flambé
Issued:	1. to 4. 1917-1936
	5. c.1913
Derivative:	Flambé on onyx base

Colourways	U.S. $	Can. $	U.K. £
1. Dark blue	300.00	350.00	150.00
2. Green-turquoise	300.00	350.00	150.00
3. White	300.00	350.00	150.00
4. Yellow	300.00	350.00	150.00
5. Flambé	750.00	900.00	400.00

HN 145C
Fledgling
Style Five

Model No.:	1237
Height:	2", 5.1 cm
Colour:	1. Blue and yellow, black wing tips
	2. Yellow, black wing tips
	3. Yellow, brown wing tips
Issued:	1917-by 1946

Colourways	U.S. $	Can. $	U.K. £
1. Blue/yellow	200.00	250.00	100.00
2. Yellow/black	200.00	250.00	100.00
3. Yellow/brown	200.00	250.00	100.00

HN 146
Bulldog with Helmet and Haversack (Old Bill)

Model No.:	Unknown
Height:	6 ½", 16.5 cm
Size:	Large
Colour:	See below
Issued:	1. 1918-c.1925
	2. Unknown

Colourways	U.S. $	Can. $	U.K. £
1. Brown/bronze helmet	1,500.00	1,800.00	750.00
2. Titanian	Extremely Rare		

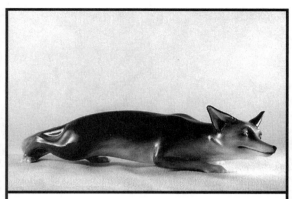

HN 147A
Fox, Stalking - large

Model No.:	29A
Size:	2 ½" x 12 ½", 6.4 x 31.7 cm
Size:	Large
Colour:	See below
Issued:	1. 1918-by 1946
	2. c.1912-1962

Colourways	U.S. $	Can. $	U.K. £
1. Light and dark brown	1,200.00	1,450.00	650.00
2. Flambé	1,000.00	1,200.00	525.00

HN 147A-1
Fox, Stalking - small

Model No.:	29B
Size:	1" x 5 ¼", 2.5 x 13.3 cm
Colour:	See below
Issued:	1. 1918-by 1946
	2. and 4. Unknown
	3. c.1912-1996

Colourways	U.S. $	Can. $	U.K. £
1. Natural colours	500.00	600.00	275.00
2. Chinese Jade	2,200.00	2,600.00	1,100.00
3. Flambé	200.00	250.00	100.00
4. Sung	700.00	850.00	375.00

HN 147B
Fox, Seated - Style Two - small

Model No.:	14
Height:	4 ½", 12.1 cm
Colour:	See below
Issued:	1. 1918-by 1946
	2. 1912-1996
	3. c.1920

Colourways	U.S. $	Can. $	U.K. £
1. Brown/cream/black	300.00	350.00	160.00
2. Flambé	200.00	250.00	100.00
3. Sung	600.00	725.00	325.00

HN 147C
Fox, Seated - Style One - medium

Model No.:	12
Height:	4 ¾", 12.1 cm
Colour:	See below
Issued:	1. 1918-by 1946
	2. and 3. c.1912-1946
Varieties:	Also decorated with transfer prints of grapes and vines

Colourways	U.S. $	Can. $	U.K. £
1. Brown/white/black	600.00	725.00	325.00
2. Flambé (illustrated)	600.00	725.00	325.00
3. Sung	1,000.00	1,200.00	525.00

HN 147C-1
Fox
Seated - Style One - small

Model No.:	12A
Height:	3", 7.6 cm
Colour:	See below
Issued:	1. 1918-by 1946
	2. 1912-1938
Derivative:	Fox seated on sterling silver tray

Colourways	U.S. $	Can. $	U.K. £
1. Browns/black	600.00	725.00	325.00
2. Flambé	700.00	850.00	390.00

HN 147D
Fox
Curled - Style One

Model No.:	15
Height:	4 ¾", 12.1 cm
Colour:	See below
Issued:	1. 1918-by 1946
	2. and 3. c.1912

Colourways	U.S. $	Can. $	U.K. £
1. Brown/black	700.00	850.00	390.00
2. Flambé	900.00	1,100.00	475.00
3. Holbien	500.00	600.00	275.00

HN 147E
Fox
Stalking - medium

Model No.:	29
Size:	1 ½" x 8 ¼", 5.1 x 21.0 cm
Size:	Medium
Colour:	See below
Issued:	1. 1918-by 1946
	2. c.1912-1962

Colourways	U.S. $	Can. $	U.K. £
1. Browns	700.00	850.00	390.00
2. Flambé	500.00	600.00	275.00

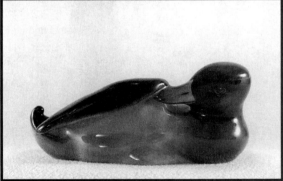

HN 148A
Duck
Preening - Style Two

Model No.:	4
Size:	1 ½" x 3 ½", 3.8 x 8.9 cm
Colour:	See below
Issued:	1. 1913-1936
	2. c.1912
Varieties:	HN 271, 299

Colourways	U.S. $	Can. $	U.K. £
1. Blue/green/brown (china)	400.00	475.00	225.00
2. Flambé	500.00	600.00	275.00

HN 148B
Duck
Resting

Model No.:	112
Height:	2", 5.1 cm
Size:	Small
Colour:	See below
Issued:	1. 1918-by 1946
	2. 1912-1996

Colourways	U.S. $	Can. $	U.K. £
1. Blue/green/brown	500.00	600.00	275.00
2. Flambé (illustrated)	150.00	175.00	80.00

HN 149
Swallow on Rock

Model No.:	196
Height:	4 ¾", 12.1 cm
Colour:	Dark blue-black feathers, red markings on head, white breast, beige rock
Issued:	1918-by 1946
Varieties:	HN 136; Also called 'Blue Bird on Rock' HN 269

Description	U.S. $	Can. $	U.K. £
Dark blue swallow	350.00	425.00	200.00

HN 150
Duck
Head stretched forward

Model No.:	207
Height:	4", 10.1 cm
Size:	Large
Colour:	See below
Issued:	1. 1918-by 1946
	2. c.1917
Varieties:	HN 229, 2556

Colourways	U.S. $	Can. $	U.K. £
1. Browns/cream/blue	500.00	600.00	275.00
2. Flambé	700.00	850.00	375.00

HN 151
Lop-eared Rabbit

Model No.:	113
Height:	4", 10.1 cm
Colour:	See below
Issued:	1. 1918-by 1946
	2. Unknown
Varieties:	HN 108, 276

Colourways	U.S. $	Can. $	U.K. £
1. White/black patches	750.00	900.00	425.00
2. Flambé		Very Rare	

HN 152
Kingfisher on Rock
Style One

Model No.:	44
Height:	4", 10.1 cm
Colour:	See below
Issued:	1. 1918-1936
	2. c.1913-by 1946
Varieties:	HN 131, Flambé

Colourways	U.S. $	Can. $	U.K. £
1. Turquoise/yellow/beige	300.00	375.00	150.00
2. Flambé	750.00	900.00	400.00

HN 153
Bulldog With Tam O'Shanter and Haversack

Model No.:	Unknown
Height:	7", 17.8 cm
Colour:	See below
Issued:	1. 1918-c.1925
	2. Unknown

Colourways	U.S. $	Can. $	U.K. £
1. Brown/bronze tam	2,000.00	2,500.00	1,000.00
2. Titanian		Extremely Rare	

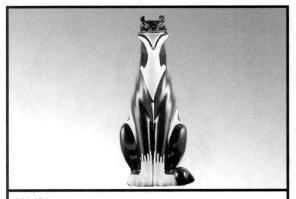

HN 154
'Kateroo' Character Cat

Model No.:	214	
Designer:	Charles Noke	
Height:	12 ¾", 32.0 cm	
Colour:	1.	Black and white (china)
	2.	Green
	3.	Yellow
Issued:	1918-c.1925	

Colourways	U.S. $	Can. $	U.K. £
1. Black and white		Extremely Rare	
2. Green		In all	
3. Yellow		Colourways	

HN 155
Owl
Style One

Model No.:	153
Designer:	Charles Noke
Height:	5", 12.7 cm
Colour:	Light and dark brown
Issued:	1918-by 1946

Description	U.S. $	Can. $	U.K. £
Owl		Very Rare	

HN 156
Monkey
Hand raised to ear

Model No.:	156
Height:	3 ½", 8.9 cm
Colour:	See below
Issued:	1. 1918-by 1946
	2. c.1912

Colourways	U.S. $	Can. $	U.K. £
1. Natural colours	800.00	975.00	450.00
2. Flambé	1,000.00	1,200.00	550.00

Note: A model is known in an experimental Sung-like glaze.

HN 157
Cockerel
Seated - Style One

Model No.:	50
Height:	Unknown
Colour:	Blue and purple
Issued:	1918-1936

Description	U.S. $	Can. $	U.K. £
Cockerel		Extremely Rare	

HN 158
Toucan on Perch - green

Model No.:	212
Height:	7 ½", 19.1 cm
Colour:	Green, blue and black plumage, orange and black beak, black perch
Issued:	1918-1936
Varieties:	HN 159, 196, 294

Colourways	U.S. $	Can. $	U.K. £
Green/blue/black	750.00	900.00	400.00

HN 159
Toucan on Perch - black

Model No.:	212
Height:	7 ½", 19.1 cm
Colour:	Black, green, yellow and orange
Issued:	1918-1936
Varieties:	HN 158, 196, 294

Colourways	U.S. $	Can. $	U.K. £
Black/green/yellow	750.00	900.00	400.00

HN 160
Owl With Owlet Under Wing

Model No.:	71
Designer:	Charles Noke
Height:	4 ¾", 12.1 cm
Colour:	See below
Issued:	1. 1918-1936
	2. c.1912-1936
Derivative:	Flambé, on onyx base

Colourways	U.S. $	Can. $	U.K. £
1. Browns		Extremely Rare	
2. Flambé (illustrated)		Extremely Rare	

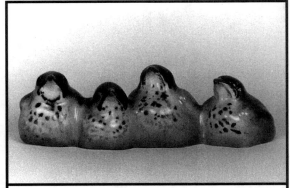

HN 161
Thrush Chicks (four)

Model No.:	208
Size:	2" x 5 ½", 5.1 x 14.0 cm
Colour:	See below
Issued:	1. 1918-by 1946
	2. c.1912
Varieties:	Also called 'Four Fledglings' HN 171

Colourways	U.S. $	Can. $	U.K. £
1. Yellow/black/brown	450.00	525.00	250.00
2. Flambé		Rare	

HN 162
Butterfly on Stump

Model No.:	141
Height:	3", 7.6 cm
Colour:	Light blue wings, dark blue markings, gold body, beige rock
Issued:	1918-1936

Description	U.S. $	Can. $	U.K. £
Blue butterfly	650.00	1,100.00	350.00

HN 163
Budgerigar on Tree Stump

Model No.:	221
Height:	7", 17.8 cm
Colour:	See below
Issued:	1. and 2. 1918-1936; 3. and 4. c.1918-1936
Varieties:	HN 199
Derivative:	Onyx pin tray

Colourways	U.S. $	Can. $	U.K. £
1. Green/yellow/black	500.00	600.00	275.00
2. White/green/pearl	500.00	600.00	275.00
3. Flambé	900.00	1,075.00	500.00
4. Sung	1,200.00	1,450.00	650.00

HN 164
Rooster
Style One

Model No.:	225
Height:	9", 22.9 cm
Colour:	Orange back, brown breast, red head
Issued:	1918-by 1946
Varieties:	HN 184

Description	U.S. $	Can. $	U.K. £
Orange rooster		Extremely Rare	

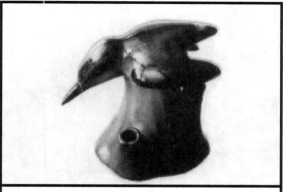

HN 165
Kingfisher on Tree Stump (flower holder)
Style One

Model No.:	227
Height:	3", 7.6 cm
Colour:	See below
Issued:	1. 1918-1936
	2. c.1918-1936
Varieties:	HN 858

Colourways	U.S. $	Can. $	U.K. £
1. Blue/turquoise/orange	600.00	725.00	335.00
2. Flambé	1,000.00	1,200.00	550.00

HN 166
Foxhound, Seated - Style One

Model No.:	209
Height:	1 4", 10.1 cm
	2. 3", 7.6 cm
Colour:	See below
Issued:	1. 1918-by 1946
	2. c.1917

Colourways	U.S. $	Can. $	U.K. £
1. White/brown	750.00	900.00	400.00
2. Flambé	1,000.00	1,200.00	550.00

Note: A Foxhound on a plinth is model 40A.

HN 167
Tern (female)

Model No.:	231
Size:	2 ½" x 8 ½", 6.4 x 21.6 cm
Colour:	See below
Issued:	1. 1918-by 1946
	2. c.1912
Varieties:	HN 1194; Also called 'Tern (male)'
	HN 168, 1193

Colourways	U.S. $	Can. $	U.K. £
1. Grey/white/red	450.00	550.00	250.00
2. Flambé	1,000.00	1,200.00	550.00

HN 168
Tern (male)

Model No.:	231
Size:	2 ½" x 8 ½", 6.4 x 21.6 cm
Colour:	See below
Issued:	1. 1918-by 1946
	2. c.1912
Varieties:	HN 1193; Also called 'Tern (female)'
	HN 167, 1194

Colourways	U.S. $	Can. $	U.K. £
1. Blue-grey/white/black	450.00	550.00	250.00
2. Flambé	1,000.00	1,200.00	550.00

HN 169
Barn Owl
Style One

Model No.:	148
Designer:	Harry Tittensor
Height:	3", 7.6 cm
Colour:	See below)
Issued:	1. 1918-by 1946
	2. c.1913

Colourways	U.S. $	Can. $	U.K. £
1. Cream/brown (china)	1,000.00	1,200.00	550.00
2. Flambé	1,200.00	1,500.00	650.00

HN 170
Comic Brown Bear

Model No.:	58
Designer:	Charles Noke
Height:	5", 12.7 cm
Colour:	See below
Issued:	1. 1918-1936
	2. and 3. c.1918-1936
Varieties:	HN 270

Colourways	U.S. $	Can. $	U.K. £
1. Brown	1,000.00	1,200.00	550.00
2. Blue	1,200.00	1,500.00	650.00
3. Flambé	1,500.00	1,800.00	800.00

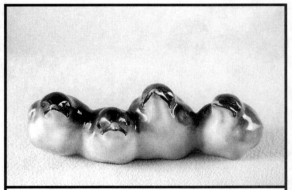

HN 171
Four Fledglings

Model No.:	208
Size:	2" x 5 ½", 5.1 x 14.0 cm
Colour:	See below
Issued:	1. 1918-by 1946
	2. c.1912
Varieties:	Also called 'Thrush Chicks (four)' HN 161

Colourways	U.S. $	Can. $	U.K. £
1. Browns/cream	450.00	525.00	250.00
2. Flambé		Rare	

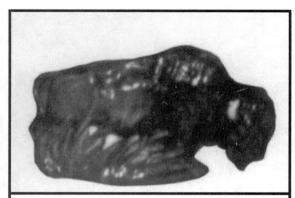

HN 172
Bison
Style One

Model No.:	136
Height:	5", 12.7 cm
Colour:	Light and dark brown
Issued:	1918-1936

Description	U.S. $	Can. $	U.K. £
Bison		Very Rare	

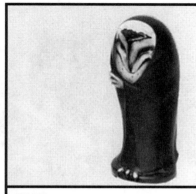

HN 173
Granny Owl

Model No.:	228
Designer:	Charles Noke
Height:	7 ½", 19.1 cm
Colour:	Red cloak and ermine collar
Issued:	1918-1936
Varieties:	HN 187; Also called 'Wise Old Owl'

Description	U.S. $	Can. $	U.K. £
Granny owl	4,000.00	4,750.00	2,200.00

*

HN 175
Great-Crested Grebe

Model No.:	233
Height:	12", 30.5 cm
Colour:	Green back and beak, pale breast
Issued:	1918-by 1946

Description	U.S. $	Can. $	U.K. £
Great-crested grebe		Extremely Rare	

HN 176
Bloodhound

Model No.:	48
Height:	5 ¾", 14.6 cm
Colour:	See below
Issued:	1. 1919-by 1946
	2. c.1926

Colourways	U.S. $	Can. $	U.K. £
1. Brown	1,250.00	1,500.00	700.00
2. Flambé	2,000.00	2,500.00	1,100.00

*

HN 178
Cockerel, Crouching - green

Model No.:	30
Height:	3 ¼", 8.3 cm
Colour:	Green
Issued:	1. 1919-1936; 2. c.1912
Varieties:	HN 124, 180, 267
Derivative:	Cockerel bowl with hollow centre and sterling silver rim (flambé)

Colourways	U.S. $	Can. $	U.K. £
1. Green	350.00	425.00	200.00
2. Flambé	600.00	725.00	325.00

HN 179
Foxes, Curled - Style One

Model No.:	6
Height:	4", 10.1 cm
Colour:	See below
Issued:	1. 1919-by 1946
	2. 3. and 4. c.1912
Varieties:	HN 117

Colourways	U.S. $	Can. $	U.K. £
1. Brown/orange	1,500.00	1,800.00	800.00
2. Flambé	1,000.00	1,200.00	550.00
3. Holbien	600.00	725.00	325.00
4. Sung	2,000.00	2,500.00	1,100.00

HN 180
Cockerel, Crouching - red

Model No.:	30
Height:	3 ¼", 8.3 cm
Colour:	See below
Issued:	1. 1919-1936 2. c.1912
Varieties:	HN 124, 178, 267
Derivative:	Cockerel bowl with hollow centre and sterling silver rim (flambé)

Colourways	U.S. $	Can. $	U.K. £
1. Red/orange	350.00	425.00	200.00
2. Flambé	600.00	725.00	325.00

HN 181
Elephant, Trunk down, curled

Model No.:	65
Designer:	Charles Noke
Height:	4", 10.1 cm (small)
Colour:	See below
Issued:	1. 1920-by 1946
	2. and 3. c.1913-by 1946
Varieties:	HN 186

Colourways	U.S. $	Can. $	U.K. £
1. Grey/black (china)	500.00	600.00	275.00
2. Flambé	700.00	850.00	375.00
3. Sung	1,000.00	1,200.00	550.00

HN 182
Character Monkey - green

Model No.:	213		
Designer:	Charles Noke		
Height:	7", 17.8 cm		
Colour:	See below		
Issued:	1. 1920-1936		
	2. c.1920		
Varieties:	HN 183		

Colourways	U.S. $	Can. $	U.K. £
1. Green jacket/hat		Very Rare	
2. Flambé		Very Rare	

HN 183
Character Monkey - blue

Model No.:	213		
Designer:	Charles Noke		
Height:	7", 17.8 cm		
Colour:	See below		
Issued:	1. 1920-1936		
	2. c.1920		
Varieties:	HN 182		

Colourways	U.S. $	Can. $	U.K. £
1. Blue jacket/hat		Very Rare	
2. Flambé		Very Rare	

HN 184
Rooster
Style One

Model No.:	225
Height:	9", 22.9 cm
Colour:	White and grey body, black tail feathers, red comb
Issued:	1920-by 1946
Varieties:	HN 164

Description	U.S. $	Can. $	U.K. £
White/grey rooster		Extremely Rare	

HN 185
Cockatoo on a Rock - yellow

Model No.:	68
Designer:	Leslie Harradine
Height:	6", 15.2 cm
Colour:	See below
Issued:	1. 1920-1936
	2. c.1912-1936
Varieties:	HN 191, 192, 200, 877
Derivative:	Onyx pin tray

Colourways	U.S. $	Can. $	U.K. £
1. Yellow/white	600.00	700.00	325.00
2. Flambé	1,200.00	1,450.00	650.00

HN 186
Elephant, Trunk down, curled

Model No.:	65
Designer:	Charles Noke
Height:	4", 10.1 cm (small)
Colour:	See below
Issued:	1. 1920-by 1946
	2. and 3. c.1913-by 1946
Varieties:	HN 181

Colourways	U.S. $	Can. $	U.K. £
1. Brown	500.00	600.00	275.00
2. Flambé	700.00	850.00	375.00
3. Sung	1,000.00	1,200.00	550.00

HN 187
Granny Owl

Model No.:	228
Designer:	Charles Noke
Height:	7 ½", 19.1 cm
Colour:	Blue-grey check shawl with white mob cap
Issued:	1920-by 1946
Varieties:	HN 173; Also called 'Wise Old Owl'

Description	U.S. $	Can. $	U.K. £
Granny owl	4,000.00	4,750.00	2,200.00

HN 188
Duckling
New born - yellow/brown

Model No.:	3
Height:	3", 7.6 cm
Colour:	See below
Issued:	1. 1920-1936
	2. c.1912
Varieties:	HN 189, 190

Colourways	U.S. $	Can. $	U.K. £
1. Yellow/brown		Rare	
2. Flambé		Rare	

HN 189
Duckling
New born - yellow/black

Model No.:	3
Height:	3", 7.6 cm
Colour:	See below
Issued:	1. 1920-1936
	2. c.1912
Varieties:	HN 188, 190

Colourways	U.S. $	Can. $	U.K. £
1. Black/yellow		Rare	
2. Flambé		Rare	

HN 190
Duckling
New born - green

Model No.:	3
Height:	3", 7.6 cm
Colour:	See below
Issued:	1. 1920-1936
	2. c.1912
Varieties:	HN 188, 189

Colourways	U.S. $	Can. $	U.K. £
1. Green/blue		Rare	
2. Flambé (illustrated)		Rare	

HN 191
Cockatoo on a Rock - blue

Model No.:	68
Designer:	Leslie Harradine
Height:	6", 15.2 cm
Colour:	See below
Issued:	1. 1920-1936
	2. c.1912-1936
Varieties:	HN 185, 192, 200, 877
Derivative:	Onyx pin tray

Colourways	U.S. $	Can. $	U.K. £
1. Blue/purple	600.00	700.00	325.00
2. Flambé	1,200.00	1,450.00	650.00

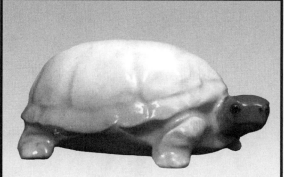

HN 192
Cockatoo on a Rock - red

Model No.:	68
Designer:	Leslie Harradine
Height:	6", 15.2 cm
Colour:	See below
Issued:	1. 1920-1936
	2. c.1912-1936
Varieties:	HN 185, 191, 200, 877
Derivative:	Onyx pin tray

Colourways	U.S. $	Can. $	U.K. £
1. Red/orange	600.00	700.00	325.00
2. Flambé	1,200.00	1,450.00	650.00

HN 193
Tortoise

Model No.:	101
Size:	2" x 4 ¾", 5.1 x 12.1 cm
Size:	Large
Colour:	See below
Issued:	1. 1920-by 1946
	2. c.1912

Colourways	U.S. $	Can. $	U.K. £
1. Grey/red head	800.00	950.00	450.00
2. Flambé	2,000.00	2,500.00	1,100.00
3. Sung	2,500.00	3,000.00	1,250.00

HN 194
Terrier Puppy
Lying

Model No.:	121
Size:	3" x 7 ¾", 7.6 x 19.7 cm
Colour:	See below
Issued:	1. 1920-by 1946
	2. c.1913

Colourways	U.S. $	Can. $	U.K. £
1. White/black	1,200.00	1,450.00	650.00
2. Flambé		Very Rare	

HN 195
Gannet

Model No.:	243
Height:	6 ½", 16.5 cm
Colour:	See below
Issued:	1. 1920-by 1946
	2. c.1919
Varieties:	HN 1197

Colourways	U.S. $	Can. $	U.K. £
1. Blue-grey/white	800.00	950.00	450.00
2. Flambé		Very Rare	

HN 196
Toucan on Perch

Model No.:	212
Height:	7 ½", 19.1 cm
Colour:	Blue and purple toucan on brown perch
Issued:	1920-1936
Varieties:	HN 158, 159, 294

Description	U.S. $	Can. $	U.K. £
Blue toucan	750.00	900.00	400.00

HN 197
Weaver Bird on Rock

Model No.:	251
Height:	5" 12.7 cm
Colour:	Black with orange breast
Issued:	1920-by 1946
Varieties:	HN 220

Description	U.S. $	Can. $	U.K. £
Black/orange weaver bird	1,000.00	1,200.00	550.00

HN 198
King Penguin and Chick

Model No.:	239
Height:	5 ½", 14.0 cm
Colour:	See below
Issued:	1. 1920-by 1946
	2. c.1918-1961
Varieties:	HN 297, 998

Colourways	U.S. $	Can. $	U.K. £
1. Black/white	1,200.00	1,450.00	650.00
2. Flambé (illustrated)	1,200.00	1,450.00	650.00

HN 199
Budgerigar on Tree Stump

Model No.:	221
Height:	6 ¾", 17.2 cm
Colour:	See below
Issued:	1. 1920-1936
	2. and 3. c.1918-1936
Varieties:	HN 163
Derivative:	Onyx pin tray

Colourways	U.S. $	Can. $	U.K. £
1. Light blue/yellow	500.00	600.00	275.00
2. Flambé (illustrated)	900.00	1,075.00	500.00
3. Sung	1,200.00	1,450.00	650.00

HN 200
Cockatoo on a Rock

Model No.:	68
Designer:	Leslie Harradine
Height:	6", 15.2 cm
Colour:	See below
Issued:	1. 1920-1936
	2. c.1912-1936
Varieties:	HN 185, 191, 192, 877
Derivative:	Onyx pin tray

Colourways	U.S. $	Can. $	U.K. £
1. Blue/green	600.00	700.00	325.00
2. Flambé	1,200.00	1,450.00	650.00

HN 201
Cat with Mouse on Tail
Tabby

Model No.:	216
Height:	4 ¼", 10.8 cm
Colour:	See below
Issued:	1. 1920-by 1946
	2 and 3. c.1920
Varieties:	HN 202

Colourways	U.S. $	Can. $	U.K. £
1. Tabby	3,500.00	4,000.00	1,750.00
2. Flambé (illustrated)	4,000.00	4,750.00	2,000.00
3. Sung	4,000.00	4,750.00	2,000.00

HN 202
Cat with Mouse on Tail
Black

Model No.:	216
Height:	4 ¼", 10.8 cm
Colour:	See below
Issued:	1. 1920-by 1946
	2 and 3. c.1920
Varieties:	HN 201

Colourways	U.S. $	Can. $	U.K. £
1. Black/white/grey	3,500.00	4,000.00	1,750.00
2. Flambé	4,000.00	4,750.00	2,000.00
3. Sung	4,000.00	4,750.00	2,000.00

HN 203
Cat on a Column/or Plinth - tabby cat

Model No.:	240
Height:	1. On column - 7", 17.8 cm
	2. On plinth - 4", 10.1 cm
Colour:	Tabby cat on column or plinth
Issued:	1920-by 1946
Varieties:	HN 244, 245

Description	U.S. $	Can. $	U.K. £
1. On column (illustrated)	3,500.00	4,000.00	1,750.00
2. On plinth	3,500.00	4,000.00	1,750.00

HN 204
Persian Kitten
Style One

Model No.:	242
Height:	5", 12.7 cm
Colour:	See below
Issued:	1. 1920-by 1946
	2. c.1920
Varieties:	HN 221

Colurways	U.S. $	Can. $	U.K. £
1. Tabby		Extremely rare	
2. Sung		Extremely rare	

HN 205
Ducklings
Standing - black

Model No.:	247
Height:	2 ¾", 7.0 cm
Colour:	See below
Issued:	1. 1920-by 1946
	2. c.1919
Varieties:	HN 206, 275

Colourways	U.S. $	Can. $	U.K. £
1. Black/light yellow	600.00	725.00	350.00
2. Flambé		Rare	

HN 206
Ducklings
Standing - brown

Model No.:	247		
Height:	2 ¾", 7.0 cm		
Colour:	See below		
Issued:	1. 1920-by 1946		
	2. c.1919		
Varieties:	HN 205, 275		

Colourways	U.S. $	Can. $	U.K. £
1. Browns/white	600.00	725.00	350.00
2. Flambé		Rare	

HN 207
Country Mouse

Model No.:	250
Designer:	Charles Noke
Height:	Unknown
Colour:	Cream coat, brown head and tail
Issued:	1920-1936

Description	U.S. $	Can. $	U.K. £
Country mouse		Extremely rare	

HN 208
Toucan in Tail Coat and Bow Tie

Model No.:	234
Designer:	Charles Noke
Height:	4 ½", 11.4 cm
Colour:	Black and white
Issued:	1920-by 1946
Derivative:	Place name holder

Description	U.S. $	Can. $	U.K. £
Toucan	2,500.00	3,000.00	1,250.00

HN 209
Rabbits
Brown, one with Dark Head

Model No.:	249
Height:	3 ½", 8.9 cm
Colour:	See below
Issued:	1. 1920-by 1946
	2. c.1919
Varieties:	HN 217, 218, 219, 969

Colourways	U.S. $	Can. $	U.K. £
1. Brown	1,500.00	1,750.00	750.00
2. Flambé		Very Rare	

HN 210
Cat Asleep, Head on Paw

Model No.:	23
Height:	1 ½", 3.8 cm
Colour:	See below
Issued:	1. 1920-1936
	2. Unknown
Varieties:	HN 227

Description	U.S. $	Can. $	U.K. £
1. Black/white cat	1,000.00	1,250.00	550.00
2. Flambé	1,500.00	1,800.00	750.00

HN 211
Black-Headed Gull (male)

Model No.:	235
Height:	4", 10.1 cm
Colour:	Black-head, grey feathers, white breast
Issued:	1920-by 1946
Varieties:	HN 1195; Also called 'Seagull (female)'
	HN 212, 1196

Description	U.S. $	Can. $	U.K. £
Black-headed gull (male)	600.00	725.00	325.00

HN 212
Seagull (female)

Model No.:	235
Height:	4", 10.1 cm
Colour:	White head and breast, grey feathers, red beak
Issued:	1920-by 1946
Varieties:	HN 1196; Also called 'Black-headed Gull (male)' HN 211, 1195

Description	U.S. $	Can. $	U.K. £
Seagull (female)	600.00	725.00	325.00

HN 213
Pigs
Snoozing - Both Pigs' Ears Up

Model No.:	61
Size:	4" x 7", 10.1 x 17.8 cm
Colour:	See below
Issued:	1. 1920-1936
	2. 1912-1936
Varieties:	HN 238, 802

Colourways	U.S. $	Can. $	U.K. £
1. Green/mauve		Very Rare	
2. Flambé (illustrated)	2,000.00	2,500.00	1,000.00

HN 214
Bird with Five Chicks - black

Model No.:	246
Height:	3 ¼", 8.3 cm
Colour:	Black, pink and brown
Issued:	1920-1936
Varieties:	HN 215, 216, 272

Colourways	U.S. $	Can. $	U.K. £
1. Black	500.00	600.00	250.00
2. Flambé	1,200.00	1,450.00	650.00

HN 215
Bird with Five Chicks - grey

Model No.:	246
Height:	3 ¼", 8.3 cm
Colour:	Grey, blue and lemon
Issued:	1920-1936
Varieties:	HN 214, 216, 272

Colourways	U.S. $	Can. $	U.K. £
1. Grey	500.00	600.00	250.00
2. Flambé	1,200.00	1,450.00	650.00

HN 216
Bird with Five Chicks - green

Model No.:	246
Height:	3 ¼", 8.3 cm
Colour:	Green, blue and lemon
Issued:	1920-1936
Varieties:	HN 214, 215, 272

Colourways	U.S. $	Can. $	U.K. £
1. Green	500.00	600.00	250.00
2. Flambé	1,200.00	1,450.00	650.00

HN 217
Rabbits
Brown patches on Faces

Model No.:	249
Height:	3 ½", 8.9 cm
Colour:	See below
Issued:	1. 1920-by 1946
	2. c.1919
Varieties:	HN 209, 218, 219, 969

Colourways	U.S. $	Can. $	U.K. £
1. Brown	1,500.00	1,750.00	750.00
2. Flambé		Very Rare	

HN 218
Rabbits
Black patches on Face

Model No.:	249
Height:	3 ½", 8.9 cm
Colour:	See below
Issued:	1. 1920-by 1946
	2. c.1919
Varieties:	HN 209, 217, 219, 969

Colourways	U.S. $	Can. $	U.K. £
1. Brown/black patches	1,500.00	1,750.00	750.00
2. Flambé		Very Rare	

HN 219
Rabbits
Black and Yellow patches on Face

Model No.:	249
Height:	3 ½", 8.9 cm
Colour:	See below
Issued:	1. 1920-by 1946
	2. c.1919
Varieties:	HN 209, 217, 218, 969

Colourways	U.S. $	Can. $	U.K. £
1. Brown/black/yellow	1,500.00	1,750.00	750.00
2. Flambé		Very Rare	

HN 220
Weaver Bird on Rock

Model No.:	251
Height:	5", 12.7 cm
Colour:	Red and brown
Issued:	1920-by 1946
Varieties:	HN 197

Description	U.S. $	Can. $	U.K. £
Red/brown Weaver bird	1,000.00	1,200.00	550.00

HN 221
Persian Kitten
Style One

Model No.:	242
Height:	5", 12.7 cm
Colour:	See below
Issued:	1. 1920-by 1946
	2. c.1920
Varieties:	HN 204

Colourways	U.S. $	Can. $	U.K. £
1. Black/white		Extremely Rare	
2. Sung (illustrated)		Extremely Rare	

HN 222
Owl in a Crescent Moon-Shaped Dish

Model No.:	37			
Height:	4", 10.1 cm			
Colour:	See below			
Issued:	1. and 2. 1920-1936			
	3. c.1912			

Colourways	U.S. $	Can. $	U.K. £
1. White/gold highlights		Very Rare	
2. Yellow/green lustre		Very Rare	
3. Flambé		Very Rare	

HN 223
Lion
Seated

Model No.:	59			
Height:	6 ½", 16.5 cm			
Colour:	See below			
Issued:	1. 1920-by 1946			
	2 and 3. c.1912			

Colourways	U.S. $	Can. $	U.K. £
1. Brown		Very Rare	
2. Flambé		Very Rare	
3. Holbien		Very Rare	

HN 224
Kingfisher on Rock
Style Two

Model No.:	258			
Height:	3 ½", 8.9 cm			
Colour:	Blue			
Issued:	1920-by 1946			

Description	U.S. $	Can. $	U.K. £
Kingfisher	1,200.00	1,450.00	650.00

HN 225
Tiger
Crouching

Model No.:	111			
Designer:	Charles Noke			
Size:	2" x 9 ½", 5.1 x 24.0 cm			
Colour:	See below			
Issued:	1. 1920-1936; 2. c.1912-1968			

Colourways	U.S. $	Can. $	U.K. £
1. Browns	800.00	950.00	450.00
2. Flambé (illustrated)	1,000.00	1,200.00	550.00

Note: Model No. 111 was also used to produce flambé panther.

HN 226
Town Mouse - blue

Model No.:	256
Designer:	Charles Noke
Height:	2 ½", 6.4 cm
Colour:	Blue coat, blue hat with yellow and green feather, green and yellow scarf
Issued:	1920-by 1946
Varieties:	HN 228

Description	U.S. $	Can. $	U.K. £
Blue coat and hat	1,500.00	1,750.00	800.00

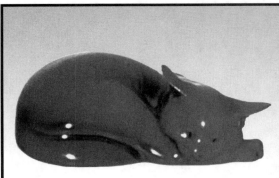

HN 227
Cat Asleep, Head on Paw

Model No.:	23
Height:	1 ½", 3.8 cm
Colour:	See below
Issued:	1. 1920-1936
	2. Unknown
Varieties:	HN 210

Description	U.S. $	Can. $	U.K. £
1. Tabby	1,000.00	1,250.00	550.00
2. Flambé (illustrated)	1,500.00	1,800.00	750.00

HN 228
Town Mouse - yellow

Model No.:	256
Designer:	Charles Noke
Height:	2 ½", 6.4 cm
Colour:	Yellow coat
Issued:	1920-by 1946
Varieties:	HN 226

Description	U.S. $	Can. $	U.K. £
Yellow coat	1,600.00	1,900.00	850.00

HN 229
Duck
Head stretched forward

Model No.:	207
Height:	4", 10.1 cm
Colour:	See below
Issued:	1. 1920-by 1946
	2. c.1917
Varieties:	HN 150, 2556

Colourways	U.S. $	Can. $	U.K. £
1. Browns/green	500.00	600.00	275.00
2. Flambé	700.00	850.00	375.00

HN 231
English St. Bernard
Model No.:   262
Height: 1. 7", 17.8 cm
             2. 7 ¾", 19.7 cm
Colour: See below
Issued: 1. 1920-by 1946
             2. c.1919

Colourways	U.S. $	Can. $	U.K. £
1. Natural colours	2,000.00	2,500.00	1,100.00
2. Flambé	2,500.00	3,000.00	1,300.00

HN 232
Puppy with Bone
Model No.:   118
Height: 4", 10.1 cm
Colour: See below
Issued: 1. 1920-by 1946
             2. c.1913

Colourways	U.S. $	Can. $	U.K. £
1. Light/dark brown		Extremely Rare	
2. Flambé		Extremely Rare	

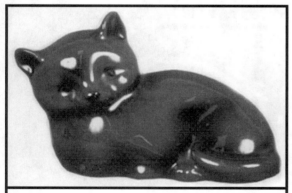

HN 233
Cat
Lying
Model No.:   70
Height: 3 ½", 8.9 cm
Colour: See below
Issued: 1. 1920-1936
             2. c.1920-1936

Colourways	U.S. $	Can. $	U.K. £
1. Yellow/orange/black	1,500.00	1,800.00	850.00
2. Flambé (illustrated)	2,000.00	2,500.00	1,100.00

HN 234
Cats
Model No.:   259
Height: 5", 12.7 cm
Colour: Black, brown and white
Issued: 1920-1936

Description	U.S. $	Can. $	U.K. £
Cats	2,000.00	2,500.00	1,100.00

HN 235
Duck
Preening - Style One

Model No.:	2
Height:	2 ½", 6.4 cm
Colour:	See below
Issued:	1. 1920-1936
	2. c.1912-1936
Varieties:	HN 298

Colourways	U.S. $	Can. $	U.K. £
1. Orange/black	1,000.00	1,200.00	550.00
2. Flambé	900.00	1,075.00	425.00

HN 236
Chicks (two)

Model No.:	1163A
Designer:	Charles Noke
Height:	2 ½", 6.4 cm
Colour:	See below
Issued:	1. 1920-by 1946
	2 and 3. c.1908-by 1946

Colourways	U.S. $	Can. $	U.K. £
1. Dark blue/turquoise	600.00	725.00	325.00
2. Black	600.00	725.00	325.00
3. Flambé (illustrated)	600.00	725.00	325.00
4. Sung	900.00	1,075.00	500.00

NOTES ON PRICING

- Animal figures are not as plentiful as pretty ladies or character figures and caution in pricing must prevail.

- In the pricing tables N/I (not issued) indicates that the animal figure was not available in that particular market.

- Rarity classification provides a range for the collector to work with.

- Always remember that when dealing with rare animal figures you need two willing parties, a buyer and a seller. One without the other will not work and only when they agree do you have a market price.

Rarity Class	Rare	Very Rare	Extremely Rare
U.S. $	1,850.-2,750.	2,750.-4,500.	4,500. - Up
Can. $	2,250.-3,500.	3,500.-5,500.	5,500. - Up
U.K. £	1,000.-1,500.	1,500.-2,500.	2,500. - Up

HN 237
Mrs Gamp Mouse

Model No.:	257
Designer:	Charles Noke
Height:	Unknown
Colour:	Unknown
Issued:	1920-by 1946

Description	U.S. $	Can. $	U.K. £
Mrs Gamp Mouse		Extremely Rare	

HN 238
Pigs
Snoozing - Both Pigs' Ears Up

Model No.:	61			
Size:	4" x 7", 10.1 x 17.8 cm			
Colour:	See below			
Issued:	1. 1920-1936			
	2. 1912-1936			
Varieties:	HN 213, 802			

Colourways	U.S. $	Can. $	U.K. £
1. Unknown		Very Rare	
2. Flambé (illustrated)	2,000.00	2,500.00	1,000.00

HN 239
Ducklings
Resting

Model No.:	97
Size:	1 ¾" x 5 ½", 4.5 x 14.0 cm
Colour:	See below
Issued:	1. 1920-by 1946
	2. c.1913

Colourways	U.S. $	Can. $	U.K. £
1. Light brown	500.00	600.00	275.00
2. Red (matt)	600.00	725.00	325.00
3. Flambé	800.00	950.00	425.00

HN 240
Thrush on Rock

Model No.:	253
Height:	5 ½", 14.0 cm
Colour:	Blue, red, black and green
Issued:	1920-1936

Description	U.S. $	Can. $	U.K. £
Thrush	1,000.00	1,200.00	550.00

HN 241
Eagle Crouching on Rock - brown

Model No.:	265
Height:	5", 12.7 cm
Colour:	Brown and gold
Issued:	1920-by 1946
Varieties:	HN 242

Colourways	U.S. $	Can. $	U.K. £
Brown eagle	1,500.00	1,800.00	825.00

HN 242
Eagle Crouching on Rock - light brown

Model No.:	265
Height:	5", 12.7 cm
Colour:	Light brown and gold, white head and neck
Issued:	1920-by 1946
Varieties:	HN 241

Description	U.S. $	Can. $	U.K. £
Light brown eagle	1,500.00	1,800.00	825.00

HN 243
Pig Bowl, Style One

Model No.:	Unknown
Size:	2 ½" x 5 ½", 6.4 x 14.0 cm
Colour:	See below
Issued:	1. 1920-1936
	2. c.1920
	3. 1934

Colourways	U.S. $	Can. $	U.K. £
1. Brown/cream/silver	600.00	725.00	325.00
2. Flambé	1,000.00	1,200.00	550.00
3. Titanian	1,200.00	1,450.00	650.00
4. Kingsware	500.00	600.00	275.00

HN 244
Cat on a Column/or Plinth - black and white cat

Model No.:	240
Height:	1. On column - 7", 17.8 cm
	2. On plinth - 4", 10.1 cm
Colour:	Black and white cat on brown column or plinth
Issued:	1920-by 1946
Varieties:	HN 203, 245

Description	U.S. $	Can. $	U.K. £
1. On column	3,000.00	3,750.00	1,750.00
2. On plinth (illustrated)	3,000.00	3,750.00	1,750.00

HN 245
Cat on a Column/or Plinth - black

Model No.:	240
Height:	1. On column - 7", 17.8 cm
	2. On plinth - 4", 10.1 cm
Colour:	Black cat on brown column or plinth
Issued:	1920-by 1946
Varieties:	HN 203, 244

Description	U.S. $	Can. $	U.K. £
1. On column (illustrated)	3,000.00	3,750.00	1,750.00
2. On plinth	3,000.00	3,750.00	1,750.00

HN 246
Comic Pig

Model No.:	57
Designer:	Charles Noke
Height:	5 ½", 14.0 cm
Colour:	See below
Issued:	1. 1920-1936
	2 and 3. Unknown

Colourways	U.S. $	Can. $	U.K. £
1. Unknown		Very Rare	
2. Flambé	2,500.00	3,000.00	1,250.00
3. Titanian	3,000.00	3,600.00	1,500.00

HN 247
Peahen

Model No.:	270
Height:	4 ½", 11.4 cm
Colour:	See below
Issued:	1. 1921-by 1946
	2. c.1920

Colourways	U.S. $	Can. $	U.K. £
1. Grey/pink/black/red	600.00	1,000.00	350.00
2. Flambé		Very Rare	

HN 248
Duck
Standing - white / blue

Model No.:	307
Height:	13", 33.0 cm
Size:	Large
Colour:	White and blue
Issued:	1921-by 1946
Varieties:	HN 249, 252, 1198, 2635

Description	U.S. $	Can. $	U.K. £
White and blue duck	2,000.00	2,500.00	1,100.00

HN 249
Drake
Standing - blue / white

Model No.:	307
Height:	13", 33.0 cm
Size:	Large
Colour:	Blue and white
Issued:	1921-by 1946
Varieties:	HN 248, 252, 1198, 2635

Description	U.S. $	Can. $	U.K. £
Blue and white duck	2,000.00	2,500.00	1,100.00

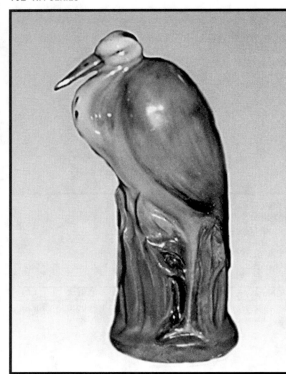

HN 250
Heron

Model No.:	314
Height:	5 ½", 14.0 cm
Colour:	See below
Issued:	1. 1921-1936
	2. c.1921
Varieties:	HN 251

Colourways	U.S. $	Can. $	U.K. £
1. Unknown		Very Rare	
2. Flambé		Very Rare	

HN 251
Heron

Model No.:	314
Height:	5 ½", 14.0 cm
Colour:	See below
Issued:	1. 1921-1936
	2. c.1921
Varieties:	HN 250

Colourways	U.S. $	Can. $	U.K. £
1. Grey/green/white		Very Rare	
2. Flambé		Very Rare	

HN 252
Duck
Standing - white

Model No.:	307
Height:	13", 33.0 cm
Size:	Large
Colour:	White
Issued:	1921-by 1946
Varieties:	HN 248, 249, 1198, 2635

Description	U.S. $	Can. $	U.K. £
White duck	2,000.00	2,500.00	1,100.00

HN 253
Monkey, Seated, arms folded

Model No.:	53
Height:	3", 7.6 cm
Colour:	See below
Issued:	1. 1921-by 1946
	2. and 3. c.1912-by 1946
Varieties:	HN 118
Derivative:	On alabaster base

Colourways	U.S. $	Can. $	U.K. £
1. Brown/orange	600.00	725.00	325.00
2. Flambé	700.00	850.00	375.00
3. Titanian		Very Rare	

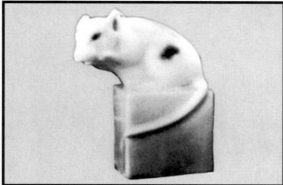

HN 254
Monkeys (Mother and Baby)

Model No.:	52
Designer:	Leslie Harradine
Height:	3", 7.6 cm
Colour:	See below
Issued:	1. 1921-by 1946
	2 and 3. c.1912-1962

Colourways	U.S. $	Can. $	U.K. £
1. Brown/orange	500.00	600.00	275.00
2. Flambé	600.00	725.00	325.00
3. Sung	2,500.00	3,000.00	1,500.00

HN 255
Mouse on a Cube

Model No.:	1164
Designer:	Charles Noke
Height:	2 ½", 6.4 cm
Colour:	See below
Issued:	1. 1921-by 1946
	2. c.1912-by 1946

Colourways	U.S. $	Can. $	U.K. £
1. White/green cube	1,000.00	1,200.00	550.00
2. Flambé	2,000.00	2,500.00	1,000.00

For an illustration of HN 256
see page 105

For an illustration of HN 257
see page 105

HN 256
Character Bird
Style One - green / blue

Model No.:	333
Height:	1", 2.5 cm
Colour:	Green and blue
Issued:	1922-by 1946
Varieties:	HN 283

Colourways	U.S. $	Can. $	U.K. £
Green/blue	850.00	1,000.00	475.00

HN 257
Character Bird
Style Two - yellow / red

Model No.:	334
Height:	1 ½", 3.8 cm
Colour:	Yellow with red head
Issued:	1922-by 1946
Varieties:	HN 284

Colourways	U.S. $	Can. $	U.K. £
Yellow/red	850.00	1,000.00	475.00

For an illustration of HN 258
see page 105

For an illustration of HN 259
see page 105

HN 258
Character Bird
Style Three - yellow / black

Model No.:	335		
Height:	1", 2.5 cm		
Colour:	Yellow with black head		
Issued:	1922-by 1946		
Varieties:	HN 285		

Colourways	U.S. $	Can. $	U.K. £
Yellow/black	850.00	1,000.00	475.00

HN 259
Character Bird
Style Four - grey / red

Model No.:	336		
Height:	1", 2.5 cm		
Colour:	Grey with red head and beak and green eyes		
Issued:	1922-by 1946		
Varieties:	HN 286		

Colourways	U.S. $	Can. $	U.K. £
Grey/red	850.00	1,000.00	475.00

HN 260
Character Bird
Style Five - orange

Model No.:	337		
Height:	1", 2.5 cm		
Colour:	Orange		
Issued:	1922-by 1946		
Varieties:	HN 287		
Derivative:	Ashtray		

Colourways	U.S. $	Can. $	U.K. £
Orange	850.00	1,000.00	475.00

HN 261
Character Bird
Style Six - green / red

Model No.:	338		
Height:	1", 2.5 cm		
Colour:	Green with red beak		
Issued:	1922-by 1946		
Varieties:	HN 288		

Colourways	U.S. $	Can. $	U.K. £
Green/red	850.00	1,000.00	475.00

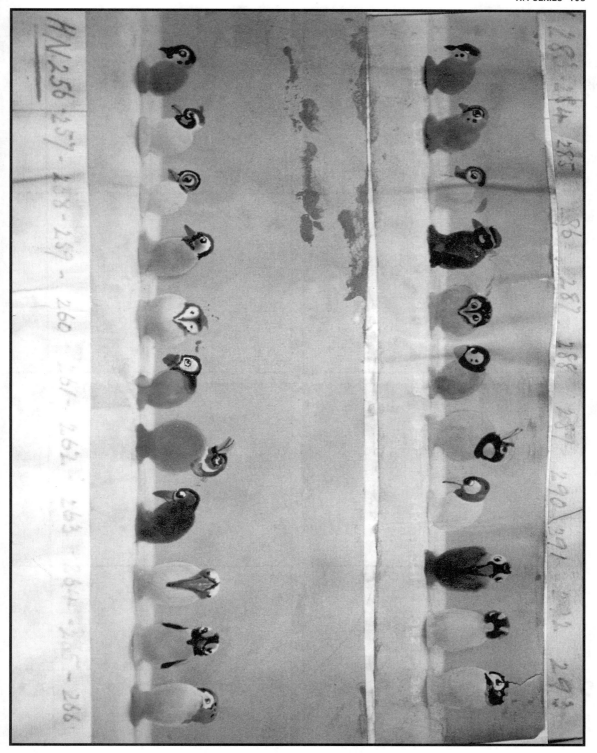

For an illustration of HN 262
see page 105

For an illustration of HN 263
see page 105

HN 262
Character Bird
Style Seven - orange

Model No.:	339
Height:	1", 2.5 cm
Colour:	Orange
Issued:	1922-by 1946
Varieties:	HN 289

Colourways	U.S. $	Can. $	U.K. £
Orange	850.00	1,000.00	475.00

HN 263
Character Bird
Style Eight - turquoise

Model No.:	340
Height:	1", 2.5 cm
Colour:	Turquoise
Issued:	1922-by 1946
Varieties:	HN 290

Colourways	U.S. $	Can. $	U.K. £
Turquoise	850.00	1,000.00	475.00

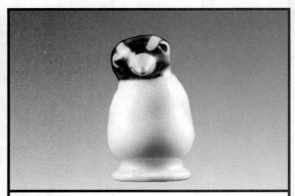

HN 264
Character Bird
Style Nine - orange / black

Model No.:	341
Height:	1 ¾", 4.4 cm
Colour:	Pale orange with black highlights
Issued:	1922-by 1946
Varieties:	HN 291
Derivative:	Onyx pin tray

Colourways	U.S. $	Can. $	U.K. £
Orange/black	850.00	1,000.00	475.00

HN 265
Character Bird
Style Ten - grey / black

Model No.:	342
Height:	1 ½", 3.8 cm
Colour:	Grey, black and orange
Issued:	1922-by 1946
Varieties:	HN 292

Colourways	U.S. $	Can. $	U.K. £
Grey/black	850.00	1,000.00	475.00

For an illustration of HN 266
see page 105

HN 266
Character Bird
Style Eleven - orange / black

Model No.:	343
Height:	1", 2.5 cm
Colour:	Pale orange with black beak
Issued:	1922-by 1946
Varieties:	HN 293

Colourways	U.S. $	Can. $	U.K. £
Orange/black	850.00	1,000.00	475.00

HN 267
Cockerel, Crouching

Model No.:	30
Height:	3 ¼", 8.3 cm
Colour:	See below
Issued:	1. 1922-1936
	2. c.1912
Varieties:	HN 124, 178, 180
Derivative:	Cockerel Bowl with hollow centre and sterling silver rim (flambé)

Colourways	U.S. $	Can. $	U.K. £
1. Brown/blue/black	350.00	425.00	200.00
2. Flambé	600.00	725.00	325.00

HN 268
Kingfisher
Style One

Model No.:	91
Height:	2 ½", 6.4 cm
Colour:	See below
Issued:	1. 1922-by 1946
	2. c.1912

Colourways	U.S. $	Can. $	U.K. £
1. Blue/yellow		Very Rare	
2. Flambé (illustrated)	600.00	725.00	325.00

HN 269
Blue Bird on Rock

Model No.:	196
Height:	4 ½", 11.4 cm
Colour:	Blue and yellow
Issued:	1922-by 1946
Varieties:	Also called 'Swallow on Rock' HN 136, 149

Description	U.S. $	Can. $	U.K. £
Blue bird	600.00	725.00	325.00

HN 270
Comic Brown Bear

Model No.:	58
Designer:	Charles Noke
Height:	5", 12.7 cm
Colour:	See below
Issued:	1. 1922-1936
	2 and 3. c.1918-1936
Varieties:	HN 170

Colourways	U.S. $	Can. $	U.K. £
1. Brown	1,000.00	1,200.00	550.00
2. Blue	1,200.00	1,500.00	650.00
3. Flambé	1,500.00	1,800.00	800.00

HN 271
Duck
Preening - Style Two

Model No.:	4
Size:	1 ½" x 3 ½", 3.8 x 8.9 cm
Colour:	See below
Issued:	1. 1922-1936
	2. c.1912
Varieties:	HN 148A, 299

Colourways	U.S. $	Can. $	U.K. £
1. Green	450.00	550.00	250.00
2. Flambé	500.00	600.00	275.00

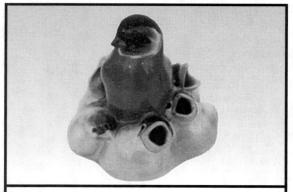

HN 272
Bird with Five Chicks - Jade

Model No.:	246
Height:	3 ¼", 8.3 cm
Colour:	Bird: jade green and brown with red head
	Chicks: pale blue with brown heads
Issued:	1922-1936
Varieties:	HN 214, 215, 216

Colourways	U.S. $	Can. $	U.K. £
1. Jade		Rare	
2. Flambé	1,200.00	1,450.00	650.00

HN 273
Hare
Crouching - Style One

Model No.:	119
Size:	2" x 4 ½", 5.1 x 11.4 cm
Colour:	See below
Issued:	1. 1922-by 1946
	2. and 3. 1913-by 1946
Varieties:	HN 107, 126, 142, 803

Colourways	U.S. $	Can. $	U.K. £
1. Yellow/black	650.00	800.00	350.00
2. Flambé	850.00	1,000.00	450.00
3. Sung	1,250.00	1,500.00	700.00

HN 274
Chick

Model No.:	1163B			
Designer:	Charles Noke			
Height:	2 ¼", 5.7 cm			
Colour:	See below			
Issued:	1. 1922-by 1946			
	2. c.1908			
Varieties:	HN 282			

Colourways	U.S. $	Can. $	U.K. £
1. Green	450.00	525.00	250.00
2. Flambé (illustrated)	450.00	525.00	250.00

HN 275
Ducklings
Standing - orange

Model No.:	247
Height:	2 ¾", 7.0 cm
Colour:	See below
Issued:	1. 1922-by 1946
	2. c.1919
Varieties:	HN 205, 206

Colourways	U.S. $	Can. $	U.K. £
1. Orange	600.00	725.00	350.00
2. Flambé		Rare	

HN 276
Lop-eared Rabbit

Model No.:	113
Height:	Large - 4", 10.1 cm
Colour:	See below
Issued:	1. 1922-by 1946
	2. Unknown
Varieties:	HN 108, 151

Colourways	U.S. $	Can. $	U.K. £
1. Yellow/black	750.00	900.00	425.00
2. Flambé		Very Rare	

HN 277
Wren
Style One

Model No.:	104
Height:	2", 5.1 cm
Colour:	See below
Issued:	1. 1922-by 1946
	2. c.1913-by 1946
Varieties:	Also called 'Robin' HN 144

Colourways	U.S. $	Can. $	U.K. £
1. Unknown	400.00	475.00	200.00
2. Flambé	750.00	900.00	400.00

Photograph not
available
at press time

HN 278
Finches (two)

Model No.:	263
Height:	2 ¾", 7.0 cm
Colour:	See below
Issued:	1. 1922-by 1946
	2. c.1922

Colourways	U.S. $	Can. $	U.K. £
1. Green/yellow	700.00	850.00	400.00
2. Flambé		Rare	

HN 279
Fledgling on Rock
Style Two - green

Model No.	140
Designer:	Charles Noke
Height:	4 ½", 11.4 cm
Colour:	Green
Issued:	1922-1936
Varieties:	HN 281

Description	U.S. $	Can. $	U.K. £
Green fledgling	450.00	525.00	225.00

HN 280
Finches (three)

Model No.:	264
Designer:	Charles Noke
Size:	2" x 3 ¾", 5.1 x 9.5 cm
Colour:	See below
Issued:	1. 1922-by 1946
	2. c.1913

Colourways	U.S. $	Can. $	U.K. £
1. Yellow/brown	500.00	600.00	250.00
2. Flambé		Rare	

HN 281
Fledgling on Rock
Style Two - yellow

Model No.:	140
Designer:	Charles Noke
Height:	4 ½", 11.4 cm
Colour:	Yellow
Issued:	1922-1936
Varieties:	HN 279

Description	U.S. $	Can. $	U.K. £
Yellow fledgling	450.00	525.00	225.00

HN 282
Chick

Model No.:	1163B			
Designer:	Charles Noke			
Height:	2 ¼", 5.7 cm			
Colour:	See below			
Issued:	1. 1922-by 1946			
	2. c.1908			
Varieties:	HN 274			

Colourways	U.S. $	Can. $	U.K. £
1. Blue	450.00	525.00	225.00
2. Flambé (illustrated)	450.00	525.00	225.00

For an illustration of HN 283
see page 105

HN 283
Character Bird
Style One - green

Model No.:	333
Height:	1", 2.5 cm
Colour:	Green with green beak
Issued:	1922-by 1946
Varieties:	HN 256

Colourways	U.S. $	Can. $	U.K. £
Green	850.00	1,000.00	475.00

For an illustration of HN 284
see page 105

HN 284
Character Bird
Style Two - mauve / green

Model No.:	334
Height:	1 ½", 3.8 cm
Colour:	Mauve and green head with orange beak
Issued:	1922-by 1946
Varieties:	HN 257

Colourways	U.S. $	Can. $	U.K. £
Mauve/green	850.00	1,000.00	475.00

For an illustration of HN 285
see page 105

HN 285
Character Bird
Style Three - yellow / green

Model No.:	335
Height:	1", 2.5 cm
Colour:	Yellow with green head
Issued:	1922-by 1946
Varieties:	HN 258

Colourways	U.S. $	Can. $	U.K. £
Yellow/green	850.00	1,000.00	475.00

For an illustration of HN 286
see page 105

HN 286
Character Bird
Style Four - blue / red

Model No.:	336
Height:	1", 2.5 cm
Colour:	Blue with red head and beak
Issued:	1922-by 1946
Varieties:	HN 259

Colourways	U.S. $	Can. $	U.K. £
Blue/red	850.00	1,000.00	475.00

HN 287
Character Bird
Style Five - green / black

Model No.:	337
Height:	1", 2.5 cm
Colour:	Green with black head
Issued:	1922-by 1946
Varieties:	HN 260
Derivative:	Ashtray

Colourways	U.S. $	Can. $	U.K. £
Green/black	850.00	1,000.00	475.00

HN 288
Character Bird
Style Six - purple / green

Model No.:	338
Height:	1", 2.5 cm
Colour:	Purple with green beak
Issued:	1922-by 1946
Varieties:	HN 261

Colourways	U.S. $	Can. $	U.K. £
Purple/green	850.00	1,000.00	475.00

For an illustration of HN 289
see page 105

HN 289
Character Bird
Style Seven - orange / green

Model No.:	339
Height:	1", 2.5 cm
Colour:	Orange with green beak
Issued:	1922-by 1946
Varieties:	HN 262

Colourways	U.S. $	Can. $	U.K. £
Orange/green	850.00	1,000.00	475.00

For an illustration of HN 290
see page 105

HN 290
Character Bird
Style Eight - yellow / green

Model No.:	340
Height:	1", 2.5 cm
Colour:	Yellow with green head and orange beak
Issued:	1922-by 1946
Varieties:	HN 263

Colourways	U.S. $	Can. $	U.K. £
Yellow/green	850.00	1,000.00	475.00

HN 291
Character Bird
Style Nine - blue / green

Model No.:	341
Height:	1 ¾", 4.5 cm
Colour:	Blue with green head and yellow eyes
Issued:	1922-by 1946
Varieties:	HN 264
Derivative:	Onyx pin tray

Colourways	U.S. $	Can. $	U.K. £
Blue/green	850.00	1,000.00	475.00

HN 292
Character Bird
Style Ten - yellow / blue

Model No.:	342
Height:	1 ½", 3.8 cm
Colour:	Yellow with blue and yellow striped head
Issued:	1922-by 1946
Varieties:	HN 265

Colourways	U.S. $	Can. $	U.K. £
Yellow/blue	850.00	1,000.00	475.00

For an illustration of HN 293
see page 105

HN 293
Character Bird
Style Eleven - yellow / orange

Model No.:	343
Height:	1", 2.5 cm
Colour:	Yellow with orange spot on head
Issued:	1922-by 1946
Varieties:	HN 266

Colourways	U.S. $	Can. $	U.K. £
Yellow/orange	850.00	1,000.00	475.00

HN 294
Toucan on Perch

Model No.:	212
Height:	7 ½", 19.1 cm
Colour:	Black and white, red beak
Issued:	1922-by 1946
Varieties	HN 158, 159, 196

Colourways	U.S. $	Can. $	U.K. £
Black/white/red	750.00	900.00	400.00

HN 295
Pelican
Beak Down

Model No.:	125
Height:	6 ¼", 15.9 cm
Colour:	See below
Issued:	1 and 2. 1922-by 1946
	3. c.1920

Colourways	U.S. $	Can. $	U.K. £
1. Black/green/brown beak	1,000.00	1,200.00	550.00
2. Black/green/red beak	1,000.00	1,200.00	550.00
3. Pale brown	700.00	825.00	375.00
4. Flambé		Rare	

HN 296
Emperor Penguin

Model No.:	84
Height:	6", 15.2 cm
Colour:	See below
Issued:	1. 1922-by 1946
	2. 1913-1996
Varieties:	HN 113

Colourways	U.S. $	Can. $	U.K. £
1. Black/grey	1,000.00	1,200.00	550.00
2. Flambé (illustrated)	300.00	375.00	150.00

HN 297
King Penguin and Chick

Model No.:	239
Height:	5 ½", 14.0 cm
Colour:	See below
Issued:	1. 1922-by 1946
	2. c.1918-1961
Varieties:	HN 198, 998

Colourways	U.S. $	Can. $	U.K. £
1. Black/white	1,200.00	1,450.00	650.00
2. Flambé (illustrated)	1,200.00	1,450.00	650.00

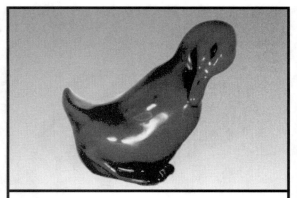

HN 298
Duck
Preening - Style One

Model No.:	2
Height:	2 ½", 6.4 cm
Colour:	See below
Issued:	1. 1922-1936
	2. c.1912-1936
Varieties:	HN 235

Colourways	U.S. $	Can. $	U.K. £
1. Unknown	1,000.00	1,200.00	550.00
2. Flambé (illustrated)	900.00	1,075.00	425.00

HN 299
Drake
Preening - Style Two

Model No.:	4
Size:	1 ½" x 3 ½", 3.8 x 8.9 cm
Colour:	See below
Issued:	1. 1922-by 1946
	2. c.1912
Varieties:	HN 148A, 271

Colourways	U.S. $	Can. $	U.K. £
1. Green/brown/white	450.00	550.00	250.00
2. Flambé	500.00	600.00	275.00

HN 800
Pig Snoozing - large

Model No.:	110
Size:	2 ½" x 5 ½", 6.4 x 14.0 cm
Size:	Large
Colour:	See below
Issued:	1. 1922-by 1946
	2. and 3. c.1912

Colourways	U.S. $	Can. $	U.K. £
1. Unknown	1,000.00	1,200.00	550.00
2. Flambé (illustrated)	1,000.00	1,200.00	550.00
3. Sung	2,000.00	2,500.00	1,000.00

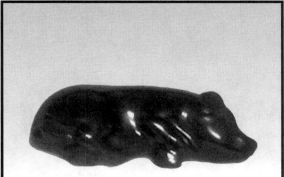

HN 801
Pig Snoozing - small

Model No.:	110A
Size:	1 ¼" x 3 ¾", 3.1 x 9.5 cm
Size:	Small
Colour:	See below
Issued:	1. 1922-by 1946
	2. 3. and 4. c.1912

Colourways	U.S. $	Can. $	U.K. £
1. Tan	600.00	725.00	300.00
2. Blue (illustrated)	600.00	725.00	300.00
3. Flambé	600.00	725.00	300.00
4. Sung	2,000.00	2,500.00	1,000.00

HN 802
Pigs
Snoozing - Both Pigs' Ears Up

Model No.:	61	
Size:	4" x 7", 10.1 x 17.8 cm	
Colour:	See below	
Issued:	1. 1923-1936	
	2. 1912-1936	
Varieties:	HN 213, 238	

Colourways	U.S. $	Can. $	U.K. £
1. Black/white		Very Rare	
2. Flambé (illustrated)	2,000.00	2,500.00	1,000.00

HN 803
Hare
Crouching - Style One

Model No.:	119	
Size:	2" x 4 ½", 5.1 x 11.4 cm	
Colour:	See below	
Issued:	1. 1923-by 1946	
	2. and 3. 1913-by 1946	
Varieties:	HN 107, 126, 142, 273	

Colourways	U.S. $	Can. $	U.K. £
1. Black/white	650.00	800.00	350.00
2. Flambé	850.00	1,000.00	450.00
3. Sung (illustrated)	1,250.00	1,500.00	700.00

HN 804
'Bonzo' Character Dog
Style One - lying - orange / cream

Model No.:	392	
Designer:	Charles Noke	
Height:	1", 2.5 cm	
Colour:	Pale orange and cream	
Issued:	1922-1936	

Description	U.S. $	Can. $	U.K. £
Style one, orange/cream	1,800.00	2,150.00	975.00

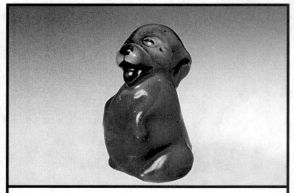

HN 805A
'Bonzo' Character Dog
Style Two - large mouth - green / purple

Model No.:	389	
Designer:	Charles Noke	
Height:	2 ½", 6.4 cm	
Colour:	Green and purple	
Issued:	1923-1936	
Varieties:	HN 809, 811	

Description	U.S. $	Can. $	U.K. £
Style two, green/purple	1,800.00	2,150.00	975.00

HN 805B
'Bonzo' Character Dog
Style Three - small mouth - blue

Model No.:	387
Designer:	Charles Noke
Height:	2", 5.1 cm
Colour:	Blue with brown face and highlights
Issued:	1923-1936
Varieties:	HN 808, 810, 812

Description	U.S. $	Can. $	U.K. £
Style three, blue	1,800.00	2,150.00	975.00

HN 806
Duck
Standing - white

Model No.:	395
Height:	2 ½", 6.4 cm
Size:	Small
Colour:	See below
Issued:	1. 1923-1968
	2. 1922-1996
Varieties:	HN 807, 2591

Colourways	U.S. $	Can. $	U.K. £
1. White/brown/black	150.00	175.00	80.00
2. Flambé	150.00	175.00	80.00

HN 807
Drake
Standing - green

Model No.:	395
Height:	2 ½", 6.4 cm
Size:	Small
Colour:	See below
Issued:	1. 1923-1977
	2. 1922-1996
Varieties:	HN 806, 2591

Colourways	U.S. $	Can. $	U.K. £
1. Green/brown/white	150.00	175.00	80.00
2. Flambé	150.00	175.00	80.00

HN 808
'Bonzo' Character Dog
Style Three - small mouth - yellow / brown

Model No.:	387
Designer:	Charles Noke
Height:	2", 5.1 cm
Colour:	Yellow with brown spots
Issued:	1923-1936
Varieties:	HN 805B, 810, 812

Description	U.S. $	Can. $	U.K. £
Style three, yellow/brown	1,800.00	2,150.00	975.00

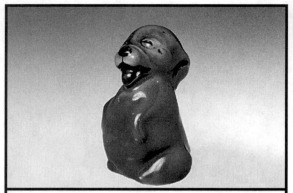

HN 809
'Bonzo' Character Dog
Style Two - large mouth - yellow

Model No.:	389	
Designer:	Charles Noke	
Height:	2 ½", 6.4 cm	
Colour:	Yellow	
Issued:	1933-1936	
Varieties:	HN 805A, 811	

Description	U.S. $	Can. $	U.K. £
Style two, yellow	1,800.00	2,150.00	975.00

HN 810
'Bonzo' Character Dog
Style Three - small mouth - green

Model No.:	387	
Designer:	Charles Noke	
Height:	2", 5.1 cm	
Colour:	Green	
Issued:	1923-1936	
Varieties:	HN 805B, 808, 812	

Description	U.S. $	Can. $	U.K. £
Style three, green	1,800.00	2,150.00	975.00

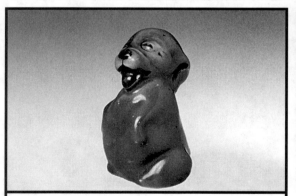

HN 811
'Bonzo' Character Dog
Style Two - large mouth - blue

Model No.:	389	
Designer:	Charles Noke	
Height:	2 ½", 6.4 cm	
Colour:	Blue	
Issued:	1923-1936	
Varieties:	HN 805A, 809	

Description	U.S. $	Can. $	U.K. £
Style two, blue	1,800.00	2,150.00	975.00

HN 812
'Bonzo' Character Dog
Style Three - small mouth - orange

Model No.:	387	
Designer:	Charles Noke	
Height:	2", 5.1 cm	
Colour:	Orange	
Issued:	1923-1936	
Varieties:	HN 805B, 808, 810	

Description	U.S. $	Can. $	U.K. £
Style three, orange	1,800.00	2,150.00	975.00

HN 813
Miniature Bird

Model No.:	396
Height:	Unknown
Colour:	White
Issued:	1923-by 1946
Varieties:	HN 867, 868, 869, 870, 871, 872, 873, 874

Description	U.S. $	Can. $	U.K. £
Miniature bird		Rare	

HN 814
'Bonzo' Character Dog
Style Four - black buttons

Model No.:	393
Designer:	Charles Noke
Height:	2", 5.1 cm
Colour:	Cream-yellow with black buttons and jacket edge
Issued:	1923-by 1946
Varieties:	HN 815, 826

Description	U.S. $	Can. $	U.K. £
Style four, black buttons	1,800.00	2,150.00	975.00

HN 815
'Bonzo' Character Dog
Style Four - red buttons

Model No.:	393
Designer:	Charles Noke
Height:	2", 5.1 cm
Colour:	Cream-yellow with red buttons and jacket edge
Issued:	1923-by 1946
Varieties:	HN 814, 826

Description	U.S. $	Can. $	U.K. £
Style four, red buttons	1,800.00	2,150.00	975.00

*

HN 818
'Ooloo' Character Cat
Black

Model No.:	400
Designer:	Charles Noke
Height:	3", 7.6 cm
Colour:	Black with white face
Issued:	1923-1932
Varieties:	HN 819, 827, 828, 829; Also called 'Lucky' K12, HN 971 on ashtray

Description	U.S. $	Can. $	U.K. £
Black cat	750.00	900.00	375.00

HN 819
'Ooloo' Character Cat
White

Model No.:	400
Designer:	Charles Noke
Height:	3", 7.6 cm
Colour:	White
Issued:	1923-1932
Varieties:	HN 818, 827, 828, 829; Also called 'Lucky' K12, HN 971 on ashtray

Description	U.S. $	Can. $	U.K. £
White cat	1,500.00	1,800.00	825.00

HN 820
Character Kitten
Curled - Style One - ginger head

Model No.:	397
Height:	1", 2.5 cm
Colour:	White body, ginger head
Issued:	1923-1936
Varieties:	HN 821, 822
Derivative:	Onyx pin tray (Model No. 397A)

Description	U.S. $	Can. $	U.K. £
White/ginger kitten		Rare	

HN 821
Character Kitten
Curled - Style One - brown head

Model No.:	397
Height:	1", 2.5 cm
Colour:	White front, brown back and head
Issued:	1923-1936
Varieties:	HN 820, 822
Derivative:	Onyx pin tray (Model No. 397A)

Description	U.S. $	Can. $	U.K.
White/brown kitten		Rare	

HN 822
Character Kitten
Curled - Style One - black head

Model No.:	397
Height:	1", 2.5 cm
Colour:	White body and black head
Issued:	1923-1936
Varieties:	HN 820, 821
Derivative:	Onyx pin tray (Model No. 397A)

Description	U.S. $	Can. $	U.K. £
White/black kitten		Rare	

HN 823
Character Kitten
Curled - Style Two - white

Model No.:	398		
Height:	1 ¼", 3.2 cm		
Colour:	See below		
Issued:	1. 1923-1936		
	2. c.1930		
Varieties:	HN 824, 825		

Colourways	U.S. $	Can. $	U.K. £
1. White/brown		Rare	
2. Chinese Jade		Rare	

HN 824
Character Kitten
Curled - Style Two - black

Model No.:	398		
Height:	1 ¼", 3.2 cm		
Colour:	See below		
Issued:	1. 1923-1936		
	2. c.1930		
Varieties:	HN 823, 825		

Colourways	U.S. $	Can. $	U.K. £
1. Black		Rare	
2. Chinese Jade (illustrated)		Rare	

HN 825
Character Kitten
Curled - Style Two - ginger

Model No.:	398		
Height:	1 ¼", 3.2 cm		
Colour:	See below		
Issued:	1. 1923-1936		
	2. c.1930		
Varieties:	HN 823, 824		

Colourways	U.S. $	Can. $	U.K. £
1. White/ginger		Rare	
2. Chinese Jade		Rare	

HN 826
'Bonzo' Character Dog
Style Four - red

Model No.:	393		
Designer:	Charles Noke		
Height:	2", 5.1 cm		
Colour:	Red		
Issued:	1923-1936		
Varieties:	HN 814, 815		

Description	U.S. $	Can. $	U.K. £
Style four, red	1,800.00	2,150.00	975.00

HN 827
'Ooloo' Character Cat
Ginger

Model No.:	400
Designer:	Charles Noke
Height:	3", 7.6 cm
Colour:	Ginger
Issued:	1923-1932
Varieties:	HN 818, 819, 828, 829; Also called 'Lucky' K12, HN 971 on ashtray

Description	U.S. $	Can. $	U.K. £
Ginger cat	1,500.00	1,800.00	825.00

HN 828
'Ooloo' Character Cat
Tabby

Model No.:	400
Designer:	Charles Noke
Height:	3", 7.6 cm
Colour:	Tabby
Issued:	1923-1932
Varieties:	HN 818, 819, 827, 829; Also called 'Lucky' K12, HN 971 on ashtray

Description	U.S. $	Can. $	U.K. £
Tabby cat	1,500.00	1,800.00	825.00

HN 829
'Ooloo' Character Cat
Black / white

Model No.:	400
Designer:	Charles Noke
Height:	3", 7.6 cm
Colour:	Black and white
Issued:	1923-1932
Varieties:	HN 818, 819, 827, 828; Also called 'Lucky' K12, HN 971 on ashtray

Description	U.S. $	Can. $	U.K. £
Black/white cat	800.00	950.00	400.00

*

HN 831
Beagle Puppy

Model No.:	407
Height:	2 ¼", 5.7 cm
Colour:	See below
Issued:	1. 1923-by 1946
	2. c.1925
Derivatives:	Onyx calendar, Sterling silver place card holder

Colourways	U.S. $	Can. $	U.K. £
1. White/browns	1,200.00	1,450.00	650.00
2. Chinese Jade	2,000.00	2,500.00	1,100.00

HN 832
Pekinese Puppy
Seated

Model No.:	406			
Height:	2 ½", 6.4 cm			
Colour:	See below			
Issued:	1. 1923-by 1946			
	2. and 3. c.1923			
Derivatives:	Trinket boxes, onyx calendar			

Colourways		U.S. $	Can. $	U.K. £
1.	Golden brown/black	400.00	500.00	225.00
2.	Chinese Jade		Rare	
3.	Flambé		Rare	

HN 833
Pekinese Puppy
Standing

Model No.:	405			
Height:	2", 5.1 cm			
Colour:	See below			
Issued:	1. 1923-by 1946			
	2. and 3. c.1923			
Derivatives:	Trinket boxes			

Colourways		U.S. $	Can. $	U.K. £
1.	Brown/black/tan	400.00	500.00	225.00
2.	Chinese Jade		Rare	
3.	Flambé		Rare	

HN 834
Pekinese Puppy
Curled - dark brown

Model No.:	403			
Height:	1", 2.5 cm			
Colour:	Pale brown with dark brown nose and tips of ears			
Issued:	1923-by 1946			
Varieties:	HN 835, 836			
Derivative:	Ashtray			

Description	U.S. $	Can. $	U.K. £
Dark brown puppy	1,000.00	1,200.00	500.00

HN 835
Pekinese Puppy
Curled - light brown

Model No.:	403			
Height:	1", 2.5 cm			
Colour:	Light brown			
Issued:	1923-by 1946			
Varieties:	HN 834, 836			
Derivative:	Ashtray			

Description	U.S. $	Can. $	U.K. £
Light brown puppy	1,000.00	1,200.00	500.00

HN 836
Pekinese Puppy
Curled - pale brown

Model No.:	403
Height:	1", 2.5 cm
Colour:	Pale brown
Issued:	1923-by 1946
Varieties:	HN 834, 835
Derivative:	Ashtray

Description	U.S. $	Can. $	U.K. £
Pale brown puppy	1,000.00	1,200.00	500.00

HN 837
Pomeranian
Curled - brown

Model No.:	402
Height:	1", 2.5 cm
Colour:	Brown
Issued:	1923-by 1946
Varieties:	HN 838, 839

Colourways	U.S. $	Can. $	U.K. £
Brown	1,200.00	1,450.00	600.00

HN 838
Pomeranian
Curled - light brown

Model No.:	402
Height:	1", 2.5 cm
Colour:	Light brown
Issued:	1923-by 1946
Varieties:	HN 837, 839

Colourways	U.S. $	Can. $	U.K. £
Light brown	1,200.00	1,450.00	600.00

HN 839
Pomeranian
Curled - white / grey

Model No.:	402
Height:	1", 2.5 cm
Colour:	White and grey
Issued:	1923-by 1946
Varieties:	HN 837, 838

Colourways	U.S. $	Can. $	U.K. £
White/grey	1,200.00	1,450.00	600.00

HN 840
Character Duck
Style One - Large - yellow / white

Model No.:	415
Height:	3", 7.6 cm
Size:	Large
Colour:	Pale yellow body, white head
Issued:	1924-by 1946
Varieties:	HN 842, 844

Colourways	U.S. $	Can. $	U.K. £
Yellow/white, large	1,000.00	1,200.00	500.00

HN 841
Character Duck
Style One - Small - yellow / black

Model No.:	415A
Height:	2 ½", 6.4 cm
Size:	Small
Colour:	Pale yellow body, black wings, white head
Issued:	1924-by 1946
Varieties:	HN 843, 845
Derivative:	Onyx pin tray (square, round and oblong bases)

Colourways	U.S. $	Can. $	U.K. £
Yellow/black, small	800.00	950.00	400.00

HN 842
Character Duck
Style One - Large - yellow / brown

Model No.:	415
Height:	3", 7.6 cm
Size:	Large
Colour:	Yellow body, black wings, brown head
Issued:	1924-by 1946
Varieties:	HN 840, 844

Colourways	U.S. $	Can. $	U.K. £
Yellow/brown, large	1,000.00	1,200.00	500.00

HN 843
Character Duck
Style One - Small - yellow / brown

Model No.:	415A
Height:	2 ½", 6.4 cm
Size:	Small
Colour:	Yellow body with brown highlights
Issued:	1924-by 1946
Varieties:	HN 841, 845
Derivative:	Onyx pin tray (square, round and oblong bases)

Colourways	U.S. $	Can. $	U.K. £
Yellow/brown, small	800.00	950.00	400.00

HN 844
Character Duck
Style One - Large - orange / black

Model No.:	415
Height:	3", 7.6 cm
Size:	Large
Colour:	Orange body, black and brown highlights
Issued:	1924-by 1946
Varieties:	HN 840, 842

Colourways	U.S. $	Can. $	U.K. £
Orange/black, large	1,000.00	1,200.00	500.00

HN 845
Character Duck
Style One - Small - orange / black

Model No.:	415A
Height:	2 ½", 6.4 cm
Size:	Small
Colour:	Orange body, black / brown highlights
Issued:	1924-by 1946
Varieties:	HN 841, 843
Derivative:	Onyx pin tray (square, round and oblong bases)

Colourways	U.S. $	Can. $	U.K. £
Orange/black, small	800.00	950.00	400.00

HN 846
Toucan on Tree Stump (flower holder)

Model No.:	432
Height:	Unknown
Colour:	Unknown
Issued:	1924-1936

Description	U.S. $	Can. $	U.K. £
Toucan (flower holder)		Rare	

HN 847
Bird on Tree Stump (flower holder)

Model No.:	430
Height:	Unknown
Colour:	Yellow and orange
Issued:	1924-1936

Description	U.S. $	Can. $	U.K. £
Bird (flower holder)		Rare	

HN 848
Heron on Grass Perch (flower holder)

Model No.:	437
Height:	5 ½", 13.8 cm
Colour:	Grey with black highlights, green base
Issued:	1924-1936

Description	U.S. $	Can. $	U.K. £
Heron (flower holder)	1,800.00	2,150.00	975.00

HN 849
Duck and Ladybird (flower holder)

Model No.:	435
Height:	4 ½", 11.4 cm
Colour:	White duck, green base
Issued:	1924-1936

Description	U.S. $	Can. $	U.K. £
Duck/ladybird (flower holder)		Rare	

HN 850
Duckling on a Rock (flower holder)

Model No.:	438
Height:	Unknown
Colour:	Yellow with brown wing tips, brown white and green base
Issued:	1924-1936

Description	U.S. $	Can. $	U.K. £
Duckling (flower holder)		Rare	

HN 851
Robin on Tree Stump (flower holder)

Model No.:	Unknown
Height:	Unknown
Colour:	Red and brown robin, black base
Issued:	1924-1936
Varieties:	HN 860

Description	U.S. $	Can. $	U.K. £
Robin (flower holder)		Rare	

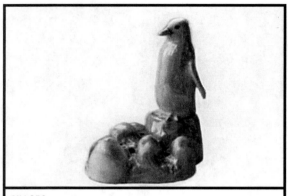

HN 852
Penguin on Rocks (flower holder)

Model No.:	441
Height:	6 ½", 16.5 cm
Colour:	1. Black and white penguin, blue rocks
	2. Pearl glaze
Issued:	1924-1936
Varieties:	HN 856

Colourways	U.S. $	Can. $	U.K. £
1. Black/white		Rare	
2. Pearl		Rare	

HN 853
Mallard Drake on Rocks (flower holder)

Model No.:	436
Height:	Unknown
Colour:	Unknown
Issued:	1924-1936

Description	U.S. $	Can. $	U.K. £
Mallard drake (flower holder)		Rare	

HN 854
Budgerigar on Branch (flower holder)

Model No.:	429
Height:	6 ½", 16.5 cm
Colour:	Pearlized budgerigar, green base
Issued:	1924-1936

Description	U.S. $	Can. $	U.K. £
Budgerigar (flower holder)		Rare	

HN 855
Wren on Tree Stump (flower holder)

Model No.:	431
Height:	Unknown
Colour:	Blue, green and grey bird on brown base
Issued:	1924-1936

Description	U.S. $	Can. $	U.K. £
Wren (flower holder)		Rare	

HN 856
Penguin on Rocks (flower holder)

Model No.:	441
Height:	6 ½", 16.5 cm
Colour:	Black and white penguin on brown and green rocks
Issued:	1924-1936
Varieties:	HN 852

Description	U.S. $	Can. $	U.K. £
Penguin (flower holder)		Rare	

HN 857
Cormorant Nesting on Tree Stump (flower holder)

Model No.:	439
Height:	Unknown
Colour:	White bird on brown base
Issued:	1924-1936

Description	U.S. $	Can. $	U.K. £
Cormorant (flower holder)		Rare	

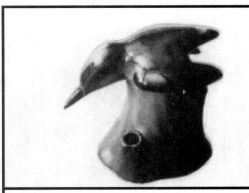

HN 858
Kingfisher on Tree Stump (flower holder)
Style One

Model No.:	227
Height:	3", 7.6 cm
Colour:	See below
Issued:	1. 1924-1936
	2. c.1918-1936
Varieties:	HN 165

Colourways	U.S. $	Can. $	U.K. £
1. Green/blue/brown	600.00	725.00	335.00
2. Flambé	1,000.00	1,200.00	550.00

HN 859
Tortoise on Rocks (flower holder)

Model No.:	434
Height:	Unknown
Colour:	Green and white
Issued:	1924-by 1946

Description	U.S. $	Can. $	U.K. £
Tortoise (flower holder)		Rare	

HN 860
Robin on Tree Stump (flower holder)

Model No.:	Unknown
Height:	Unknown
Colour:	Black and green with yellow highlights
Issued:	1924-by 1946
Varieties:	HN 851

Description	U.S. $	Can. $	U.K. £
Robin (flower holder)		Rare	

HN 861
Polar Bear
Standing - Style One

Model No.:	433
Size:	4 ½ " x 8", 11.4 x 20.3 cm
Colour:	White
Issued:	1924-by 1946

Description	U.S. $	Can. $	U.K. £
Polar Bear	1,800.00	2,150.00	975.00

HN 862A
Kingfisher on Stand with Primroses

Model No.:	44A
Height:	4 ½", 11.4 cm
Colour:	Green, malachite blue and orange bird, yellow flowers
Issued:	1924-1936
Varieties:	HN 862B with kingcup flowers

Description	U.S. $	Can. $	U.K. £
Kingfisher/primroses	700.00	850.00	375.00

HN 862B
Kingfisher on Stand with Kingcups

Model No.	44B
Height:	4 ½", 11.4 cm
Colour:	Green, malachite blue and orange bird, yellow flowers
Issued:	1924-1936
Varieties:	HN 862A with primrose flowers

Description	U.S. $	Can. $	U.K. £
Kingfisher/kingcups	700.00	850.00	375.00

HN 863
Character Duck
Style Two - yellow / white

Model No.: 425
Height: 2 ½", 6.4 cm
Colour: Yellow body, white head
Issued: 1924-by 1946
Varieties: HN 864, 865

Colourways	U.S. $	Can. $	U.K. £
Yellow/white	800.00	950.00	400.00

HN 864
Character Duck
Style Two - yellow / brown

Model No.: 425
Height: 2 ½", 6.4 cm
Colour: Yellow body, brown head
Issued: 1924-by 1946
Varieties: HN 863, 865

Colourways	U.S. $	Can. $	U.K. £
Yellow/brown	800.00	950.00	400.00

HN 865
Character Duck
Style Two - brown

Model No.: 425
Height: 2 ½", 6.4 cm
Colour: Brown body and head
Issued: 1924-by 1946
Varieties: HN 863, 864

Colourways	U.S. $	Can. $	U.K. £
Brown	800.00	950.00	400.00

HN 866
Character Fox

Model No.: 442
Height: Unknown
Colour: Light brown with dark brown highlights
Issued: 1924-by 1946
Derivatives: Onyx pin tray

Description	U.S. $	Can. $	U.K. £
Character fox		Rare	

HN 867
Miniature Bird
Grey / brown

Model No.:	396
Height:	Unknown
Colour:	Grey back and wings, brown head
Issued:	1924-by 1946
Varieties:	HN 813, 868, 869, 870, 871, 872, 873, 874

Colourways	U.S. $	Can. $	U.K. £
Grey/brown		Rare	

HN 868
Miniature Bird
Green

Model No.:	396
Height:	Unknown
Colour:	Green back and head
Issued:	1924-by 1946
Varieties:	HN 813, 867, 869, 870, 871, 872, 873, 874

Colourways	U.S. $	Can. $	U.K. £
Green		Rare	

HN 869
Miniature Bird
Green / yellow

Model No.:	396
Height:	Unknown
Colour:	Green-black back and head, yellow breast
Issued:	1924-by 1946
Varieties:	HN 813, 867, 868, 870, 871, 872, 873, 874

Colourways	U.S. $	Can. $	U.K. £
Green/yellow		Rare	

HN 870
Miniature Bird
Green / grey

Model No.:	396
Height:	Unknown
Colour:	Green-black head, grey wings, yellow breast
Issued:	1924-by 1946
Varieties:	HN 813, 867, 868, 869, 871, 872, 873, 874

Colourways	U.S. $	Can. $	U.K. £
Green/grey		Rare	

HN 871
Miniature Bird
Brown

Model No.:	396
Height:	Unknown
Colour:	Brown back and wings
Issued:	1924-by 1946
Varieties:	HN 813, 867, 868, 869, 870, 872, 873, 874

Colourways	U.S. $	Can. $	U.K. £
Brown		Rare	

HN 872
Miniature Bird
Green / red

Model No.:	396
Height:	Unknown
Colour:	Green back, red head
Issued:	1924-by 1946
Varieties:	HN 813, 867, 868, 869, 870, 871, 873, 874

Colourways	U.S. $	Can. $	U.K. £
Green/red		Rare	

HN 873
Miniature Bird
Blue

Model No.:	396
Height:	Unknown
Colour:	Blue back
Issued:	1924-by 1946
Varieties:	HN 813, 867, 868, 869, 870, 871, 872, 874

Colourways	U.S. $	Can. $	U.K. £
Blue		Rare	

HN 874
Miniature Bird
Green / mauve

Model No.:	396
Height:	Unknown
Colour:	Green back, mauve breast, blue head
Issued:	1924-by 1946
Varieties:	HN 813, 867, 868, 869, 870, 871, 872, 873

Colourways	U.S. $	Can. $	U.K. £
Green/mauve		Rare	

For an illustration of the Miniature Birds see page 132.

HN 875
Kingfisher on Tree Stump (flower holder)
Style Two

Model No.:	446	
Height:	4", 10.1 cm	
Colour:	Blue	
Issued:	1924-1936	

Description	U.S. $	Can. $	U.K. £
Kingfisher (flower holder)		Rare	

HN 876
Tiger on a Rock
Style One

Model No.:	106
Designer:	Charles Noke
Size:	3 ½" x 9", 8.9 x 22.9 cm
Colour:	See below
Issued:	1. 1924-by 1946
	2. c.1913

Colourways	U.S. $	Can. $	U.K. £
1. Browns/black	2,000.00	2,500.00	1,100.00
2. Flambé	2,000.00	2,500.00	1,100.00

Note: Charles Noke impressed on rock.

HN 877
Cockatoo on Rock

Model No.:	68
Designer:	Leslie Harradine
Height:	6", 15.2 cm
Colour:	See below
Issued:	1. 1924-1936
	2. c.1912-1936
Varieties:	HN 185, 191, 192, 200
Derivative:	Onyx pin tray

Colourways	U.S. $	Can. $	U.K. £
1. Blue/orange	600.00	700.00	325.00
2. Flambé	1,200.00	1,450.00	650.00

HN 878
Cockerel
Seated - Style Two - white

Model No.:	451
Height:	4", 10.1 cm
Colour:	White
Issued:	1924-1936
Varieties:	HN 879, 880

Description	U.S. $	Can. $	U.K. £
White cockerel	400.00	475.00	200.00

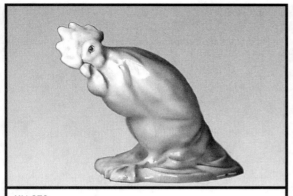

HN 879
Cockerel
Seated - Style Two - blue

Model No.:	451
Height:	4", 10.1 cm
Colour:	Blue and green
Issued:	1924-1936
Varieties:	HN 878, 880

Description	U.S. $	Can. $	U.K. £
Blue cockerel	500.00	575.00	250.00

HN 880
Cockerel
Seated - Style Two - yellow

Model No.:	451
Height:	4", 10.1 cm
Colour:	Yellow, black and red
Issued:	1924-1936
Varieties:	HN 878, 879

Description	U.S. $	Can. $	U.K. £
Yellow cockerel	500.00	575.00	250.00

HN 881
Bulldog
Seated - Style Three

Model No.:	122
Height:	2 ¾", 7.0 cm
Size:	Small
Colour:	See below
Issued:	1 and 2. 1938-by 1946
	3 and 4. c.1913-by 1946
Varieties:	On lid of lustre bowl HN 987

Colourways	U.S. $	Can. $	U.K. £
1. Brindle		Very Rare	
2. Cream/brown	2,500.00	3,000.00	1,350.00
3. Chinese Jade	3,000.00	3,600.00	1,650.00
4. Flambé	1,800.00	2,150.00	975.00

HN 882
Penguin
Style Two

Model No.:	459
Height:	6 ¾', 17.2 cm
Colour:	See below
Issued:	1. 1925-by 1946
	2. c.1925-by 1961

Colourways	U.S. $	Can. $	U.K. £
1. Green head		Rare	
2. Flambé	1,000.00	1,200.00	550.00

HN 883
Two Cuddling Orang-Outangs

Model No.:	486
Designer:	Leslie Harradine
Size:	5 ½" x 7", 14.0 x 17.8 cm
Colour:	See below
Issued:	1. 1925-1936
	2. c.1913-1936

Colourways	U.S. $	Can. $	U.K. £
1. Natural colours		Very Rare	
2. Flambé (illustrated)	4,000.00	4,750.00	2,200.00
3. Sung	5,000.00	6,000.00	2,750.00

HN 884
Character Parrot on Pillar
Style One

Model No.:	465
Height:	Unknown
Colour:	Blue and orange
Issued:	1925-1936

Description	U.S. $	Can. $	U.K. £
HN 884, Style One		Rare	

Character Parrot on Pillar
Style Two
Model No.:   466
Height: Unknown

HN 885
Colour: Pink, purple and orange
Issued: 1925-1936
Varieties: HN 886, 888

HN 886
Colour: Red, blue and orange
Issued: 1925-1936
Varieties: HN 885, 888

HN 888
Colour: Pale blue and yellow
Issued: 1925-1936
Varieties: HN 885, 886

Description	U.S. $	Can. $	U.K. £
HN 885		Rare	
HN 886		Rare	
HN 888		Rare	

*HN 887 Cockatoo not issued.

HN 889
Greyhound
Seated - black/white
Model No.:   80
Designer: Charles Noke
Height: 5", 12.7 cm
Colour: See below
Issued: 1. 1925-by 1946; 2. c.1913-by 1946
Varieties: HN 890

Colourways	U.S. $	Can. $	U.K. £
1. Black/white	1,200.00	1,450.00	675.00
2. Flambé	1,500.00	1,800.00	800.00

Note: First produced in the 1890s as part of a vellum piece.

HN 890
Greyhound
Seated - brown /cream
Model No.:   80
Designer: Charles Noke
Height: 5", 12.7 cm
Colour: See below
Issued: 1. 1925-by 1946; 2. c.1913-by 1946
Varieties: HN 889

Colourways	U.S. $	Can. $	U.K. £
1. Brown/cream	1,200.00	1,450.00	675.00
2. Flambé	1,500.00	1,800.00	800.00

Note: First produced in the 1890s as part of a vellum piece.

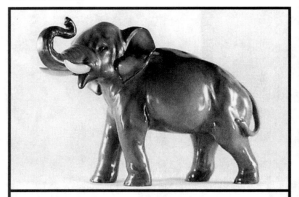

HN 891A
Elephant, Trunk in salute - Style One - medium

Model No.:	489A
Designer:	Charles Noke
Height:	6", 15.2 cm
Colour:	See below
Issued:	1. 1926-1943; 2a. c.1926-1950; 2b. 1962-1996

Colourways	U.S. $	Can. $	U.K. £
1. Olive-grey (earthenware)	700.00	875.00	400.00
2a. Flambé (original)	600.00	725.00	350.00
2b. Flambé (re-issue)	300.00	350.00	150.00
3. Sung	1,500.00	1,800.00	800.00

HN 891B
Elephant, Trunk in salute - Style One - small

Model No.:	489B
Designer:	Charles Noke
Height:	4 ½", 11.4 cm
Size:	Small
Colour:	See below
Issued:	1. 1926-1943; 2. c.1926-1962; 3. c.1926
Varieties:	HN 941, 2644

Colourways	U.S. $	Can. $	U.K. £
1. Silver-grey (china)	600.00	725.00	350.00
2. Flambé	600.00	725.00	350.00
3. Sung	1,500.00	1,800.00	825.00

HN 892
Character Pig - Laughing
Style One - red

Model No.:	494
Height:	2 ½", 6.4 cm
Colour:	See below
Issued:	1. 1926-by 1946
	2. Unknown
Varieties:	HN 893

Colourways	U.S. $	Can. $	U.K. £
1. Red/black spots		Rare	
2. Flambé		Rare	

HN 893
Character Pig - Laughing
Style One - green

Model No.:	494
Height:	2 ½", 6.4 cm
Colour:	See below
Issued:	1. 1926-by 1946
	2. Unknown
Varieties:	HN 892

Colourways	U.S. $	Can. $	U.K. £
1. Green/black spots		Rare	
2. Flambé		Rare	

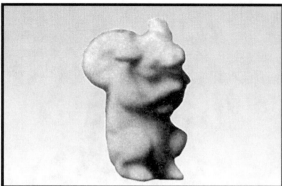

HN 894
Character Pig - Crying
Style Two

Model No.: 495
Height: 2 ½", 6.4 cm
Colour: See below
Issued: 1. 1926-by 1946
2. Unknown

Colourways	U.S. $	Can. $	U.K. £
1. Unknown		Rare	
2. Flambé (illustrated)		Rare	

HN 895
Character Pig
Style Three

Model No.: 496
Height: 2 ½", 6.4 cm
Colour: Unknown
Issued: 1926-by 1946

Description	U.S. $	Can. $	U.K. £
Style three		Rare	

Photograph
not available
at press time

Photograph
not available
at press time

HN 896
Character Pig
Style Four

Model No.: Unknown
Height: Unknown
Colour: Unknown
Issued: 1926-by 1946

Description	U.S. $	Can. $	U.K. £
Style four		Rare	

HN 897
Character Pig
Style Five

Model No.: Unknown
Height: Unknown
Colour: Unknown
Issued: 1926-1936

Description	U.S. $	Can. $	U.K. £
Style five		Rare	

HN 898
Alsatian's Head
Pencil Holder

Model No.:	509
Height:	3", 7.6 cm
Colour:	Brown
Issued:	1926-1936
Derivative:	Onyx pin tray

Description	U.S. $	Can. $	U.K. £
Pencil holder	1,000.00	1,200.00	550.00

HN 899
Alsatian
Seated, with collar

Model No.:	497
Height:	3 ¾", 9.5 cm
Colour:	See below
Issued:	1926-by 1946
Varieties:	On lid of lustre bowl HN 986 (Flambé)
Derivatives:	Onyx calendar, onyx pin tray

Colourways		U.S. $	Can. $	U.K. £
1.	Natural colours	1,000.00	1,200.00	550.00
2.	Flambé (illustrated)	900.00	1,100.00	500.00

HN 900
Fox Terrier
Seated - Style One - white/brown/ginger

Model No.:	511
Height:	3 ½", 8.9 cm
Colour:	White, brown and ginger
Issued:	1926-by 1946
Varieties:	HN 901
Derivative:	Onyx pin tray

Colourways	U.S. $	Can. $	U.K. £
White/brown/ginger	750.00	900.00	425.00

HN 901
Fox Terrier
Seated - Style One - white/black/brown

Model No.:	511
Height:	3 ½", 8.9 cm
Colour:	White, black and brown
Issued:	1926-by 1946
Varieties:	HN 900
Derivative:	Card holder; Onyx pin tray

Colourways	U.S. $	Can. $	U.K. £
White/black/brown	750.00	900.00	425.00

HN 902
Character Pig
Style Six - black

Model No.:	510
Height:	Unknown
Colour:	White with black patches
Issued:	1926-1936
Varieties:	HN 903

Description	U.S. $	Can. $	U.K. £
Style six - black		Rare	

HN 903
Character Pig
Style Six - brown

Model No.:	510
Height:	Unknown
Colour:	White with brown patches
Issued:	1926-1936
Varieties:	HN 902

Description	U.S. $	Can. $	U.K. £
Style six - brown		Rare	

HN 904
Terrier Puppy
Begging - Style One

Model No.:	515
Height:	3 ¼", 8.3 cm
Colour:	White with black and brown patches
Issued:	1926-by 1946
Derivatives:	Marble ashtray

Description	U.S. $	Can. $	U.K. £
Terrier puppy	750.00	900.00	425.00

HN 905
Frog
Style Two

Model No.:	516
Height:	1 ½", 3.8 cm
Colour:	See below
Issued:	1. 1926-1936
	2. Unknown

Colourways	U.S. $	Can. $	U.K. £
1. Green/ivory throat		Rare	
2. Flambé (illustrated)		Rare	

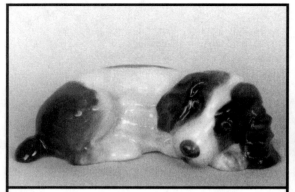

HN 906
Spaniel Puppy - Dark Brown Patches

Model No.:	514
Height:	1 ½", 3.8 cm
Colour:	White with dark brown patches
Issued:	1926-1936
Varieties:	HN 907

Colourways	U.S. $	Can. $	U.K. £
Dark brown patches	1,200.00	1,450.00	650.00

HN 907
Spaniel Puppy - Light Brown Patches

Model No.:	514
Height:	1 ½", 3.8 cm
Colour:	White with light brown patches
Issued:	1926-1936
Varieties:	HN 906

Colourways	U.S. $	Can. $	U.K. £
Light brown patches	1,200.00	1,450.00	650.00

NOTES ON PRICING

- Animal figures are not as plentiful as pretty ladies or character figures and caution in pricing must prevail.

- In the pricing tables N/I (not issued) indicates that the animal figure was not available in that particular market.

- Rarity classification provides a range for the collector to work with.

- Always remember that when dealing with rare animal figures you need two willing parties, a buyer and a seller. One without the other will not work and only when they agree do you have a market price.

Rarity Class	Rare	Very Rare	Extremely Rare
U.S. $	1,850./2,750.	2,750./4,500.	4,500./Up
Can. $	2,250./3,500.	3,500./5,500.	5,500./Up
U.K. £	1,000./1,500.	1,500./2,500.	2,500./Up

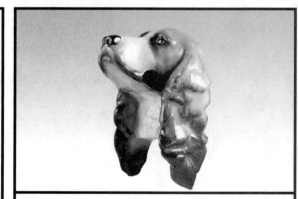

HN 908
Spaniel Puppy's Head
Pencil Holder

Model No.:	520
Height:	3", 7.6 cm
Colour:	1. Blue roan
	2. Liver and white
Issued:	1926-1936

Colourways	U.S. $	Can. $	U.K. £
1. Blue roan	1,000.00	1,200.00	550.00
2. Liver and white	1,000.00	1,200.00	550.00

HN 909
Fox Terrier
Standing - Style One

Model No.:	554			
Height:	4", 10.1 cm			
Size:	Medium			
Colour:	See below			
Issued:	1. 1927-by 1946			
	2. Unknown			
Varieties:	HN 923			

Colourways	U.S. $	Can. $	U.K. £
1. White/dark brown	700.00	850.00	375.00
2. Flambé	900.00	1,100.00	500.00

HN 910
Fox Terrier
Seated- Style Two

Model No.:	553	
Height:	1. 5 ¼", 13.3 cm	
	2. 4 ½", 11.4 cm	
Size:	Medium	
Colour:	See below	
Issued:	1. 1927-by 1946	
	2. c.1927	
Varieties:	HN 924	

Colourways	U.S. $	Can. $	U.K. £
1. White/black/brown	700.00	850.00	375.00
2. Flambé	900.00	1,100.00	500.00

HN 911
Tiger
Lying

Model No.:	533
Designer:	Charles Noke
Size:	2 ½" x 7 ½", 6.4 cm x 19.1 cm
Colour:	See below
Issued:	1. 1927-by 1946
	2. c.1926

Colourways	U.S. $	Can. $	U.K. £
1. Browns	900.00	1,100.00	500.00
2. Flambé	1,500,00	1,800.00	825.00

HN 912
Tiger, Seated

Model No.:	530
Designer:	Charles Noke
Height:	6 ¼", 15.9 cm
Colour:	See below
Issued:	1. 1927-1940 2. c.1926-1940

Colourways	U.S. $	Can. $	U.K. £
1. Golden brown/brown	1,000.00	1,200.00	550.00
2. Flambé	1,600.00	2,000.00	875.00
3. Sung	4,500.00	5,500.00	2,500.00

Note: Model 530 was also used to produced HN 919 Leopard.

HN 913
Character Toucan With Hat
Style One

Model No.:	548
Height:	1 ½", 3.84 cm
Colour:	Green and black body, yellow beak, red and yellow hat
Issued:	1927-by 1946

Description	U.S. $	Can. $	U.K. £
Style one		Rare	

HN 914
Character Toucan With Hat
Style Two

Model No.:	546
Height:	1 ½", 3.84 cm
Colour:	Green and black body, red and yellow hat
Issued:	1927-by 1946

Description	U.S. $	Can. $	U.K. £
Style two		Rare	

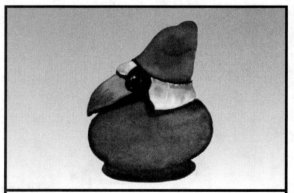

HN 915
Character Toucan With Hat
Style Three

Model No.:	549
Height:	1 ½", 3.84 cm
Colour:	Turquoise body, red hat
Issued:	1927-by 1946

Description	U.S. $	Can. $	U.K. £
Style three		Rare	

HN 916
Character Toucan With Hat
Style Four

Model No.:	550
Height:	1 ½", 3.84 cm
Colour:	Black and orange body, brown hat
Issued:	1927-by 1946

Description	U.S. $	Can. $	U.K. £
Style four		Rare	

HN 917
Character Toucan With Hat
Style Five

Model No.:	551
Height:	1 ½", 3.84 cm
Colour:	Blue body, red and yellow hat
Issued:	1927-by 1946

Description	U.S. $	Can. $	U.K. £
Style five		Rare	

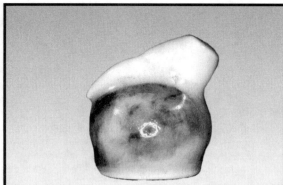

HN 918
Character Toucan With Hat
Style Six

Model No.:	547
Height:	1 ½", 3.84 cm
Colour:	See below
Issued:	1. 1927-by 1946
	2. c.1930

Colourways	U.S. $	Can. $	U.K. £
1. Purple/black/yellow/red		Rare	
2. Chinese Jade (illustrated)		Rare	

HN 919
Leopard
Seated

Model No.:	530
Designer:	Charles Noke
Height:	6 ½", 16.5 cm
Colour:	Brown with black spots
Issued:	1927-1940

Description	U.S. $	Can. $	U.K. £
Leopard	1,500.00	1,800.00	800.00

Note: Model 530 was also used to produce HN 912 Tiger.

HN 920
Foxes
Curled - Style Two

Model No.:	528
Size:	3" x 6", 7.6 x 15.2 cm
Colour:	See below
Issued:	1. 1927-by 1946
	2. c.1926
Varieties:	HN 925

Description	U.S. $	Can. $	U.K. £
1. Brown/black	3,750.00	4,500.00	2,000.00
2. Flambé		Rare	

HN 921
Alsatian
Seated, without collar

Model No.:	525
Height:	1. 7", 17.8 cm
	2. 8 ¼", 21.0 cm
Colour:	See below
Issued:	1. 1927-by 1946
	2. c.1927

Colourways	U.S. $	Can. $	U.K. £
1. Natural colours	900.00	1,100.00	500.00
2. Flambé	1,500.00	1,800.00	825.00

HN 922
Wilfred the Rabbit

Model No.:	559
Designer:	Charles Noke
Height:	4", 10.1 cm
Colour:	Light brown and white rabbit, yellow trumpet
Issued:	1927-1936

Description	U.S. $	Can. $	U.K. £
Wilfred the rabbit	2,000.00	2,500.00	1,100.00

HN 923
Fox Terrier
Standing - Style One

Model No.:	554
Height:	4", 10.1 cm
Size:	Medium
Colour:	See below
Issued:	1. 1927-by 1946
	2. Unknown
Varieties:	HN 909

Colourways	U.S. $	Can. $	U.K. £
1. White/light brown	700.00	850.00	375.00
2. Flambé	900.00	1,100.00	500.00

HN 924
Fox Terrier
Seated - Style Two

Designer:	553
Height:	1. 5 ¼", 13.3 cm
	2. 4 ½", 11.4 cm
Size:	Medium
Colour:	See below
Issued:	1. 1927-by 1946
	2. c.1927
Varieties:	HN 910

Colourways	U.S. $	Can. $	U.K. £
1. White/light brown	700.00	850.00	375.00
2. Flambé	900.00	1,100.00	500.00

DOGS

HN 809
'Bonzo' Character Dog
Style Two

HN 833
Pekinese Puppy, Standing

HN 128
Puppy, Seated

HN 958
King Charles Spaniel

HN 127
Cavalier King Charles Spaniel, Style One

HN 106
Collie, Seated

DOGS

HN 1069
Smooth-Haired Terrier
Ch. 'Chosen Don of Notts'

HN 943
Fox Terrier, Standing
Style Two

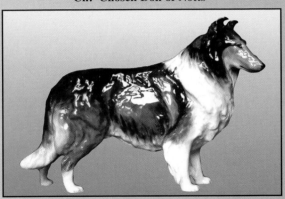

HN 1057
Collie Ch. 'Ashstead Applause'

HN 2667
Labrador Ch. 'Bumblikite Of Mansergh'

HN 1110
Scottish Terrier, Standing, Style Four

HN 1054
Irish Setter Ch. 'Pat O'Moy'

DOGS

HN 2515
Springer Spaniel Ch. 'Dry Toast'

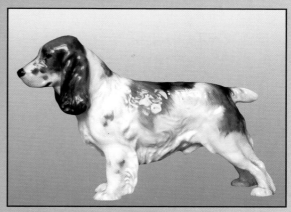

HN 1136
Cocker Spaniel

HN 1072
Bulldog, Standing

HN 948
Bulldog, Seated, Style Four

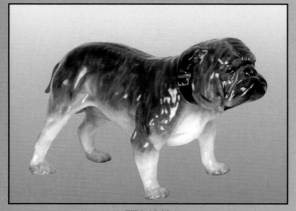

HN 1043
Bulldog, Standing

HN 1046
Bulldog, Standing

DOGS

HN 2508
Sealyham, Seated

HN 1075
Greyhound, Standing

HN 1012
Pekinese Ch. 'Biddee of Ifield'

HN 2643
Boxer Ch. 'Warlord of Mazelaine'

HN 2624
Pointer, Style One

HN 2529
English Setter with Pheasant

DOGS

HN 2585
Cocker Spaniel Lying in Basket

HN 2590
Cocker Spaniels Sleeping

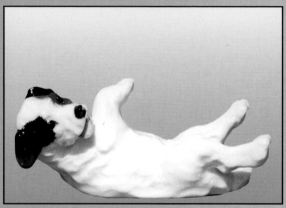

HN 1098
Character Dog Lying on Back

HN 1103
Character Dog with Ball

HN 1099
Character Dog Yawning

HN 1159
Character Dog with Bone

ROYAL ADDERLEY BIRD STUDIES

Hummingbird

American Blue Bird

Blue Tit
Style Two

Blue Tits (Two)
Style One

English Robin
Style Two

Painted Bunting

Blue Jay
Style One

Black-Headed Gouldian Finch

Chaffinch
Style Three

ROYAL ADDERLEY BIRD STUDIES

Cardinals

Virginia Cardinal

**Cardinal (Female)
Style Four**

**Cardinal (Male)
Style Five**

Budgerigars

**Budgerigar
Style Two**

Budgerigars

**Budgerigar
Style Two**

IMAGES

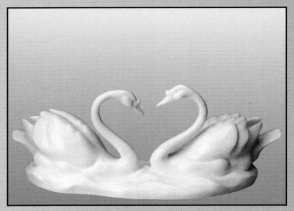

HN 4440
'Endless Love' Swans

HN 4176
'Pride' Lions

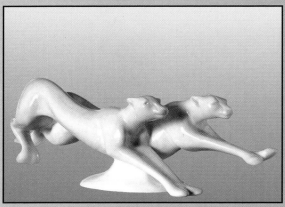

HN 4172
'Running Wild' Cheetahs

HN 4173
'Dedication' Polar Bears

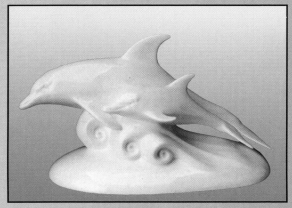

HN 4181
'Crest of A Wave' Dolphins

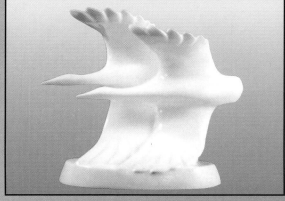

HN 3527
'Going Home' Flying Geese

HN 925
Foxes
Curled - Style Two

Model No.:	528
Size:	3" x 6", 7.6 x 15.2 cm
Colour:	See below
Issued:	1. 1927-by 1946
	2. c.1926
Varieties:	HN 920

Colourways	U.S. $	Can. $	U.K. £
1. Grey/brown	3,750.00	4,500.00	2,000.00
2. Flambé		Rare	

HN 926
Foxes
Curled - Style Three

Model No.:	545
Height:	1 ¾", 5.1 cm
Size:	Miniature
Colour:	See below
Issued:	1. 1927-by 1946
	2. c.1927

Colourways	U.S. $	Can. $	U.K. £
1. Brown/black	1,000.00	1,200.00	500.00
2. Flambé	1,500.00	1,750.00	750.00

HN 927
Pekinese (two)

Model No.:	544
Size:	2 ½" x 4 ½", 6.4 cm x 11.4 cm
Colour:	See below
Issued:	1. 1927-by 1946
	2 and 3. c.1927

Colourways	U.S. $	Can. $	U.K. £
1. Natural colours	1,200.00	1,500.00	650.00
2. Chinese Jade		Rare	
3. Flambé		Rare	

HN 928
Ousel Bowl

Model No.:	Unknown
Height:	7", 17.8 cm
Colour:	Green, blue, brown and orange
Issued:	1927-by 1946

Description	U.S. $	Can. $	U.K. £
Ousel bowl	2,000.00	2,500.00	1,350.00

Note: The bird forms a covered bowl.

HN 929
Fox Terrier Puppy
Seated - white/black patches

Model No.:	570		
Height:	Unknown		
Colour:	White with black patches		
Issued:	1927-by 1946		
Varieties:	HN 931		

Colourways	U.S. $	Can. $	U.K. £
White, black patches		Rare	

HN 930
Alsatian Puppy

Model No.:	568		
Height:	2 ½", 6.4 cm		
Colour:	Brown		
Issued:	1927-by 1946		

Description	U.S. $	Can. $	U.K. £
Alsatian puppy		Rare	

HN 931
Fox Terrier Puppy
Seated - brown

Model No.:	570		
Height:	Unknown		
Colour:	Brown		
Issued:	1927-by 1946		
Varieties:	HN 929		

Colourways	U.S. $	Can. $	U.K. £
Brown		Rare	

HN 932
Scottish Terrier
Seated - Style One - steel grey

Model No.:	569		
Height:	Unknown		
Colour:	Steel grey		
Issued:	1927-by 1946		
Varieties:	HN 933, 934		

Colourways	U.S. $	Can. $	U.K. £
Steel grey		Rare	

HN 933
Scottish Terrier
Seated - Style One - black

Model No.:	569	
Height:	Unknown	
Colour:	Black	
Issued:	1927-by 1946	
Varieties:	HN 932, 934	

Colourways	U.S. $	Can. $	U.K. £
Black		Rare	

HN 934
Scottish Terrier
Seated - Style One - brown

Model No.:	569	
Height:	Unknown	
Colour:	Brown	
Issued:	1927-by 1946	
Varieties:	HN 932, 933	

Colourways	U.S. $	Can. $	U.K. £
Brown		Rare	

HN 935
Pip, Squeak and Wilfred Tray

Model No.:	564	
Designer:	Charles Noke	
Height:	4", 10.1 cm	
Colour:	Brown, black and white, cream tray	
Issued:	1927-1936	

Description	U.S. $	Can. $	U.K. £
Pip, Squeak, Wilfred	3,500.00	4,250.00	1,750.00

Note: On base "Daily Mirror."

HN 936
Teal Duck

Model No.:	Unknown	
Height:	Unknown	
Colour:	Unknown	
Issued:	1927-by 1946	

Description	U.S. $	Can. $	U.K. £
Teal duck		Rare	

HN 937
Alsatian
Standing on plinth

Model No.: 572
Height: Unknown
Colour: Brown
Issued: 1927-by 1946

Description	U.S. $	Can. $	U.K. £
Alsatian, standing		Very Rare	

HN 938
Alsatian
Lying on plinth

Model No.: 571
Height: Unknown
Colour: Brown
Issued: 1927-by 1946

Description	U.S. $	Can. $	U.K. £
Alsatian, lying		Very Rare	

HN 939
Bears Drinking - dark brown

Model No.: 561
Height: 3", 7.6 cm
Colour: Dark brown
Issued: 1927-1936
Varieties: HN 940

Colourways	U.S. $	Can. $	U.K. £
Dark brown	4,000.00	4,750.00	2,250.00

HN 940
Bears Drinking - light brown

Model No.: 561
Height: 3", 7.6 cm
Colour: Light brown
Issued: 1927-1936
Varieties: HN 939

Colourways	U.S. $	Can. $	U.K. £
Light brown	4,000.00	4,750.00	2,250.00

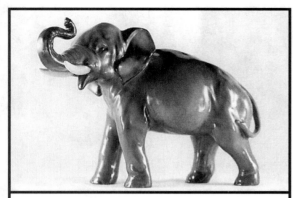

HN 941
Elephant, Trunk in salute - Style One

Model No.:	489B
Designer:	Charles Noke
Height:	4 ½", 11.4 cm
Size:	Small
Colour:	See below
Issued:	1. 1927-by 1946; 2. and 3. c.1926-1962
Varieties:	HN 891B, 2644

Colourways	U.S. $	Can. $	U.K. £
1. Black/white	600.00	725.00	325.00
2. Flambé	600.00	725.00	325.00
3. Sung	1,500.00	1,800.00	800.00

HN 942
Fox Terrier
Standing - Style Three - light brown patches

Model No.:	581
Height:	6", 15.2 cm
Size:	Large
Colour:	White with light brown patches
Issued:	1927-1936
Varieties:	HN 944

Colourways	U.S. $	Can. $	U.K. £
Light brown patches	800.00	950.00	400.00

HN 943
Fox Terrier
Standing - Style Two - light brown patches

Model No.:	580
Height:	5 ½", 14.0 cm - Large
Colour:	See below
Issued:	1. 1927-1940
	2. and 3. c.1927-by 1946
Varieties:	HN 945

Colourways	U.S. $	Can. $	U.K. £
1. White/light brown	800.00	950.00	400.00
2. Chinese Jade		Rare	
3. Flambé	1,500.00	1,800.00	800.00

HN 944
Fox Terrier
Standing - Style Three - dark brown patches

Model No.:	581
Height:	6", 15.2 cm
Size:	Large
Colour:	White with dark brown patches
Issued:	1927-1936
Varieties:	HN 942

Colourways	U.S. $	Can. $	U.K. £
Dark brown patches	800.00	950.00	400.00

HN 945
Fox Terrier
Standing - Style Two - black-brown patches

Model No.:	580
Height:	5 ½", 14.0 cm
Size:	Large
Colour:	See below
Issued:	1. 1927-1940, 2. c.1927-by 1946
Varieties:	HN 943

Colourways	U.S. $	Can. $	U.K. £
1. White/black-brown	800.00	950.00	400.00
2. Chinese Jade		Rare	
3. Flambé	1,500.00	1,800.00	800.00

HN 946
Peruvian Penguin - Medium

Model No.:	585
Designer:	Charles Noke
Height:	7 ¾", 19.7 cm - medium
Colour:	See below
Issued:	1. 1927-by 1946; 2. c.1936-1961
Varieties:	HN 1190

Colourways	U.S. $	Can. $	U.K. £
1. Black/white	1,200.00	1,450.00	650.00
2. Flambé	1,000.00	1,200.00	550.00

Note: Flambé models incorporate a rock as the base. Naturalistic models are free standing,

HN 947
King Penguin

Model No.:	591
Height:	7 ½", 19.0 cm
Colour:	See below
Issued:	1. 1927-by 1946
	2. c.1927
Varieties:	HN 1189

Colourways	U.S. $	Can. $	U.K. £
1. Silver-grey	1,200.00	1,450.00	650.00
2. Flambé	1,000.00	1,200.00	550.00

HN 948
Bulldog
Seated - Style Four

Model No.:	135
	Flambé: 135A
Height:	6", 15.2 cm
Colour:	See below
Issued:	1. 1927-by 1946 2. and 3. c.1913
Varieties:	HN 129

Colourways	U.S. $	Can. $	U.K. £
1. Dark brown	4,000.00	5,000.00	2,200.00
2. Flambé	3,000.00	3,600.00	1,700.00
3. Sung	4,000.00	5,000.00	2,200.00

CHARACTER ELEPHANT

Height: Unknown
Issued: 1928-by 1946

	HN 949 Style One	HN 950 Style Two	HN 951 Style Two	HN 952 Style One
Model No.:	596	595	595	596
Colour:	Orange	Yellow	Brown and blue	Pink
Varieties:	HN 952	HN 951	HN 950	HN 949

Currency	HN 949	HN 950	HN 951	HN 952
U.S. $				
Can. $	Very Rare	Very Rare	Very Rare	Very Rare
U.K. £				

Terrier Puppy
Seated

HN 953

Model No.:	597
Height:	Unknown
Colour:	Black, brown and white
Issued:	1928-by 1946
Varieties:	HN 954

HN 954

Model No.:	597
Height:	Unknown
Colour:	Black, dark brown and white
Issued:	1928-by 1946
Varieties:	HN 953

Description	U.S. $	Can. $	U.K. £
HN 953		Very Rare	
HN 954		Very Rare	

HN 955
Brown Bear
Style One

Model No.:	592
Height:	5", 12.7 cm
Colour:	See below
Issued:	1. 1928-by 1946
	2. c.1928

Colourways	U.S. $	Can. $	U.K. £
1. Brown	1,500.00	1,800.00	800.00
2. Flambé		Very Rare	

HN 956
Mallard Drake, Standing

Model No.:	137
Height:	1. 5 ½", 14.0 cm
	2. 6 ½", 16.5 cm
Size:	Medium
Colour:	See below
Issued:	1. 1928-by 1946
	2. 1913-1996
Varieties:	HN 114, 115, 116, 1191, 2555, 2647

Colourways	U.S. $	Can. $	U.K. £
1. Unknown	450.00	550.00	250.00
2. Flambé	300.00	375.00	150.00

HN 957
King Charles Spaniel - liver and white

Model No.:	532
Height:	4 ¾" 12.1 cm
Colour:	Liver and white
Issued:	1928-by 1946
Varieties:	HN 958

Colourways	U.S. $	Can. $	U.K. £
Liver and white	750.00	900.00	400.00

HN 958
King Charles Spaniel - black and white

Model No.:	532
Height:	4 ¾", 12.1 cm
Colour:	Black and white
Issued:	1928-by 1946
Varieties:	HN 957

Colourways	U.S. $	Can. $	U.K. £
Black and white	750.00	900.00	400.00

*

HN 960
Character Ape with Book
Eyes open

Model No.:	604
Designer:	Charles Noke
Height:	4", 10.1 cm
Colour:	Brown
Issued:	1928-1936

Description	U.S. $	Can. $	U.K. £
Ape, eyes open	2,500.00	3,000.00	1,250.00

HN 961
Character Ape with Book
Eyes closed

Model No.:	604
Designer:	Charles Noke
Height:	4", 10.1 cm
Colour:	Brown
Issued:	1928-1936

Description	U.S. $	Can. $	U.K. £
Ape, eyes closed	2,500.00	3,000.00	1,250.00

HN 962
Great Dane's Head
Pencil Holder

Model No.:	529
Height:	3", 7.6 cm
Colour:	Grey and white
Issued:	1928-1936
Derivative:	Onyx calendar

Description	U.S. $	Can. $	U.K. £
Pencil holder	1,200.00	1,450.00	600.00

HN 963
Fox
Seated - Style Four

Model No.:	599
Height:	5 ½", 14.0 cm
Size:	Medium
Colour:	Brown with black ear tips
Issued:	1928-by 1946

Description	U.S. $	Can. $	U.K. £
Fox, seated	800.00	950.00	425.00

HN 964
Scottish Terrier
Standing - Style One - black

Model No.:	78
Height:	4", 10.1 cm
Colour:	See below
Issued:	1. 1928-by 1946
	2. c.1913
Varieties:	HN 965

Colourways	U.S. $	Can. $	U.K. £
1. Black	1,250.00	1,500.00	700.00
2. Flambé		Rare	

HN 965
Scottish Terrier
Standing - Style One - brown

Model No.:	78
Height:	4", 10.1 cm
Colour:	See below
Issued:	1. 1928-by 1946
	2. c.1913
Varieties:	HN 964

Colourways	U.S. $	Can. $	U.K. £
1. Brown	1,250.00	1,500.00	700.00
2. Flambé		Rare	

HN 966
Elephant, Trunk in salute

Model No.:	489
Designer:	Charles Noke
Height:	7", 17.8 cm
Size:	Large
Colour:	See below
Issued:	1. 1928-by 1946
	2. and 3. c.1926-1962

Colourways	U.S. $	Can. $	U.K. £
1. Brown/grey (matt)	2,500.00	3,000.00	1,400.00
2. Chinese Jade	2,500.00	3,000.00	1,400.00
3. Flambé	750.00	900.00	375.00

HN 967
Cat, Seated - Style One

Model No.:	9
Designer:	Charles Noke
Height:	4 ½", 11.4 cm
Colour:	See below
Issued:	1. 1928-by 1946
	2. 1920-1996
Varieties:	HN 109, 120

Colourways	U.S. $	Can. $	U.K. £
1. Brown/white	1,000.00	1,200.00	550.00
2. Flambé	200.00	250.00	110.00
3. Sung		Extremely Rare	

HN 968
Pig
Snorting - large

Model No.:	72
Size:	2 ½" x 5 ½", 6.4 x 14.0 cm
Size:	Large
Colour:	See below
Issued:	1. 1928-1936
	2. c.1912-1936

Colourways	U.S. $	Can. $	U.K. £
1. Black/white	900.00	1,100.00	500.00
2. Flambé	1,000.00	1,200.00	550.00

HN 968A
Pig
Snorting - small

Model No.:	72A
Size:	2" x 4 ½", 5.0 x 11.9 cm
Size:	Small
Colour:	See below
Issued:	1. 1928-1936
	2. c.1928-1936

Colourways	U.S. $	Can. $	U.K. £
1. Black/white	800.00	950.00	400.00
2. Flambé	1,000.00	1,200.00	500.00

HN 969
Rabbits

Model No.:	249
Height:	3 ½", 8.9 cm
Colour:	See below
Issued:	1. 1928-by 1946
	2. c.1919
Varieties:	HN 209, 217, 218, 219

Colourways	U.S. $	Can. $	U.K. £
1. White/brown	1,500.00	1,750.00	750.00
2. Flambé		Very Rare	

HN 970
Dachshund
Standing - Style Two

Model No.:	36
Size:	4 ½" x 6 ½", 11.4 x 6.5 cm
Colour:	See below
Issued:	1928-by 1946

Colourways	U.S. $	Can. $	U.K. £
Brown	650.00	775.00	350.00

HN 971
'Ooloo' Character Cat
Ashtray

Model No.:	400
Height:	3", 7.6 cm
Colour:	Black and white cat, yellow tray
Issued:	1928-by 1946

Description	U.S. $	Can. $	U.K. £
Ashtray	750.00	900.00	400.00

HN 972
Character Ape in Dunce's Cap with Book

Model No.:	640
Designer:	Charles Noke
Height:	5 ½", 14.0 cm
Colour:	See below
Issued:	1. 1928-1936
	2. c.1929-1937

Colourways	U.S. $	Can. $	U.K. £
1. Dark brown/white	3,000.00	3,600.00	1,500.00
2. Flambé (illustrated)	3,000.00	3,600.00	1,500.00

HN 973
Character Duck
Style Three - yellow/brown/black

Model No.:	647
Height:	6", 15.2 cm
Size:	Large
Colour:	See below
Issued:	1. 1930-by 1946
	2. c.1930
Varieties:	HN 974

Colourways	U.S. $	Can. $	U.K. £
1. Yellow/brown/black	1,200.00	1,500.00	675.00
2. Flambé		Very Rare	

HN 974
Character Duck
Style Three - lemon-yellow

Model No.:	647
Height:	6", 15.2 cm
Size:	Large
Colour:	See below
Issued:	1. 1930-by 1946
	2. c.1930
Varieties:	HN 973

Colourways	U.S. $	Can. $	U.K. £
1. Lemon-yellow	1,200.00	1,500.00	675.00
2. Flambé		Very Rare	

HN 975
English Setter with Collar

Model No.:	646
Height:	6", 15.2 cm
Colour:	Black and white
Issued:	1930-by 1946
Varieties:	Also called 'Red Setter with Collar'
	HN 976

Description	U.S. $	Can. $	U.K. £
English setter	1,500.00	1,800.00	850.00

HN 976
Red Setter with Collar

Model No.:	646
Height:	6", 15.2 cm
Colour:	Light brown
Issued:	1930-by 1946
Varieties:	Also called 'English Setter with Collar' HN 975

Description	U.S. $	Can. $	U.K. £
Red setter	1,500.00	1,800.00	850.00

HN 977
Drake
Resting

Model No.:	654
Size:	3 ¾" x 7 ¼", 9.5 x 18.4 cm
Size:	Large
Colour:	See below
Issued:	1. 1930-by 1946
	2. c.1929-1961
Varieties:	HN 1192

Colourways	U.S. $	Can. $	U.K. £
1. Green/white/brown	750.00	900.00	400.00
2. Flambé	750.00	900.00	400.00

HN 978
Fox
Curled - Style Two

Model No.:	653
Length:	7", 17.8 cm
Colour:	See below
Issued:	2. 1930-by 1946
	2. c.1929

Colourways	U.S. $	Can. $	U.K. £
1. Brown	2,250.00	2,700.00	1,200.00
2. Flambé		Very Rare	

HN 979
Hare
Lying, legs stretched behind - brown

Model No.:	656
Size:	3" x 7 ½", 7.6 x 19.1 cm
Size:	Large
Colour:	See below
Issued:	1. 1930-by 1946
	2. 1929-1962
Varieties:	HN 984, 985, 1071, 2593

Colourways	U.S. $	Can. $	U.K. £
1. Brown/white/black	500.00	600.00	275.00
2. Flambé	600.00	725.00	325.00

HN 980
Aberdeen Terrier - black

Model No.:	657		
Size:	3" x 5", 7.6 x 12.7 cm		
Colour:	Black		
Issued:	1930-by 1946		
Varieties:	HN 981		

Colourways	U.S. $	Can. $	U.K. £
Black	775.00	950.00	425.00

HN 981
Aberdeen Terrier - grey

Model No.:	657		
Size:	3" x 5", 7.6 x 12.7 cm		
Colour:	Grey with brown highlights		
Issued:	1930-by 1946		
Varieties:	HN 980		

Colourways	U.S. $	Can. $	U.K. £
Grey	775.00	950.00	425.00

HN 982
Sealyham - Standing - Style One

Model No.:	658		
Height:	3", 7.6 cm		
Colour:	See below		
Issued:	1 to 3. 1930-1936		
	4. c.1930		
Varieties:	HN 983		

Colourways	U.S. $	Can. $	U.K. £
1. White/black patches	800.00	975.00	450.00
2. White/brown patches	800.00	975.00	450.00
3. Light tan	1,000.00	1,250.00	550.00
4. Flambé		Very Rare	

HN 983
Sealyham
Standing - Style One - light brown patches

Model No.:	658		
Height:	3", 7.6 cm		
Colour:	See below		
Issued:	1. 1930-1936		
	2. c.1930		
Varieties:	HN 982		

Colourways	U.S. $	Can. $	U.K. £
1. White/light brown	1,000.00	1,250.00	550.00
2. Flambé		Very Rare	

HN 984
Hare
Lying, legs stretched behind - white

Model No.:	656
Size:	3" x 7 ½", 7.6 x 19.1 cm
Size:	Large
Colour:	See below
Issued:	1. 1930-by 1946
	2. 1929-1962
Varieties:	HN 979, 985, 1071, 2593

Colourways	U.S. $	Can. $	U.K. £
1. White	500.00	600.00	275.00
2. Flambé	600.00	725.00	325.00

HN 985
Hare
Lying, legs stretched behind - grey

Model No.:	656
Size:	3" x 7 ½", 7.6 x 19.1 cm
Size:	Large
Colour:	See below
Issued:	1. 1930-by 1946
	2. 1929-1962
Varieties:	HN 979, 984, 1071, 2593

Colourways	U.S. $	Can. $	U.K. £
1. Grey	500.00	600.00	275.00
2. Flambé	600.00	725.00	325.00

HN 986
Alsatian Seated on Lid of a Lustre Bowl

Model No.:	497A
Height:	5", 12.7 cm (includes bowl)
Colour:	Brown dog on mother of pearl bowl
Issued:	1930-by 1946
Varieties:	HN 899 (without bowl)

Description	U.S. $	Can. $	U.K. £
Alsatian / lustre bowl	2,500.00	3,000.00	1,400.00

HN 987
Bulldog Seated on Lid of a Lustre Bowl

Model No.:	122
Height:	4", 10.1 cm (includes bowl)
Colour:	White bulldog with dark brown patches, mother of pearl bowl
Issued:	1930-by 1946
Varieties:	HN 881 (without bowl)

Description	U.S. $	Can. $	U.K. £
Bulldog / lustre bowl	3,000.00	3,600.00	1,500.00

HN 988
Airedale Terrier
Standing

Model No.:	685
Size:	8" x 8", 20.3 x 20.3 cm
Size:	Large
Colour:	Light brown
Issued:	1930-1936
Varieties:	HN 996

Colourways	U.S. $	Can. $	U.K. £
Light brown	1,800.00	2,150.00	950.00

HN 989
Scottish Terrier
Standing - Style Two - black/grey

Model No.:	Unknown
Size:	3 ½" x 6 ¾", 8.9 x 17.1 cm
Colour:	Black with grey highlights
Issued:	1930-1936
Varieties:	HN 992

Colourways	U.S. $	Can. $	U.K. £
Black/grey	1,600.00	1,900.00	850.00

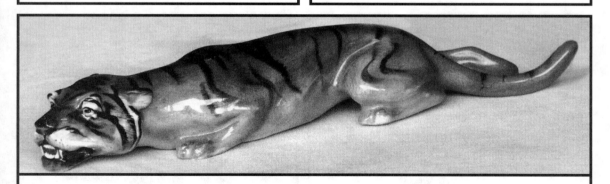

Tiger
Stalking - Style One

	HN 990	HN 991A	HN 991B
Model No.:	680	680A	680B
Designer:	Charles Noke		
Colour:	Brown		
Issued:	1930-by 1946		
Size:	Large	Medium	Small
Length:	7 ½", 19.1 cm	5 ½", 14.0 cm	Unknown

Currency	Large	Medium	Small
U.S. $	900.00	1,100.00	525.00
Can. $	800.00	975.00	450.00
U.K. £	700.00	850.00	375.00

HN 992
Scottish Terrier
Standing - Style Two - brown/black

Model No.:	Unknown
Size:	3 ½" x 6 ¾", 8.9 x 17.1 cm
Colour:	Brown and black
Issued:	1930-by 1946
Varieties:	HN 989

Colourways	U.S. $	Can. $	U.K. £
Black/brown	1,600.00	1,900.00	850.00

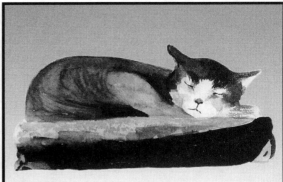

HN 993
Cat Asleep on Cushion

Model No.:	24
Height:	1 ¾", 4.4 cm
Colour:	Black and blue
Issued:	1930-1936

Description	U.S. $	Can. $	U.K. £
Cat asleep on cushion		Very Rare	

HN 994
Fox on Pedestal

Model No.:	21
Height:	6", 15.2 cm
Colour:	See below
Issued:	1. 1930-1936
	2. c.1912-1936

Colourways	U.S. $	Can. $	U.K. £
1. Brown		Very Rare	
2. Flambé		Very Rare	

HN 995
Pekinese
Standing

Model No.:	689
Size:	3 ½" x 5", 8.9 x 12.7 cm
Colour:	See below
Issued:	1. 1930-1937
	2. c.1930
Varieties:	HN 1003

Colourways	U.S. $	Can. $	U.K. £
1. Brown/black	1,500.00	1,800.00	800.00
2. Chinese Jade	2,500.00	3,000.00	1,500.00

HN 996
Airedale Terrier
Standing

Model No.:	685
Size:	8" x 8", 20.3 x 20.3 cm
Size:	Large
Colour:	Light brown with black highlights
Issued:	1930-1936
Varieties:	HN 988

Colourways	U.S. $	Can. $	U.K. £
Light brown/black	1,800.00	2,150.00	950.00

HN 997
Airedale Terrier
Seated

Model No.:	686
Height:	5", 12.7 cm
Colour:	White with black and dark brown patches on ears, eyes and body
Issued:	1930-by 1946

Description	U.S. $	Can. $	U.K. £
Airedale terrier, seated	1,600.00	1,900.00	850.00

HN 998
King Penguin and Chick

Model No.:	239
Height:	5 ½", 14.0 cm
Colour:	See below
Issued:	1. 1930-by 1946
	2. c.1918-1961
Varieties:	HN 198, 297

Colourways	U.S. $	Can. $	U.K. £
1. Green/yellow	1,200.00	1,450.00	650.00
2. Flambé (illustrated)	1,200.00	1,450.00	650.00

HN 999
Persian Cat
Seated - Style One

Model No.:	690
Height:	5", 12.7 cm
Colour:	Black and white
Issued:	1930-1985
Varieties:	HN 2539

Description	U.S. $	Can. $	U.K. £
Black/white cat	175.00	225.00	100.00

HN 1000
Cocker Spaniel Ch. 'Lucky Star of Ware'

Model No.:	709
Designer:	Frederick Daws
Height:	6 ½", 16.5 cm
Size:	Large
Colour:	Black with grey highlights
Issued:	1931-1960
Varieties:	HN 1002, 1108, 1134, 1186; Also called 'Lucky Pride of Ware'

Description	U.S. $	Can. $	U.K. £
Black, large	600.00	725.00	325.00

HN 1001
Cocker Spaniel with Pheasant

Model No.:	714
Designer:	Frederick Daws
Size:	6 ½" x 7 ¾", 16.5 x 19.7 cm
Size:	Large
Colour:	White with brown markings, reddish-brown and green pheasant
Issued:	1931-1968
Varieties:	HN 1137

Description	U.S. $	Can. $	U.K. £
White/brown, large	450.00	550.00	250.00

HN 1002
Cocker Spaniel

Model No.:	709
Designer:	Frederick Daws
Height:	6 ½", 16.5 cm
Size:	Large
Colour:	Liver and white
Issued:	1931-1960
Varieties:	HN 1000, 1108, 1134, 1186; Also called 'Lucky Star of Ware' and 'Lucky Pride of Ware'

Description	U.S. $	Can. $	U.K. £
Liver/white, large	725.00	875.00	400.00

HN 1003
Pekinese
Standing

Model No.:	689
Size:	3 ½" x 5", 8.9 x 12.7 cm
Colour:	See below
Issued:	1. 1931-1937
	2. c.1930
Varieties:	HN 995

Colourways	U.S. $	Can. $	U.K. £
1. Dark brown	1,500.00	1,800.00	800.00
2. Chinese Jade	2,500.00	3,000.00	1,500.00

HN 1004
Blue Tit and Blossom

Model No.:	721
Height:	2 ½", 6.4 cm
Colour:	Browns, white, flowers, dark brown and green base
Issued:	1931-1937

Description	U.S. $	Can. $	U.K. £
Blue tit	1,200.00	1,450.00	650.00

HN 1005
Thrush and Blossom

Model No.:	716
Height:	2 ½", 6.4 cm
Colour:	Browns, yellow, white flowers, dark brown and green base
Issued:	1931-1937

Description	U.S. $	Can. $	U.K. £
Thrush	1,200.00	1,450.00	650.00

*

HN 1007
Rough Haired Terrier Ch. 'Crackley Startler'

Model No.:	725
Designer:	Frederick Daws
Height:	7 ½", 19.1 cm
Size:	Large
Colour:	White with black and brown markings
Issued:	1931-1955
Varieties:	Also known as 'Crackley Hunter'

Description	U.S. $	Can. $	U.K. £
Rough-haired terrier	900.00	1,100.00	500.00

HN 1008
Scottish Terrier Ch. 'Albourne Arthur'

Model No.:	720
Designer:	Frederick Daws
Height:	7", 17.8 cm
Size:	Large
Colour:	Black
Issued:	1931-1955

Description	U.S. $	Can. $	U.K. £
Scottish terrier	1,250.00	1,500.00	700.00

HN 1009
Hare and Leverets
Model No.: 731
Designer: Unknown
Length: 5", 12.7 cm
Colour: Brown
Issued: 1931-1937

Description	U.S. $	Can. $	U.K. £
Hare and leverets		Rare	

PEKINESE CH. 'BIDDEE OF IFIELD'- Standing

Designer: Frederick Daws
Colour: Golden brown with black highlights

	HN 1010	HN 1011	HN 1012
Model No.:	734	734A	734B
Height:	7", 17.8 cm	6 ½", 16.5 cm	3", 11.4 cm
Size:	Extra large	Large	Medium
Issued:	1931-1955	1931-1955	1931-1985
Derivative:	–	–	Bookend

Currency	Extra Large	Large	Small
U.S. $	1,500.00	1,000.00	125.00
Can. $	1,800.00	1,250.00	150.00
U.K. £	850.00	550.00	65.00

HN 1013
Rough-Haired Terrier Ch. 'Crackley Startler'

Model No.:	725A
Designer:	Frederick Daws
Height:	5 ½", 17.8 cm
Size:	Medium
Colour:	White with black and brown markings
Issued:	1931-1960
Varieties:	Also called 'Crackley Hunter'
Derivative:	Bookend

Description	U.S. $	Can. $	U.K. £
Medium	400.00	475.00	225.00

HN 1014
Rough-Haired Terrier Ch. 'Crackley Startler'

Model No.:	725B
Designer:	Frederick Daws
Height:	3 ¾", 13.3 cm
Size:	Small
Colour:	White with black and brown markings
Issued:	1931-1985
Varieties:	Also called 'Crackley Hunter'

Description	U.S. $	Can. $	U.K. £
Small	200.00	250.00	100.00

HN 1015
Scottish Terrier Ch. 'Albourne Arthur'

Model No.:	720A
Designer:	Frederick Daws
Height:	5", 16.5 cm
Size:	Medium
Colour:	Black
Issued:	1931-1960
Derivative:	Bookend

Description	U.S. $	Can. $	U.K. £
Medium	400.00	475.00	225.00

HN 1016
Scottish Terrier Ch. 'Albourne Arthur'

Model No.:	720B
Designer:	Frederick Daws
Height:	3 ½", 12.7 cm
Size:	Small
Colour:	Black
Issued:	1931-1985

Description	U.S. $	Can. $	U.K. £
Small	200.00	250.00	100.00

SCOTTISH TERRIER - Seated - Style Two

Colour: Black

HN 1017

Model No.: 733
Height: 7", 17.8 cm
Size: Large
Issued: 1931-1946

Description	U.S. $	Can. $	U.K. £
Large	2,000.00	2,500.00	1,150.00

HN 1018

Model No.: 733A
Height: 5", 12.7 cm
Size: Medium
Issued: 1931-by 1946

Description	U.S. $	Can. $	U.K. £
1. Natural	1,200.00	1,450.00	650.00
2. Flambé	1,200.00	1,450.00	650.00

HN 1019

Model No.: 733B
Height: 3 ½", 8.9 cm
Size: Small
Issued: 1931-by 1946

Description	U.S. $	Can. $	U.K. £
Small	900.00	1,100.00	500.00

HN 1020
Cocker Spaniel Ch. 'Lucky Star of Ware'

Model No.: 709A
Designer: Frederick Daws
Height: 5", 17.8 cm
Size: Medium
Colour: See below
Issued: 1. 1931-1985 2. c.1937
Varieties: Also called 'Lucky Pride of Ware,' and Spaniel HN 1036, 1109, 1135, 1187

Colourways	U.S. $	Can. $	U.K. £
1. Black/grey	200.00	250.00	100.00
2. Flambé	1,100.00	1,350.00	600.00

HN 1021
Cocker Spaniel Ch. 'Lucky Star of Ware'

Model No.: 709B
Designer: Frederick Daws
Height: 3 ½", 8.9 cm
Size: Small
Colour: Black coat with grey markings
Issued: 1931-1968
Varieties: Also called 'Lucky Pride of Ware,' and Spaniel HN 1037, 1078, 1136, 1188

Description	U.S. $	Can. $	U.K. £
Small	175.00	225.00	100.00

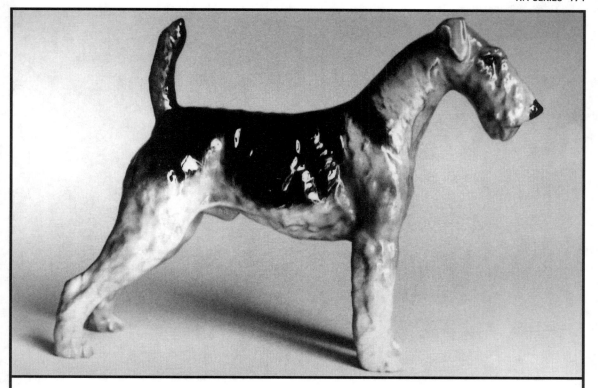

AIREDALE TERRIER CH. 'COTSFORD TOPSAIL'

Designer: Frederick Daws
Colour: 1. Natural; Dark brown and black coat, light brown underbody
2. Flambé

		HN 1022	HN 1023	HN 1024
Model No.:		738	738A	738B
Height:		8", 20.3 cm	5 ¼", 13.3 cm	4", 10.1 cm
Size:		Large	Medium	Small
Issued:	1. Natural	1931-1960	1931-1985	1931-1968
	2. Flambé	c.1931	c.1931	Unknown

Currency	Large		Medium		Small	
	Natural	Flambé	Natural	Flambé	Natural	Flambé
U.S. $	1,350.00	2,000.00	200.00	1,300.00	250.00	N/A
Can. $	1,600.00	2,500.00	250.00	1,500.00	300.00	N/A
U.K. £	750.00	1,000.00	100.00	700.00	150.00	N/A

ENGLISH FOXHOUND CH. 'TRING RATTLER'

Designer: Frederick Daws
Colour: White, black and brown

		HN 1025	HN 1026	HN 1027
Model No.:		740	740A	740B
Height:		8", 20.3 cm	5", 12.7 cm	4", 10.1 cm
Size:		Large	Medium	Small
Issued:	1. Natural	1931-1955	1931-1960	1931-1956
	2. Flambé	–	–	Unknown

	Large		Medium		Small	
Currency	Natural	Flambé	Natural	Flambé	Natural	Flambé
U.S. $	2,200.00	N/A	700.00	N/A	450.00	
Can. $	2,650.00	N/A	850.00	N/A	550.00	Rare
U.K. £	1,200.00	N/A	350.00	N/A	250.00	

COCKER SPANIEL WITH PHEASANT

Designer: Frederick Daws
Colour: White coat with dark brown markings,
              red brown and green pheasant

HN 1028

Model No.:   714A
Height: 5 ¼", 13.3 cm
Size: Medium
Issued: 1931-1985
Varieties: HN 1138
Derivative: Bookend

HN 1029

Model No.:   714B
Height: 3 ½", 8.9 cm
Size: Small
Issued: 1931-1968
Varieties: HN 1062, 2600

Description	U.S. $	Can. $	U.K. £
HN 1028 – medium	200.00	250.00	110.00
HN 1029 – small	275.00	325.00	150.00

SEALYHAM, CH. 'SCOTIA STYLIST ' - standing

Designer: Frederick Daws
Colour: White with light brown patches

HN 1030

Model No.:   748
Size: 5 ½" x 9", 14.0 x 22.9 cm
Size: Large
Issued: White - 1931-1955
              Flambé - c.1931

HN 1031

Model No.:   748A
Height: 4", 10.1 cm
Size: Medium
Issued: 1931-1955
Derivative: Bookend

HN 1032

Model No.:   748B
Height: 3", 12.7 cm
Size: Small
Issued: 1931-1960

Description	U.S. $	Can. $	U.K. £
HN 1030 – white	1,250.00	1,500.00	700.00
HN 1030 – flambé	2,500.00	3,000.00	1,400.00
HN 1031 – medium	275.00	350.00	150.00
HN 1032 – small	225.00	275.00	125.00

CAIRN CH. 'CHARMING EYES'

Designer: Frederick Daws
Colour: Grey with black markings

		HN 1033	HN 1034	HN 1035
Model No.:		750	750A	750B
Height:		7", 17.8 cm	4 ½", 11.4 cm	3 ¼", 8.3 cm
Size:		Large	Medium	Small
Issued:	1. Natural	1931-1955	1931-1960	1. 1931-1985
	2. Flambé	N/A	N/A	2. c.1931
Varieties:		HN 1104	HN 1105	HN 1106
Derivative:		–	Bookend	–

Currency	Large		Medium		Small	
	Natural	Flambé	Natural	Flambé	Natural	Flambé
U.S. $	1,250.00	N/A	450.00	N/A	150.00	900.00
Can. $	1,500.00	N/A	550.00	N/A	175.00	1,100.00
U.K. £	700.00	N/A	250.00	N/A	75.00	500.00

HN 1036
Cocker Spaniel - Medium

Model No.:	709A
Designer:	Frederick Daws
Height:	5 ¼", 13.3 cm
Colour:	See below
Issued:	1. 1931-1985; 2. c.1937
Varieties:	HN 1109, 1135, 1187, Also called 'Lucky Pride of Ware' and 'Lucky Star of Ware' HN 1020

Colourways	U.S. $	Can. $	U.K. £
1. White/light brown	150.00	175.00	85.00
2. Flambé	1,200.00	1,450.00	650.00

HN 1037
Cocker Spaniel

Model No.:	709B
Designer:	Frederick Daws
Height:	3 ½", 8.9 cm
Size:	Small
Colour:	White, light brown patches
Issued:	1931-1968
Varieties:	HN 1078, 1136, 1188; Also called 'Lucky Pride of Ware' and 'Lucky Star of Ware' HN 1021

Description	U.S. $	Can. $	U.K. £
Small	200.00	250.00	110.00

HN 1038
Scottish Terrier
Begging - Style One

Model No.:	Unknown
Height:	Unknown
Colour:	Unknown
Issued:	1931-by 1946

Description	U.S. $	Can. $	U.K. £
Scottish terrier	4,000.00	5,000.00	2,200.00

PEKINESE CH. 'BIDDEE OF IFIELD'
Seated
Designer: Frederick Daws
Colour: Butterscotch coat with black highlight

HN 1039
Model No.:   752
Height: 7", 17.8 cm
Size: Large
Issued: 1931-by 1946

HN 1040
Model No.:   752B
Height: 3", 7.6 cm
Size: Small
Issued: 1. Natural - 1931-by 1946
             2. Flambé - c.1931

Description	U.S. $	Can. $	U.K. £
HN 1039 – Natural	1,750.00	2,250.00	1,000.00
HN 1040 – Natural	900.00	1,100.00	500.00
HN 1040 – Flambé		Rare	

HN 1041
Sealyham Ch. 'Scotia Stylist' - Lying - Style One
Model No.:   753
Designer: Frederick Daws
Height: Unknown
Size: Large
Colour: White with light brown patches over
             the ears and eyes
Issued: 1931-by 1946

Description	U.S. $	Can. $	U.K. £
Large	1,750.00	2,250.00	1,000.00

BULLDOG
Standing

Designer: Frederick Daws
Colour: Brown and white

	HN 1042	HN 1043	HN 1044
Model No.:	754	754A	754B
Height:	5 ½", 14.0 cm	4 ¾", 12.1 cm	3 ¼", 8.3 cm
Size:	Large	Medium	Small
Issued:	1931-1960	1931-1960	1931-1968
Varieties:	HN 1045, 1072	HN 1046, 1073	HN 1047, 1074
Derivative:	—	Bookend	—

Currency	Large	Medium	Small
U.S. $	1,200.00	600.00	250.00
Can. $	1,450.00	725.00	300.00
U.K. £	650.00	350.00	150.00

HN 1045
Bulldog
Standing

Model No.:	754
Designer:	Frederick Daws
Height:	5 ¼", 13.3 cm
Size:	Large
Colour:	Brown and white
Issued:	1931-1960
Varieties:	HN 1042, 1072

Description	U.S. $	Can. $	U.K. £
Large	1,200.00	1,450.00	650.00

HN 1046
Bulldog
Standing

Model No.:	754A
Designer:	Frederick Daws
Height:	4 ¾", 12.1 cm
Size:	Medium
Colour:	Brown and white
Issued:	1931-1960
Varieties:	HN 1043, 1073

Description	U.S. $	Can. $	U.K. £
Medium	550.00	650.00	300.00

HN 1047
Bulldog
Standing

Model No.:	754B
Designer:	Frederick Daws
Height:	3 ¼", 8.3 cm
Size:	Small
Colour:	Brown and white
Issued:	1931-1985
Varieties:	HN 1044, 1074

Description	U.S. $	Can. $	U.K. £
Small	250.00	300.00	135.00

HN 1048
West Highland Terrier
Style One

Model No.:	756
Size:	6 ½" x 9", 16.5 x 22.9 cm
Size:	Large
Colour:	White with brown highlights
Issued:	1931-1931

Description	U.S. $	Can. $	U.K. £
Large	Only three known to exist.		

Note: Sold at auction, Phillips, London, October 2000, for £1,125.00.

ENGLISH SETTER CH. 'MAESYDD MUSTARD'

Designer:	Frederick Daws
Colour:	Off white coat with black highlights

		HN 1049	HN 1050	HN 1051
Model No.:		770	770A	770B
Height:		7 ½", 19.0 cm	5 ¼", 13.3 cm	4", 10.1 cm
Size:		Large	Medium	Small
Issued:	1.	1931-1960	1931-1985	1931-1968
	2.	Unknown (flambé)	–	–
Varieties:				
Also called:				
English Setter		HN 2620	HN 2621	HN 2622
Gordon Setter		HN 1079	HN 1080	HN 1081
Irish Setter		HN 1054	HN 1055	HN 1056
Ch. 'Pat O'Moy'				

Currency	Large		Medium		Small	
	Natural	Flambé	Natural	Flambé	Natural	Flambé
U.S. $	1,100.00	1,500.00	225.00	–	250.00	–
Can. $	1,350.00	1,800.00	275.00	–	300.00	–
U.K. £	600.00	825.00	125.00	–	150.00	–

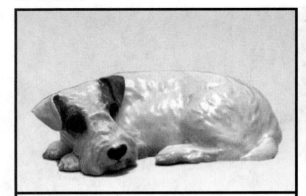

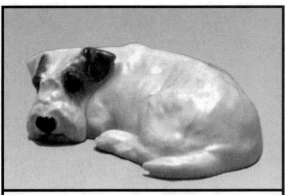

HN 1052
Sealyham Ch. 'Scotia Stylist'
Lying

Model No.:	753A
Designer:	Frederick Daws
Height:	Unknown
Size:	Medium
Colour:	White with light brown patches over ears and eyes
Issued:	1931-by 1946

Description	U.S. $	Can. $	U.K. £
Medium	1,300.00	1,600.00	750.00

HN 1053
Sealyham Ch. 'Scotia Stylist'
Lying

Model No.:	753B
Designer:	Frederick Daws
Height:	Unknown
Size:	Small
Colour:	White with light brown patches over ears and eyes
Issued:	1931-by 1946

Description	U.S. $	Can. $	U.K. £
Small	900.00	1,100.00	500.00

NOTES ON PRICING

- Animal figures are not as plentiful as pretty ladies or character figures and caution in pricing must prevail.

- In the pricing tables N/I (not issued) indicates that the animal figure was not available in that particular market.

- Rarity classification provides a range for the collector to work with.

- Always remember that when dealing with rare animal figures you need two willing parties, a buyer and a seller. One without the other will not work and only when they agree do you have a market price.

Rarity Class	Rare	Very Rare	Extremely Rare
U.S. $	1,850./2,750.	2,750./4,500.	4,500./Up
Can. $	2,250./3,500.	3,500./5,500.	5,500./Up
U.K. £	1,000./1,500.	1,500./2,500.	2,500./Up

IRISH SETTER CH. 'PAT O'MOY'

Designer: Frederick Daws
Colour: Reddish-brown

		HN 1054	HN 1055	HN 1056
Model No.:		770	770A	770B
Height:		7 ½", 19.0 cm	5", 12.7 cm	4", 10.1 cm
Size:		Large	Medium	Small
Issued:	1.	1931-1960	1931-1985	1931-1968
	2.	Unknown (flambé)	—	—
Varieties:				
Also called:				
English Setter		HN 2620	HN 2621	HN 2622
English Setter Ch.				
'Maesydd Mustard'		HN 1049	HN 1050	HN 1051
Gordon Setter		HN 1079	HN 1080	HN 1081
Derivative:		—	Bookend	—

Currency	Large		Medium		Small	
	Natural	Flambé	Natural	Flambé	Natural	Flambé
U.S. $	1,100.00	1,500.00	225.00	—	250.00	—
Can. $	1,350.00	1,800.00	275.00	—	300.00	—
U.K. £	600.00	825.00	125.00	—	140.00	—

COLLIE CH. 'ASHSTEAD APPLAUSE'

Designer: Frederick Daws
Colour: Dark and light brown coat, white chest, shoulders and feet

	HN 1057	HN 1058	HN 1059
Model No.:	779	779A	779B
Height:	7 ½", 19.1 cm	5", 12.7 cm	3 ½", 11.4 cm
Size:	Large	Medium	Small
Issued:	1931-1960	1931-1985	1931-1969

Currency	Large	Medium	Small
U.S. $	1,100.00	175.00	225.00
Can. $	1,350.00	225.00	275.00
U.K. £	600.00	100.00	125.00

*

HN 1062
Cocker Spaniel with Pheasant

Model No.:	714B
Designer:	Frederick Daws
Height:	3 ½", 8.9 cm
Size:	Small
Colour:	White with black markings, reddish-brown pheasant
Issued:	1931-1968
Varieties:	HN 1029, 2600

Description	U.S. $	Can. $	U.K. £
Cocker spaniel/pheasant	225.00	275.00	125.00

COCKER SPANIEL WITH HARE

Colour:	Brown and white dog, brown hare

HN 1063

Model No.:	784
Height:	5", 12.7 cm
Size:	Large
Issued:	1931-1935

HN 1064

Model No.:	784A
Height:	4", 10.1 cm
Size:	Small
Issued:	1931-1935

Description	U.S. $	Can. $	U.K. £
HN 1063 – large	1,750.00	2,100.00	1,000.00
HN 1064 – small	1,500.00	1,800.00	825.00

GREYHOUND
Standing

Colour: Golden brown with dark brown markings, cream chest and feet

	HN 1065	HN 1066	HN 1067
Model No.:	792	792A	792B
Height:	8 ½", 21.6 cm	6", 15.2 cm	4 ½", 11.4 cm
Size:	Large	Medium	Small
Issued:	1931-1955	1931-1955	1931-1960
Varieties:	HN 1075	HN 1076	HN 1077

Currency	Large	Medium	Small
U.S. $	1,750.00	1,000.00	800.00
Can. $	2,100.00	1,250.00	950.00
U.K. £	1,000.00	550.00	450.00

HN 1068
Smooth-Haired Terrier Ch. 'Chosen Don of Notts'

Model No.:	791
Designer:	Frederick Daws
Height:	8 ½", 21.6 cm
Size:	Large
Colour:	White, black patches on eyes, ears and back
Issued:	1931-by 1952
Varieties:	HN 2512

Description	U.S. $	Can. $	U.K. £
Large	2,500.00	3,000.00	1,400.00

HN 1069
Smooth-Haired Terrier Ch. 'Chosen Don of Notts'

Model No.:	791A
Designer:	Frederick Daws
Height:	6", 15.2 cm
Size:	Medium
Colour:	White, black patches on eyes, ears and back
Issued:	1932-1960
Varieties:	HN 2513

Description	U.S. $	Can. $	U.K. £
Medium	1,350.00	1,600.00	750.00

HN 1070
Smooth-Haired Terrier Ch. 'Chosen Don of Notts'

Model No.:	791B
Designer:	Frederick Daws
Height:	5", 12.7 cm
Size:	Small
Colour:	White, black patches on eyes, ears and back
Issued:	1931-1952
Varieties:	HN 2514

Description	U.S. $	Can. $	U.K. £
Small	1,500.00	1,800.00	825.00

HN 1071
Hare
Lying, legs stretched behind - brown

Model No.:	656
Size:	3" x 7 ½", 7.6 cm x 19.1 cm
Size:	Large
Colour:	See below
Issued:	1. 1932-1941
	2. 1929-1962
Varieties:	HN 979, 984, 985, 2593

Colourways	U.S. $	Can. $	U.K. £
1. Brown/white	500.00	600.00	275.00
2. Flambé	600.00	725.00	325.00

BULLDOG
Standing

Designer: Frederick Daws
Colour: White, brown collar, gold (tan) studs

	HN 1072	HN 1073	HN 1074
Model No.:	754	754A	754B
Height:	6", 15.2 cm	5", 12.7 cm	3 ¼", 8.2 cm
Size:	Large	Medium	Small
Issued:	1932-1960	1932-1960	1932-1985
Varieties:	HN 1042, 1045	HN 1043, 1046	HN 1044, 1047

Currency	Large	Medium	Small
U.S. $	1,200.00	650.00	200.00
Can. $	1,500.00	775.00	250.00
U.K. £	650.00	375.00	110.00

GREYHOUND
Standing

Colour: White with dark brown patches on eyes, ears and back

	HN 1075	HN 1076	HN 1077
Model No.:	792	792A	792B
Height:	8 ½", 21.6 cm	6", 15.2 cm	4 ½", 11.4 cm
Size:	Large	Medium	Small
Issued:	1932-1955	1932-1955	1932-1955
Varieties:	HN 1065	HN 1066	HN 1067

Currency	Large	Medium	Small
U.S. $	1,750.00	1,000.00	800.00
Can. $	2,100.00	1,250.00	950.00
U.K. £	1,000.00	550.00	450.00

HN 1078
Cocker Spaniel

Model No.:	709B
Designer:	Frederick Daws
Height:	3", 7.6 cm
Size:	Small
Colour:	White with black markings
Issued:	1932-1968
Varieties:	HN 1037, 1136, 1188; Also called 'Lucky Pride of Ware' and 'Lucky Star of Ware' HN 1021

Description	U.S. $	Can. $	U.K. £
Small	175.00	200.00	100.00

HN 1079
Gordon Setter - Large

Model No.:	770
Designer:	Frederick Daws
Height:	8", 20.3 cm
Colour:	Dark brown coat, light brown underbody
Issued:	1. 1932-1955; 2. Unknown
Varieties:	English Setter HN 2620, English Setter Ch. 'Maesydd Mustard' HN 1049, Irish Setter Ch. 'Pat O'Moy' HN 1054

Description	U.S. $	Can. $	U.K. £
1. Natural	4,000.00	5,000.00	2,250.00
2. Flambé	1,500.00	1,800.00	825.00

HN 1080
Gordon Setter - Medium

Model No.:	770A
Designer:	Frederick Daws
Height:	5", 12.7 cm
Colour:	Dark brown coat, light brown underbody
Issued:	1932-1955
Varieties:	English Setter HN 2621, English Setter Ch. 'Maesydd Mustard' HN 1050, Irish Setter Ch. 'Pat O'Moy' HN 1055

Description	U.S. $	Can. $	U.K. £
Medium	1,250.00	1,500.00	700.00

HN 1081
Gordon Setter - Small

Model No.:	770B
Designer:	Frederick Daws
Height:	4", 10.1 cm
Colour:	Dark brown coat, light brown underbody
Issued:	1932-1960
Varieties:	English Setter HN 2622, English Setter Ch. 'Maesydd Mustard' HN 1051, Irish Setter Ch. 'Pat O'Moy' HN 1055

Description	U.S. $	Can. $	U.K. £
Small	800.00	975.00	450.00

HN 1082
Tiger
Stalking - Style Two - extra large

Model No.:	809
Designer:	Charles Noke
Size:	5 ¾" x 13 ¼", 14.6 x 33.5 cm
Size:	Extra large
Colour:	See below
Issued:	1. 1933-by 1946 2. 1950-1996
Varieties:	HN 2646, Tiger on Alabaster Base HN 1126

Colourways	U.S. $	Can. $	U.K. £
1. Natural	1,500.00	1,800.00	850.00
2. Flambé	900.00	1,100.00	500.00

HN 1083
Tiger
Stalking - Style Two - medium

Model No.:	809A
Designer:	Charles Noke
Size:	3 ¼" x 7", 8.3 x 17.8 cm
Size:	Medium
Colour:	Brown with dark brown stripes
Issued:	1933-by 1946

Description	U.S. $	Can. $	U.K. £
Medium	1,000.00	1,200.00	550.00

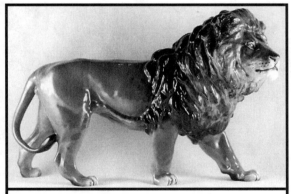

HN 1084
Tiger
Stalking - Style Two - small

Model No.:	809B
Designer:	Charles Noke
Height:	2", 5.1 cm
Size:	Small
Colour:	Brown with dark brown stripes
Issued:	1933-by 1946

Description	U.S. $	Can. $	U.K. £
Small	800.00	975.00	450.00

Note: Mould 809B was also used to produce HN 1094 Leopard.

HN 1085
Lion
Standing - Style One - large

Model No.:	801
Designer:	Charles Noke
Size:	9" x 13", 22.9 x 33.0 cm
Size:	Large
Colour:	Brown coat, dark brown mane
Issued:	1933-by 1946
Varieties:	Lion on alabaster base HN 1125

Description	U.S. $	Can. $	U.K. £
Large	2,000.00	2,500.00	1,100.00

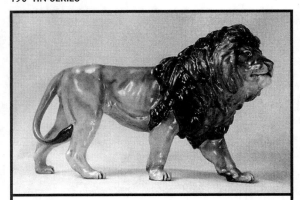

HN 1086
Lion
Standing - Style One - small

Model No.:	801A
Designer:	Charles Noke
Height:	5", 12.7 cm
Size:	Small
Colour:	Brown coat, dark brown mane
Issued:	1931-by 1946

Description	U.S. $	Can. $	U.K. £
Small	1,175.00	1,400.00	650.00

Photograph
not available
at press time

HN 1087
Drake on Ashtray

Model No.:	395
Height:	3 ½", 8.9 cm
Colour:	Green drake, cream ashtray
Issued:	1934-by 1946

Description	U.S. $	Can. $	U.K. £
HN 1087A – Fluted	225.00	275.00	125.00
HN 1087B – Plain	225.00	275.00	125.00

HN 1088
Duck on Ashtray

Model No.:	Unknown
Height:	3 ½", 8.9 cm
Colour:	White duck, cream ashtray
Issued:	1934-by 1946

Description	U.S. $	Can. $	U.K. £
HN 1088A – fluted	225.00	275.00	125.00
HN 1088B – plain	225.00	275.00	125.00

HN 1089
Robin on Ashtray

Model No.:	155
Height:	3", 7.6 cm
Colour:	Dark brown bird with red breast, cream ashtray
Issued:	1934-by 1946

Description	U.S. $	Can. $	U.K. £
HN 1089A – fluted	225.00	275.00	125.00
HN 1089B – plain	225.00	275.00	125.00

HN 1090
Mouse on Ashtray

Model No.:	1164B
Height:	3", 7.6 cm
Colour:	Grey mouse on cream ashtray
Issued:	1934-by 1946

Description	U.S. $	Can. $	U.K. £
HN 1090A – fluted	225.00	275.00	125.00
HN 1090B – plain	225.00	275.00	125.00

HN 1091
Lop-eared Rabbit on Ashtray

Model No.:	1165
Height:	3 ½", 8.9 cm
Colour:	Brown and white rabbit on cream ashtray
Issued:	1934-by 1946

Description	U.S. $	Can. $	U.K. £
HN 1091A – fluted	225.00	275.00	125.00
HN 1091B – plain	225.00	275.00	125.00

HN 1092
Comical Bird on Ashtray

Model No.:	366
Height:	Unknown
Colour:	Black, white and orange
Issued:	1934-by 1946

Description	U.S. $	Can. $	U.K. £
HN 1092A – fluted	225.00	275.00	125.00
HN 1092B – plain	225.00	275.00	125.00

Note: Model illustrated is the Comical Bird which sits on the ashtray.

HN 1093
Squirrel on Ashtray

Model No.:	115
Height:	3", 7.6 cm
Colour:	Brown squirrel on cream ashtray
Issued:	1934-by 1946

Description	U.S. $	Can. $	U.K. £
HN 1093A – fluted	225.00	275.00	125.00
HN 1093B – plain	225.00	275.00	125.00

HN 1094
Leopard
Standing

Model No.:	809B
Designer:	Charles Noke
Height:	2", 5.1 cm
Colour:	Browns
Issued:	1934-by 1946

Description	U.S. $	Can. $	U.K. £
Leopard, standing		Very Rare	

Note: Mould 809B was also used to produce HN 1084 Tiger.

HN 1095
Kingfisher on Ashtray

Model No.:	Unknown
Height:	3", 7.6 cm
Colour:	Unknown
Issued:	1934-by 1946

Description	U.S. $	Can. $	U.K. £
HN 1095A— fluted	225.00	275.00	125.00
HN 1095B — plain	225.00	275.00	125.00

HN 1096
Character Fox with Stolen Goose

Model No.:	857
Designer:	Charles Noke
Height:	4 ¾", 12.1 cm
Colour:	Green cloak and hat, brown fox
Issued:	1934-by 1946
Varieties:	HN 1102

Colourways	U.S. $	Can. $	U.K. £
Green cloak		Very Rare	

HN 1097
Character Dog Running with Ball

Model No.:	853
Height:	2 ", 12.7 cm
Colour:	White with light brown patches over eyes and ears, light and dark brown patches on back, yellow and red striped ball
Issued:	1934-1985
Varieties:	Also known with plain ball

Description	U.S. $	Can. $	U.K. £
Striped ball	100.00	125.00	60.00
Plain ball	500.00	600.00	275.00

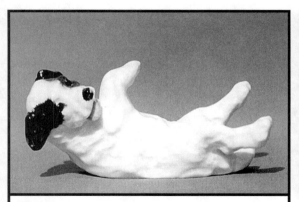

HN 1098
Character Dog Lying on Back

Model No.:	854		
Height:	2", 11.4 cm		
Colour:	White with brown and black patches over ears and eyes		
Issued:	1934-1959		

Description	U.S. $	Can. $	U.K. £
Dog, lying on back	225.00	275.00	125.00

HN 1099
Character Dog Yawning

Model No.:	856		
Height:	4", 10.1 cm		
Colour:	White with brown patches over ears and eyes, black patches on back		
Issued:	1934-1985		

Description	U.S. $	Can. $	U.K. £
Dog, yawning	100.00	125.00	60.00

Note: Model also known with left front paw tucked under.

HN 1100
Bull Terrier
Standing - Style One

Model No.:	852		
Height:	4", 10.1 cm		
Colour:	White with brown patches over eyes and ears, black patches on back		
Issued:	1934-1959		

Description	U.S. $	Can. $	U.K. £
Bull terrier	400.00	475.00	225.00

HN 1101
Character Dog Lying, Panting

Model No.:	866		
Height:	2 ¼", 5.7 cm		
Colour:	White with brown patches over ears and eyes, black patches on back		
Issued:	1934-1959		

Description	U.S. $	Can. $	U.K. £
Dog, lying/panting	200.00	250.00	110.00

HN 1102
Character Fox with Stolen Goose

Model No.:	857
Designer:	Charles Noke
Height:	4 ¾", 12.1 cm
Colour:	Red cloak, black hat, grey chicken
Issued:	1934-by 1946
Varieties:	HN 1096

Colourways	U.S. $	Can. $	U.K. £
Red cloak		Very Rare	

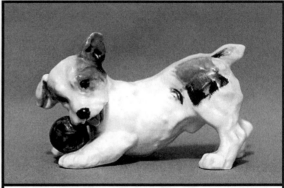

HN 1103
Character Dog with Ball

Model No.:	855
Height:	2 ½", 10.2 cm
Colour:	White with light and dark brown patches maroon ball
Issued:	1934-1985

Description	U.S. $	Can. $	U.K. £
Dog with ball	100.00	125.00	60.00

Note: This model is also known with a doll in place of the ball.

HN 1104
Cairn
Standing - Large

Model No.:	750
Designer:	Frederick Daws
Height:	7", 17.8 cm
Size:	Large
Colour:	Black (earthenware)
Issued:	1937-1955
Varieties:	Also called Cairn Ch. 'Charming Eyes' HN 1033

Description	U.S. $	Can. $	U.K. £
Large	1,250.00	1,500.00	700.00

HN 1105
Cairn
Standing - Medium

Model No.:	750A
Designer:	Frederick Daws
Height:	4 ½",11.4 cm
Size:	Medium
Colour:	Black (earthenware)
Issued:	1937-1960
Varieties:	Also called Cairn Ch. 'Charming Eyes' HN 1034

Description	U.S. $	Can. $	U.K. £
Medium	600.00	725.00	325.00

HN 1106
Cairn, Standing

Model No.:	750B
Designer:	Frederick Daws
Height:	3", 7.6 cm
Size:	Small
Colour:	See below
Issued:	1. 1937-1960; 2. c.1931
Varieties:	Also called Cairn Ch. 'Charming Eyes' HN 1035

Colourways	U.S. $	Can. $	U.K. £
1. Black (earthenware)	300.00	350.00	170.00
2. Flambé	900.00	1,100.00	500.00

HN 1107
Scottish Terrier
Standing - Style Three

Model No.:	Unknown
Size:	6 ¾" x 11", 17.2 x 27.9 cm
Size:	Large
Colour:	Black (earthenware)
Issued:	1934-by 1946

Description	U.S. $	Can. $	U.K. £
Large		Very Rare	

HN 1108
Cocker Spaniel - Large

Model No.:	709
Designer:	Frederick Daws
Height:	6 ½", 16.5 cm
Colour:	White with black markings
Issued:	1937-1960
Varieties:	HN 1002, 1134, 1186; Also called 'Lucky Star of Ware' and 'Lucky Pride of Ware' HN 1000

Description	U.S. $	Can. $	U.K. £
Large	725.00	875.00	400.00

HN 1109
Cocker Spaniel - Medium

Model No.:	709A
Designer:	Frederick Daws
Height:	5", 12.7 cm
Colour:	See below
Issued:	1. 1937-1985; 2. c.1937
Varieties:	HN 1036, 1135, 1187, Also called 'Lucky Pride of Ware' and 'Lucky Star of Ware' HN 1020
Derivative:	Bookend

Colourways	U.S. $	Can. $	U.K. £
1. White/black	150.00	175.00	85.00
2. Flambé	1,200.00	1,450.00	650.00

HN 1110
Scottish Terrier
Standing - Style Four

Model No.:	873	
Designer:	Frederick Daws	
Height:	7", 17.8 cm	
Size:	Large	
Colour:	Black (earthenware)	
Issued:	1937-by 1946	

Description	U.S. $	Can. $	U.K. £
Large	1,750.00	2,100.00	1,000.00

HN 1111
Dalmatian Ch. 'Goworth Victor'

Model No.:	900
Designer:	Frederick Daws
Height:	7 ¾", 19.7 cm
Size:	Large
Colour:	White with black spots, black ears
Issued:	1937-1955

Description	U.S. $	Can. $	U.K. £
Large	2,750.00	3,250.00	1,500.00

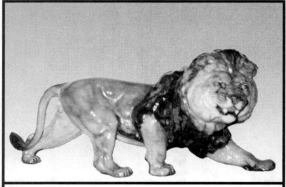

HN 1112
Lion
Standing - Style Two

Model No.:	Unknown	
Designer:	Charles Noke	
Length:	16", 40.6 cm	
Size:	Large	
Colour:	Brown with dark brown mane (china)	
Issued:	1937-1946	
Varieties:	HN 1119 Lion on the Rock	

Description	U.S. $	Can. $	U.K. £
Large	2,250.00	2,750.00	1,250.00

HN 1113
Dalmatian Ch. 'Goworth Victor'

Model No.:	900A
Designer:	Frederick Daws
Height:	5 ½", 14.0 cm
Size:	Medium
Colour:	White with black spots, black ears
Issued:	1937-1985

Description	U.S. $	Can. $	U.K. £
Medium	250.00	300.00	140.00

HN 1114
Dalmatian Ch. 'Goworth Victor'

Model No.:	900B
Designer:	Frederick Daws
Height:	4 ¼", 10.8 cm
Size:	Small
Colour:	White with black spots, black ears
Issued:	1937-1968

Description	U.S. $	Can. $	U.K. £
Small	325.00	400.00	175.00

HN 1115
Alsatian Ch. 'Benign of Picardy'

Model No.:	925
Designer:	Frederick Daws
Height:	9", 22.9 cm
Size:	Large
Colour:	Dark brown coat with light brown underbody, black highlights
Issued:	1937-1960

Description	U.S. $	Can. $	U.K. £
Large	900.00	1,100.00	500.00

HN 1116
Alsatian Ch. 'Benign of Picardy'

Model No.:	925A
Designer:	Frederick Daws
Height:	6", 15.2 cm
Size:	Medium
Colour:	Dark brown coat with light brown underbody, black highlights
Issued:	1937-1985

Description	U.S. $	Can. $	U.K. £
Medium	200.00	250.00	110.00

HN 1117
Alsatian Ch. 'Benign of Picardy'

Model No.:	925B
Designer:	Frederick Daws
Height:	4 ½", 11.4 cm
Size:	Small
Colour:	Dark brown coat with light brown underbody, black highlights
Issued:	1937-1968

Description	U.S. $	Can. $	U.K. £
Small	250.00	300.00	135.00

Photograph
not available
at press time

HN 1118
Tiger on the Rock
Style Two

Model No.:	809
Designer:	Charles Noke
Height:	12", 30.5 cm
Colour:	Brown and black (earthenware)
Issued:	1937-by 1946
Varieties:	HN 1082 (without rock)

Description	U.S. $	Can. $	U.K. £
Tiger on rock	2,250.00	2,750.00	1,250.00

HN 1119
Lion on the Rock
Style One

Model No.:	Unknown
Designer:	Charles Noke
Height:	11", 27.9 cm
Colour:	Tan, brown and black (earthenware)
Issued:	1937-by 1946
Varieties:	Lion (standing) HN 1112

Description	U.S. $	Can. $	U.K. £
Lion on rock	2,250.00	2,750.00	1,250.00

HN 1120
Fighter Elephant - Large

Model No.:	626
Designer:	Charles Noke
Size:	12" x 9", 30.5 x 22.9 cm
Colour:	See below
Issued:	1. 1937-by 1946
	2. and 3. c.1929
Varieties:	HN 2640

Colourways	U.S. $	Can. $	U.K. £
1. Grey (earthenware)	1,500.00	1,850.00	850.00
2. Flambé	3,000.00	3,500.00	1,600.00
3. Sung	4,500.00	5,500.00	2,500.00

HN 1121
Elephant
Trunk down, curled

Model No.:	600
Designer:	Charles Noke
Height:	13", 33.0 cm
Size:	Large
Colour:	See below
Issued:	1. 1937-1960
	2. and 3. c.1938-1968

Colourways	U.S. $	Can. $	U.K. £
1. Grey (earthenware)		Extremely Rare	
2. Flambé	4,000.00	4,750.00	2,250.00
3. Sung	5,500.00	6,500.00	3,000.00

Photograph
not available
at press time

HN 1125
Lion on Alabaster Base

Model No.:	801
Designer:	Charles Noke
Height:	7", 17.8 cm
Size:	Extra large
Colour:	Tan
Issued:	1937-by 1946
Varieties:	HN 1085 (without base)

Description	U.S. $	Can. $	U.K. £
Lion on alabaster base		Very Rare	

HN 1126
Tiger on Alabaster Base

Model No.:	809
Designer:	Charles Noke
Size:	5 ¾" x 13 ¼", 14.6 x 33.5 cm
Size:	Extra large
Colour:	See below
Issued:	1937-by 1946
Varieties:	HN 1082, 2646

Description	U.S. $	Can. $	U.K. £
Tiger on alabaster base		Very Rare	

HN 1127
Dachshund Ch. 'Shrewd Saint'

Model No.:	938
Designer:	Frederick Daws
Height:	6", 15.2 cm
Size:	Large
Colour:	See below
Issued:	1. 1937-1955
	2. c.1937
Varieties:	Also called Dachshund HN 1139

Colourways	U.S. $	Can. $	U.K. £
1. Browns (earthenware)	800.00	975.00	450.00
2. Flambé	1,750.00	2,250.00	1,000.00

HN 1128
Dachshund Ch. 'Shrewd Saint'

Model No.:	938A
Designer:	Frederick Daws
Height:	4", 10.1 cm
Size:	Medium
Colour:	See below
Issued:	1. 1937-1985
	2. c.1937
Varieties:	Also called Dachshund HN 1140

Colourways	U.S. $	Can. $	U.K. £
1. Dark/light brown	125.00	150.00	75.00
2. Flambé	900.00	1,100.00	500.00

HN 1129
Dachshund Ch. 'Shrewd Saint'

Model No.:	938B	
Designer:	Frederick Daws	
Height:	3", 7.6 cm	
Size:	Small	
Colour:	See below	
Issued:	1. 1937-1968	
	2. c.1937	
Varieties:	Also called Dachshund HN 1141	

Colourways	U.S. $	Can. $	U.K. £
1. Dark/light brown	225.00	275.00	125.00
2. Flambé	900.00	1,100.00	500.00

HN 1130
Fox
Seated - Style Five

Model No.:	978
Designer:	Raoh Schorr
Height:	11", 27.9 cm
Size:	Extra large
Colour:	Brown and white
Issued:	1937-by 1946
Varieties:	HN 2527

Description	U.S. $	Can. $	U.K. £
Extra large	2,000.00	2,500.00	1,100.00

HN 1131
Staffordshire Bull Terrier
Style One

Model No.:	959
Designer:	Frederick Daws
Height:	9", 22.9 cm
Size:	Large
Colour:	White
Issued:	1937-by 1946
Varieties:	Also called Bull Terrier Ch. 'Bokos Brock' HN 1142

Description	U.S. $	Can. $	U.K. £
Large	3,000.00	3,500.00	1,600.00

HN 1132
Staffordshire Bull Terrier
Style One

Model No.:	959A
Designer:	Frederick Daws
Height:	6 ½", 16.5 cm
Size:	Medium
Colour:	White
Issued:	1937-1960
Varieties:	Also called Bull Terrier Ch. 'Bokos Brock' HN 1143

Description	U.S. $	Can. $	U.K. £
Medium	1,200.00	1,450.00	675.00

HN 1133
Staffordshire Bull Terrier
Style One

Model No.:	959B
Designer:	Frederick Daws
Height:	4 ½", 11.4 cm
Size:	Small
Colour:	White
Issued:	1937-by 1946
Varieties:	Also called Bull Terrier Ch. 'Bokos Brock' HN 1144

Description	U.S. $	Can. $	U.K. £
Small	1,850.00	2,250.00	1,000.00

HN 1134
Cocker Spaniel

Model No.:	709
Designer:	Frederick Daws
Height:	6 ½", 16.5 cm
Size:	Large
Colour:	Liver and white
Issued:	1937-by 1946
Varieties:	HN 1002, 1108, 1186; Also called 'Lucky Star of Ware' HN 1000 and 'Lucky Pride of Ware'

Description	U.S. $	Can. $	U.K. £
Large	700.00	850.00	400.00

HN 1135
Cocker Spaniel

Model No.:	709A
Designer:	Frederick Daws
Height:	5", 12.7 cm
Size:	Medium
Colour:	See below
Issued:	1. 1937-by 1946; 2. c.1937
Varieties:	HN 1036, 1109, 1187; Also called 'Lucky Pride of Ware' and 'Lucky Star of Ware' HN 1020

Colourways	U.S. $	Can. $	U.K. £
1. Liver/white	225.00	275.00	125.00
2. Flambé	1,100.00	1,350.00	600.00

HN 1136
Cocker Spaniel

Model No.:	709B
Designer:	Frederick Daws
Height:	3", 7.6 cm
Size:	Small
Colour:	Liver and white
Issued:	1937-by 1946
Varieties:	HN 1037, 1078, 1188; Also called 'Lucky Pride of Ware' and 'Lucky Star of Ware' HN 1021

Description	U.S. $	Can. $	U.K. £
Small	250.00	300.00	135.00

HN 1137
Cocker Spaniel with Pheasant

Model No.:	714
Designer:	Frederick Daws
Size:	6 ½" x 7 ¾", 16.5 x 19.7 cm
Size:	Large
Colour:	White coat with black markings, red-brown pheasant
Issued:	1937-1968
Varieties:	HN 1001

Description	U.S. $	Can. $	U.K. £
Large	600.00	725.00	350.00

HN 1138
Cocker Spaniel with Pheasant

Model No.:	714A
Designer:	Frederick Daws
Height:	5 ¼", 13.3 cm
Size:	Medium
Colour:	White coat with black markings, red-brown pheasant
Issued:	1937-1985
Varieties:	HN 1028
Derivative:	Bookend

Description	U.S. $	Can. $	U.K. £
Medium	300.00	350.00	170.00

HN 1139
Dachshund
Standing - Style Three

Model No.:	938
Designer:	Frederick Daws
Height:	6", 15.2 cm
Size:	Large
Colour:	See below
Issued:	1. 1937-1955; 2. c.1937
Varieties:	Also called Dachshund Ch. 'Shrewd Saint' HN 1127

Colourways	U.S. $	Can. $	U.K. £
1. Brown	800.00	975.00	450.00
2. Flambé	1,750.00	2,250.00	1,000.00

HN 1140
Dachshund
Standing - Style Three

Model No.:	938A
Designer:	Frederick Daws
Height:	4", 10.1 cm
Size:	Medium
Colour:	See below
Issued:	1. 1937-1968; 2. c.1937
Varieties:	Also called Dachshund Ch. 'Shrewd Saint' HN 1128

Colourways	U.S. $	Can. $	U.K. £
1. Brown	300.00	350.00	170.00
2. Flambé	900.00	1,100.00	500.00

HN 1141
Dachshund
Standing - Style Three

Model No.:	938B
Designer:	Frederick Daws
Height:	2 ¾", 7.0 cm
Size:	Small
Colour:	See below
Issued:	1. 1937-1968; 2. c.1937
Varieties:	Also called Dachshund Ch. 'Shrewd Saint' HN 1129

Colourways	U.S. $	Can. $	U.K. £
1. Brown	275.00	325.00	150.00
2. Flambé	900.00	1,100.00	500.00

HN 1142
Bull Terrier Ch. 'Bokos Brock'

Model No.:	959
Designer:	Frederick Daws
Height:	9", 22.9 cm
Size:	Large
Colour:	Dark brown and white
Issued:	1937-by 1946
Varieties:	Also called Staffordshire Bull Terrier HN 1131

Description	U.S. $	Can. $	U.K. £
Large	4,500.00	5,500.00	2,500.00

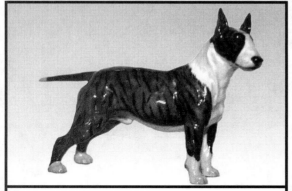

HN 1143
Bull Terrier Ch. 'Bokos Brock'

Model No.:	959A
Designer:	Frederick Daws
Height:	6 ½", 16.5 cm
Size:	Medium
Colour:	Dark brown and white
Issued:	1937-1960
Varieties:	Also called Staffordshire Bull Terrier HN 1132

Description	U.S. $	Can. $	U.K. £
Medium	1,600.00	1,900.00	900.00

HN 1144
Bull Terrier Ch. 'Bokos Brock'

Model No.:	959B
Designer:	Frederick Daws
Height:	4 ½", 11.4 cm
Size:	Small
Colour:	Dark brown and white
Issued:	1937-by 1946
Varieties:	Also called Staffordshire Bull Terrier HN 1133

Description	U.S. $	Can. $	U.K. £
Small	2,500.00	3,000.00	1,350.00

HN 1145
Moufflon
Style One

Model No.:	952
Designer:	Raoh Schorr
Height:	6", 15.2 cm
Colour:	Green-bronze
Issued:	1937-1942
Varieties:	HN 1160, 1179

Colourways	U.S. $	Can. $	U.K. £
Green-bronze	325.00	400.00	175.00

HN 1146
Calf
Style One

Model No.:	946
Designer:	Raoh Schorr
Size:	2" x 5 ½", 5.1 x 14.0 cm
Colour:	Green-bronze
Issued:	1937-1942
Varieties:	HN 1161, 1173

Colourways	U.S. $	Can. $	U.K. £
Green-bronze	325.00	400.00	175.00

HN 1147
Calf
Style Two

Model No.:	947
Designer:	Raoh Schorr
Size:	6" x 9", 15.2 x 22.9 cm
Colour:	Green-bronze
Issued:	1937-1942
Varieties:	HN 1162, 1174

Colourways	U.S. $	Can. $	U.K. £
Green-bronze	325.00	400.00	175.00

HN 1148
Water Buffalo

Model No.:	948
Designer:	Raoh Schorr
Size:	7" x 12 ½", 17.8 x 31.7 cm
Colour:	Green-bronze
Issued:	1937-1942
Varieties:	HN 1163, 1175

Colourways	U.S. $	Can. $	U.K. £
Green-bronze	475.00	575.00	275.00

HN 1149
Donkey
Style One

Model No.:	949		
Designer:	Raoh Schorr		
Height:	6", 15.2 cm		
Colour:	Green-bronze		
Issued:	1937-1942		
Varieties:	HN 1164, 1176		

Colourways	U.S. $	Can. $	U.K. £
Green-bronze	325.00	400.00	175.00

HN 1150
Young Doe

Model No.:	950		
Designer:	Raoh Schorr		
Height:	4", 10.1 cm		
Colour:	Green-bronze		
Issued:	1937-1942		
Varieties:	HN 1165, 1177		

Colourways	U.S. $	Can. $	U.K. £
Green-bronze	325.00	400.00	175.00

HN 1151
Swiss Goat

Model No.:	951		
Designer:	Raoh Schorr		
Height:	5", 12.7 cm		
Colour:	Green-bronze		
Issued:	1937-1942		
Varieties:	HN 1166, 1178		

Colourways	U.S. $	Can. $	U.K. £
Green-bronze	325.00	400.00	175.00

HN 1152
Horse
Prancing

Model No.:	953		
Designer:	Raoh Schorr		
Height:	6 ¾", 17.2 cm		
Colour:	Green-bronze		
Issued:	1937-1942		
Varieties:	HN 1167, 1180		

Colourways	U.S. $	Can. $	U.K. £
Green-bronze	325.00	400.00	175.00

HN 1153
Moufflon
Style Two

Model No.:	954
Designer:	Raoh Schorr
Height:	2", 5.1 cm
Colour:	Green-bronze
Issued:	1937-1942
Varieties:	HN 1168, 1181

Colourways	U.S. $	Can. $	U.K. £
Green-bronze	325.00	400.00	175.00

HN 1154
Jumping Goat

Model No.:	955
Designer:	Raoh Schorr
Height:	6 ¾", 17.2 cm
Colour:	Green-bronze
Issued:	1937-1942
Varieties:	HN 1169, 1182

Colourways	U.S. $	Can. $	U.K. £
Green-bronze	325.00	400.00	175.00

Photograph
not available
at press time

HN 1155
Donkey
Style Two

Model No.:	956
Designer:	Raoh Schorr
Height:	6", 15.2 cm
Colour:	Green-bronze
Issued:	1937-1942
Varieties:	HN 1170, 1183

Colourways	U.S. $	Can. $	U.K. £
Green-bronze	325.00	400.00	175.00

HN 1156
'Suspicion'
Doe

Model No.:	957
Designer:	Raoh Schorr
Height:	8 ¼", 21.0 cm
Colour:	Green-bronze
Issued:	1937-1942
Varieties:	HN 1171, 1184

Colourways	U.S. $	Can. $	U.K. £
Green-bronze	325.00	400.00	175.00

HN 1157
Antelope

Model No.:	958
Designer:	Raoh Schorr
Height:	6", 15.2 cm
Colour:	Green-bronze
Issued:	1937-1942
Varieties:	HN 1172, 1185

Colourways	U.S. $	Can. $	U.K. £
Green-bronze	325.00	400.00	175.00

HN 1158
Character Dog with Plate

Model No.:	963
Designer:	Unknown
Height:	3 ¼", 12.7 cm
Colour:	White with black and light brown patches
Issued:	1937-1985

Description	U.S. $	Can. $	U.K. £
Dog with plate	125.00	150.00	70.00

HN 1159
Character Dog with Bone

Model No.:	962
Designer:	Unknown
Height:	3 ¾", 9.5 cm
Colour:	White with black and light brown patches on back, light brown patch over left ear
Issued:	1937-1985

Description	U.S. $	Can. $	U.K. £
Dog with bone	125.00	150.00	70.00

HN 1160
Moufflon
Style One

Model No.:	952
Designer:	Raoh Schorr
Height:	6", 15.2 cm
Colour:	Cream (matt)
Issued:	1937-1942
Varieties:	HN 1145, 1179

Colourways	U.S. $	Can. $	U.K. £
Cream (matt)	325.00	400.00	175.00

HN 1161
Calf
Style One

Model No.:	946		
Designer:	Raoh Schorr		
Size:	2" x 5 ½", 5.1 x 14.0 cm		
Colour:	Cream (matt)		
Issued:	1937-1942		
Varieties:	HN 1146, 1173		

Colourways	U.S. $	Can. $	U.K. £
Cream (matt)	325.00	400.00	175.00

HN 1162
Calf
Style Two

Model No.:	947		
Designer:	Raoh Schorr		
Size:	6" x 9", 15.2 x 22.9 cm		
Colour:	Cream (matt)		
Issued:	1937-1942		
Varieties:	HN 1147, 1174		

Colourways	U.S. $	Can. $	U.K. £
Cream (matt)	325.00	400.00	175.00

HN 1163
Water Buffalo

Model No.:	948		
Designer:	Raoh Schorr		
Size:	7" x 12 ½", 17.8 x 31.7 cm		
Colour:	Cream (matt)		
Issued:	1937-1942		
Varieties:	HN 1148, 1175		

Colourways	U.S. $	Can. $	U.K. £
Cream (matt)	475.00	575.00	275.00

HN 1164
Donkey
Style One

Model No.:	949		
Designer:	Raoh Schorr		
Height:	6", 15.2 cm		
Colour:	Cream (matt)		
Issued:	1937-1942		
Varieties:	HN 1149, 1176		

Colourways	U.S. $	Can. $	U.K. £
Cream (matt)	325.00	400.00	175.00

HN 1165
Young Doe

Model No.:	950			
Designer:	Raoh Schorr			
Height:	4", 10.1 cm			
Colour:	Cream (matt)			
Issued:	1937-1942			
Varieties:	HN 1150, 1177			

Colourways	U.S. $	Can. $	U.K. £
Cream (matt)	325.00	400.00	175.00

HN 1166
Swiss Goat

Model No.:	951			
Designer:	Raoh Schorr			
Height:	5", 12.7 cm			
Colour:	Cream (matt)			
Issued:	1937-1942			
Varieties:	HN 1151, 1178			

Colourways	U.S. $	Can. $	U.K. £
Cream (matt)	325.00	400.00	175.00

HN 1167
Horse
Prancing

Model No.:	953			
Designer:	Raoh Schorr			
Height:	6 ¾", 17.2 cm			
Colour:	Cream (matt)			
Issued:	1937-1942			
Varieties:	HN 1152, 1180			

Colourways	U.S. $	Can. $	U.K. £
Cream (matt)	325.00	400.00	175.00

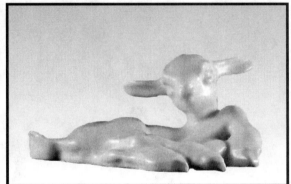

HN 1168
Moufflon
Style Two

Model No.:	954			
Designer:	Raoh Schorr			
Size:	2 ½" x 5", 6.4 x 12.7 cm			
Colour:	Cream (matt)			
Issued:	1937-1942			
Varieties:	HN 1153, 1181			

Colourways	U.S. $	Can. $	U.K. £
Cream (matt)	325.00	400.00	175.00

HN 1169
Jumping Goat

Model No.:	955
Designer:	Raoh Schorr
Height:	6 ¾", 17.2 cm
Colour:	Cream (matt)
Issued:	1937-1942
Varieties:	HN 1154, 1182

Colourways	U.S. $	Can. $	U.K. £
Cream (matt)	325.00	400.00	175.00

Photograph
not available
at press time

HN 1170
Donkey
Style Two

Model No.:	956
Designer:	Raoh Schorr
Height:	6", 15.2 cm
Colour:	Cream (matt)
Issued:	1937-1942
Varieties:	HN 1155, 1183

Colourways	U.S. $	Can. $	U.K. £
Cream (matt)	325.00	400.00	175.00

HN 1171
'Suspicion'
Doe

Model No.:	957
Designer:	Raoh Schorr
Height:	8 ¼", 21.0 cm
Colour:	Cream (matt)
Issued:	1937-1942
Varieties:	HN 1156, 1184

Colourways	U.S. $	Can. $	U.K. £
Cream (matt)	325.00	400.00	175.00

HN 1172
Antelope

Model No.:	958
Designer:	Raoh Schorr
Height:	6", 15.2 cm
Colour:	Cream (matt)
Issued:	1937-1942
Varieties:	HN 1157, 1185

Colourways	U.S. $	Can. $	U.K. £
Cream (matt)	325.00	400.00	175.00

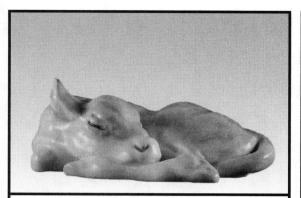

HN 1173
Calf
Style One

Model No.:	946
Designer:	Raoh Schorr
Size:	2" x 5 ½", 5.1 x 14.0 cm
Colour:	Light brown
Issued:	1937-1942
Varieties:	HN 1146, 1161

Colourways	U.S. $	Can. $	U.K. £
Natural colours	325.00	400.00	175.00

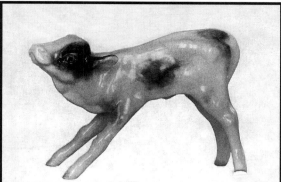

HN 1174
Calf
Style Two

Model No.:	947
Designer:	Raoh Schorr
Size:	6" x 9", 15.2 x 22.9 cm
Colour:	Natural colours
Issued:	1937-1942
Varieties:	HN 1147, 1162

Colourways	U.S. $	Can. $	U.K. £
Natural colours	325.00	400.00	175.00

HN 1175
Water Buffalo

Model No.:	948
Designer:	Raoh Schorr
Size:	7" x 12 ½", 17.8 x 31.7 cm
Colour:	Brown with black highlights
Issued:	1937-1942
Varieties:	HN 1148, 1163

Colourways	U.S. $	Can. $	U.K. £
Natural colours	475.00	575.00	275.00

HN 1176
Donkey
Style One

Model No.:	949
Designer:	Raoh Schorr
Height:	6", 15.2 cm
Colour:	Natural colours
Issued:	1937-1942
Varieties:	HN 1149, 1164

Colourways	U.S. $	Can. $	U.K. £
Natural colours	325.00	400.00	175.00

HN 1177
Young Doe

Model No.:	950
Designer:	Raoh Schorr
Height:	4", 10.1 cm
Colour:	Natural colours
Issued:	1937-1942
Varieties:	HN 1150, 1165

Colourways	U.S. $	Can. $	U.K. £
Natural colours	325.00	400.00	175.00

HN 1178
Swiss Goat

Model No.:	951
Designer:	Raoh Schorr
Height:	5", 12.7 cm
Colour:	Natural colours
Issued:	1937-1942
Varieties:	HN 1151, 1166

Colourways	U.S. $	Can. $	U.K. £
Natural colours	325.00	400.00	175.00

HN 1179
Moufflon
Style One

Model No.:	952
Designer:	Raoh Schorr
Height:	6", 15.2 cm
Colour:	Natural colours
Issued:	1937-1942
Varieties:	HN 1145, 1160

Colourways	U.S. $	Can. $	U.K. £
Natural colours	325.00	400.00	175.00

HN 1180
Horse
Prancing

Model No.:	953
Designer:	Raoh Schorr
Height:	6 ¾", 17.2 cm
Colour:	White and brown body, grey mane
Issued:	1937-1942
Varieties:	HN 1152, 1167

Colourways	U.S. $	Can. $	U.K. £
Natural colours	325.00	400.00	175.00

HN 1181
Moufflon
Style Two

Model No.:	954
Designer:	Raoh Schorr
Height:	2", 5.1 cm
Colour:	Natural colours
Issued:	1937-1942
Varieties:	HN 1153, 1168

Colourways	U.S. $	Can. $	U.K. £
Natural colours	325.00	400.00	175.00

HN 1182
Jumping Goat

Model No.:	955
Designer:	Raoh Schorr
Height:	6 ¾", 17.2 cm
Colour:	Brown and white goat on grey base
Issued:	1937-1942
Varieties:	HN 1154, 1169

Colourways	U.S. $	Can. $	U.K. £
Natural colours	325.00	400.00	175.00

Photograph
not available
at press time

HN 1183
Donkey
Style Two

Model No.:	956
Designer:	Raoh Schorr
Height:	6", 15.2 cm
Colour:	Natural colours
Issued:	1937-1942
Varieties:	HN 1155, 1170

Colourways	U.S. $	Can. $	U.K. £
Natural colours	325.00	400.00	175.00

HN 1184
'Suspicion'
Doe

Model No.:	957
Designer:	Raoh Schorr
Height:	8 ¼", 21.0 cm
Colour:	Natural colours
Issued:	1937-1942
Varieties:	HN 1156, 1171

Colourways	U.S. $	Can. $	U.K. £
Natural colours	325.00	400.00	175.00

HN 1185
Antelope

Model No.: 958
Designer: Raoh Schorr
Height: 6", 15.2 cm
Colour: Brown with black highlights
Issued: 1937-1942
Varieties: HN 1157, 1172

Colourways	U.S. $	Can. $	U.K. £
Natural colours	325.00	400.00	175.00

HN 1186
Cocker Spaniel

Model No.: 709
Designer: Frederick Daws
Height: 6 ¼", 15.9 cm
Size: Large
Colour: Golden brown with dark brown highlights
Issued: 1937-1960
Varieties: HN 1002, 1108, 1134; Also called 'Lucky Pride of Ware' and 'Lucky Star of Ware' HN 1000

Description	U.S. $	Can. $	U.K. £
Large	750.00	900.00	400.00

HN 1187
Cocker Spaniel

Model No.: 709A
Designer: Frederick Daws
Height: 5", 12.7 cm
Size: Medium
Colour: See below
Issued: 1937-1985
Varieties: HN 1036, 1135, 1109; Also called 'Lucky Pride of Ware' and 'Lucky Star of Ware' HN 1020

Colourways	U.S. $	Can. $	U.K. £
1. Browns	175.00	200.00	100.00
2. Flambé	1,100.00	1,350.00	600.00

HN 1188
Cocker Spaniel

Model No.: 709B
Designer: Frederick Daws
Height: 3 ½", 8.9 cm
Size: Small
Colour: Golden brown with dark brown highlights
Issued: 1937-1969
Varieties: HN 1037, 1078, 1136; Also called 'Lucky Pride of Ware' and 'Lucky Star of Ware' HN 1021

Description	U.S. $	Can. $	U.K. £
Small	150.00	175.00	90.00

HN 1189
King Penguin

Model No.:	591
Height:	7 ½", 19.0 cm
Colour:	See below
Issued:	1. 1937-by 1946
	2. c.1927
Varieties:	HN 947

Description	U.S. $	Can. $	U.K. £
1. Black/white/orange	1,200.00	1,450.00	650.00
2. Flambé	1,000.00	1,200.00	550.00

HN 1190
Peruvian Penguin

Model No.:	585
Designer:	Charles Noke
Height:	7 ¾", 19.7 cm
Size:	Medium
Colour:	See below
Issued:	1. 1936-by 1946
	2. c.1936-1961
Varieties:	HN 946

Colourways	U.S. $	Can. $	U.K. £
1. Black/white	1,200.00	1,450.00	650.00
2. Flambé	1,000.00	1,200.00	550.00

Note: Naturalistic models have no base.

HN 1191
Mallard Drake
Standing - Green head

Model No.:	137
Height:	5 ½", 14.0 cm
Size:	Medium
Colour:	See below
Issued:	1. 1937-by 1960
	2. 1913-1996
Varieties:	HN 114, 115, 116, 956, 2555, 2647

Colourways	U.S. $	Can. $	U.K. £
1. Green/brown/white	450.00	550.00	250.00
2. Flambé	300.00	375.00	150.00

HN 1192
Drake
Resting

Model No.:	654
Height:	3 ¾" x 7 ¼", 9.5 x 18.4 cm
Size:	Large
Colour:	See below
Issued:	1. 1937-by 1946
	2. c.1929-1961
Varieties:	HN 977

Colourways	U.S. $	Can. $	U.K. £
1. White/black/green	750.00	900.00	400.00
2. Flambé	750.00	900.00	400.00

HN 1193
Tern (male)

Model No.:	231
Size:	2 ½" x 8 ½", 6.4 x 21.6 cm
Colour:	See below
Issued:	1. 1937-by 1946
	2. c.1912
Varieties:	HN 168; Also called 'Tern' (female)
	HN 167, 1194

Colourways	U.S. $	Can. $	U.K. £
1. White/black	450.00	550.00	250.00
2. Flambé	1,000.00	1,200.00	550.00

HN 1194
Tern (female)

Model No.:	231
Size:	2 ½" x 8 ½", 6.4 x 21.6 cm
Colour:	See below
Issued:	1. 1937-by 1946
	2. c.1912
Varieties:	HN 167; Also called 'Tern' (male)
	HN 168, 1193

Colourways	U.S. $	Can. $	U.K. £
1. White/grey	450.00	550.00	250.00
2. Flambé	1,000.00	1,200.00	550.00

HN 1195
Black-Headed Gull (male)

Model No.:	235
Height:	3 ¾", 9.5 cm
Colour:	White with black head and wing tips
Issued:	1937-by 1946
Varieties:	HN 212, Also called 'Seagull' (female)
	HN 212, 1196

Description	U.S. $	Can. $	U.K. £
Black-headed gull (male)	600.00	725.00	325.00

HN 1196
Seagull (female)

Model No.:	235
Height:	3 ¾", 9.5 cm
Colour:	White with grey wings and black tail
	feathers
Issued:	1937-by 1946
Varieties:	HN 212; Also called 'Black-Headed Gull'
	(male) HN 211, 1195

Description	U.S. $	Can. $	U.K. £
Seagull (female)	600.00	725.00	325.00

HN 1197
Gannet

Model No.:	243
Height:	6 ½", 16.5 cm
Colour:	See below
Issued:	1. 1937-by 1946
	2. c.1919
Varieties:	HN 195

Colourways	U.S. $	Can. $	U.K. £
1. Lemon/grey	800.00	950.00	450.00
2. Flambé		Very Rare	

HN 1198
Drake
Standing

Model No.:	307
Height:	13", 33.0 cm
Size:	Large
Colour:	Green, brown and cream
Issued:	1937-by 1952
Varieties:	HN 248, 249, 252, 2635

Description	U.S. $	Can. $	U.K. £
Drake	2,000.00	2,500.00	1,100.00

HN 1199
Peruvian Penguin - large

Model No.:	769
Designer:	Charles Noke
Height:	12", 30.1 cm (large)
Colour:	See below
Issued:	1. 1937-by 1946; 2. c.1946-1962
Varieties:	HN 2633

Colourways	U.S. $	Can. $	U.K. £
1. Black/white	2,250.00	2,750.00	1,250.00
2. Flambé	3,000.00	3,500.00	1,650.00

Note: Flambé models incorporate a rock as the base.
Naturalistic models are free standing.

HN 1407
The Winner
Style One

Model No.:	Unknown
Designer:	G. D'Illiers
Height:	6 ¾", 17.2 cm
Colour:	Grey horse
Issued:	1930-1938

Description	U.S. $	Can. $	U.K. £
The Winner		Extremely Rare	

*

HN 2500
Cerval

Model No.	966
Designer:	Raoh Schorr
Height:	5", 12.7 cm
Colour:	White (matt)
Issued:	1937-1937

Colourways	U.S. $	Can. $	U.K. £
White (matt)	325.00	400.00	175.00

HN 2501
Lynx

Model No.	966
Designer:	Raoh Schorr
Size:	4 ½" x 7", 11.4 x17.8 cm
Colour:	White-cream (matt)
Issued:	1937-1937

Colourways	U.S. $	Can. $	U.K. £
White-cream (matt)	325.00	400.00	175.00

HN 2502
Deer
Style One - green

Model No.	994
Designer:	Raoh Schorr
Height:	2 ½", 6.4 cm
Colour:	Green (matt)
Issued:	1937-1937
Varieties:	HN 2503

Colourways	U.S. $	Can. $	U.K. £
Green (matt)	325.00	400.00	175.00

HN 2503
Deer
Style One - white

Model No.:	994
Designer:	Raoh Schorr
Height:	2", 5.1 cm
Colour:	White (matt)
Issued:	1937-1937
Varieties:	HN 2502

Colourways	U.S. $	Can. $	U.K. £
White (matt)	325.00	400.00	175.00

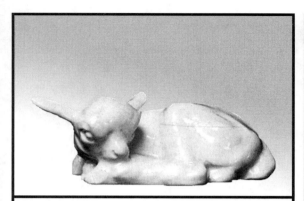

HN 2504
Lamb
Style One - green

Model No.:	995
Designer:	Raoh Schorr
Height:	1 ½", 3.8 cm
Colour:	Green (matt)
Issued:	1937-1937
Varieties:	HN 2505

Colourways	U.S. $	Can. $	U.K. £
Green (matt)	325.00	400.00	175.00

HN 2505
Lamb
Style One - white

Model No.:	995
Designer:	Raoh Schorr
Height:	1 ½", 3.8 cm
Colour:	White (matt)
Issued:	1937-1937
Varieties:	HN 2504

Colourways	U.S. $	Can. $	U.K. £
White (matt)	325.00	475.00	225.00

HN 2506
Asiatic Elephant

Model No.:	993
Designer:	Raoh Schorr
Height:	12", 30.5 cm
Colour:	Green (matt)
Issued:	1937-1937

Colourways	U.S. $	Can. $	U.K. £
Green (matt)	1,850.00	2,250.00	1,000.00

HN 2507
Zebu Cow

Model No.:	997
Designer:	Raoh Schorr
Height:	11 ½", 29.2 cm
Colour:	Green (matt)
Issued:	1937-1937

Colourways	U.S. $	Can. $	U.K. £
Green (matt)	450.00	550.00	250.00

HN 2508
Sealyham
Seated

Model No.:	986
Designer:	Unknown
Height:	3", 7.6 cm
Colour:	White with brown patches over eyes and ears
Issued:	1938-1959

Description	U.S. $	Can. $	U.K. £
Sealyham, seated	200.00	250.00	110.00

HN 2509
Sealyham
Standing - Style Two

Model No.:	985
Designer:	Unknown
Height:	2 ½", 6.3 cm
Colour:	White with light brown patches over eyes and ears
Issued:	1938-1959

Description	U.S. $	Can. $	U.K. £
Sealyham, standing	200.00	250.00	110.00

HN 2510
Character Dog Running

Model No.:	989
Designer:	Unknown
Height:	2 ¾", 7.0 cm
Colour:	White with light brown patches over ears and eyes, black and brown patch on back
Issued:	1938-1959

Description	U.S. $	Can. $	U.K. £
Dog, running	400.00	475.00	225.00

HN 2511
Bull Terrier
Standing - Style Two

Model No.:	988
Designer:	Unknown
Height:	4", 10.1 cm
Colour:	White with light and dark brown patches over eyes, ears and back
Issued:	1938-1959

Description	U.S. $	Can. $	U.K. £
Bull terrier	400.00	475.00	225.00

SMOOTH-HAIRED TERRIER CH. 'CHOSEN DON OF NOTTS'

Designer: Frederick Davis
Colour: White with dark brown patches on ears

	HN 2512	**HN 2513**	**HN 2514**
Model No.:	791	791A	791B
Height:	8 ½", 21.6 cm	6", 15.2 cm	4 ½", 11.4 cm
Size:	Large	Medium	Small
Issued:	1938-1952	1938-1960	1938-1952
Varieties:	HN 1068	HN 1069	HN 1070

Currency	Large	Medium	Small
U.S. $	2,750.00	1,500.00	1,500.00
Can. $	3,250.00	1,800.00	1,800.00
U.K. £	1,600.00	850.00	850.00

HN 2515
Springer Spaniel Ch. 'Dry Toast'
Model No.: 1009
Designer: Frederick Daws
Height: 8", 20.3 cm
Size: Large
Colour: White coat with dark brown markings
Issued: 1938-1955

Description	U.S. $	Can. $	U.K. £
Large	1,200.00	1,500.00	700.00

HN 2516
Springer Spaniel Ch. 'Dry Toast'
Model No.: 1009A
Designer: Frederick Daws
Height: 5", 12.7 cm
Size: Medium
Colour: White coat with dark brown markings
Issued: 1938-1968

Description	U.S. $	Can. $	U.K. £
Medium	400.00	475.00	225.00

HN 2517
Springer Spaniel Ch. 'Dry Toast'
Model No.: 1009B
Designer: Frederick Daws
Height: 3 ¾", 9.5 cm
Size: Small
Colour: White coat with dark brown markings
Issued: 1938-1985

Description	U.S. $	Can. $	U.K. £
Small	225.00	275.00	125.00

HN 2518
Pride of the Shires and Foal
Model No.: 1018
Designer: W. M. Chance
Size: 9 ¾" x 14", 24.8 x 35.5 cm
Size: Large
Colour: Brown mare, light brown foal
Issued: 1938-1960
Varieties: HN 2523, 2528

Description	U.S. $	Can. $	U.K. £
Large	1,500.00	1,750.00	800.00

HN 2519
Gude Grey Mare and Foal

Model No.:	1016
Designer:	W. M. Chance
Height:	7 ½", 19.0 cm
Size:	Large
Colour:	White mare with grey markings on legs, light brown foal with white stockings,
Issued:	1938-1960

Description	U.S. $	Can. $	U.K. £
Large	1,250.00	2,200.00	700.00

HN 2520
Farmer's Boy

Model No.:	1013
Designer:	W. M. Chance
Height:	8 ½", 21.6 cm
Size:	Large
Colour:	White horse, rider in brown and green
Issued:	1938-1960

Description	U.S. $	Can. $	U.K. £
Farmer's Boy	2,250.00	2,750.00	1,200.00

HN 2521
Dapple Grey and Rider

Model No.:	1017
Designer:	W. M. Chance
Height:	7 ¼", 18.4 cm
Size:	Large
Colour:	White horse, rider in red and brown
Issued:	1938-1960

Description	U.S. $	Can. $	U.K. £
Dapple grey/rider	4,000.00	4,750.00	2,200.00

HN 2522
Chestnut Mare and Foal

Model No.:	1020
Designer:	W. M. Chance
Height:	6 ½", 16.5 cm
Size:	Large
Colour:	Chestnut mare with white stockings, fawn coloured foal with white stockings
Issued:	1938-1960

Description	U.S. $	Can. $	U.K. £
Large	1,250.00	2,200.00	700.00

HN 2523
Pride of the Shires and Foal

Model No.:	1018
Designer:	W. M. Chance
Size:	9 ¾" x 14", 24.8 x 35.5 cm
Size:	Large
Colour:	White mare, grey markings on legs and hind quarters, light brown foal with white stockings
Issued:	1938-1960
Varieties:	HN 2518, 2528

Description	U.S. $	Can. $	U.K. £
Large	1,500.00	1,750.00	800.00

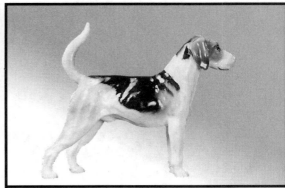

HN 2524
American Foxhound - large

Model No.:	1026
Designer:	Frederick Daws
Height:	8", 20.3 cm
Size:	Large
Colour:	White with black and brown markings
Issued:	1938-1955

Description	U.S. $	Can. $	U.K. £
Large	2,500.00	3,000.00	1,350.00

HN 2525
American Foxhound - medium

Model No.:	1026A
Designer:	Frederick Daws
Height:	5", 12.7 cm
Size:	Medium
Colour:	White with black and brown markings
Issued:	1938-1960

Description	U.S. $	Can. $	U.K. £
Medium	1,000.00	1,250.00	575.00

HN 2526
American Foxhound - small

Model No.:	1026B
Designer:	Frederick Daws
Height:	4", 10.1 cm
Size:	Small
Colour:	White with black and brown markings
Issued:	1938-1952

Description	U.S. $	Can. $	U.K. £
Small	750.00	900.00	425.00

HN 2527
Fox
Seated - Style Five

Model No.:	978
Designer:	Raoh Schorr
Height:	11", 27.9 cm
Size:	Extra large
Colour:	Brown and white
Issued:	1938-by 1946
Varieties:	HN 1130

Description	U.S. $	Can. $	U.K. £
Extra large	2,000.00	2,500.00	1,100.00

HN 2528
Pride of the Shires and Foal

Model No.:	1018
Designer:	W. M. Chance
Size:	9 ¾" x 14", 24.8 x 35.5 cm
Size:	Large
Colour:	Brown mare, light fawn foal
Issued:	1939-1960
Varieties:	HN 2518, 2523

Description	U.S. $	Can. $	U.K. £
Large	1,500.00	1,750.00	800.00

HN 2529
English Setter with Pheasant

Model No.:	1028
Designer:	Frederick Daws
Height:	8", 20.3 cm
Colour:	Grey with black markings, red-brown pheasant, yellow-brown leaves on base
Issued:	1939-1985
Varieties:	HN 2599

Description	U.S. $	Can. $	U.K. £
English setter/pheasant	900.00	1,100.00	500.00

HN 2530
Merely a Minor - brown

Model No.:	1039
Designer:	Frederick Daws
Height:	12", 30.5 cm
Size:	Large
Colour:	Brown with white stockings and nose
Issued:	1939-1960
Varieties:	HN 2531

Colourways	U.S. $	Can. $	U.K. £
Brown	1,000.00	1,200.00	550.00

HN 2531
Merely a Minor - grey

Model No.:	1039
Designer:	Frederick Daws
Height:	12", 30.5 cm
Size:	Large
Colour:	Grey
Issued:	1939-1960
Varieties:	HN 2530

Colourways	U.S. $	Can. $	U.K. £
Grey	1,000.00	1,200.00	550.00

HN 2532
Gude Grey Mare and Foal

Model No.:	1016A
Designer:	W. M. Chance
Height:	5 ½", 14.0 cm
Size:	Small
Colour:	White mare with grey markings on legs, light brown foal with white stockings
Issued:	1940-1967

Description	U.S. $	Can. $	U.K. £
Small	800.00	950.00	450.00

HN 2533
Chestnut Mare and Foal

Model No.:	1020B
Designer:	W. M. Chance
Height:	5", 12.7 cm
Size:	Small
Colour:	Chestnut brown mare with white stockings, fawn coloured foal with white stockings
Issued:	1940-1960

Description	U.S. $	Can. $	U.K. £
Small	750.00	900.00	400.00

HN 2534
Pride of the Shires and Foal

Model No.:	1018A
Designer:	W. M. Chance
Height:	6 ½", 16.5 cm
Size:	Small
Colour:	Brown mare, light brown foal
Issued:	1940-1960
Varieties:	HN 2536

Description	U.S. $	Can. $	U.K. £
Small	750.00	900.00	400.00

HN 2535
Tiger on a Rock
Style Three

Model No.:	1038
Designer:	Charles Noke
Size:	4" x 9", 10.1 x 22.9 cm
Colour:	Browns, charcoal rock
Issued:	1940-1960

Description	U.S. $	Can. $	U.K. £
Tiger on rock	1,250.00	1,500.00	700.00

HN 2536
Pride of the Shires and Foal

Model No.:	1018A
Designer:	W. M. Chance
Height:	6 ½", 16.5 cm
Size:	Small
Colour:	White mare, grey markings on legs and hind quarters, light brown foal white stockings
Issued:	1940-1960
Varieties:	HN 2534

Description	U.S. $	Can. $	U.K. £
Small	750.00	900.00	400.00

HN 2537
Merely a Minor - brown

Model No.:	1039A
Designer:	Frederick Daws
Height:	9 ¼", 24.0 cm
Size:	Medium
Colour:	Brown with white stockings and nose
Issued:	1940-1960
Varieties:	HN 2538

Colourways	U.S. $	Can. $	U.K. £
Brown	800.00	950.00	450.00

HN 2538
Merely a Minor - white

Model No.:	1039A
Designer:	Frederick Daws
Height:	9 ¼", 24.0 cm
Size:	Medium
Colour:	White with dark grey markings on legs and neck
Issued:	1940-1960
Varieties:	HN 2537

Colourways	U.S. $	Can. $	U.K. £
White	800.00	950.00	450.00

HN 2539
Persian Cat
Seated - Style One

Model No.:	690
Height:	5", 12.7 cm
Colour:	1. Dark grey with white highlights
	2. White
Issued:	1940-1968
Varieties:	HN 999

Colourways	U.S. $	Can. $	U.K. £
1. Dark grey	500.00	600.00	275.00
2. White	500.00	600.00	275.00

HN 2540
Kingfisher on a Tree Stump - large

Model No.:	1053
Height:	4 ½", 11.4 cm
Size:	Large
Colour:	Sea-green and blue feathers, brown breast, green and grey base
Issued:	1940-1946

Description	U.S. $	Can. $	U.K. £
Large	350.00	425.00	200.00

NOTES ON PRICING

- Animal figures are not as plentiful as pretty ladies or character figures and caution in pricing must prevail.

- In the pricing tables N/I (not issued) indicates that the animal figure was not available in that particular market.

- Rarity classification provides a range for the collector to work with.

- Always remember that when dealing with rare animal figures you need two willing parties, a buyer and a seller. One without the other will not work and only when they agree do you have a market price.

Rarity Class	Rare	Very Rare	Extremely Rare
U.S. $	1,850./2,750.	2,750./4,500.	4,500./Up
Can. $	2,250./3,500.	3,500./5,500.	5,500./Up
U.K. £	1,000./1,500.	1,500./2,500.	2,500./Up

HN 2541
Kingfisher on a Tree Stump – small

Model No.:	1053A
Height:	3 ½", 8.9 cm
Size:	Small
Colour:	Sea-green and blue feathers, brown breast, green and grey base
Issued:	1940-1946

Description	U.S. $	Can. $	U.K. £
Small	325.00	425.00	200.00

HN 2542A
Baltimore Oriole
Style One

Model No.:	1051
Height:	4 ¼", 10.8 cm
Colour:	Black and orange bird, brown base, white flowers, green leaves
Issued:	1940-1946

Description	U.S. $	Can. $	U.K. £
Style one	325.00	400.00	180.00

HN 2542B
Baltimore Oriole
Style Two

Model No.:	1051
Height:	4 ¼", 10.8 cm
Colour:	Black and orange bird, brown base, white flowers
Issued:	1940-1946

Description	U.S. $	Can. $	U.K. £
Style two	325.00	400.00	180.00

HN 2543
Bluebird with Lupins
Style Two

Model No.:	1062
Height:	6", 15.2 cm
Colour:	Blue and pink bird with mauve and green stump
Issued:	1941-1946

Description	U.S. $	Can. $	U.K. £
Bluebird with lupins	325.00	400.00	180.00

HN 2544
Mallard Drake with Spill Vase

Model No.:	1057
Height:	8", 20.3 cm
Colour:	Green head, brown and white feathers, green spill and reeds
Issued:	1941-1946

Description	U.S. $	Can. $	U.K. £
Drake with spill vase	1,500.00	1,800.00	850.00

HN 2545
Cock Pheasant

Model No.:	1063
Height:	7", 17.8 cm
Size:	Small
Colour:	Red-brown plumage, blue-green head
Issued:	1941-1952
Varieties:	HN 2632

Description	U.S. $	Can. $	U.K. £
Cock pheasant	450.00	550.00	250.00

HN 2546
Yellow-Throated Warbler
Style Two

Model No.:	1058
Height:	4 ¾", 12.1 cm
Colour:	Blue feathers, black wing tips, yellow throat
Issued:	1941-1946

Description	U.S. $	Can. $	U.K. £
Yellow-throated warbler	325.00	400.00	180.00

HN 2547
Budgerigars on a Tree Stump

Model No.:	1054
Height:	6", 15.2 cm
Colour:	Green and yellow birds with black markings, green and beige base
Issued:	1941-1946

Description	U.S. $	Can. $	U.K. £
Budgerigars	500.00	600.00	275.00

HN 2548
Golden-Crested Wren
Style Two

Model No.:	1052
Height:	4 ½", 11.4 cm
Colour:	Green feathers with black markings, white flowers, brown base
Issued:	1941-1946

Description	U.S. $	Can. $	U.K. £
Golden-crested wren	325.00	400.00	180.00

HN 2549
English Robin
Style One

Model No.:	1060
Height:	2 ½", 6.4 cm
Colour:	Brown feathers, red breast, yellow flowers, green leaves, beige base
Issued:	1941-1946

Description	U.S. $	Can. $	U.K. £
English robin	325.00	400.00	180.00

HN 2550
Chaffinch
Style One

Model No.:	1066
Height:	2 ½", 6.4 cm
Colour:	Brown with black, pink and blue wing tips, blue head, yellow flowers, green base
Issued:	1941-1946

Description	U.S. $	Can. $	U.K. £
Chaffinch	375.00	400.00	180.00

HN 2551
Bullfinch
Style Two

Model No.:	1070
Height:	5 ½", 14.0 cm
Colour:	Blue and pale blue feathers, red breast
Issued:	1941-1946

Description	U.S. $	Can. $	U.K. £
Bullfinch	325.00	400.00	180.00

HN 2552
Thrush Chicks (two)

Model No.:	1071
Height:	3", 7.6 cm
Colour:	See below
Issued:	1. 1941-1946
	2. c.1941

Colourways	U.S. $	Can. $	U.K. £
1. Brown/yellow/green	325.00	400.00	180.00
2. Flambé	700.00	850.00	375.00

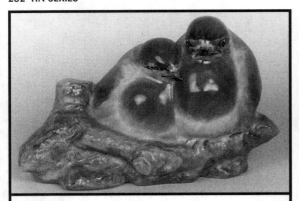

HN 2553
Robin Chicks (two)

Model No.:	1069		
Height:	3", 7.6 cm		
Colour:	Brown feathers, red breast, green base		
Issued:	1941-1946		

Description	U.S. $	Can. $	U.K. £
Robin chicks	325.00	400.00	180.00

HN 2554
Cardinal
Style Two

Model No.:	1059		
Height:	6 ¾", 17.1 cm		
Colour:	Red feathers with black markings, green leaves and stump, white flowers		
Issued:	1941-1946		

Description	U.S. $	Can. $	U.K. £
Cardinal	750.00	900.00	425.00

HN 2555
Mallard Drake
Standing - Green head

Model No.:	137		
Height:	5 ½", 14.0 cm		
Size:	Medium		
Colour:	See below		
Issued:	1. 1941-1946		
	2. 1913-1996		
Varieties:	HN 114, 115, 116, 956, 1191, 2647		

Colourways	U.S. $	Can. $	U.K. £
1. Green/brown/white	450.00	550.00	250.00
2. Flambé	300.00	375.00	150.00

HN 2556
Duck
Head stretched forward

Model No.:	207		
Height:	4", 10.1 cm		
Colour:	See below		
Issued:	1. 1941-1946		
	2. c.1917		
Varieties:	HN 150, 229		

Colourways	U.S. $	Can. $	U.K. £
1. Brown/turquoise	500.00	600.00	275.00
2. Flambé	700.00	850.00	375.00

HN 2557
Welsh Corgi Ch. 'Spring Robin'
Large

Model No.:	1050	
Designer:	Frederick Daws	
Height:	8", 20.3 cm	
Size:	Large	
Colour:	Golden brown with white and brown underbody	
Issued:	1941-1955	

Description	U.S. $	Can. $	U.K. £
Large	1,500.00	1,800.00	800.00

HN 2558
Welsh Corgi Ch. 'Spring Robin'
Medium

Model No.:	1050A	
Designer:	Frederick Daws	
Height:	5", 12.7 cm	
Size:	Medium	
Colour:	Golden brown with white and brown underbody	
Issued:	1941-1968	

Description	U.S. $	Can. $	U.K. £
Medium	500.00	600.00	275.00

HN 2559
Welsh Corgi Ch. 'Spring Robin'
Small

Model No.:	1050B	
Designer:	Frederick Daws	
Height:	3 ½", 8.9 cm	
Size:	Small	
Colour:	Golden brown with white and brown underbody	
Issued:	1941-1985	

Description	U.S. $	Can. $	U.K. £
Small	200.00	250.00	110.00

HN 2560
Great Dane Ch. 'Rebeller of Ouborough'

Model No.:	1077	
Designer:	Frederick Daws	
Height:	8 ½", 21.6 cm	
Size:	Large	
Colour:	Light brown	
Issued:	1941-1955	

Description	U.S. $	Can. $	U.K. £
Large	1,750.00	2,100.00	1,000.00

HN 2561
Great Dane Ch. 'Rebeller of Ouborough'

Model No.:	1077A		
Designer:	Frederick Daws		
Height:	6", 15.2 cm		
Size:	Medium		
Colour:	Light brown		
Issued:	1941-1960		

Description	U.S. $	Can. $	U.K. £
Medium	800.00	950.00	450.00

HN 2562
Great Dane Ch. 'Rebeller of Ouborough'

Model No.:	1077B		
Designer:	Frederick Daws		
Height:	4 ½", 11.3 cm		
Size:	Small		
Colour:	Light brown		
Issued:	1941-1952		

Description	U.S. $	Can. $	U.K. £
Small	800.00	950.00	450.00

HN 2563
Pride of the Shires

Model No.:	1073		
Designer:	W. M. Chance		
Height:	9", 22.9 cm		
Size:	Large		
Colour:	Grey		
Issued:	1941-1960		

Description	U.S. $	Can. $	U.K. £
Large	1,250.00	1,500.00	700.00

HN 2564
Pride of the Shires

Model No.:	1073A	
Designer:	W. M. Chance	
Height:	6 3/8", 16.5 cm	
Size:	Small	
Colour:	Light brown horse, black mane, tail and legs, white nose and feet, green-brown base	
Issued:	1941-1960	

Description	U.S. $	Can. $	U.K. £
Small	900.00	1,100.00	500.00

HN 2565
Chestnut Mare - large
Model No.:	1074
Designer:	W. M. Chance
Height:	6 ½", 16.5 cm
Size:	Large
Colour:	Brown
Issued:	1941-1960

Description	U.S. $	Can. $	U.K. £
Large	1,250.00	1,500.00	700.00

HN 2566
Chestnut Mare - small
Model No.:	1074A
Designer:	W. M. Chance
Height:	5 ¼", 13.3 cm
Size:	Small
Colour:	Brown
Issued:	1941-1960

Description	U.S. $	Can. $	U.K. £
Small	900.00	1,100.00	500.00

HN 2567
Merely a Minor - small
Model No.:	1039B
Designer:	Frederick Daws
Height:	6 ½", 16.5 cm
Size:	Small
Colour:	White with grey markings on legs
Issued:	1941-1967
Varieties:	HN 2571

Description	U.S. $	Can. $	U.K. £
Small	650.00	775.00	350.00

HN 2568
Gude Grey Mare - large
Model No.:	1072
Designer:	W. M. Chance
Height:	8", 20.3 cm
Size:	Large
Colour:	White with grey markings on legs
Issued:	1941-1967

Description	U.S. $	Can. $	U.K. £
Large	1,250.00	1,500.00	700.00

HN 2569
Gude Grey Mare - medium

Model No.:	1072A
Designer:	W. M. Chance
Height:	5", 12.7 cm
Size:	Medium
Colour:	White with grey markings on legs
Issued:	1941-1967

Description	U.S. $	Can. $	U.K. £
Medium	750.00	900.00	400.00

HN 2570
Gude Grey Mare - small

Model No.:	1072B
Designer:	W. M. Chance
Height:	3 ¾", 9.5 cm
Size:	Small
Colour:	White with grey markings on legs
Issued:	1941-1967

Description	U.S. $	Can. $	U.K. £
Small	650.00	775.00	350.00

HN 2571
Merely a Minor - small

Model No.:	1039B
Designer:	Frederick Daws
Height:	6 ½", 16.5 cm
Size:	Small
Colour:	Light brown, white nose and feet, black tail
Issued:	1941-1967
Varieties:	HN 2567

Colourways	U.S. $	Can. $	U.K. £
Brown/white	600.00	725.00	325.00

HN 2572
Mallard Drake
Resting

Model No.:	1102
Size:	1 ½" x 2 ¾", 5.1 x 7.0 cm
Size:	Small
Colour:	Green head, brown wings, brown breast, white underbody white tail
Issued:	1941-1946

Description	U.S. $	Can. $	U.K. £
Mallard drake	150.00	175.00	85.00

HN 2573
Kingfisher
Style Two

Model No.:	1103
Height:	2 ½", 6.4 cm
Colour:	Turquoise, green and light brown feathers, black beak
Issued:	1941-1946

Description	U.S. $	Can. $	U.K. £
Kingfisher	350.00	425.00	200.00

HN 2574
Seagull on Rock

Model No.:	1108
Height:	2 ¼", 5.7 cm
Colour:	White head and breast, grey wings with black tail feathers
Issued:	1941-1946

Description	U.S. $	Can. $	U.K. £
Seagull on rock	350.00	425.00	200.00

HN 2575
Swan

Model No.:	1105
Height:	2 ¼", 5.7 cm
Colour:	White, black and orange beak
Issued:	1941-1946

Description	U.S. $	Can. $	U.K. £
Swan	500.00	600.00	300.00

HN 2576
Pheasant

Model No.:	1107
Height:	2 ½", 6.4 cm
Colour:	Red-brown feathers with green tail feathers, blue-green head, brown and green base
Issued:	1941-1946

Description	U.S. $	Can. $	U.K. £
Pheasant	350.00	425.00	200.00

HN 2577
Peacock

Model No.:	1106
Height:	2 ¾", 7.0 cm
Colour:	Dark turquoise breast, yellow, green and brown tail feathers
Issued:	1941-1946

Description	U.S. $	Can. $	U.K. £
Peacock	350.00	425.00	200.00

HN 2578
Dapple Grey

Model No.:	1134
Designer:	W. M. Chance
Height:	7 ½", 19.1 cm
Colour:	White with grey markings on legs
Issued:	1941-1960
Varieties:	Also called "Punch Peon," Chestnut Shire HN 2623

Description	U.S. $	Can. $	U.K. £
Dapple grey	1,250.00	1,500.00	700.00

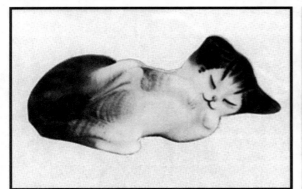

HN 2579
Character Kitten
Lying on back

Model No.:	1080
Designer:	Peggy Davies
Height:	1 ½", 3.8 cm
Colour:	Brown and white
Issued:	1941-1985

Description	U.S. $	Can. $	U.K. £
Kitten, on back	100.00	125.00	55.00

HN 2580
Character Kitten
Licking hind paw

Model No.:	1079
Designer:	Peggy Davies
Height:	2 ¼", 5.7 cm
Colour:	Brown and white
Issued:	1941-1985

Description	U.S. $	Can. $	U.K. £
Kitten, licking hind paw	100.00	125.00	55.00

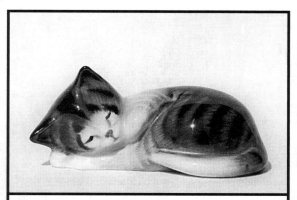

HN 2581
Character Kitten
Sleeping

Model No.:	1085
Designer:	Peggy Davies
Height:	1 ½", 3.8 cm
Colour:	Brown and white
Issued:	1941-1985

Description	U.S. $	Can. $	U.K. £
Kitten, sleeping	100.00	125.00	55.00

HN 2582
Character Kitten
On hind legs

Model No.:	1087
Designer:	Peggy Davies
Height:	2 ¾", 7.0 cm
Colour:	Light brown and black coat with white underbody
Issued:	1941-1985

Description	U.S. $	Can. $	U.K. £
Kitten, on hind legs	100.00	125.00	55.00

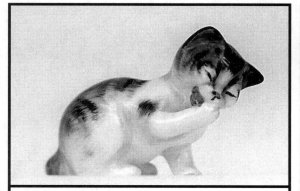

HN 2583
Character Kitten
Licking front paw

Model No.:	1086
Designer:	Peggy Davies
Height:	2", 5.1 cm
Colour:	Tan and white
Issued:	1941-1985

Description	U.S. $	Can. $	U.K. £
Kitten, licking front paw	100.00	125.00	55.00

HN 2584
Character Kitten
Looking up

Model No.:	1081
Designer:	Peggy Davies
Height:	2", 5.1 cm
Colour:	Tan and white
Issued:	1941-1985

Description	U.S. $	Can. $	U.K. £
Kitten, looking up	100.00	125.00	55.00

HN 2585
Cocker Spaniel Lying in Basket

Model No.: 1155
Height: 2", 5.1 cm
Colour: White with brown and black markings, light brown basket
Issued: 1941-1985

Description	U.S. $	Can. $	U.K. £
Spaniel in basket	100.00	125.00	55.00

HN 2586
Cocker Spaniel Chewing Handle of Basket

Model No.: 1153
Height: 2 ¾", 7.0 cm
Colour: White with dark brown ears and patches on back, light brown patches over eyes, light brown basket
Issued: 1941-1985

Description	U.S. $	Can. $	U.K. £
Spaniel chewing basket	100.00	125.00	55.00

HN 2587
Terrier Sitting in Basket

Model No.: 1152
Height: 3", 7.6 cm
Colour: White with brown markings, brown basket
Issued: 1941-1985

Description	U.S. $	Can. $	U.K. £
Terrier in basket	100.00	125.00	55.00

HN 2588
Terrier Puppies in a Basket

Model No.: 1154
Height: 3", 7.6 cm
Colour: White with light and dark brown markings, brown basket
Issued: 1941-1985

Description	U.S. $	Can. $	U.K. £
Puppies in basket	100.00	125.00	55.00

HN 2589
Cairn Terrier
Begging

Model No.:	1131
Height:	4", 10.1 cm
Colour:	Beige with black highlights
Issued:	1941-1985

Description	U.S. $	Can. $	U.K. £
Cairn terrier	100.00	125.00	55.00

HN 2590
Cocker Spaniels Sleeping

Model No.:	1132
Height:	1 ¾", 4.5 cm
Colour:	White dog with brown markings and golden brown dog
Issued:	1941-1969

Description	U.S. $	Can. $	U.K. £
Spaniels, sleeping	100.00	125.00	55.00

HN 2591
Duck
Standing

Model No.:	395
Height:	2 ½", 6.4 cm
Size:	Small
Colour:	See below
Issued:	1. 1941-1968
	2. 1922-1996
Varieties:	HN 806, 807

Colourways	U.S. $	Can. $	U.K. £
1. Green/white/brown	150.00	175.00	80.00
2. Flambé	150.00	175.00	80.00

HN 2592
Hare
Crouching - Style Three

Model No.:	1157
Height:	2 ¾", 7.0 cm
Colour:	See below
Issued:	1. 1941-1968
	2. 1945-1996

Colourways	U.S $	Can. $	U.K. £
1. Light brown/white	175.00	200.00	100.00
2. Flambé	175.00	200.00	100.00

HN 2593
Hare
Lying, legs stretched behind - large

Model No.:	656
Size:	3" x 7 ½", 7.6 x 19.1 cm
Size:	Large
Colour:	See below
Issued:	1. 1941-1968
	2. 1929-1962
Varieties:	HN 979, 984, 985, 1071

Colourways	U.S $	Can. $	U.K. £
1. Light brown/white	350.00	425.00	200.00
2. Flambé	600.00	725.00	325.00

HN 2594
Hare
Lying, legs stretched behind - small

Model No.:	656A
Size:	1 ¾" x 5 ¼", 4.4 x 13.3 cm
Size:	Small
Colour:	See below
Issued:	1. 1941-1985
	2. 1929-1996

Colourways	U.S $	Can. $	U.K. £
1. Light brown/white	150.00	180.00	85.00
2. Flambé	150.00	180.00	85.00

HN 2595
Lamb
Style Two

Model No.:	1117
Designer:	Peggy Davies
Height:	Unknown
Colour:	White
Issued:	Modelled 1941

Description	U.S $	Can. $	U.K. £
Lamb, style two	1,000.00	1,250.00	500.00

HN 2596
Lamb
Style Three

Model No.:	1112
Designer:	Peggy Davies
Height:	Unknown
Colour:	White
Issued:	Modelled 1941

Description	U.S $	Can. $	U.K. £
Lamb, style three	1,000.00	1,250.00	500.00

HN 2597
Lamb
Style Four

Model No.:   1115
Designer: Peggy Davies
Height: 3 ¼", 8.3 cm
Colour: Black lamb on white base
Issued: Modelled 1941

Description	U.S $	Can. $	U.K. £
Lamb, style four	1,000.00	1,250.00	500.00

HN 2598
Lamb
Style Five

Model No.:   1116
Designer: Peggy Davies
Height: Unknown
Colour: White
Issued: Modelled 1941

Description	U.S $	Can. $	U.K. £
Lamb, style five	1,000.00	1,250.00	500.00

HN 2599
English Setter with Pheasant

Model No.:   1028
Designer: Frederick Daws
Height: 8", 20.3 cm
Colour: Red-brown
Issued: 1941
Varieties: HN 2529

Description	U.S $	Can. $	U.K. £
English setter/pheasant	2,000.00	2,500.00	1,100.00

HN 2600
Cocker Spaniel with Pheasant

Model No.:   714B
Designer: Frederick Daws
Height: 3 ½", 8.9 cm
Size: Small
Colour: Black
Issued: 1941
Varieties: HN 1029, 1062

Description	U.S $	Can. $	U.K. £
Cocker spaniel/pheasant	Only one known to exist.		

AMERICAN GREAT DANE

	Colour:	Light brown	

	HN 2601	**HN 2602**	**HN 2603**
Model No.:	1171	1171A	1171B
Height:	8 ½", 21.6 cm	6 ½", 16.5 cm	4 ½", 11.4 cm
Size:	Large	Medium	Small
Issued:	1941-1955	1941-1960	1941-1960

Currency	Large	Medium	Small
U.S $	1,850.00	1,000.00	950.00
Can. $	2,250.00	1,250.00	1,200.00
U.K. £	1,100.00	575.00	550.00

HN 2604
Peacock Butterfly

Model No.:	1178
Height:	2", 5.1 cm
Colour:	Tan, black, yellow, blue, white and green
Issued:	1941-by 1946

Description	U.S $	Can. $	U.K. £
Peacock butterfly	1,500.00	1,800.00	850.00

HN 2605
Camberwell Beauty Butterfly

Model No.:	1181
Height:	2", 5.1 cm
Colour:	Purple, blue, white and green
Issued:	1941-by 1946

Description	U.S $	Can. $	U.K. £
Camberwell beauty	1,500.00	1,800.00	850.00

HN 2606
Swallowtail Butterfly

Model No.:	1175
Height:	2 ¾", 7.0 cm
Colour:	Yellow, black, blue, green and white
Issued:	1941-by 1946

Description	U.S $	Can. $	U.K. £
Swallowtail butterfly	1,500.00	1,800.00	850.00

HN 2607
Red Admiral Butterfly

Model No.:	1179
Height:	2", 5.1 cm
Colour:	Brown, black, red, yellow, white and green
Issued:	1941-by 1946

Description	U.S $	Can. $	U.K. £
Red admiral butterfly	1,500.00	1,800.00	850.00

HN 2608
Copper Butterfly

Model No.: 1177
Height: 2", 5.1 cm
Colour: Unknown
Issued: 1941-by 1946

Description	U.S $	Can. $	U.K. £
Copper butterfly	1,500.00	1,800.00	850.00

HN 2609
Tortoiseshell Butterfly

Model No.: 1180
Height: 2", 5.1 cm
Colour: Unknown
Issued: 1941-by 1946

Description	U.S $	Can. $	U.K. £
Tortoiseshell butterfly	1,500.00	1,800.00	850.00

HN 2610
Pheasant Hen

Model No.: 1195
Height: 6", 15.2 cm
Colour: Light brown with dark brown markings, green base
Issued: 1942-1950

Description	U.S $	Can. $	U.K. £
Pheasant hen	600.00	725.00	325.00

HN 2611
Chaffinch
Style Two

Model No.: 1200
Height: 2", 5.1 cm
Colour: Brown feathers, blue, yellow and black markings, green base
Issued: c.1945-1950

Description	U.S $	Can. $	U.K. £
Chaffinch	350.00	425.00	200.00

HN 2612
Baltimore Oriole
Style Three

Model No.:	1201
Height:	4", 10.1 cm
Colour:	Yellow with black head and wing tips, green base
Issued:	c.1945-1950

Description	U.S $	Can. $	U.K. £
Baltimore oriole	350.00	425.00	200.00

HN 2613
Golden-Crested Wren
Style Three

Model No.:	1202
Height:	2 ½", 6.4 cm
Colour:	Green with black markings, yellow and white breast, brown base
Issued:	c.1945-1950

Description	U.S $	Can. $	U.K. £
Golden-crested wren	350.00	425.00	200.00

HN 2614
Blue Bird

Model No.:	1203
Height:	5", 12.7 cm
Colour:	Blue with pink and white breast, green base
Issued:	c.1945-1950

Description	U.S $	Can. $	U.K. £
Blue bird	350.00	425.00	200.00

HN 2615
Cardinal
Style Three

Model No.:	1204
Height:	4 ½", 11.4 cm
Colour:	Red feathers with black markings, green base
Issued:	c.1945-1950

Description	U.S $	Can. $	U.K. £
Cardinal	350.00	425.00	200.00

HN 2616
Bullfinch
Style Three

Model No.:	1205
Height:	4", 10.1 cm
Colour:	Mauve and black feathers, pink breast, green base
Issued:	c.1945-1950

Description	U.S $	Can. $	U.K. £
Bullfinch	350.00	425.00	200.00

HN 2617
Robin
Style Two

Model No.:	1206
Height:	2", 5.1 cm
Colour:	Brown feathers, red breast, green base
Issued:	c.1945-1950

Description	U.S $	Can. $	U.K. £
Robin	350.00	425.00	200.00

HN 2618
Yellow-Throated Warbler
Style Three

Model No.:	1207
Height:	4 ½", 11.4 cm
Colour:	Blue feathers with black markings, yellow breast, green base
Issued:	c.1945-1950

Description	U.S $	Can. $	U.K. £
Yellow-throated warbler	350.00	425.00	200.00

Photograph
not available
at press time

HN 2619
Grouse

Model No.:	1161
Height:	Unknown
Colour:	Unknown
Issued:	Unknown

Description	U.S $	Can. $	U.K. £
Grouse		Not known to exist	

HN 2620
English Setter - large

Model No.:	770
Designer:	Frederick Daws
Size:	7 ½" x 12 ¼", 19.1 x 31.1 cm
Colour:	White with liver highlights
Issued:	1. 1950-c.1960; 2. Unknown
Varieties:	English Setter Ch. 'Maesydd Mustard'
	HN 1049, Gordon Setter HN 1079,
	Irish Setter Ch. 'Pat O'Moy' HN 1054

Colourways		U.S $	Can. $	U.K. £
1.	Natural	3,000.00	3,600.00	1,750.00
2.	Flambé	1,500.00	1,800.00	825.00

HN 2621
English Setter - medium

Model No.:	770A
Designer:	Frederick Daws
Height:	5 ¼", 13.3 cm
Colour:	Liver and white
Issued:	1950-c.1960
Varieties:	English Setter Ch. 'Maesydd Mustard'
	HN 1050, Gordon Setter HN 1080,
	Irish Setter Ch. 'Pat O'Moy' HN 1055
Derivative:	Bookend

Description	U.S $	Can. $	U.K. £
Medium	2,000.00	2,500.00	1,100.00

HN 2622
English Setter - small

Model No.:	770B
Designer:	Frederick Daws
Height:	3 ¾", 9.5 cm
Size:	Small
Colour:	Liver and white
Issued:	1950-c.1960
Varieties:	English Setter Ch. 'Maesydd Mustard'
	HN 1051, Gordon Setter HN 1081,
	Irish Setter Ch. 'Pat O'Moy' HN 1056

Description	U.S $	Can. $	U.K. £
Small	1,500.00	1,800.00	850.00

HN 2623
Punch Peon, Chestnut Shire

Model No.:	1134
Designer:	W. M. Chance
Height:	7 ½", 19.1 cm
Colour:	Brown with black mane and black and
	white markings on legs
Issued:	1950-1960
Varieties:	Also called 'Dapple Grey' HN 2578

Description	U.S $	Can. $	U.K. £
Punch Peon	1,500.00	1,800.00	800.00

HN 2624
Pointer
Style One

Model No.:	1312
Designer:	Peggy Davies
Size:	5 ½" x 11 ½", 14.0 cm x 29.2 cm
Colour:	White with dark brown markings, yellow and green leaves, brown tree stump
Issued:	1952-1985

Description	U.S $	Can. $	U.K. £
Pointer	550.00	650.00	300.00

HN 2625
French Poodle - large

Model No.:	1212
Designer:	Peggy Davies
Size:	9" x 10", 22.9 x 25.4 cm
Size:	Large
Colour:	White
Issued:	Modelled 1952

Description	U.S $	Can. $	U.K. £
Large	Only two known to exist.		

*

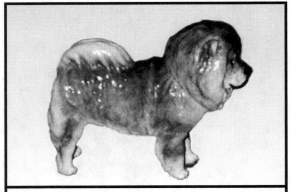

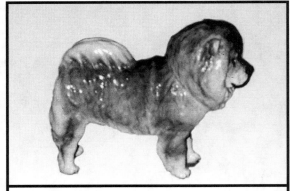

HN 2628
Chow Ch. 'T'Sioh of Kin-Shan'
Large

Model No.:	1209
Height:	Unknown
Size:	Large
Colour:	Golden brown
Issued:	Modelled 1952

Description	U.S $	Can. $	U.K. £
Large	Only one known to exist.		

HN 2629
Chow Ch. 'T'Sioh of Kin-Shan'
Medium

Model No.:	1209A
Height:	Unknown
Size:	Medium
Colour:	Golden brown
Issued:	Modelled 1952

Description	U.S $	Can. $	U.K. £
Medium	Not known to exist.		

HN 2630
Chow Ch. 'T'Sioh of Kin-Shan'
Small

Model No.:	1209B
Height:	Unknown
Size:	Small
Colour:	Golden brown
Issued:	Modelled 1952

Description	U.S $	Can. $	U.K. £
Small		Not known to exist.	

HN 2631
French Poodle - medium

Model No.:	1212A
Designer:	Peggy Davies
Height:	5 ¼", 13.3 cm
Size:	Medium
Colour:	White with pink, grey and black markings
Issued:	1952-1985

Description	U.S $	Can. $	U.K. £
Medium	150.00	200.00	90.00

HN 2632
Cock Pheasant

Model No.:	1063
Height:	6 ¾", 17.2 cm
Colour:	Red-brown feathers, dark blue markings, green-blue head, green-brown base (china)
Issued:	1952-1968
Varieties:	HN 2545
Series:	Prestige

Description	U.S $	Can. $	U.K. £
Cock pheasant	450.00	550.00	250.00

HN 2633
Peruvian Penguin - large

Model No.:	769
Designer:	Charles Noke
Height:	12", 30.1 cm (large)
Colour:	See below
Issued:	1. 1952-1973; 2. c.1946-1962
Varieties:	HN 1199
Series:	Prestige

Colourways	U.S $	Can. $	U.K. £
1. Black/white (china)	2,250.00	2,750.00	1,250.00
2. Flambé	3,000.00	3,500.00	1,650.00

Note: Naturalistic models are free standing.
Flambé models incorporate a rock as the base.

HN 2634
Fox
Seated - Style Six

Model No.:	767
Height:	10 ½", 26.7 cm
Colour:	Golden brown with black highlights (china)
Issued:	1952-1992
Series:	Prestige

Description	U.S $	Can. $	U.K. £
Fox, seated	2,000.00	2,500.00	1,000.00

HN 2635
Drake
Standing

Model No.:	307
Height:	13 ½", 34.3 cm
Size:	Large
Colour:	White with light brown shading (china)
Issued:	1952-1974
Series:	Prestige
Varieties:	HN 248, 249, 252, 1198

Description	U.S $	Can. $	U.K. £
White drake	2,000.00	2,500.00	1,100.00

HN 2636
Indian Runner Drake

Model No.:	1327
Designer:	Peggy Davies
Height:	18", 45.7 cm
Size:	Large
Colour:	White
Issued:	1952-c.1960

Description	U.S $	Can. $	U.K. £
Indian runner drake	1,750.00	2,100.00	950.00

HN 2637
Polar Bear and Cub on Base - Large

Model No.:	613
Designer:	Charles Noke
Height:	15", 38.1 cm
Colour:	See below
Issued:	1. 1952-c.1960
	2. 3. and 4. c.1929

Colourways	U.S $	Can. $	U.K. £
1. White/green	8,000.00	10,000.00	4,500.00
2. Flambé	8,000.00	10,000.00	4,500.00
3. Chang		Extremely Rare	
4. Sung		Extremely Rare	

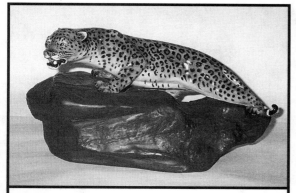

HN 2638
Leopard on Rock

Model No.:	1036
Designer:	Charles Noke
Size:	9" x 11 ½", 22.9 x 29.2 cm
Colour:	Golden brown with dark brown spots, charcoal rock (earthenware)
Issued:	1952-1981
Series:	Prestige

Description	U.S $	Can. $	U.K. £
Leopard on rock	1,500.00	1,800.00	850.00

HN 2639
Tiger on a Rock
Style Five

Model No.:	1038
Designer:	Charles Noke
Size:	12" x 10 ¼", 30.5 x 26.0 cm
Colour:	Golden brown with dark brown stripes, charcoal rock (earthenware)
Issued:	1952-1992
Series:	Prestige

Description	U.S $	Can. $	U.K. £
Tiger on rock	1,500.00	1,800.00	850.00

HN 2640
Fighter Elephant - Large

Model No.:	626
Designer:	Charles Noke
Size:	12" x 9", 30.5 x 22.9 cm
Colour:	See below
Issued:	1. 1952-1992 2. and 3. c.1929
Varieties:	HN 1120
Series:	Prestige

Colourways	U.S $	Can. $	U.K. £
1. Grey (earthenware)	1,100.00	1,300.00	600.00
2. Flambé	3,000.00	3,500.00	1,600.00
3. Sung	4,500.00	5,500.00	2,500.00

HN 2641
Lion on Rock
Style Two

Model No.:	1033
Designer:	Charles Noke
Height:	10 ½", 26.7 cm
Colour:	Golden brown lion, charcoal rock (earthenware)
Issued:	1952-1992
Series:	Prestige

Description	U.S $	Can. $	U.K. £
Lion on rock	1,500.00	1,800.00	850.00

HN 2642
Red Squirrel in a Pine Tree
Prototype

Model No.:	1292		
Designer:	Peggy Davies		
Length:	8", 20.3 cm		
Colour:	Nut brown		
Issued:	Modelled 1945		

Description	U.S $	Can. $	U.K. £
Red squirrel		Prototype	

HN 2643
Boxer Ch. 'Warlord of Mazelaine'

Model No.:	1412A
Designer:	Peggy Davies
Height:	6 ½", 16.5 cm
Size:	Medium
Colour:	Golden brown coat with white bib
Issued:	1952-1985

Description	U.S $	Can. $	U.K. £
Boxer	150.00	175.00	80.00

HN 2644
Elephant
Trunk in salute - Style One

Model No.:	489B
Designer:	Charles Noke
Height:	4 ½", 11.4 cm (small)
Colour:	See below
Issued:	1. 1952-1985; 2. and 3. c.1926-1962
Varieties:	HN 891B, 941

Colourways	U.S $	Can. $	U.K. £
1. Grey/black (china)	250.00	300.00	140.00
2. Flambé	500.00	600.00	275.00
3. Sung	1,500.00	1,800.00	800.00

HN 2645
Doberman Pinscher Ch. 'Rancho Dobe's Storm'

Model No.:	1508
Designer:	Peggy Davies
Size:	6 ¼" x 6 ½", 15.9 x 16.5 cm
Size:	Medium
Colour:	See below
Issued:	1. 1955-1985
	2. c.1955

Colourways	U.S $	Can. $	U.K. £
1. Black/brown	200.00	250.00	100.00
2. Flambé		Rare	

HN 2646
Tiger, Stalking - Style Two - extra large

Model No.:	809
Designer:	Charles Noke
Size:	5 ¾" x 13 ¼", 14.6 x 33.5 cm (extra large)
Colour:	See below
Issued:	1. 1955-1992; 2. 1950-1996
Varieties:	HN 1082; Also Tiger on Alabaster Base HN 1126
Series:	Prestige

Colourways	U.S $	Can. $	U.K. £
1. Natural	1,000.00	1,200.00	550.00
2. Flambé	900.00	1,100.00	500.00

HN 2647
Drake, Standing - Medium

Model No.:	137
Height:	1. 5 ½", 14.0 cm
	2. 6 ½", 16.5 cm
Size:	Medium
Colour:	See below
Issued:	1. 1959-1962
	2. 1913-1996
Varieties:	HN 114, 115, 116, 956, 1191, 2555

Colourways	U.S $	Can. $	U.K. £
1. Green/grey/brown (china)	450.00	550.00	250.00
2. Flambé	300.00	375.00	150.00

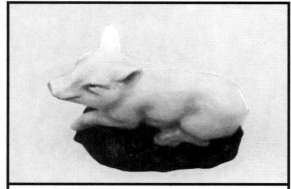

HN 2648
Piglet
Style One

Model No.:	1279
Designer:	Peggy Davies
Height:	2", 5.1 cm
Colour:	Pink piglet on green grassy mound
Issued:	1959-1967

Description	U.S $	Can. $	U.K. £
Style one	150.00	175.00	85.00

HN 2649
Piglet
Style Two

Model No.:	1275
Designer:	Peggy Davies
Height:	2", 5.1 cm
Colour:	Pink piglet on green grassy mound
Issued:	1959-1967

Description	U.S $	Can. $	U.K. £
Style two	150.00	175.00	85.00

HN 2650
Piglet
Style Three

Model No.:	1282
Designer:	Peggy Davies
Height:	1", 2.5 cm
Colour:	Pink piglet on green grassy mound
Issued:	1959-1967

Description	U.S $	Can. $	U.K. £
Style three	150.00	175.00	85.00

HN 2651
Piglet
Style Four

Model No.:	1280
Designer:	Peggy Davies
Height:	1", 2.5 cm
Colour:	Pink piglet on green grassy mound
Issued:	1959-1967

Description	U.S $	Can. $	U.K. £
Style four	150.00	175.00	85.00

HN 2652
Piglet
Style Five

Model No.:	1281
Designer:	Peggy Davies
Height:	2", 5.1 cm
Colour:	Pink piglet on green grassy mound
Issued:	1959-1967

Description	U.S $	Can. $	U.K. £
Style five	150.00	175.00	85.00

HN 2653
Piglet
Style Six

Model No.:	1278
Designer:	Peggy Davies
Height:	2", 5.1 cm
Colour:	Pink piglet on green grassy mound
Issued:	1959-1967

Description	U.S $	Can. $	U.K. £
Style six	150.00	175.00	85.00

HN 2654
Character Dog with Slipper
Model No.:   1673
Designer: Unknown
Height: 3", 7.6 cm
Colour: White with black and brown patches,
               grey slipper
Issued: 1959-1985

Description	U.S $	Can. $	U.K. £
Dog with slipper	100.00	125.00	55.00

HN 2655
Siamese Cat
Seated - Style One
Model No.:   1672
Designer: Joseph Ledger
Modeller: Peggy Davies
Height: 5 ½", 14.0 cm
Colour: Cream with black markings
Issued: 1960-1985
Series: Chatcull Range

Description	U.S $	Can. $	U.K. £
Siamese cat, seated	125.00	150.00	70.00

HN 2656
Pine Marten
Model No.:   1689
Designer: Joseph Ledger
Height: 4", 10.1 cm
Colour: See below
Issued: 1. 1960-1969
               2. c.1960
Series: Chatcull Range

Colourways	U.S $	Can. $	U.K. £
1. Natural colours	400.00	475.00	225.00
2. Flambé		Rare	

HN 2657
Langur Monkey
Model No.:   1703
Designer: Joseph Ledger
Height: 4 ½", 11.4 cm
Colour: Long-haired brown and white coat
Issued: 1960-1969
Series: Chatcull Range

Description	U.S $	Can. $	U.K. £
Langur monkey	300.00	375.00	175.00

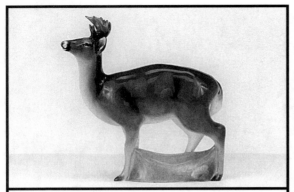

HN 2658
White -Tailed Deer

Model No.:	1707
Designer:	Joseph Ledger
Height:	6", 15.2 cm
Colour:	Brown and grey
Issued:	1960-1969
Series:	Chatcull Range

Description	U.S $	Can. $	U.K. £
White-tailed deer	300.00	375.00	175.00

HN 2659
Brown Bear
Style Two

Model No.:	1688
Designer:	Joseph Ledger
Height:	4", 10.1 cm
Colour:	See below
Issued:	1. 1960-1969
	2. c.1960
Series:	Chatcull Range

Colourways	U.S $	Can. $	U.K. £
1. Brown/black	250.00	300.00	150.00
2. Mandarin		Rare	

HN 2660
Siamese Cat
Standing - Style One

Model No.:	1709
Designer:	Joseph Ledger
Modeller:	Peggy Davies
Height:	5", 12.7 cm
Colour:	Cream with black markings
Issued:	1960-1985
Series:	Chatcull Range

Description	U.S $	Can. $	U.K. £
Siamese cat, standing	125.00	150.00	70.00

HN 2661
Mountain Sheep

Model No.:	1692
Designer:	Joseph Ledger
Height:	5", 12.7 cm
Colour:	Brown with white highlights, green base
Issued:	1960-1969
Series:	Chatcull Range

Description	U.S $	Can. $	U.K. £
Mountain sheep	300.00	375.00	175.00

HN 2662
Siamese Cat
Lying - Style One

Model No.:	1710
Designer:	Joseph Ledger
Modeller:	Peggy Davies
Height:	3 ¾", 9.5 cm
Colour:	Cream with black markings
Issued:	1960-1985
Series:	Chatcull Range

Description	U.S $	Can. $	U.K. £
Siamese cat, lying	125.00	150.00	70.00

HN 2663
River Hog

Model No.:	1704
Designer:	Joseph Ledger
Height:	3 ½", 8.9 cm
Colour:	Dark brown with light brown and white highlights
Issued:	1960-1969
Series:	Chatcull Range

Description	U.S $	Can. $	U.K. £
River hog	300.00	375.00	175.00

HN 2664
Nyala Antelope

Model No.:	1705
Designer:	Joseph Ledger
Height:	5 ¾", 14.6 cm
Colour:	Mushroom coloured coat with black and brown highlights
Issued:	1960-1969
Series:	Chatcull Range

Description	U.S. $	Can. $	U.K. £
Nyala antelope	300.00	375.00	175.00

HN 2665
Llama
Style Two

Model No.:	1687
Designer:	Joseph Ledger
Height:	6 ½", 16.5 cm
Colour:	Brown with turquoise highlights
Issued:	1960-1969
Series:	Chatcull Range

Description	U.S $	Can. $	U.K. £
Llama	300.00	375.00	175.00

HN 2666
Badger
Style One

Model No.:	1708
Designer:	Joseph Ledger
Height:	2 ¾", 7.0 cm
Colour:	See below
Issued:	1. 1960-1969
	2. c.1960
Series:	Chatcull Range

Colourways	U.S $	Can. $	U.K. £
1. Natural colours	300.00	375.00	175.00
2. Mandarin		Rare	

HN 2667
Labrador Ch. 'Bumblikite of Mansergh'

Model No.:	1946
Designer:	John Bromley
Height:	5 ¼", 13.3 cm
Size:	Medium
Colour:	Black
Issued:	1967-1985

Description	U.S $	Can. $	U.K. £
Labrador	175.00	200.00	100.00

HN 2668
Puffins

Model No.:	2289
Designer:	Robert Jefferson
Height:	9 ¾", 24.8 cm
Colour:	Dark grey and white birds with red, yellow and blue beaks
Issued:	1974 in a limited edition of 250
Series:	Jefferson Sculptures

Description	U.S $	Can. $	U.K. £
Puffins		900.00	1,100.00	500.00

HN 2669
Snowy Owl (male)

Model No.:	2264
Designer:	Robert Jefferson
Height:	16", 40.1 cm
Colour:	White with grey markings
Issued:	1976 in a limited edition of 150
Series:	Jefferson Sculptures

Description	U.S $	Can. $	U.K. £
Snowy owl (male)	900.00	1,100.00	500.00

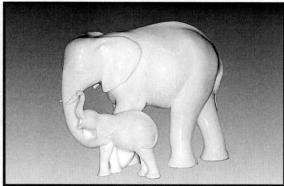

HN 2670
Snowy Owl (female)

Model No.:	2389		
Designer:	Robert Jefferson		
Height:	9 ½", 24.0 cm		
Colour:	White with grey markings		
Issued:	1976 in a limited edition of 150		
Series:	Jefferson Sculptures		

Description	U.S $	Can. $	U.K. £
Snowy owl (female)	900.00	1,100.00	500.00

*

HN 3463
'Motherhood' Elephants

Model No.:	Unknown
Designer:	Adrian Hughes
Height:	8 ¾", 22.2 cm
Colour:	White
Issued:	1995-1998
Series:	Images of Nature
Varieties:	HN 3464

Colourways	U.S $	Can. $	U.K. £
White	225.00	275.00	125.00

HN 3464
'Motherhood' Elephants

Model No.:	Unknown
Designer:	Adrian Hughes
Height:	8 ¾", 22.2 cm
Colour:	Flambé
Issued:	1995-1997
Series:	Images of Fire
Varieties:	HN 3463

Colourways	U.S $	Can. $	U.K. £
Flambé	750.00	900.00	400.00

*

HN 3466
'Twilight' Barn Owls

Model No.:	Unknown
Designer:	Adrian Hughes
Height:	5 ¾", 14.6 cm
Colour:	White
Issued:	1996-1999
Series:	Images of Nature

Description	U.S $	Can. $	U.K. £
'Twilight'	100.00	125.00	50.00

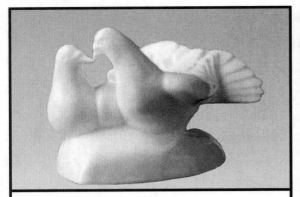

HN 3467
'Devotion' Doves

Designer:	Adrian Hughes
Height:	2 ½", 6.3 cm
Colour:	White
Issued:	1996 to the present
Series:	Images of Nature

Description	U.S $	Can. $	U.K. £
'Devotion'	50.00	120.00	40.00

HN 3468
'First Born' Whales

Designer:	Adrian Hughes
Height:	6", 15.2 cm
Colour:	White
Issued:	1997-2002
Series:	Images of Nature

Description	U.S $	Can. $	U.K. £
'First Born'	125.00	150.00	75.00

*

HN 3500
Black-Throated Loon

Model No.:	2268
Designer:	Robert Jefferson
Size:	9 ½" x 20", 24.0 x 50.8 cm
Colour:	Green head, black and white wings, white underbody
Issued:	1974 in a limited edition of 150
Series:	Jefferson Sculptures

Description	U.S $	Can. $	U.K. £
Black-throated loon	1,000.00	1,200.00	550.00

HN 3501
White-Winged Cross Bills

Model No.:	2208
Designer:	Robert Jefferson
Height:	8", 20.3 cm
Colour:	Red bird with white and brown wings, dull yellow bird with brown and white wings
Issued:	1974 in a limited edition of 250
Series:	Jefferson Sculptures

Description	U.S $	Can. $	U.K. £
White-winged cross bills	900.00	1,100.00	500.00

HN 3502
King Eider

Model No.:	2302
Designer:	Robert Jefferson
Height:	10", 25.4 cm
Colour:	Dark brown, grey head, red and yellow beak
Issued:	1974 in a limited edition of 150
Series:	Jefferson Sculptures

Description	U.S $	Can. $	U.K. £
King eider	1,000.00	1,200.00	550.00

HN 3503
Roseate Terns

Model No.:	2319
Designer:	Robert Jefferson
Height:	11", 27.9 cm
Colour:	Grey and white large bird, light brown chicks
Issued:	1974 in a limited edition of 150
Series:	Jefferson Sculptures

Description	U.S $	Can. $	U.K. £
Roseate terns	1,000.00	1,200.00	550.00

HN 3504
Golden-Crowned Kinglet

Model No.:	2406
Designer:	Robert Jefferson
Height:	8 ¼", 21.0 cm
Colour:	Brown branch and acorn, yellow, brown and red bird
Issued:	1974 in an unlimited number
Series:	Jefferson Sculptures

Description	U.S $	Can. $	U.K. £
Golden-crowned kinglet	550.00	650.00	300.00

HN 3505
Winter Wren

Model No.:	2405
Designer:	Robert Jefferson
Height:	5", 12.7 cm
Colour:	Brown with cream breast
Issued:	1974 in an unlimited number
Series:	Jefferson Sculptures

Description	U.S $	Can. $	U.K. £
Winter wren	550.00	650.00	300.00

HN 3506
Colorado Chipmunks

Model No.:	2404
Designer:	Robert Jefferson
Height:	13", 33.0 cm
Colour:	Brown with black patches
Issued:	1974 in a limited edition of 75
Series:	Jefferson Sculptures

Description	U.S $	Can. $	U.K. £
Colorado chipmunks	1,500.00	1,800.00	825.00

HN 3507
Harbour Seals

Model No.:	2434
Designer:	Robert Jefferson
Height:	8 ½", 21.6 cm
Colour:	Greys and browns
Issued:	1975 in a limited edition of 75
Series:	Jefferson Sculptures

Description	U.S $	Can. $	U.K. £
Harbour seals	1,500.00	1,800.00	825.00

HN 3508
Snowshoe Hares

Model No.:	2446
Designer:	Robert Jefferson
Height:	10 ¾", 27.3 cm
Colour:	Browns and white
Issued:	1975 in a limited edition of 75
Series:	Jefferson Sculptures

Description	U.S $	Can. $	U.K. £
Snowshoe hares	1,500.00	1,800.00	825.00

HN 3509
Downy Woodpecker

Model No.:	2469
Designer:	Robert Jefferson
Height:	7 ¼", 18.4 cm
Colour:	Black and white bird, green leaves, blue flower
Issued:	1975 in an unlimited number
Series:	Jefferson Sculptures

Description	U.S $	Can. $	U.K. £
Downy woodpecker	550.00	650.00	300.00

HN 3510
Eastern Bluebird Fledgling

Model No.:	2481
Designer:	Robert Jefferson
Height:	5 ¾", 14.6 cm
Colour:	Brown with light brown highlights, green leaves, purple flower, tan trowel
Issued:	1976 in a limited edition of 250
Series:	Jefferson Sculptures

Description	U.S $	Can. $	U.K. £
Bluebird fledgling	550.00	650.00	300.00

Photograph
not available
at press time

HN 3511
Chipping Sparrow

Model No.:	2466
Designer:	Robert Jefferson
Height:	7 ½", 19.1 cm
Colour:	Brown and yellow, red head
Issued:	1976 in a limited edition of 200
Series:	Jefferson Sculptures

Description	U.S $	Can. $	U.K. £
Chipping sparrow	550.00	650.00	300.00

HN 3512
Mallard (male)

Model No.:	2614
Designer:	Harry Sales from Lem Ward originals
Height:	4", 10.1 cm
Colour:	Light and dark brown, green head, yellow beak
Issued:	1979-1985
Series:	Wildlife Decoys

Description	U.S $	Can. $	U.K. £
Mallard (male)	175.00	200.00	100.00

HN 3513
Pintail (male)

Model No.:	Unknown
Designer:	Harry Sales from Lem Ward originals
Height:	4", 10.1 cm
Colour:	Light and dark brown with cream markings
Issued:	1979-1985
Series:	Wildlife Decoys

Description	U.S $	Can. $	U.K. £
Pintail (male)	175.00	200.00	100.00

HN 3514
Greater Scaup (male)

Model No.:	2620
Designer:	Harry Sales from Lem Ward originals
Height:	3 ¾", 9.5 cm
Colour:	Dark green with light green and beige, blue bill
Issued:	1979-1985
Series:	Wildlife Decoys

Description	U.S $	Can. $	U.K. £
Greater scaup (male)	175.00	200.00	100.00

HN 3515
Mallard (female)

Model No.:	2603
Designer:	Harry Sales from Lem Ward originals
Height:	4", 101. cm
Colour:	Dark brown, orange-brown
Issued:	1979-1985
Series:	Wildlife Decoys

Description	U.S $	Can. $	U.K. £
Mallard (female)	175.00	200.00	100.00

HN 3516
Pintail (female)

Model No.:	2612
Designer:	Harry Sales from Lem Ward originals
Height:	4", 10.1 cm
Colour:	Light brown, dark brown and cream
Issued:	1979-1985
Series:	Wildlife Decoys

Description	U.S $	Can. $	U.K. £
Pintail (female)	175.00	200.00	100.00

HN 3517
Greater Scaup (female)

Model No.:	2621
Designer:	Harry Sales from Lem Ward originals
Height:	4", 10.1 cm
Colour:	Dark brown, light brown, blue bill
Issued:	1979-1985
Series:	Wildlife Decoys

Description	U.S $	Can. $	U.K. £
Greater scaup (female)	175.00	200.00	100.00

HORSES

DA 35B
'Moonlight'

DA 179
Black Bess

DA 239
Spirit of Tomorrow

DA 238
Shire Horse, Style Two

DA 182
First Born

DA 236
The Flight of the Trakehner

HORSES

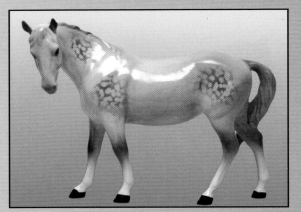

DA 46
Mare (facing left)

DA 42
'Bois Roussel' Race Horse

DA 50
Arab Horse 'Xayal'

DA 185
Shetland Pony, Style Two

DA 43
Shire Mare

DA 45
Trotting Horse (Cantering Shire)

HORSES

DA 47
Shetland Pony (Woolly Shetland Mare), Style One

DA 67
Pinto Pony

DA 164
Welsh Mountain Pony, Style One

DA 48
Horse (Swish Tail)

DA 163A
Quarter Horse (not on plinth)

DA 68
Appaloosa

HORSES

DA 57A
Spirit of the Wild

DA 59A
Spirit of Youth

DA 55
Mare (small, facing right, head up)

DA 58A
Spirit of Freedom

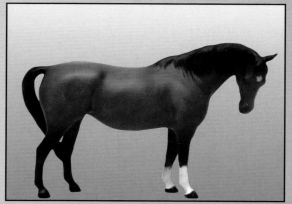

DA 54
Mare (facing right, head down)

DA 56
Horse (small thoroughbred stallion)

HORSES

DA 188
Mr. Frisk, Style One

DA 190
Mr. Frisk, Style Two

DA 154B
The Winner, Style Two

DA 193A
Horse of the Year 1992

DA 134
Desert Orchid, Style One

DA 218
'Red Rum', Style Two

HORSES FROM
GREEK MYTHOLOGY

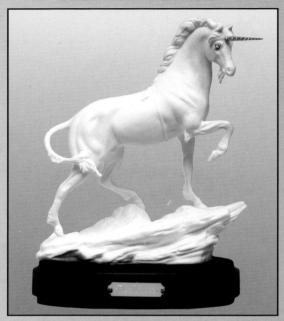

HN 3549
Unicorn

FROM THE
"SPIRITED HORSE" SERIES

DA 183
Spirit of the Wild

HN 3547
Pegasus

NEW ISSUES FOR 2004

RDA 5
Standard Schnauzer

RDA 4
Jack Russell

RDA 9
Rough Collie

RDA 7
Dalmatian

RDA 15
Pointer

RDA 11
Beagle

NEW ISSUES FOR 2004

RDA 18
Maine Coon

RDA 6
Chow Chow

RDA 19
Persian

RDA 31
Palomino

RDA 33
My First Horse

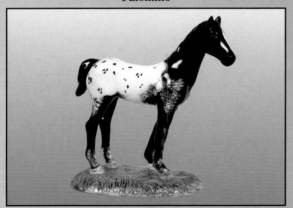

RDA 35
Appaloosa Foal

RDA 32
Appaloosa

HN 3518
Merganser (male)

Model No.:	Unknown
Designer:	Harry Sales from Lem Ward originals
Height:	4", 10.1 cm
Colour:	Charcoal, light brown and green
Issued:	1980-1985
Series:	Wildlife Decoys

Description	U.S $	Can. $	U.K. £
Merganser (male)	175.00	200.00	100.00

HN 3519
Merganser (female)

Model No.:	2643
Designer:	Harry Sales from Lem Ward originals
Height:	4", 10.1 cm
Colour:	Brown, light brown and black
Issued:	1980-1985
Series:	Wildlife Decoys

Description	U.S $	Can. $	U.K. £
Merganser (female)	175.00	200.00	100.00

HN 3520
Green Wing Teal (male)

Model No.:	2683
Designer:	Harry Sales from Lem Ward originals
Height:	4", 10.1 cm
Colour:	Brown, green and black
Issued:	1979-1986

Description	U.S. $	Can. $	U.K. £
Green wing teal (male)	175.00	200.00	100.00

HN 3521
Green Wing Teal (female)

Model No.:	2684
Designer:	Harry Sales from Lem Ward originals
Height:	4", 10.1 cm
Colour:	Beige, brown and green
Issued:	1979-1986

Description	U.S. $	Can. $	U.K. £
Green wing teal (female)	175.00	200.00	100.00

HN 3522
'The Leap' Dolphin

Model No.: 2949
Designer: Adrian Hughes
Height: 9", 22.9 cm
Colour: See below
Issued: 1. 1982-1999 2. 1983
Series: Images of Nature

Colourways	U.S. $	Can. $	U.K. £
1. White	175.00	225.00	100.00
2. Flambé	1,000.00	1,250.00	550.00

Note: The flambé model was test marketed at selected Royal Doulton outlet stores in the U.K.

HN 3523
'Capricorn' Mountain Goat

Model No.: 2959
Designer: Adrian Hughes
Height: 9 ¾", 24.8 cm
Colour: See below
Issued: 1. 1982-1988
        2. 1983
Series: Images of Nature

Colourways	U.S. $	Can. $	U.K. £
1. White	175.00	225.00	100.00
2. Flambé	1,200.00	1,500.00	675.00

HN 3524
'The Gift of Life' Mare and Foal

Model No.: 2923
Designer: Russell Willis
Height: 8 ¼", 21.0 cm
Colour: White
Issued: 1982-1996
Varieties: HN 3536 (flambé)
Series: Images of Nature

Colourways	U.S. $	Can. $	U.K. £
White	600.00	725.00	325.00

HN 3525
'Courtship' Terns

Model No.: 2930
Designer: Russell Willis
Height: 14 ¼", 36.2 cm
Colour: White
Issued: 1982-2003
Varieties: HN 3535 (flambé)
Series: Images of Nature

Colourways	U.S. $	Can. $	U.K. £
White	600.00	725.00	350.00

HN 3526
'Shadow Play' Cat

Model No.:	2936
Designer:	Russell Willis
Height:	10", 25.4 cm
Colour:	See below
Issued:	1. 1982-1999
	2. c.1983
Series:	Images of Nature

Colourways	U.S. $	Can. $	U.K. £
1. White	175.00	225.00	100.00
2. Flambé	1,350.00	1,600.00	750.00

HN 3527
'Going Home' Flying Geese

Model No.:	2925
Designer:	Adrian Hughes
Height:	6 ¼", 15.9 cm
Colour:	See below
Issued:	1982-2002
Series:	Images of Nature
Varieties:	HN 3546

Colourways	U.S. $	Can. $	U.K. £
1. White	125.00	150.00	70.00
2. Flambé	1,350.00	1,600.00	750.00

Note: Another style, a prototype, exists in flambé.

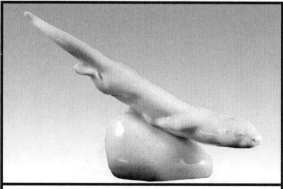

HN 3528
'Freedom' Otters

Model No.:	3058
Designer:	Robert Jefferson
Height:	8 ½", 21.6 cm
Colour:	White
Issued:	1983-1986
Series:	Images of Nature

Description	U.S. $	Can. $	U.K. £
White otters	225.00	275.00	125.00

HN 3529
'Bright Water' Otter

Model No.:	3058A
Designer:	Robert Jefferson
Size:	7 ½" x 11", 19.1 x 27.9 cm
Colour:	White
Issued:	1983-1986
Series:	Images of Nature

Description	U.S. $	Can. $	U.K. £
White otter	225.00	275.00	125.00

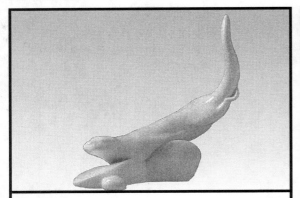

HN 3530
'Clear Water' Otter

Model No.:	3058B
Designer:	Robert Jefferson
Height:	8 ¼", 21.0 cm
Colour:	White
Issued:	1983-1986
Series:	Images of Nature

Description	U.S. $	Can. $	U.K. £
White otter	225.00	275.00	125.00

HN 3531
'Nestling Down' Swans

Model No.:	3198
Designer:	Adrian Hughes
Size:	8 ½" x 12", 21.6 x 30.5 cm
Colour:	White
Issued:	1985-1994
Series:	Images of Nature
Varieties:	HN 3538 (flambé)

Colourways	U.S. $	Can. $	U.K. £
White	400.00	475.00	225.00

HN 3532
'The Homecoming' Doves

Model No.:	3304
Designer:	Russell Willis
Height:	14 ¾", 37.5 cm
Colour:	White
Issued:	1987-1998
Series:	Images of Nature
Varieties:	HN 3539 (flambé)

Colourways	U.S. $	Can. $	U.K. £
White	450.00	550.00	250.00

HN 3533
'Patience' Heron

Model No.:	3467
Designer:	Peter Gee
Height:	12 ¼", 31.1 cm
Colour:	White
Issued:	1987-1995
Series:	Images of Nature

Description	U.S. $	Can. $	U.K. £
White heron	125.00	150.00	70.00

HN 3534
'Playful' Lion Cubs

Model No.:	3432
Designer:	Adrian Hughes
Height:	8", 20.3 cm
Colour:	White
Issued:	1987-1993
Series:	Images of Nature

Description	U.S. $	Can. $	U.K. £
White lion cubs	175.00	225.00	100.00

HN 3535
'Courtship' Terns

Model No.:	2930
Designer:	Russell Willis
Height:	15", 38.1 cm
Colour:	Flambé
Issued:	1987-1996
Series:	Images of Fire
Varieties:	HN 3525

Colourways	U.S. $	Can. $	U.K. £
Flambé	1,100.00	1,350.00	600.00

HN 3536
'The Gift of Life' Mare and Foal

Model No.:	2923
Designer:	Russell Willis
Height:	9", 22.9 cm
Colour:	Flambé
Issued:	1987-1996
Series:	Images of Fire
Varieties:	HN 3524

Colourways	U.S. $	Can. $	U.K. £
Flambé	1,100.00	1,350.00	600.00

*

HN 3538
'Nestling Down' Swans

Model No.:	3198
Designer:	Adrian Hughes
Size:	8 ½" x 12", 21.6 x 30.5 cm
Colour:	Flambé
Issued:	1988-1996
Series:	Images of Fire
Varieties:	HN 3531

Colourways	U.S. $	Can. $	U.K. £
Flambé	1,100.00	1,350.00	600.00

HN 3539
'The Homecoming' Doves

Model No.:	3304
Designer:	Russell Willis
Height:	14 ¾", 37.5 cm
Colour:	Flambé
Issued:	1989-1996
Series:	Images of Fire
Varieties:	HN 3532

Colourways	U.S. $	Can. $	U.K. £
Flambé	1,100.00	1,350.00	600.00

HN 3540
'Graceful' Panthers

Model No.:	3573
Designer:	John Ablitt
Size:	4 ½" x 11", 11.4 x 27.9 cm
Colour:	White
Issued:	1989-1992
Series:	Images of Nature

Description	U.S. $	Can. $	U.K. £
White panthers	250.00	300.00	150.00

HN 3541
Peregrine Falcon

Model No.:	3140
Designer:	Graham Tongue
Height:	11 ½", 29.2 cm
Colour:	Dark brown and cream
Issued:	1990 in a limited edition of 2,500
Series:	Artist's Signature Edition
Varieties:	DA 40

Description	U.S. $	Can. $	U.K. £
Peregrine falcon	225.00	275.00	125.00

HN 3542
'Serenity' Tropical Shoal of Fish

Model No.:	3660
Designer:	John Ablitt
Height:	11", 27.9 cm
Colour:	White
Issued:	1990-1995
Series:	Images of Nature

Description	U.S. $	Can. $	U.K. £
White fish	175.00	225.00	100.00

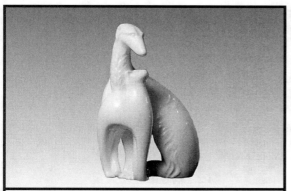

HN 3543
'Friendship' Borzoi Dog and Cat

Model No.:	3658
Designer:	John Ablitt
Height:	8 ¼", 21.0 cm
Colour:	White
Issued:	1990-1992
Series:	Images of Nature

Description	U.S. $	Can. $	U.K. £
White dog and cat	150.00	175.00	85.00

HN 3544
'Playtime' Cat with Kitten

Model No.:	3864
Designer:	John R. Ablitt
Height:	8", 20.3 cm
Colour:	White
Issued:	1990-1992
Series:	Images of Nature

Description	U.S. $	Can. $	U.K. £
White cat/kitten	150.00	175.00	85.00

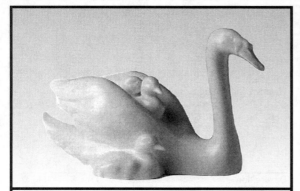

HN 3545
'Motherly Love' Swan and Two Cygnets

Model No.:	3901
Designer:	Adrian Hughes
Height:	6", 15.2 cm
Colour:	White
Issued:	1990-1999
Series:	Images of Nature

Description	U.S. $	Can. $	U.K. £
White swan/cygnets	175.00	225.00	100.00

HN 3546
'Going Home' Flying Geese

Model No.:	2925
Designer:	Adrian Hughes
Height:	6 ¼", 15.9 cm
Colour:	White
Issued:	1987 for Nabisco Foods Canada

Colourways	U.S. $	Can. $	U.K. £
White	125.00	150.00	70.00

Note: A corporate commission of HN 3527

HN 3547
Pegasus

Model No.: 3187
Designer: Alan Maslankowski
Height: 10", 25.4 cm
Colour: White
Issued: 1990-1993

Description	U.S. $	Can. $	U.K. £
Pegasus	500.00	600.00	275.00

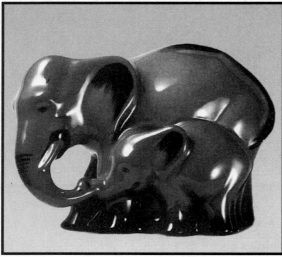

HN 3548
Elephant and Young

Model No.: 3789
Designer: Eric Griffiths
Height: 3 ¼", 8.3 cm
Colour: Flambé
Issued: 1990-1996
Series: Images of Fire

Description	U.S. $	Can. $	U.K. £
Flambé elephants	375.00	450.00	200.00

HN 3549
Unicorn

Model No.:	3927
Designer:	Alan Maslankowski
Height:	10", 25.4 cm
Colour:	White unicorn, gold horn
Issued:	1991-1993

Description	U.S. $	Can. $	U.K. £
Unicorn	500.00	600.00	275.00

HN 3550
'Always and Forever' Doves

Model No.:	4188
Designer:	Adrian Hughes
Height:	4 ½", 11.4 cm
Colour:	White
Issued:	1993 to the present
Series:	Images of Nature

Description	U.S. $	Can. $	U.K. £
White doves	50.00	135.00	40.00

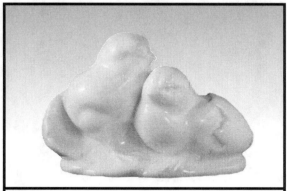

HN 3551
'New Arrival' Chicks

Model No.:	4300
Designer:	Alan Maslankowski
Height:	3", 7.6 cm
Colour:	White
Issued:	1994-1998
Series:	Images of Nature

Description	U.S. $	Can. $	U.K. £
White chicks	75.00	90.00	40.00

HN 3552
Dragon
Style Two

Model No.:	4315			
Designer:	Robert Tabbenor			
Height:	5 ¼", 13.3 cm			
Colour:	Flambé			
Issued:	1993-1995			
Series:	RDICC			

Description	U.S. $	Can. $	U.K. £
Flambé Dragon	300.00	375.00	175.00

*

HN 3893
'Playtime' Two Kittens

Designer:	Robert Tabbenor
Height:	4 ¾", 11.5 cm
Colour:	White
Issued:	1997-2000
Series:	Images of Nature

Description	U.S. $	Can. $	U.K. £
White kittens	75.00	90.00	40.00

HN 3894
'Sleepy Heads' Two Cats

Designer:	Robert Tabbenor
Height:	3 ½", 8.9 cm
Colour:	White
Issued:	1. 1998 to the present
	2. Unknown
Series:	Images of Nature

Description	U.S. $	Can. $	U.K. £
1. White	52.00	185.00	40.00
2. Flambé	750.00	900.00	400.00

HN 3895
'Night Watch' Owls

Designer:	Robert Tabbenor
Height:	6", 15.0 cm
Colour:	White
Issued:	1998-2002
Series:	Images of Nature

Description	U.S. $	Can. $	U.K. £
White owls	75.00	90.00	40.00

HN 3896
'Running Free' Rabbits

Designer:	Robert Tabbenor
Height:	8", 20.3 cm
Colour:	White
Issued:	1999-2001
Series:	Images of Nature

Description	U.S. $	Can. $	U.K. £
Hares	150.00	175.00	85.00

*

HN 3898
'Standing Tall' Giraffes

Designer:	Robert Tabbenor
Height:	13", 33.0 cm
Colour:	White
Issued:	1999 to the present
Series:	Images of Nature

Description	U.S. $	Can. $	U.K. £
Giraffes	N/A	315.00	99.00

*

HN 4087
'Soaring High' Eagle

Designer:	Alan Maslankowski
Height:	11", 27.9 cm
Colour:	White
Issued:	2000-2002
Series:	Images of Nature

Description	U.S. $	Can. $	U.K. £
Eagle	250.00	300.00	125.00

*

HN 4170
The Ox

Designer:	Robert Tabbenor
Height:	3", 7.5 cm
Colour:	White
Issued:	1999 in a limited edition of 2000
Series:	The Christmas Story

Description	U.S. $	Can. $	U.K. £
Ox	50.00	60.00	30.00

Note: Sold as part of the Christmas Story in a limited
edition of 2,000 sets. Ten pieces comprise the set,
all carrying the millennium backstamp. For
other figures in the set see Royal Doulton Figurines.

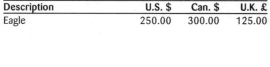

HN 4171
The Ass

Designer:	Robert Tabbenor
Height:	3 ¾", 9.4 cm
Colour:	White
Issued:	1999 in a limited edition of 2,000
Series:	The Christmas Story

Description	U.S. $	Can. $	U.K. £
Ass	50.00	60.00	30.00

Note: Sold as part of the Christmas Story in a limited edition of 2,000 sets. Ten pieces comprise the set, all carrying the millennium backstamp. For other pieces in the set see Royal Doulton Figurines.

HN 4172
'Running Wild' Cheetahs

Designer:	Robert Tabbenor
Height:	4", 10.1 cm
Colour:	White
Issued:	2000-2002
Series:	Images of Nature

Description	U.S. $	Can. $	U.K. £
Cheetahs	175.00	200.00	100.00

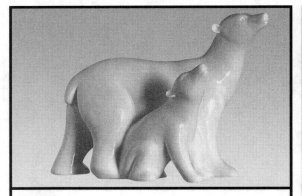

HN 4173
'Dedication' Polar Bears

Designer:	Robert Tabbenor
Height:	6", 15.2 cm
Colour:	White
Issued:	2000-2003
Series:	Images of Nature

Description	U.S. $	Can. $	U.K. £
Polar Bears	175.00	200.00	100.00

*

HN 4176
'Pride' Lions

Designer:	Robert Tabbenor
Size:	4 ½" x 10", 11.4 x 25.4 cm
Colour:	White
Issued:	2001-2002
Series:	1. Images of Nature
	2. WWF Charity Figures

Description	U.S. $	Can. $	U.K. £
Lions	175.00	200.00	100.00

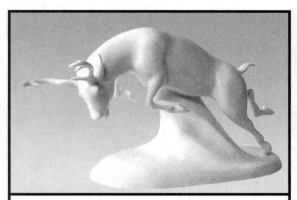

HN 4177
'Majestic' The Stag

Designer:	Robert Tabbenor
Size:	5 ¼" x 11 ¾", 13.3 x 29.4 cm
Colour:	White
Issued:	2001-2002
Series:	Images of Nature

Description	U.S. $	Can. $	U.K. £
Stag	250.00	300.00	140.00

HN 4178
Polar Bear and Cub

Designer:	Robert Tabbenor after Charles Noke
Height:	9 ½", 24.0 cm
Colour:	White
Issued:	2001 in a limited edition of 200
Series:	The Noke Collection

Description	U.S. $	Can. $	U.K. £
Polar bear and cub	1,600.00	2,000.00	900.00

Note: HN 4178 is based on the original model designed by Charles Noke in the 1920s. *

HN 4181
'Crest of A Wave' Dolphins

Designer:	Robert Tabbenor
Height:	6 ¼", 15.9 cm
Colour:	White
Issued:	2002-2002
Series:	1. Images of Nature
	2. WWF Charity Figure
	3. Image of the year

Description	U.S. $	Can. $	U.K. £
Dolphins	175.00	200.00	100.00

HN 4182
'Playfulness' Otters

Designer:	Robert Tabbenor
Length:	4", 10.1 cm
Colour:	White
Issued:	2002-2003
Series:	Images of Nature

Description	U.S. $	Can. $	U.K. £
Otters	175.00	200.00	100.00

*

HN 4184
A New Life' (Mare and Foal)

Designer: Robert Tabbemor
Height: 7 ¼", 18.4 cm
Colour: White
Issued: 2003 to the present
Series: Images of Nature

Description	U.S. $	Can. $	U.K. £
Horses	N/I	280.00	N/A

*

HN 4359
'Tumbling Waters' Otters

Designer: Alan Maslankowski
Height: 14 ½", 36.8 cm
Colour: White
Issued: 2001 in a limited edition of 750
Series: Images of Nature

Description	U.S. $	Can. $	U.K. £
Otters	1,000.00	1,200.00	550.00

*

HN 4440
'Endless Love' Swans

Designer: Alan Maslankowski
Size: 5 ¼" x 13 ½", 13.3 x 34.3 cm
Colour: White
Issued: 2002-2003
Series: Images of Nature

Description	U.S. $	Can. $	U.K. £
Swans	175.00	200.00	100.00

HN 4441
'Contentment' Cat

Designer: Alan Maslankowski
Height: 6 ¾", 17.2 cm
Colour: White
Issued: 2002-2003
Series: Images of Nature

Description	U.S. $	Can. $	U.K. £
Cat	100.00	125.00	50.00

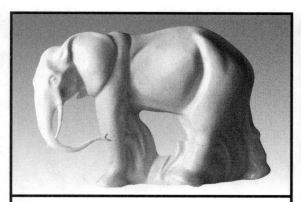

HN 4489
Elephant Mother

Designer:	Alan Maslankowski
Height:	8", 20.3 cm
Colour:	White
Issued:	2003 to the present
Series:	Images

Description	U.S. $	Can. $	U.K. £
Elephant	155.00	275.00	65.00

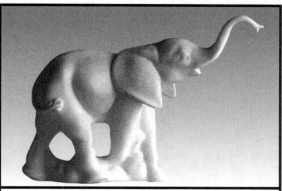

HN 4490
Elephant Young

Designer:	Alan Maslankowski
Height:	5 ½", 14.0 cm
Colour:	White
Issued:	2003 to the present
Series:	Images

Description	U.S. $	Can. $	U.K. £
Elephant	75.00	135.00	N/A

HN 4512
Puppy Love

Designer:	Martyn Alcock
Height:	2 ¼", 5.7 cm
Colour:	White
Issued:	2003 to the present
Series:	Images

Description	U.S. $	Can. $	U.K. £
Puppies	50.00	135.00	30.00

HN 4513
Soul Mates

Designer:	Martyn Alcock
Height:	6 ¼", 15.9 cm
Colour:	White
Issued:	2003 to the present
Series:	Images

Description	U.S. $	Can. $	U.K. £
Cats	70.00	135.00	45.00

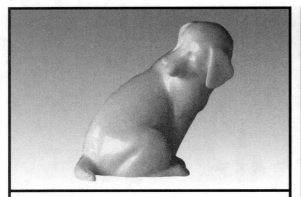

HN 4514
Faithful

Designer:	Martyn Alcock
Height:	5 ½", 14.0 cm
Colour:	White
Issued:	2003 to the present
Series:	Images

Description	U.S. $	Can. $	U.K. £
Dog	55.00	135.00	35.00

HN 4630
Kissing Cats

Designer:	Shane Ridge
Height:	4 ¾",12.1 cm
Colour:	White
Issued:	2004 to the present
Series:	Images

Description	U.S. $	Can. $	U.K. £
Cats	N/I	125.00	35.00

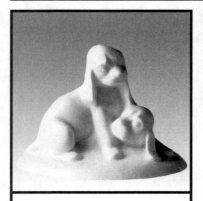

HN 4631
Playful Puppies

Designer: Shane Ridge
Height: 3 ½", 8.9 cm
Colour: White
Issued: 2004 to the present
Series: Images
U.S. N/I
Can. $125.00
U.K. £ 39.00

HN 4705
Ox
Style Two

Designer: Unknown
Height: 5", 12.7 cm
Colour: Cream, brown and gold
Issued: 2004 to the present
Series: Nativity Collection
U.S. $43.00
Can. N/I
U.K. N/I

Note: For other pieces in the Nativity
Collection see the Royal
Doulton Figurines catalogue.

HN 4706
Donkey
Style Three

Designer: Unknown
Height: 4 ½", 11.9 cm
Colour: Grey, gold and pink
Issued: 2004 to the present
Series: Nativity Collection
U.S. $43.00
Can. N/I
U.K. N/I

Note: For other pieces in the Nativity
Collection see the Royal
Doulton Figurines catalogue.

K1
Bulldog
Seated - Style Five
Model No.:   762
Designer: Unknown
Height: 2 ½", 6.3 cm
Colour: Tan; brown
               patches
Issued: 1931-1977
U.S. $125.00
Can. $150.00
U.K.   £ 70.00

K2
Bulldog Puppy
Model No.:   763
Designer: Unknown
Height: 2", 5.1 cm
Colour: Tan, dark brown
               patches
Issued: 1931-1977
Varieties: The patch can
               be on either the
               left or right side
               of face.
U.S. $125.00
Can. $150.00
U.K.   £ 70.00

K3
Sealyham
Begging
Model No.:   760
Designer: Unknown
Height: 2 ¾", 7.0 cm
Colour: White, light brown
               patches
Issued: 1931-1977
U.S. $125.00
Can. $150.00
U.K.   £ 70.00

K4
Sealyham
Lying - Style Two
Model No.:   765
Designer: Unknown
Size: 1 ½" x 3 ¼",
               3.8 x 8.3 cm
Colour: White, light brown
               patches
Issued: 1931-1959
U.S. $350.00
Can. $425.00
U.K.   £200.00

K5
Airedale Terrier
Lying
Model No.:   757
Designer: Unknown
Size: 1 ¼" x 2 ¼",
               3.1 x 5.7 cm
Colour: Dark and light
               brown
Issued: 1931-1959
U.S. $350.00
Can. $425.00
U.K.   £200.00

K6
Pekinese
Seated
Model No.:   758
Designer: Unknown
Height: 2", 5.1 cm
Colour: Golden brown;
               black markings
Issued: 1931-1977
U.S $100.00
Can. $125.00
U.K.   £ 55.00

K7
Foxhound
Seated - Style Two
Model No.:   764
Designer: Unknown
Height: 2 ½", 6.4 cm
Colour: White; dark brown
               and black patches
Issued: 1931-1977
Derivative: On ashtray
U.S. $150.00
Can. $175.00
U.K.   £ 85.00

K8
Fox Terrier
Seated - Style Three
Model No.:   759
Designer: Unknown
Height: 2 ½", 6.4 cm
Colour: White; black and
               brown patches
Issued: 1931-1977
U.S. $150.00
Can. $175.00
U.K.   £ 85.00

K9A
Cocker Spaniel
Seated - Style One
Model No.: 755
Designer: Unknown
Height: 2 ½", 6.4 cm
Colour: Golden brown;
black highlights
Issued: 1931-1977
Varieties: K9B
U.S. $100.00
Can. $125.00
U.K. £ 55.00

K9B
Cocker Spaniel
Seated - Style One
Model No.: 755
Designer: Unknown
Height: 2 ½", 6.4 cm
Colour: Black and brown
Issued: 1931-1977
Varieties: K9A
U.S.
Can. Rare
U.K.

K10
Scottish Terrier
Begging - Style Two
Model No.: 761
Designer: Unknown
Height: 2 ¾", 7.0 cm
Colour: Grey; black
highlights
Issued: 1931-1977
U.S. $125.00
Can. $150.00
U.K. £ 75.00

K11
Cairn Terrier
Seated
Model No.: 766
Designer: Unknown
Height: 2 ½", 6.4 cm
Colour: Grey; black
highlights
Issued: 1931-1977
U.S. $125.00
Can. $150.00
U.K. £ 75.00

K12
'Lucky' Black Cat
Model No.: 400
Designer: Charles Noke
Height: 2 ¾", 7.0 cm
Colour: Black; white face
Issued: 1932-1975
Varieties: Also called
'Ooloo' HN 818,
819, 827, 828,
829, HN 971 on
ashtray
U.S. $125.00
Can. $150.00
U.K. £ 75.00

K13
Alsatian
Seated - Style One
Model No.: 787
Designer: Unknown
Height: 3", 7.6 cm
Colour: Dark and light
brown
Issued: 1931-1977
U.S. $150.00
Can. $175.00
U.K. £ 85.00

K14
Bull Terrier
Lying
Model No.: 1093
Designer: Unknown
Size: 1 ¼" x 2 ¾",
3.2 x 7.0 cm
Colour: White
Issued: 1940-1959
U.S. $450.00
Can. $550.00
U.K. £250.00

K15
Chow (Shibu Ino)
Model No.: 1095
Designer: Unknown
Height: 2 ½", 6.3 cm
Colour: Golden brown
Issued: 1940-1977
U.S. $150.00
Can. $175.00
U.K. £ 85.00

K16
Welsh Corgi
Model No.: 1094
Designer: Unknown
Size: 2 ½" x 2 ¼",
6.3 x 5.7 cm
Colour: Golden brown
Issued: 1940-1977
U.S. $175.00
Can. $200.00
U.K. £100.00

K17
Dachshund
Seated
Model No.: 1096
Designer: Unknown
Size: 1 ¾" x 2 ¾",
4.4 x 7.0 cm
Colour: Golden brown;
dark brown
highlights
Issued: 1940-1977
U.S. $125.00
Can. $150.00
U.K. £ 70.00

K18
Scottish Terrier
Seated - Style Three
Model No.: 1092
Designer: Unknown
Size: 2 ¼" x 2 ¾",
5.7 x 7.0 cm
Colour: Black; grey
highlights
Issued: 1940-1977
U.S. $125.00
Can. $150.00
U.K. £ 70.00

K19
St. Bernard
Lying
Model No.: 1097
Designer: Unknown
Size: 1 ½" x 2 ½",
3.8 x 6.3 cm
Colour: Brown and cream;
black highlights
Issued: 1940-1977
U.S. $125.00
Can. $150.00
U.K. £ 70.00

K20
Penguin with Chick Under
Wing
Model No.: 1084
Designer: Peggy Davies
Height: 2 ¼", 5.7 cm
Colour: Black and white
Issued: 1940-1968
U.S. $200.00
Can. $250.00
U.K. £110.00

K21
Penguin
Style Four
Model No.: 1099
Designer: Peggy Davies
Height: 2", 5.1 cm
Colour: Black and white
Issued: 1940-1968
U.S. $200.00
Can. $250.00
U.K. £110.00

K22
Penguin
Style Five
Model No.: 1098
Designer: Peggy Davies
Height: 1 ¾", 5.1 cm
Colour: Grey, white
and black
Issued: 1940-1968
U.S. $200.00
Can. $250.00
U.K. £110.00

K23
Penguin
Style Six
Model No.: 1101
Designer: Peggy Davies
Height: 1 ½", 3.8 cm
Colour: Grey, white and
black
Issued: 1940-1968
U.S. $200.00
Can. $250.00
U.K. £110.00

K24
Penguin
Style Seven
Model No.: 1100
Designer: Peggy Davies
Height: 2", 5.1 cm
Colour: Black and white
Issued: 1940-1968
U.S. $200.00
Can. $250.00
U.K. £110.00

K25
Penguin
Style Eight
Model No.: 1083
Designer: Peggy Davies
Height: 2 ¼", 5.7 cm
Colour: Grey, white and black
Issued: 1940-1968
U.S. $200.00
Can. $250.00
U.K. £110.00

K26
Mallard Duck
Model No.: 1133
Designer: Unknown
Height: 1 ½", 3.8 cm
Colour: Yellow, brown and green
Issued: 1940-1946
U.S. $700.00
Can. $850.00
U.K. £400.00

K27
Yellow-Throated Warbler
Style One
Model No.: 1128
Designer: Unknown
Height: 2", 5.1 cm
Colour: Blue, black and yellow bird; pink and white flowers
Issued: 1940-1946
U.S. $1,000.00
Can. $1,250.00
U.K. £ 600.00

K28
Cardinal
Style One
Model No.: 1127
Designer: Unknown
Height: 2 ¾", 7.0 cm
Colour: Red with black markings; white flowers
Issued: 1940-1946
U.S. $1,000.00
Can. $1,250.00
U.K. £ 600.00

K29
Baltimore Oriole
Style Four
Model No.: 1130
Designer: Unknown
Height: 2 ¾", 7.0 cm
Colour: Orange; black head and wings; white flowers
Issued: 1940-1946
U.S. $1,000.00
Can. $1,250.00
U.K. £ 600.00

K30
Bluebird with Lupins
Style One
Model No.: 1129
Designer: Unknown
Height: 2 ½", 6.4 cm
Colour: Blue; pink highlights; green leaves
Issued: 1940-1946
U.S. $1,000.00
Can. $1,250.00
U.K. £ 600.00

K31
Bullfinch
Style One
Model No.: 1126
Designer: Unknown
Height: 2 ¼", 5.7 cm
Colour: Blue; black head and wing tips, red breast; pink flowers
Issued: 1940-1946
U.S. $1,000.00
Can. $1,250.00
U.K. £ 600.00

K32
Budgerigar
Style One
Model No.: 1144
Designer: Unknown
Height: Unknown
Colour: Unknown
Issued: 1940-1946
U.S.
Can. Extremely
U.K. Rare

K33
Golden-Crested Wren
Style One
Model No.: 1135
Designer: Unknown
Height: Unknown
Colour: Unknown
Issued: 1940-1946
U.S.
Can. Extremely
U.K. Rare

K34
Magpie
Model No.: 1151
Designer: Unknown
Height: Unknown
Colour: Unknown
Issued: 1940-1946
U.S.
Can. Extremely
U.K. Rare

K35
Jay
Model No.: 1146
Designer: Unknown
Height: 2 ¼", 5.7 cm
Colour: Brown and white
with blue wing
Issued: 1940-1946
U.S. $1,000.00
Can. $1,250.00
U.K. £ 600.00

K36
Goldfinch
Model No.: 1145
Designer: Unknown
Height: Unknown
Colour: Unknown
Issued: 1940-1946
U.S.
Can. Extremely
U.K. Rare

K37
Hare
Crouching - Style Two
Model No.: 1148
Designer: Unknown
Height: 1 ½", 3.8 cm
Colour: Brown and white;
black highlights
Issued: 1940-1977
U.S. $100.00
Can. $125.00
U.K. £ 55.00

K38
Hare
Seated, ears down
Model No.: 1150
Designer: Unknown
Height: 2 ½", 6.4 cm
Colour: Dark brown and
white
Issued: 1940-1977
U.S. $100.00
Can. $125.00
U.K. £ 55.00

K39
Hare
Seated, ears up
Model No.: 1149
Designer: Unknown
Height: 2 ¼", 5.7 cm
Colour: Light brown and
white
Issued: 1940-1977
U.S. $100.00
Can. $125.00
U.K. £ 55.00

D SERIES

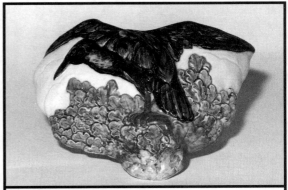

D 5772A
Owl Wall Pocket

Model No.:	Unknown
Height:	7 ½", 19.0 cm
Colour:	Brown owl, green oak leaves, cream wall pocket
Issued:	1937

Description	U.S. $	Can. $	U.K. £
Owl wall pocket	500.00	600.00	275.00

D 5772B
Crow Wall Pocket

Model No.:	Unknown
Height:	7 ¼", 18.4 cm
Colour:	Black crow, green oak leaves, cream wall pocket
Issued:	1937

Description	U.S. $	Can. $	U.K. £
Crow wall pocket	500.00	600.00	275.00

D 5913
Bulldog Draped in Union Jack

Model No.:	Unknown
Designer:	Charles Noke
Height:	Large – 6", 15.2 cm
	Medium – 4", 10.1 cm
	Small – 2 ¼", 5.7 cm
Colour:	1. Cream dog with black collar, red, white and blue Union Jack
	2. White
Issued:	Large – 1941-1961
	Medium – 1941-1961
	Small – 1941

Description	U.S. $	Can. $	U.K. £
Large	900.00	1,100.00	500.00
Medium	300.00	350.00	170.00
Small	200.00	250.00	110.00

Note:
1. All-white models exist of the medium and large sizes. An all-white model of the small size is not known.
   Large, white, sold at Phillips 6/99 for £1,200.
   Medium, white, sold at Phillips 6/99 for £950.
2. A Khaki dog with Union Jack sold at Phillips 6/99 for £1,125.

Bulldog Draped in Union Jack with Derby Hat

Model No.:	Unknown
Designer:	Charles Noke
Colour:	Cream dog, beige hat with brown band, blue spotted bow tie, brown cigar, red, white and blue Union Jack

D 6178

Height:	7 ½", 19.1 cm
Size:	Large
Issued:	1941

D 6179

Height:	5", 12.7 cm
Size:	Medium
Issued:	1941

D 6180

Height:	3", 7.6 cm
Size:	Small
Issued:	1941

Description	U.S. $	Can. $	U.K. £
Large	3,000.00	3,600.00	1,650.00
Medium	2,000.00	2,500.00	1,100.00
Small	1,250.00	1,500.00	700.00

Bulldog Draped in Union Jack With Trinity Cap

Model No.:	Unknown
Designer:	Charles Noke
Colour:	Cream dog, navy cap, red, white and blue Union Jack

D 6181

Height:	7", 17.8 cm
Size:	Large
Issued:	1941

D 6182

Height:	5", 12.7 cm
Size:	Medium
Issued:	1941

D 6183

Height:	2 ¾", 6.9 cm
Size:	Small
Issued:	1941

Description	U.S. $	Can. $	U.K. £
Large	3,000.00	3,600.00	1,650.00
Medium	2,250.00	2,750.00	1,250.00
Small	1,600.00	2,000.00	9000.00

6193
Bulldog Wearing Sailor Suit and Hat

Model No.:	Unknown
Designer:	Charles Noke
Height:	Large – 6", 15.2 cm
	Medium – 4 ¾", 12.1 cm
	Small – 2 ¾", 6.9 cm
Colour:	Cream dog, navy and white sailor's suit and hat
Issued:	1941

Description	U.S. $	Can. $	U.K. £
Large	4,000.00	4,750.00	2,200.00
Medium	3,600.00	4,300.00	2,000.00
Small	2,250.00	2.750.00	1,250.00

D 6448
Huntsman Fox

Model No.:	Unknown
Height:	4 ½", 11.4 cm
Colour:	Brown fox wearing a maroon jacket, white jodhpurs, black hat and boots
Issued:	1956-1981

Description	U.S. $	Can. $	U.K. £
Huntsman fox	175.00	200.00	100.00

D 6449
Christmas Turkey

Model No.:	Unknown
Designer:	Graham Tongue
Height:	6 ¼", 15.9 cm
Colour:	White feathers, red head
Issued:	1990-1990
Varieties:	DA 161

Description	U.S. $	Can. $	U.K. £
Christmas turkey	125.00	150.00	70.00

Note: Commissioned by Sir Bernard Matthews, Norfolk. A turkey was given to each member of his staff.

ROYAL ADDERLEY
(BIRD STUDIES)

American Blue Bird

Height:	3 ¾", 9.5 cm
Colour:	Blue, orange, brown and white
Issued:	1979-1983
U.S.	$150.00
Can.	$175.00
U.K.	£ 85.00

Baltimore Oriole
Style Five

Height:	4 ½", 11.4 cm
Colour:	Orange, black and yellow
Issued:	1979-1983
U.S.	$150.00
Can.	$175.00
U.K.	£ 85.00

Black-Headed Gouldian Finch

Height:	4", 10.1 cm
Colour:	Black, pink, yellow, green, white, black and blue
Issued:	1979-1982
Varieties:	Also called 'Red-Headed Gouldian Finch'
U.S.	$150.00
Can.	$175.00
U.K.	£ 85.00

Blue Gnatcatcher

Height:	4", 10.1 cm
Colour:	Blue, pink, black , and yellow
Issued:	1979-1982
U.S.	$150.00
Can.	$170.00
U.K.	£ 85.00

Blue Jay
Style One

Height:	4 ¾", 12.1 cm
Colour:	Blue, black, white and pink
Issued:	1979-1983
U.S.	$150.00
Can.	$175.00
U.K.	£ 85.00

Blue Tit
Style One

Height:	3 ¾", 9.5 cm
Colour:	Yellow, blue, black, white and pink
Issued:	1979-1983
Varieties:	Also called 'Chicadee, Style One'
U.S.	$150.00
Can.	$175.00
U.K.	£ 85.00

Blue Tit
Style Two

Height:	3 ¼", 9.5 cm
Colour:	Yellow, blue, black, white and pink
Issued:	1979-1983
Varieties:	Also called 'Chicadee, Style Two'
U.S.	$150.00
Can.	$175.00
U.K.	£ 85.00

Blue Tit and Young

Height:	4 ¾", 12.1 cm
Colour:	Yellow, brown, green, blue and white
Issued:	1979-1983
U.S.	$350.00
Can.	$425.00
U.K.	£200.00

Blue Tits (two)
Style One

Height:	5 ¼", 13.3 cm
Colour:	Yellow, light blue, white and pink
Issued:	1979-1983
Varieties:	Also called 'Great Tits' and 'Hudsonian Chicadees'
U.S.	$225.00
Can.	$275.00
U.K.	£125.00

Blue Tits (three)
Style Two

Height:	4 ¾", 12.1 cm
Colour:	Yellow, light blue, white and pink
Issued:	1979-1983
Varieties:	Also called 'Chicadees'
U.S.	$300.00
Can.	$360.00
U.K.	£170.00

Budgerigar
Style Two - large

Height:	5 ¼", 13.3 cm	
Size:	Large	
Colour:	Yellow, green, black and blue	
Issued:	1979-1983	
	Gloss	Matt
U.S.	$150.00	150.00
Can.	$175.00	175.00
U.K.	£ 85.00	85.00

Budgerigar
Style Two - medium

Height:	4 ¾", 12.1 cm	
Size:	Medium	
Colour:	Blue, white, black, yellow and pink	
Issued:	1979-1983	
	Gloss	Matt
U.S.	$150.00	150.00
Can.	$175.00	175.00
U.K.	£ 85.00	85.00

Budgerigars

Height:	4 ½", 11.4 cm	
Colour:	Yellow, green, blue, white and black	
Issued:	1979-1983	
	Gloss	Matt
U.S.	$225.00	225.00
Can.	$275.00	275.00
U.K.	£125.00	125.00

Canary - orange

Height:	5 ¼", 13.3 cm
Colour:	Orange, black and red
Issued:	1979-1983
Varieties:	Also called 'Canary, Yellow'
U.S.	$150.00
Can.	$175.00
U.K.	£ 85.00

Canary - yellow

Height:	5 ¼", 13.3 cm	
Colour:	Yellow, black, white and red	
Issued:	1979-1983	
Varieties:	Also called 'Canary, orange'	
	Gloss	Matt
U.S.	$150.00	150.00
Can.	$175.00	175.00
U.K.	£ 85.00	85.00

Cardinal (female)
Style Four

Colour:	Yellow face and breasts, red head and wings
Issued:	1979-1983
Varieties:	Also called 'Cardinal, male,' 'Red-Crested Cardinal' and 'Virginia Cardinal'

Large	4 ½", 11.4 cm
Medium	4", 10.1 cm
Small	3 ½", 8.9 cm

Currency	Large	Medium	Small
U.S. $	300.00	200.00	150.00
Can. $	360.00	250.00	175.00
U.K. £	170.00	110.00	85.00

Cardinal (male)
Style Five

Colour:	Red feathers with yellow highlights, yellow tail feathers, pink flower
Issued:	1979-1983
Varieties:	Also called 'Cardinal, female,' 'Red-Crested Cardinal' and 'Virginia Cardinal'

Large	5", 12.7 cm
Medium	4 ½", 11.4 cm
Small	3 ½", 8.9 cm

Currency	Large	Medium	Small
U.S. $	300.00	200.00	150.00
Can. $	360.00	250.00	175.00
U.K. £	170.00	110.00	85.00

Cardinals (Two)
Height: 5 ¼", 13.3 cm
Colour: Red and yellow, purple flowers
Issued: 1979-1983
U.S. $225.00
Can. $275.00
U.K. £125.00

Chaffinch
Style Three
Height: 4 ¼", 10.8 cm
Colour: Yellow, pink, black and white
Issued: 1979-1983
Varieties: Also called 'Coppersmith Barbet'
U.S. $150.00
Can. $175.00
U.K. £ 85.00

Chicadee
Style One - head up
Height: 3 ¾", 9.5 cm
Colour: Dark blue, white, brown, black and pink
Issued: 1979-1983
Varieties: Also called 'Blue Tit, Style One'
U.S. $150.00
Can. $175.00
U.K. £ 85.00

Chicadee
Style Two - head down
Height: 3 ½', 8.9 cm
Colour: Dark blue, white, brown, black and pink
Issued: 1979-1983
Varieties: Also called 'Blue Tit, Style Two'
U.S. $150.00
Can. $175.00
U.K. £ 85.00

Photograph not available at press time

Chicadees
Height: 4 ¾", 12.1 cm
Colour: Dark blue, white, brown, pink and yellow
Issued: 1979-1983
Varieties: Also called 'Blue Tits, Style Two'
U.S. $300.00
Can. $360.00
U.K. £170.00

Coppersmith Barbet
Height: 4 ½", 11.4 cm
Colour: Yellow, black and red
Issued: 1979-1983
Varieties: Also called 'Chaffinch, Style Three'
U.S. $150.00
Can. $175.00
U.K. £ 85.00

English Robin
Style Two
Height: 4 ½", 11.4 cm
Colour: Red and brown
Issued: 1979-1983
Varieties: Also called 'Pekin Robin'

	Gloss	Matt
U.S.	$150.00	150.00
Can.	$175.00	175.00
U.K.	£ 85.00	85.00

Goldfinch
Style Two
Height: 3 ¾", 9.5 cm
Colour: Unknown
Issued: 1979-1983
U.S. $150.00
Can. $175.00
U.K. £ 85.00

Great Tits

Height:	5 ¼", 13.3 cm
Colour:	Yellow, dark blue, black, white and pink
Issued:	1979-1983
Varieties:	Also called 'Blue Tits, Style One' and 'Hudsonian Chicadees'
U.S.	$225.00
Can.	$275.00
U.K.	£125.00

Hudsonian Chicadees

Height:	5 ¼", 13.3 cm
Colour:	Yellow, red, black and pink
Issued:	1979-1983
Varieties:	Also called 'Blue Tits, Style One' and 'Great Tits'
U.S.	$225.00
Can.	$275.00
U.K.	£125.00

Hummingbird

Height:	3 ¾", 9.5 cm
Colour:	Blue, green, black and pink
Issued:	1979-1983
U.S.	$150.00
Can.	$175.00
U.K.	£ 85.00

Mallard Landing

Height:	3 ½", 8.9 cm
Colour:	Orange, red, black, yellow and green
Issued:	1979-1983
U.S.	$150.00
Can.	$175.00
U.K.	£ 85.00

Painted Bunting

Height:	3", 7.6 cm	
Colour:	Red, green, blue, maroon and pink	
Issued:	1979-1983	
	Gloss	**Matt**
U.S.	$150.00	150.00
Can.	$175.00	175.00
U.K.	£ 85.00	85.00

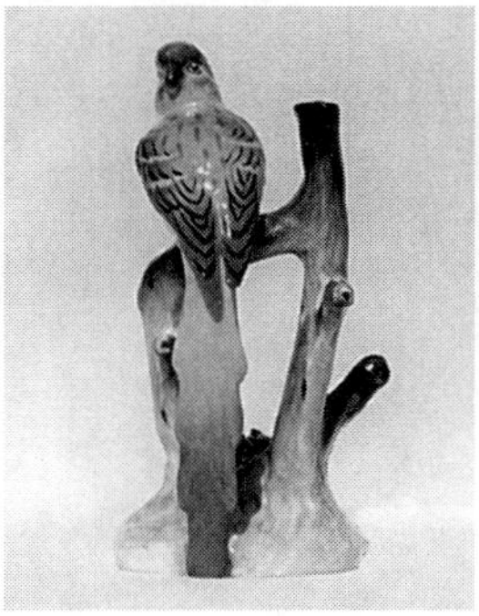

Parakeet

Height:	5", 12.7 cm
Colour:	Green, red, blue and pink
Issued:	1979-1982
U.S.	$150.00
Can.	$175.00
U.K.	£ 85.00

Parakeets

Height:	6", 15.2 cm
Colour:	Blue, green, red yellow and pink
Issued:	1979-1982
U.S.	$225.00
Can.	$275.00
U.K.	£125.00

Pekin Robin

Height:	4 ½", 11.5 cm
Colour:	Brown, red and yellow
Issued:	1979-1982
Varieties:	Also called 'English Robin, Style Two'
U.S.	$150.00
Can.	$175.00
U.K.	£ 85.00

Red Crested Cardinal

Colour:	Grey, red and black
Issued:	1979-1983
Varieties:	Also called 'Cardinal, female,' 'Cardinal, male' and 'Virginia Cardinal'

Medium

Height:	4", 10.1 cm

Small

Height:	3 1/3", 8.9 cm

Currency	Medium	Small
U.S. $	200.00	150.00
Can. $	250.00	175.00
U.K. £	110.00	85.00

Red-Headed Gouldian Finch

Height:	4", 10.1 cm
Colour:	Green, black, red, pink and yellow
Issued:	1979-1983
Varieties:	Also called 'Black-Headed Gouldian Finch'

Finish	U.S. $	Can. $	U.K. £
Gloss	150.00	175.00	85.00

Robin with Can

Height:	4", 10.1 cm
Colour:	Brown, red, green, pink, white and yellow
Issued:	1979-1983

Finish	U.S. $	Can. $	U.K. £
Gloss	300.00	360.00	170.00
Matt	300.00	360.00	170.00

Tanager

Height:	4", 10.1 cm		
Colour:	Yellow, black and red		
Issued:	1979-1983		

Finish	U.S. $	Can. $	U.K. £
Gloss	150.00	175.00	85.00

Warbler Tall

Height:	6 ½", 16.5 cm		
Colour:	Orange, yellow, blue, black and purple		
Issued:	1979-1983		

Finish	U.S. $	Can. $	U.K. £
Gloss	225.00	275.00	125.00

Virginia Cardinal

Colour:	Red, black and lilac
Issued:	1979-1982
Varieties:	Also called 'Cardinal, female,' 'Cardinal, male' and 'Red-Crested Cardinal'
Large	5", 12.7 cm
Medium	4 ½", 11.4 cm
Small	3 ½", 8.9 cm

Currency	Large	Medium	Small
U.S. $	250.00	200.00	150.00
Can. $	300.00	250.00	175.00
U.K. £	140.00	110.00	85.00

DA SERIES

DA 1
Barn Owl (Tyto Alba)
Style Two

Model No.:	Unknown
Designer:	Graham Tongue
Height:	11", 27.9 cm
Colour:	Golden feathers with dark brown markings
Issued:	1989-1996
Series:	Wildlife Collection / Connoisseur

Description	U.S. $	Can. $	U.K. £
Barn owl	1,000.00	1,250.00	550.00

DA 2
Robin on Branch

Model No.:	Unknown
Designer:	Graham Tongue
Height:	6 ¼", 15.9 cm
Colour:	Red breast, red-brown feathers with black highlights
Issued:	1989-1992
Series:	Garden Birds

Description	U.S. $	Can. $	U.K. £
Robin on branch	150.00	175.00	80.00

DA 3
Suspended Blue Tit

Model No.:	Unknown
Designer:	Martyn C. R. Alcock
Height:	5", 12.7 cm
Colour:	Yellow breast, blue feathers with black markings
Issued:	1989-1992
Series:	Garden Birds

Description	U.S. $	Can. $	U.K. £
Blue tit	150.00	175.00	80.00

DA 4
Wren
Style Two

Model No.:	Unknown
Designer:	Martyn C. R. Alcock
Height:	5 ¼", 13.3 cm
Colour:	Light brown feathers with dark brown markings
Issued:	1989-1992
Series:	Garden Birds

Description	U.S. $	Can. $	U.K. £
Wren	150.00	175.00	80.00

DA 5
Chaffinch
Style Four

Model No.:	Unknown
Designer:	Warren Platt
Height:	6", 15.2 cm
Colour:	Reddish-brown with yellow and black highlights
Issued:	1989-1992
Series:	Garden Birds

Description	U.S. $	Can. $	U.K. £
Chaffinch	150.00	175.00	80.00

DA 6
Hare
Standing - Style Two

Model No.:	Unknown
Designer:	Warren Platt
Height:	8 ½", 21.6 cm
Colour:	Golden brown hare with white highlights
Issued:	1989-1992
Series:	Wildlife Collection

Description	U.S. $	Can. $	U.K. £
Hare	175.00	200.00	100.00

DA 7
Otter

Model No.:	Unknown
Designer:	Amanda Hughes-Lubeck
Height:	9", 22.9 cm
Colour:	Black and white
Issued:	1989-1992
Series:	Wildlife Collection

Description	U.S. $	Can. $	U.K. £
Otter	200.00	250.00	110.00

DA 8
Badger
Style Two

Model No.:	Unknown
Designer:	Amanda Hughes-Lubeck
Height:	5 ½", 14.0 cm
Colour:	Black with black and white striped face
Issued:	1989-1992
Series:	Wildlife Collection

Description	U.S. $	Can. $	U.K. £
Badger	175.00	200.00	100.00

DA 9
Fox
Standing

Model No.:	Unknown
Designer:	Warren Platt
Height:	7 ½", 19.1 cm
Colour:	Brown fox with dark brown highlights, white neck and tail end
Issued:	1989-1992
Series:	Wildlife Collection

Description	U.S. $	Can. $	U.K. £
Fox, standing	200.00	250.00	110.00

DA 10
Fox with Cub

Model No.:	Unknown
Designer:	Warren Platt
Height:	6 ½", 16.5 cm
Colour:	Brown
Issued:	1989-1992
Series:	Wildlife Collection

Description	U.S. $	Can. $	U.K. £
Fox with cub	150.00	175.00	80.00

DA 11
Wood Mice

Model No.:	Unknown
Designer:	Amanda Hughes-Lubeck
Height:	7 ½", 19.1 cm
Colour:	Brown mice, cream mushroom
Issued:	1989-1992
Series:	Wildlife Collection

Description	U.S. $	Can. $	U.K. £
Wood mice	150.00	175.00	80.00

DA 12
Robin on Apple

Model No.:	Unknown
Designer:	Graham Tongue
Height:	6 ¼", 15.9 cm
Colour:	Red breast, red-brown feathers with black markings, yellow apple
Issued:	1989-1992
Series:	Garden Birds

Description	U.S. $	Can. $	U.K. £
Robin	150.00	175.00	80.00

DA 13
Blue Tit with Matches

Model No.:	Unknown
Designer:	Martyn C. R. Alcock
Height:	6 ¾", 17.2 cm
Colour:	Blue and yellow bird, brown and cream box of matches
Issued:	1989-1992
Series:	Garden Birds

Description	U.S. $	Can. $	U.K. £
Blue tit	150.00	175.00	85.00

DA 14
Arab Colt 'Xayal'

Beswick No.:	1265
Designer:	Arthur Gredington
Height:	7 ¼", 18.4 cm
Colour:	Dark brown (matt)
Issued:	1989-1990
Series:	Connoisseur Horses
Varieties:	DA 50

Description	U.S. $	Can. $	U.K. £
'Xayal'	200.00	250.00	110.00

DA 15
'Arkle'
Style One

Beswick No.:	2065
Designer:	Arthur Gredington
Height:	12", 30.5 cm
Colour:	Bay (matt)
Issued:	1989-1999
Series:	Connoisseur Horses

Description	U.S. $	Can. $	U.K. £
'Arkle'	275.00	325.00	150.00

DA 16
'Nijinsky'

Beswick No.:	2345
Designer:	Albert Hallam
Height:	11", 27.9 cm
Colour:	Bay (matt)
Issued:	1989-1999
Series:	Connoisseur Horses

Description	U.S. $	Can. $	U.K. £
'Nijinsky'	275.00	325.00	150.00

DA 17
'Black Beauty' and Foal

Beswick No.:	2466/2536
Designer:	Graham Tongue
Height:	8", 20.3 cm
Colour:	Black (Gloss or matt)
Issued:	1. Gloss – 1989-1990
	2. Matt – 1989-1999
Series:	Connoisseur Horses

Description	U.S. $	Can. $	U.K. £
1. gloss	250.00	300.00	150.00
2. Matt	200.00	250.00	110.00

Note: Gloss model available only from catalogue firm.

DA 18
'Red Rum'
Style One

Beswick No.:	2510
Designer:	Graham Tongue
Height:	12 ½", 31.7 cm
Colour:	Bay (matt)
Issued:	1989-1999
Series:	Connoisseur Horses

Description	U.S. $	Can. $	U.K. £
Style one	275.00	350.00	150.00

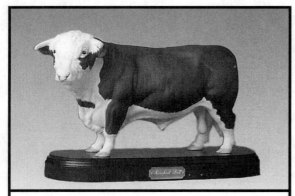

DA 19
Hereford Bull

Beswick No:	A2542
Designer:	Graham Tongue
Size:	7 ½" x 11", 19.1 x 27.9 cm
Colour:	Brown and cream (matt)
Issued:	1989-1996
Series:	Connoisseur Cattle

Description	U.S. $	Can. $	U.K. £
Hereford bull	300.00	360.00	175.00

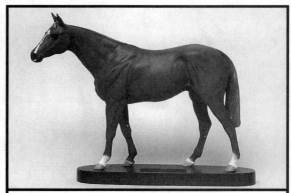

DA 20
'Grundy'

Beswick No.:	2558
Designer:	Graham Tongue
Height:	11 ¼", 28.9 cm
Colour:	Chestnut (matt)
Issued:	1989-1997
Series:	Connoisseur Horses

Description	U.S. $	Can. $	U.K. £
'Grundy'	275.00	350.00	150.00

DA 21
Polled Hereford Bull

Beswick No.:	A2574
Designer:	Graham Tongue
Height:	7 ½", 19.1 cm
Colour:	Brown and white (matt)
Issued:	1989-1996
Series:	Connoisseur Cattle

Description	U.S. $	Can. $	U.K. £
Polled Hereford bull	300.00	360.00	175.00

DA 22
Lifeguard

Beswick No.:	2562
Designer:	Graham Tongue
Height:	14 ½", 36.8 cm
Colour:	Black horse, Guardsman wears scarlet silver, white and black uniform (matt)
Issued:	1989-1996
Series:	Connoisseur Horses
Varieties:	Also called 'Blues and Royals' DA 25

Description	U.S. $	Can. $	U.K. £
Life guard	775.00	950.00	425.00

DA 23
Friesian Bull

Beswick No.:	A2580
Designer:	Graham Tongue
Size:	7" x 11 ½", 17.8 x 29.2 cm
Colour:	Black and white (matt)
Issued:	1989-1997
Series:	Connoisseur Cattle

Description	U.S. $	Can. $	U.K. £
Friesian bull	300.00	360.00	175.00

DA 24
Collie
Standing

Beswick No.:	2581
Designer:	Graham Tongue
Height:	8 ¼", 21.0 cm
Colour:	Golden brown and white (matt)
Issued:	1989-1994
Series:	Connoisseur Dogs

Description	U.S. $	Can. $	U.K. £
Collie	150.00	175.00	85.00

DA 25
Blues and Royals

Beswick No.:	2582
Designer:	Graham Tongue
Height:	14 ½", 36.8 cm
Colour:	Black horse, Guardsman wears blue, silver, white and red uniform (matt)
Issued:	1989-1996
Series:	Connoisseur Horses
Varieties:	Also called 'Lifeguard' DA 22

Description	U.S. $	Can. $	U.K. £
Blues and Royals	775.00	950.00	425.00

DA 26
Alsatian
Standing - Style One

Beswick No.:	2587
Designer:	Graham Tongue
Height:	9", 22.9 cm
Colour:	Dark and sandy brown (matt)
Issued:	1989-1994
Series:	Connoisseur Dogs

Description	U.S. $	Can. $	U.K. £
Alsatian	150.00	175.00	85.00

DA 27
Charolais Bull

Beswick No.:	A2600
Designer:	Graham Tongue
Size:	7 ½" x 12", 19.1 x 30.5 cm
Colour:	Light golden brown
Issued:	1989-1996
Series:	Connoisseur Cattle

Description	U.S. $	Can. $	U.K. £
Charolais bull	300.00	360.00	175.00

DA 28
Morgan Horse

Beswick No.:	2605	
Designer:	Graham Tongue	
Height:	11 ½", 29.2 cm	
Colour:	Black (matt)	
Issued:	1989-1996	
Series:	Connoisseur Horses	

Description	U.S. $	Can. $	U.K. £
Morgan horse	350.00	425.00	200.00

DA 29
Friesian Cow

Beswick No.:	A2607	
Designer:	Graham Tongue	
Height:	7 ½", 19.1 cm	
Colour:	Black and white (matt)	
Issued:	1989-1997	
Series:	Connoisseur Cattle	

Description	U.S. $	Can. $	U.K. £
Friesian cow	300.00	360.00	175.00

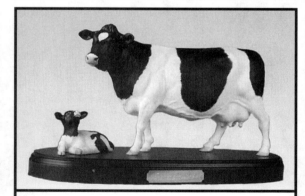

DA 30
Friesian Cow and Calf

Beswick No.:	A2607/2690	
Designer:	Graham Tongue	
Height:	7 ½", 19.1 cm	
Colour:	Black and white (matt)	
Issued:	1989-1997	
Series:	Connoisseur Cattle	

Description	U.S. $	Can. $	U.K. £
Friesian cow/calf	350.00	425.00	200.00

DA 31
'The Minstrel'

Beswick No.:	2608	
Designer:	Graham Tongue	
Height:	13 ¼", 33.5 cm	
Colour:	Chestnut (matt)	
Issued:	1989-1997	
Series:	Connoisseur Horses	

Description	U.S. $	Can. $	U.K. £
'The Minstrel'	300.00	360.00	175.00

DA 32
Majestic Stag

Beswick No.:	2629
Designer:	Graham Tongue
Height:	13 ½", 34.3 cm
Colour:	Golden brown (matt)
Issued:	1989-1996
Series:	Connoisseur

Description	U.S. $	Can. $	U.K. £
Majestic stag	350.00	425.00	200.00

DA 33
Charolais Cow and Calf

Beswick No.:	A2648/2652
Designer:	Graham Tongue
Height:	7 ¼", 18.4 cm
Colour:	Cream (matt)
Issued:	1989-1996
Series:	Connoisseur Cattle

Description	U.S. $	Can. $	U.K. £
Charolais cow/calf	350.00	425.00	200.00

DA 34
Hereford Cow and Calf

Beswick No.:	A2667\2669
Designer:	Graham Tongue
Height:	7", 17.8 cm
Colour:	Brown and white (matt)
Issued:	1989-1996
Series:	Connoisseur Cattle

Description	U.S. $	Can. $	U.K. £
Hereford cow/calf	350.00	425.00	200.00

DA 35A
'Champion'

Beswick No.:	2671
Designer:	Graham Tongue
Height:	11 ¼", 28.9 cm
Colour:	Chestnut (matt)
Issued:	1989-1996
Series:	Connoisseur Horses
Varieties:	Also called 'Moonlight' DA 35B, 'Sunburst' DA 36

Description	U.S. $	Can. $	U.K. £
'Champion'	300.00	360.00	175.00

DA 35B
'Moonlight'

Beswick No.:	2671
Designer:	Graham Tongue
Height:	11 ¼", 28.9 cm
Colour:	Grey (matt)
Issued:	1989-1996
Series:	Connoisseur Horses
Varieties:	Also called 'Champion' DA 35A, 'Sunburst' DA 36

Description	U.S. $	Can. $	U.K. £
'Moonlight'	300.00	360.00	175.00

DA 36
'Sunburst' Palomino Horse

Beswick No.:	2671
Designer:	Graham Tongue
Height:	11 ¼", 28.9 cm
Colour:	Light brown, white mane and tail (matt)
Issued:	1989-1995
Series:	Connoisseur Horses
Varieties:	Also called 'Champion' DA 35A, 'Moonlight' DA 35B

Description	U.S. $	Can. $	U.K. £
'Sunburst'	300.00	360.00	175.00

DA 37
'Troy'

Beswick No.:	2674
Designer:	Graham Tongue
Height:	11 ¾", 29.8 cm
Colour:	Bay (matt)
Issued:	1989-1997
Series:	Connoisseur Horses

Description	U.S. $	Can. $	U.K. £
'Troy'	300.00	360.00	175.00

DA 38
'Open Ground' (Pheasant)

Beswick No.:	2760
Designer:	Graham Tongue
Height:	11 ½", 29.2 cm
Colour:	Golden brown with black and red head (matt)
Issued:	1989-1994
Series:	Connoisseur

Description	U.S. $	Can. $	U.K. £
Pheasant	350.00	425.00	200.00

DA 39
'The Watering Hole' (Leopard)

Model No.:	Unknown
Designer:	Graham Tongue
Height:	6 ½", 16.5 cm
Colour:	Pale brown with dark brown spots
Issued:	1989-1994
Series:	Connoisseur

Description	U.S. $	Can. $	U.K. £
Leopard	350.00	425.00	200.00

DA 40
Peregrine Falcon

Model No.:	3140
Designer:	Graham Tongue
Height:	11", 27.9 cm
Colour:	Browns and creams
Issued:	1989-1996
Series:	Connoisseur
Varieties:	HN 3541

Description	U.S. $	Can. $	U.K. £
Peregrine falcon	225.00	275.00	125.00

DA 41
Prancing Horse (rearing horse)

Beswick No.:	1014
Designer:	Arthur Gredington
Height:	10 ¼", 26.0 cm
Colour:	1. Black (gloss and matt)
	2. Brown (gloss)
Issued:	1. 1994-1994
	2. 1989-1990

Colourways	U.S. $	Can. $	U.K. £
1. Black (gloss)	275.00	350.00	150.00
2. Black (matt)	275.00	350.00	150.00
3. Brown (gloss)	175.00	200.00	100.00

DA 42
'Bois Roussel' Race Horse

Beswick No.:	701
Designer:	Arthur Gredington
Height:	8", 20.3 cm
Colour:	See below (gloss and matt)
Issued:	1. Brown – 1989-1999
	2. Dapple grey – 1989-1995

Colourways	U.S. $	Can. $	U.K. £
1. Brown (gloss)	125.00	150.00	70.00
2. Brown (matt)	125.00	150.00	70.00
3. Dapple grey (gloss)	150.00	180.00	85.00

DA 43
Shire Mare

Beswick No.:	818
Designer:	Arthur Gredington
Height:	8 ½", 21.6 cm
Colour:	Brown with white feet (gloss and matt)
Issued:	1A. Gloss – 1989-1999
	1B. Matt – 1989-1996

Colourways	U.S. $	Can. $	U.K. £
1. Brown (gloss)	125.00	150.00	70.00
2. Brown (matt)	150.00	180.00	85.00

DA 44
Horse
Stocky, jogging mare

Beswick No.:	855
Designer:	Arthur Gredington
Height:	6", 15.2 cm
Issued:	1. Black - 1998
	2. Brown - 1989-1999

Description	U.S. $	Can. $	U.K. £
1. Black	125.00	150.00	70.00
2. Brown	125.00	150.00	70.00

Note: The black colourway was exclusive to Index Catalogue.

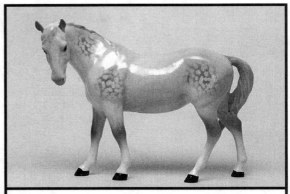

DA 45
Trotting Horse (cantering shire)

Beswick No.:	975
Designer:	Arthur Gredington
Height:	8 ¾", 22.2 cm
Colour:	Brown (gloss)
Issued:	1989-1999
Varieties:	Flambé prototype

Description	U.S. $	Can. $	U.K. £
Cantering shire	125.00	150.00	70.00

DA 46
Mare (facing left)

Beswick No.:	976
Designer:	Arthur Gredington
Height:	6 ¾", 17.2 cm
Colour:	See below (gloss and matt)
Issued:	1989 -1997

Colourways	U.S. $	Can. $	U.K. £
1. Brown (gloss)	125.00	150.00	70.00
2. Brown (matt)	125.00	150.00	70.00
3. Dapple grey (gloss)	150.00	180.00	85.00

DA 47
Shetland Pony (Woolly Shetland Mare)
Style One

Beswick No.:	1033
Designer:	Arthur Gredington
Height:	5 ¾", 14.6 cm
Colour:	Brown (gloss)
Issued:	1989-1999

Description	U.S. $	Can. $	U.K. £
Shetland pony	75.00	90.00	40.00

DA 48
Horse (Swish Tail)

Beswick No:	1182
Designer:	Arthur Gredington
Height:	8 ¾", 22.2 cm
Colour:	Brown (gloss and matt)
Issued:	1. Brown (gloss) – 1989-1999
	2. Brown (matt) – 1989-1997

Colourways	U.S. $	Can. $	U.K. £
1. Brown (gloss)	125.00	150.00	70.00
2. Brown (matt)	125.00	150.00	70.00

DA 49
Palomino Horse (prancing Arab type)

Beswick No.: 1261
Designer: Arthur Gredington
Height: 6 ¾", 17.2 cm
Colour: See below (gloss and matt)
Issued: 1. Brown (gloss), Dapple grey - 1989-1999
2. Brown (matt), Palomino - 1989-1998

Colourways	U.S. $	Can. $	U.K. £
1. Brown (gloss)	125.00	150.00	70.00
2. Brown (matt)	125.00	150.00	70.00
3. Dapple grey (gloss)	125.00	150.00	70.00
4. Palomino (gloss)	125.00	150.00	70.00

DA 50
Arab Horse 'Xayal'

Beswick No.: 1265
Designer: Arthur Gredington
Height: 6 ¼", 15.9 cm
Colour: See below (gloss)
Issued: 1. Brown − 1989-1996
2. Dapple grey, Palomino − 1989-1997
Varieties: DA 14

Colourways	U.S. $	Can. $	U.K. £
1. Brown	125.00	150.00	70.00
2. Dapple grey	150.00	180.00	85.00
3. Palomino	150.00	180.00	85.00

DA 51
Horse (head tucked, leg up)

Beswick No.: 1549
Designer: Pal Zalmen
Height: 7 ½", 19.1 cm
Colour: Brown (gloss)
Issued: 1989-1999

Description	U.S. $	Can. $	U.K. £
Head tucked, leg up	125.00	150.00	70.00

DA 52
Arab Horse

Beswick No.: 1771
Designer: Arthur Gredington
Height: 7 ½", 19.1 cm
Colour: Brown (gloss and matt)
Issued: 1989-1997

Description	U.S. $	Can. $	U.K. £
1. Gloss	125.00	150.00	70.00
2. Matt	125.00	150.00	70.00

DA 53
Thoroughbred Horse

Beswick No.:	1772A
Designer:	Arthur Gredington
Height:	8", 20.3 cm
Colour:	See below (gloss)
Issued:	1. Brown – 1989-1999
	2. Dapple grey – 1989-1998
Varieties:	Also called 'Appaloosa' DA 68

Colourways	U.S. $	Can. $	U.K. £
1. Brown	125.00	150.00	70.00
2. Dapple grey	150.00	180.00	85.00

DA 54
Mare (facing right, head down)

Beswick No.:	1812
Designer:	Arthur Gredington
Height:	5 ¾", 14.6 cm
Colour:	Brown (gloss)
Issued:	1989-1989

Description	U.S. $	Can. $	U.K. £
Mare (facing right)	125.00	150.00	75.00

DA 55
Mare (small, facing right, head up)

Beswick No.:	1991
Designer:	Arthur Gredington
Height:	5 ½", 14.0 cm
Colour:	See below (gloss and matt)
Issued:	1. Brown (gloss) – 1989-1999
	2. Other colours – 1989-1995

Colourways	U.S. $	Can. $	U.K. £
1. Brown (gloss)	100.00	125.00	55.00
2. Brown (matt)	100.00	125.00	55.00
3. Dapple grey (gloss)	125.00	150.00	70.00
4. Palomino (gloss)	125.00	150.00	70.00

DA 56
Horse (small thoroughbred stallion)

Beswick No.:	1992
Designer:	Arthur Gredington
Height:	5 ½", 14.0 cm
Colour:	See below (gloss and matt)
Issued:	1. Brown – 1989-1999
	2. Dapple grey – 1989-1998

Colourways	U.S. $	Can. $	U.K. £
1. Brown (gloss)	100.00	125.00	55.00
2. Brown (matt)	100.00	125.00	55.00
3. Dapple grey (gloss)	125.00	150.00	70.00

DA 57A
Spirit of the Wind (not on plinth)

Beswick No.: 2688
Designer: Graham Tongue
Height: 8", 20.3 cm
Colour: Brown (gloss and matt)
Issued: 1989-1996
Series: Spirited Horses

Colourways	U.S. $	Can. $	U.K. £
1. Brown (gloss)	125.00	150.00	70.00
2. Brown (matt)	125.00	150.00	70.00

DA 57B
Spirit of the Wind (on plinth)

Beswick No.: 2688
Designer: Graham Tongue
Height: 9", 22.9 cm
Colour: See below (gloss and matt)
Issued: 1. Black – 1989-1990
2. Other colours – 1989-1999
Series: Spirited Horses

Colourways	U.S. $	Can. $	U.K. £
1. Black (matt)	150.00	180.00	85.00
2. Brown (gloss)	150.00	180.00	85.00
3. Brown (matt)	150.00	180.00	85.00
4. White (matt)	125.00	150.00	70.00

DA 58A
Spirit of Freedom (not on plinth)

Beswick No.: 2689
Designer: Graham Tongue
Height: 7", 17.8 cm
Colour: Brown (gloss and matt)
Issued: 1989-1997
Series: Spirited Horses

Colourways	U.S. $	Can. $	U.K. £
1. Brown (gloss)	125.00	150.00	70.00
2. Brown (matt)	125.00	150.00	70.00

DA 58B
Spirit of Freedom (on plinth)

Beswick No.: 2689
Designer: Graham Tongue
Height: 8", 20.3 cm
Colour: See below (gloss and matt)
Issued: 1. Black – 1989-1993
2. Other colours – 1989-1999
Series: Spirited Horses

Colourways	U.S. $	Can. $	U.K. £
1. Black (matt)	150.00	180.00	85.00
2. Brown (gloss)	150.00	180.00	85.00
3. Brown (matt)	150.00	180.00	85.00
4. White (matt)	125.00	150.00	70.00

DA 59A
Spirit of Youth (not on plinth)

Beswick No.:	2703
Designer:	Graham Tongue
Height:	7", 17.8 cm
Colour:	Brown (gloss and matt)
Issued:	1989-1996
Series:	Spirited Horses

Colourways	U.S. $	Can. $	U.K. £
1. Brown (gloss)	125.00	150.00	70.00
2. Brown (matt)	125.00	150.00	70.00

DA 59B
Spirit of Youth (on wooden plinth)

Beswick No.:	2703
Designer:	Graham Tongue
Height:	8", 20.3 cm
Colour:	See below (matt)
Issued:	See below
Series:	Spirited Horses

Colourways	U.S. $	Can. $	U.K. £
1. Black (matt) 1989-1993	150.00	180.00	85.00
2. Brown (gloss) 1989-1999	150.00	180.00	85.00
3. Brown (matt) 1989-1996	150.00	180.00	85.00
4. White (matt) 1989-1995	125.00	150.00	70.00

DA 60A
Spirit of Fire (not on plinth)

Beswick No.:	2829
Designer:	Graham Tongue
Height:	8", 20.3 cm
Colour:	See below (gloss and matt)
Issued:	1989-1994
Varieties:	Spirited Horses

Colourways	U.S. $	Can. $	U.K. £
1. Brown (gloss)	125.00	150.00	70.00
2. Brown (matt)	125.00	150.00	70.00

DA 60B
Spirit of Fire (on plinth)

Beswick No.:	2829
Designer:	Graham Tongue
Height:	9", 22.9 cm
Colour:	See below (matt)
Issued:	See below
Series:	Spirited Horses

Colourways	U.S. $	Can. $	U.K. £
1. Black (matt) 1989-1994	125.00	150.00	70.00
2. Brown (matt) 1989-1994	125.00	150.00	70.00
3. White (matt) 1989-1993	125.00	150.00	70.00

DA 61A
Spirit of Earth (not on plinth)

Beswick No.:	2914
Designer:	Graham Tongue
Height:	7 ½", 19.1 cm
Colour:	Brown (gloss and matt)
Issued:	1989-1993

Colourways	U.S. $	Can. $	U.K. £
1. Brown (gloss)	150.00	180.00	85.00
2. Brown (matt)	150.00	180.00	85.00

DA 61B
Spirit of Earth (on plinth)

Beswick No.:	2914
Designer:	Graham Tongue
Height:	8 ½", 21.6 cm
Colour:	See below (matt)
Issued:	1989-1993
Series:	Spirited Horses

Colourways	U.S. $	Can. $	U.K. £
1. Black	175.00	200.00	100.00
2. Brown	175.00	200.00	100.00
3. White	175.00	200.00	100.00

DA 62A
Shire Horse (not on plinth)
Style One

Beswick No.:	2578
Designer:	Alan Maslankowski
Height:	8 ¼", 21.0 cm
Colour:	Brown (matt)
Issued:	1989 -1997
Series:	Connoisseur Horses

Colourways	U.S. $	Can. $	U.K. £
Brown	250.00	300.00	150.00

DA 62B
Shire Horse (on wooden plinth)
Style One

Beswick No.:	2578
Designer:	Alan Maslankowski
Height:	8 ¾", 22.2 cm
Colour:	Brown (matt)
Issued:	1994-1996
Series:	Connoisseur Horses

Colourways	U.S. $	Can. $	U.K. £
Brown	275.00	325.00	150.00

DA 63A
Spirit of Peace (not on plinth)

Beswick No.:	2916	
Designer:	Graham Tongue	
Height:	4 ¾", 12.1 cm	
Colour:	Brown (matt)	
Issued:	1989-1997	

Colourways	U.S. $	Can. $	U.K. £
Brown	125.00	150.00	70.00

DA 63B
Spirit of Peace (on wooden plinth)

Beswick No.:	2916	
Designer:	Graham Tongue	
Height:	5 ¾", 14.6 cm	
Colour:	See below (matt)	
Issued:	1989 -1997	
Series:	Spirited Horses	

Colourways	U.S. $	Can. $	U.K. £
1. Brown	150.00	180.00	85.00
2. White	150.00	180.00	85.00

DA 64A
Spirit of Affection (not on plinth)

Beswick No.:	H2689/2536	
Designer:	Graham Tongue	
Height:	7", 17.8 cm	
Colour:	White (matt)	
Issued:	1989-1996	
Series:	Spirited Horses	

Colourways	U.S. $	Can. $	U.K. £
White	150.00	180.00	85.00

DA 64B
Spirit of Affection (on wooden plinth)

Beswick No.:	H2689/2536	
Designer:	Graham Tongue	
Height:	8", 20.3 cm	
Colour:	See below (matt)	
Issued:	1. Brown –1989-1996	
	2. White – 1989-1999	
Series:	Spirited Horses	

Colourways	U.S. $	Can. $	U.K. £
1. Brown	175.00	200.00	100.00
2. White	175.00	200.00	100.00

DA 65
'Black Beauty'

Beswick No.:	2466		
Designer:	Graham Tongue		
Height:	7", 17.8 cm		
Colour:	Black (matt)		
Issued:	1989-1999		

Description	U.S. $	Can. $	U.K. £
'Black Beauty'	125.00	150.00	70.00

DA 66
'Black Beauty' as a Foal

Beswick No.:	2536		
Designer:	Graham Tongue		
Height:	5 ¾", 14.6 cm		
Colour:	Black (matt)		
Issued:	1989-1999		

Description	U.S. $	Can. $	U.K. £
'Black Beauty' as Foal	75.00	90.00	40.00

DA 67
Pinto Pony

Beswick No.:	1373		
Designer:	Arthur Gredington		
Height:	6 ½", 16.5 cm		
Colour:	See below (gloss and matt)		
Issued:	1989-1990		

Colourways	U.S. $	Can. $	U.K. £
1. Piebald (gloss)	150.00	180.00	85.00
2. Piebald (matt)	150.00	180.00	85.00
3. Skewbald (gloss)	150.00	180.00	85.00
4. Skewbald (matt)	150.00	180.00	85.00

DA 68
Appaloosa

Beswick No.:	1772B		
Designer:	Arthur Gredington		
Height:	8", 20.3 cm		
Colour:	Black and white (gloss)		
Issued:	1989-1996		
Varieties:	Also called 'Thoroughbred Horse' DA 53		

Colourways	U.S. $	Can. $	U.K. £
Black and white	150.00	180.00	85.00

DA 69A
Springtime (not on plinth)

Beswick No.:	2837
Designer:	Graham Tongue
Height:	4 ½", 11.4 cm
Colour:	Brown (gloss)
Issued:	1989-1999
Series:	Spirited Foals

Colourways	U.S. $	Can. $	U.K. £
Brown	75.00	90.00	40.00

Note: Beswick model illustrated.

DA 69B
Springtime (on wooden plinth)

Beswick No.:	2837
Designer:	Graham Tongue
Height:	5 ½", 14.0 cm
Colour:	See below (matt)
Issued:	1989-1999
Series:	Spirited Foals

Colourways	U.S. $	Can. $	U.K. £
1. Brown	75.00	90.00	40.00
2. White	75.00	90.00	40.00

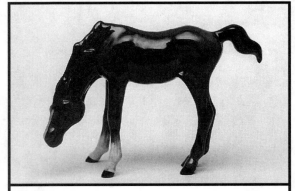

DA 70A
Young Spirit (not on plinth)

Beswick No.:	2839
Designer:	Graham Tongue
Height:	3 ½", 8.9 cm
Colour:	Brown (gloss)
Issued:	1989-1993
Series:	Spirited Foals

Colourways	U.S. $	Can. $	U.K. £
Brown	75.00	90.00	40.00

DA 70B
Young Spirit (on wooden plinth)

Beswick No.:	2839
Designer:	Graham Tongue
Height:	4 ¼", 10.7 cm
Colour:	See below (matt)
Issued:	1. Black – 1989-1996
	2. Brown and white – 1989-1995
Series:	Spirited Foals

Colourways	U.S. $	Can. $	U.K. £
1. Black	75.00	90.00	40.00
2. Brown	75.00	90.00	40.00
3. White	75.00	90.00	40.00

DA 71A
Sunlight (not on plinth)

Beswick No.:	2875
Designer:	Graham Tongue
Height:	3 ½", 8.9 cm
Colour:	Brown (gloss)
Issued:	1989-1996
Series:	Spirited Foals

Colourways	U.S. $	Can. $	U.K. £
Brown	75.00	90.00	40.00

DA 71B
Sunlight (on wooden plinth)

Beswick No.:	2875
Designer:	Graham Tongue
Height:	4 ¼", 10.7 cm
Colour:	See below (matt)
Issued:	1989-1996
Series:	Spirited Foals

Colourways		U.S. $	Can. $	U.K. £
1.	Black	75.00	90.00	40.00
2.	Brown	75.00	90.00	40.00
3.	White	75.00	90.00	40.00

DA 72A
Adventure (not on plinth)

Beswick No.:	2876
Designer:	Graham Tongue
Height:	4 ½", 11.4 cm
Colour:	Brown (gloss)
Issued:	1989-1997
Series:	Spirited Foals

Colourways	U.S. $	Can. $	U.K. £
Brown	75.00	90.00	40.00

DA 72B
Adventure (on plinth)

Beswick No.:	2876
Designer:	Graham Tongue
Height:	5 ½", 14.0 cm
Colour:	See below (matt)
Issued:	1989-1997
Series:	Spirited Foals

Colourways		U.S. $	Can. $	U.K. £
1.	Brown	75.00	90.00	40.00
2.	White	75.00	90.00	40.00

DA 73
Spirit of Nature (on wooden plinth)

Beswick No.:	2935
Designer:	Graham Tongue
Height:	6 ¼", 15.9 cm
Colour:	Brown (matt)
Issued:	1989-1996
Series:	Spirited Horses

Colourways	U.S. $	Can. $	U.K. £
Brown	125.00	150.00	70.00

Note: Beswick model illustrated.

DA 74
Foal (small, stretched, facing right)

Beswick No:	815
Designer:	Arthur Gredington
Height:	3 ¼", 8.3 cm
Colour:	See below
Issued:	1. Brown (gloss) – 1989-1999
	2. Brown (matt) – 1989-1996
	3. Dapple grey – 1989-1995

Colourways	U.S. $	Can. $	U.K. £
1. Brown (gloss)	50.00	60.00	30.00
2. Brown (matt)	50.00	60.00	30.00
3. Dapple grey (gloss)	60.00	75.00	35.00

DA 75
Foal (lying)

Beswick No:	915
Designer:	Arthur Gredington
Height:	3 ¼", 8.3 cm
Colour:	See below (gloss and matt)
Issued:	1. Brown (gloss) – 1989-1999
	2. Brown (matt) – 1989-1996
	3. Dapple grey – 1989-1995

Colourways	U.S. $	Can. $	U.K. £
1. Brown (gloss)	50.00	60.00	30.00
2. Brown (matt)	55.00	65.00	30.00
3. Dapple grey (gloss)	65.00	80.00	35.00

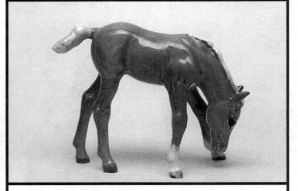

DA 76
Foal (grazing)

Beswick No.:	946
Designer:	Arthur Gredington
Height:	3 ¼", 8.3 cm
Colour:	See below (gloss and matt)
Issued:	1. Brown (gloss) – 1989-1999
	2. Other colours – 1989-1996

Colourways	U.S. $	Can. $	U.K. £
1. Brown (gloss)	50.00	60.00	30.00
2. Brown (matt)	55.00	65.00	30.00
3. Dapple grey (gloss)	65.00	80.00	35.00
4. Palomino (gloss)	60.00	75.00	35.00

DA 77
Foal (large, head down)

Beswick No.:	947
Designer:	Arthur Gredington
Height:	4 ½", 11.4 cm
Colour:	Brown (gloss and matt)
Issued:	1. Brown (gloss) −1989-1999
	2. Brown (matt) − 1989-1996

Colourways	U.S. $	Can. $	U.K. £
1. Brown (gloss)	60.00	75.00	35.00
2. Brown (matt)	60.00	75.00	35.00

DA 78
Foal (small, stretched, facing left)

Beswick No.:	997
Designer:	Arthur Gredington
Height:	3 ¼", 8.3 cm
Colour:	See below

Colourways	U.S. $	Can. $	U.K. £
1. Black (gloss) 1995-1997	60.00	75.00	35.00
2. Brown (gloss) 1989-1999	40.00	50.00	20.00
3. Brown (matt) 1989-1996	55.00	65.00	30.00
4. Grey (gloss) 1989-1997	60.00	75.00	35.00

DA 79
Shetland Foal

Beswick No.:	1034
Designer:	Arthur Gredington
Height:	3 ¾", 9.5 cm
Colour:	Brown (gloss and matt)
Issued:	1. Brown (gloss) − 1989-1999
	2. Brown (matt) − 1989-1996

Colourways	U.S. $	Can. $	U.K. £
1. Brown (gloss)	50.00	60.00	25.00
2. Brown (matt)	65.00	80.00	35.00

DA 80
Foal (Arab type)

Beswick No.:	1407
Designer:	Arthur Gredington
Height:	4 ½", 11.4 cm
Colour:	1. Brown, Dapple grey (gloss) - 1989-1999
	2. Brown (matt) - 1989-1996
	3. Palomino (gloss) - 1989-1995

Colourways	U.S. $	Can. $	U.K. £
1. Brown (gloss)	50.00	60.00	25.00
2. Brown (matt)	65.00	80.00	35.00
3. Dapple grey (gloss)	85.00	100.00	50.00
4. Palomino (gloss)	70.00	85.00	40.00

DA 81
Foal (larger, thoroughbred type)

Beswick No.: 1813
Designer: Arthur Gredington
Height: 4 ½", 11.4 cm
Colour: Brown (gloss and matt)
Issued: 1. Brown (gloss) − 1989-1999
2. Brown (matt) − 1989-1995

Colourways	U.S. $	Can. $	U.K. £
1. Brown (gloss)	60.00	75.00	35.00
2. Brown (matt)	60.00	75.00	35.00

DA 82
Foal (smaller thoroughbred type, facing left)

Beswick No.: 1816
Designer: Arthur Gredington
Height: 3 ½", 8.9 cm
Colour: See below
Issued: 1. Brown (gloss) − 1989-1999
2. Brown (matt) − 1989-1996
3. Palomino (gloss) − 1989-1996

Colourways	U.S. $	Can. $	U.K. £
1. Brown (gloss)	50.00	60.00	25.00
2. Brown (matt)	50.00	60.00	25.00
3. Palomino (gloss)	65.00	80.00	35.00

DA 83
Siamese Cat
Seated - Style Two

Beswick No.: 2139
Designer: Mr. Garbet
Height: 13 ¾", 34.9 cm
Colour: Cream and black (gloss)
Issued: 1989-1996
Series: Fireside Models

Description	U.S. $	Can. $	U.K. £
Siamese cat	150.00	175.00	90.00

DA 84
Old English Sheepdog
Seated

Beswick No.: 2232
Designer: Albert Hallam
Height: 11 ½", 29.2 cm
Colour: Grey and white (gloss)
Issued: 1989-1994
Series: Fireside Models

Description	U.S. $	Can. $	U.K. £
Old English Sheepdog	275.00	325.00	150.00

DA 85
Dalmatian

Beswick No.:	2271
Designer:	Graham Tongue
Height:	13 ¾", 34.9 cm
Colour:	White with black spots (gloss)
Issued:	1989-1996
Series:	Fireside Models

Description	U.S. $	Can. $	U.K. £
Dalmatian	350.00	425.00	200.00

DA 86
Labrador (seated)

Beswick No.:	2314
Designer:	Graham Tongue
Height:	13 ¼", 33.6 cm
Colour:	See below (gloss)
Issued:	1989-1996
Series:	Fireside Models
Varieties:	'Black Labrador' HN 86B

Colourways	U.S. $	Can. $	U.K. £
1. Black	275.00	325.00	150.00
2. Golden	275.00	325.00	150.00

DA 87
Yorkshire Terrier
Seated - Style One

Beswick No.:	2377
Designer:	Graham Tongue
Height:	10 ¼", 26.0 cm
Colour:	Dark and light brown (gloss)
Issued:	1989-1994
Series:	Fireside Models

Description	U.S. $	Can. $	U.K. £
Yorkshire terrier	325.00	400.00	175.00

DA 88
Alsatian
Seated - Style Two

Beswick No.:	2410
Designer:	Graham Tongue
Height:	14", 35.5 cm
Colour:	Dark and sandy brown (gloss)
Issued:	1989-1996
Series:	Fireside Models

Description	U.S. $	Can. $	U.K. £
Alsatian	300.00	360.00	165.00

OLD ENGLISH DOGS (left and right facing pairs)

Colour: White and gold (gloss)
Series: Traditional Staffordshire dogs

	DA 89 - 90	DA 91 - 92	DA 93 - 94	DA 95 - 96	DA 97 - 98
Beswick No.:	M1378 / 3	M1378 / 4	M1378 / 5	M1378 / 6	M1378 / 7
Height:	10", 25.4 cm	9", 22.9 cm	7 ½", 19.1 cm	5 ½", 14.0 cm	3 ½", 8.9 cm
Issued:	1989-1997	1989-1999	1989-1997	1989-1999	1989-1999
Currency	DA 89 - 90	DA91 - 92	DA 93 - 94	DA 95 - 96	DA 97 - 98
U.S. $	110.00	90.00	65.00	55.00	35.00
Can. $	135.00	110.00	80.00	65.00	40.00
U.K. £	60.00	50.00	35.00	30.00	20.00

DA 99
Rottweiler

Beswick No.:	3056
Designer:	Alan Maslankowski
Height:	5 ¼", 13.3 cm
Colour:	Brown and black (gloss and matt)
Issued:	1. Gloss –1990-1999
	2. Matt – 1990-1996

Description	U.S. $	Can. $	U.K. £
1. Gloss	100.00	125.00	60.00
2. Matt	100.00	125.00	60.00

DA 100
Old English Sheepdog
Standing

Beswick No.:	3058
Designer:	Warren Platt
Height:	5 ½", 14.0 cm
Colour:	Grey and white
Issued:	1. Gloss – 1990-1999
	2. Matt – 1990-1995

Description	U.S. $	Can. $	U.K. £
1. Gloss	100.00	125.00	60.00
2. Matt	125.00	150.00	70.00

DA 101
Staffordshire Bull Terrier - Style Two

Beswick No.:	3060
Designer:	Alan Maslankowski
Height:	4", 10.1 cm
Colour:	1. Brindle – 1990-1996
	2. White/tan (gloss) – 1990-1995
	3. White/tan (matt) –1990-1997

Colourways	U.S. $	Can. $	U.K. £
1. Brindle (gloss)	125.00	150.00	70.00
2. Brindle (matt)	125.00	150.00	70.00
3. White/tan (gloss)	125.00	150.00	70.00
4. White/tan (matt)	125.00	150.00	70.00

DA 102
Afghan Hound

Beswick No.:	3070
Designer:	Alan Maslankowski
Height:	5 ½", 14.0 cm
Colour:	Light brown and cream (gloss and matt)
Issued:	1990-1996

Description	U.S. $	Can. $	U.K. £
1. Gloss	125.00	150.00	70.00
2. Matt	125.00	150.00	70.00

DA 103
Alsatian
Standing - Style Two

Beswick No.: 3073
Designer: Alan Maslankowski
Height: 5 ¾", 14.6 cm
Colour: Dark and light brown
Issued: 1. Gloss – 1990-1999
2. Matt – 1990-1996

Description	U.S. $	Can. $	U.K. £
1. Gloss	60.00	75.00	35.00
2. Matt	75.00	90.00	40.00

DA 104
Boxer

Beswick No.: 3081
Designer: Alan Maslankowski
Height: 5 ½", 14.0 cm
Colour: Golden brown and white
Issued: 1. Gloss – 1990-1999
2. Matt – 1990-1995

Description	U.S. $	Can. $	U.K. £
1. Gloss	75.00	90.00	40.00
2. Matt	100.00	125.00	55.00

DA 105
Doberman

Beswick No.: 3121
Designer: Alan Maslankowski
Height: 5 ¼", 13.3 cm
Colour: Dark brown
Issued: 1990-1996

Description	U.S. $	Can. $	U.K. £
1. Gloss	100.00	125.00	55.00
2. Matt	100.00	125.00	55.00

DA 106
Rough Collie

Beswick No.: 3129
Designer: Warren Platt
Height: 5 ½", 14.0 cm
Colour: Golden brown and white
Issued: 1. Gloss –1990-1995
2. Matt –1990-1996

Description	U.S. $	Can. $	U.K. £
1. Gloss	100.00	125.00	55.00
2. Matt	100.00	125.00	55.00

DA 107
Springer Spaniel

Beswick No.:	3135
Designer:	Amanda Hughes-Lubeck
Height:	5", 12.7 cm
Colour:	Dark brown and white
Issued:	1. Gloss – 1990-1999
	2. Matt – 1990-1996

Description	U.S. $	Can. $	U.K. £
1. Gloss	100.00	125.00	55.00
2. Matt	100.00	125.00	55.00

DA 108
The Spaniel (on ceramic plinth)

Beswick No.:	2980
Designer:	Alan Maslankowski
Height:	8 ¼", 21.0 cm
Colour:	See below (matt)
Issued:	1990-1995
Series:	Spirited Dogs

Colourways	U.S. $	Can. $	U.K. £
1. Black/white	200.00	250.00	110.00
2. Golden	200.00	250.00	110.00
3. Liver/white	200.00	250.00	110.00

DA 109
The Setter (on ceramic plinth)

Beswick No.:	2986
Designer:	Graham Tongue
Height:	8 ½", 21.6 cm
Colour:	See below (matt)
Issued:	1990-1995
Series:	Spirited Dogs

Description	U.S. $	Can. $	U.K. £
1. English Setter	200.00	250.00	110.00
2. Gordon Setter	200.00	250.00	110.00
3. Red Setter	200.00	250.00	110.00

DA 110
The Pointer (on ceramic plinth)
Style Two

Beswick No.:	3011
Designer:	Graham Tongue
Height:	8 ½", 21.6 cm
Colour:	White with dark brown patches (matt)
Issued:	1990-1995
Series:	Spirited Dogs

Description	U.S. $	Can. $	U.K. £
Pointer	175.00	200.00	100.00

DA 111
The Labrador (on ceramic plinth)
Standing - Style One
Beswick No.:   3062A
Designer: Alan Maslankowski
Height: 7 ½", 19.1 cm
Colour: See below (matt)
Issued: 1990-1995
Series: Spirited Dogs

Colourways	U.S. $	Can. $	U.K. £
1. Black	150.00	175.00	85.00
2. Golden	150.00	175.00	85.00

DA 112
The Retriever (on ceramic plinth)
Beswick No.:   3066
Designer: Graham Tongue
Height: 7 ½", 19.1 cm
Colour: Golden brown (matt)
Issued: 1990-1995
Series: Spirited Dogs

Colourways	U.S. $	Can. $	U.K. £
Golden brown	175.00	200.00	100.00

DA 113
Pekinese
Begging
Beswick No.:   2982
Designer: Alan Maslankowski
Height: 5 ½", 14.0 cm
Colour: Cream (gloss and matt)
Issued: 1990-1995
Series: Good Companions

Description	U.S. $	Can. $	U.K. £
1. Gloss	75.00	90.00	40.00
2. Matt	75.00	90.00	40.00

DA 114
Norfolk Terrier
Beswick No.:   2984
Designer: Alan Maslankowski
Height: 4", 10.1 cm
Colour: Dark brown (gloss and matt)
Issued: 1990-1995
Series: Good Companions

Description	U.S. $	Can. $	U.K. £
1. Gloss	65.00	80.00	35.00
2. Matt	65.00	80.00	35.00

DA 115
Poodle on Blue Cushion
Beswick No.: 2985
Designer: Alan Maslankowski
Height: 5", 12.7 cm
Colour: White poodle, blue cushion (gloss and matt)
Issued: 1990-1995
Series: Good Companions

Description	U.S. $	Can. $	U.K. £
1. Gloss	125.00	150.00	65.00
2. Matt	125.00	150.00	65.00

DA 116
Dachshund
Standing - Style Four
Beswick No.: 3013
Designer: Alan Maslankowski
Height: 4 ½", 11.4 cm
Colour: See below (gloss and matt)
Issued: 1990-1995
Series: Good Companions

Colourways	U.S. $	Can. $	U.K. £
1. Black/tan (gloss)	65.00	80.00	35.00
2. Black/tan (matt)	65.00	80.00	35.00
3. Tan (gloss)	65.00	80.00	35.00

DA 117
Shetland Sheepdog
Beswick No.: 3080
Designer: Alan Maslankowski
Height: 5", 12.7 cm
Colour: Golden brown and white (gloss and matt)
Issued: 1990-1995
Series: Good Companions

Description	U.S. $	Can. $	U.K. £
1. Gloss	75.00	90.00	40.00
2. Matt	75.00	90.00	40.00

DA 118
Cairn Terrier
Standing
Beswick No.: 3082
Designer: Warren Platt
Height: 4 ½", 11.4 cm
Colour: Light brown (gloss and matt)
Issued: 1990-1995
Series: Good Companions

Description	U.S. $	Can. $	U.K. £
1. Gloss	75.00	90.00	40.00
2. Matt	75.00	90.00	40.00

DA 119
Yorkshire Terrier
Seated - Style Two

Beswick No.:   3083
Designer: Warren Platt
Height: 5", 12.7 cm
Colour: Light brown and cream (gloss and matt)
Issued: 1990-1995
Series: Good Companions

Description	U.S. $	Can. $	U.K. £
1. Gloss	75.00	90.00	40.00
2. Matt	75.00	90.00	40.00

DA 120
West Highland Terrier
Style Two

Beswick No.:   3149
Designer: Martyn C. R. Alcock
Height: 5", 12.7 cm
Colour: White (gloss and matt)
Issued: 1990-1995
Series: Good Companions

Description	U.S. $	Can. $	U.K. £
1. Gloss	75.00	90.00	40.00
2. Matt	75.00	90.00	40.00

DA 121
Cavalier King Charles Spaniel - Style Two

Beswick No.:   3155
Designer: Warren Platt
Height: 5", 12.7 cm
Colour: See below (gloss and matt)
Issued: 1990-1995
Series: Good Companions

Colourways	U.S. $	Can. $	U.K. £
1. Black/tan/white (gloss)	75.00	90.00	40.00
2. Black/tan/white (matt)	75.00	90.00	40.00
3. Tan/white (gloss)	75.00	90.00	40.00

DA 122
Siamese Kittens

Beswick No.:   1296
Designer: Miss Granoska
Height: 2 ¾", 7.0 cm
Colour: Cream and black (gloss)
Issued: 1990-1999

Colourways	U.S. $	Can. $	U.K. £
Cream / black	50.00	60.00	25.00

Note: Flambé prototype exists.

DA 123
Kitten

Beswick No.:	1436
Designer:	Colin Melbourne
Height:	3 ¼", 8.3 cm
Colour:	See below (gloss)
Issued:	1990-1999

Colourways	U.S. $	Can. $	U.K. £
1. Ginger	30.00	35.00	15.00
2. Grey	30.00	35.00	15.00
3. White	30.00	35.00	15.00

DA 124
Siamese Cat
Lying - Style Two

Beswick No.:	1558B
Designer:	Pal Zalmen
Remodelled:	Albert Hallam
Length:	7 ¼", 18.4 cm
Colour:	Cream and black (gloss)
Issued:	1990-1999

Description	U.S. $	Can. $	U.K. £
Gloss	45.00	55.00	25.00

DA 125
Siamese Cat
Lying - Style Three

Beswick No.:	1559B
Designer:	Pal Zalmen
Remodelled:	Albert Hallam
Length:	7 ¼", 18.4 cm
Colour:	Cream and black (gloss)
Issued:	1990-1999

Colourways	U.S. $	Can. $	U.K. £
Cream / black	45.00	55.00	25.00

DA 126
Persian Cat
Seated - Style Two

Beswick No.:	1867
Designer:	Albert Hallam
Height:	6 ¼", 15.9 cm
Colour:	See below (gloss)
Issued:	See below

Colourways	U.S. $	Can. $	U.K. £
1. Ginger 1990-1996	100.00	125.00	55.00
2. Grey 1990-1999	100.00	125.00	55.00
3. White 1990-1996	100.00	125.00	55.00

DA 127
Siamese Cat
Seated - Style Three

Beswick No.:	1882	
Designer:	Albert Hallam	
Height:	9", 22.9 cm	
Size:	Large	
Colour:	Cream and black (gloss)	
Issued:	1990-1999	

Description	U.S. $	Can. $	U.K. £
Gloss	100.00	125.00	55.00

DA 128
Persian Kitten
Style Two

Beswick No.:	1886
Designer:	Albert Hallam
Height:	4", 10.1 cm
Colour:	See below (gloss)
Issued:	1990-1999

Colourways	U.S. $	Can. $	U.K. £
1. Ginger	40.00	50.00	20.00
2. Grey	40.00	50.00	20.00
3. White	40.00	50.00	20.00

DA 129
Siamese Cat
Seated - Style Four

Beswick No.:	1887
Designer:	Albert Hallam
Height:	4", 10.1 cm
Size:	Small
Colour:	Cream and black (gloss)
Issued:	1990-1999

Description	U.S. $	Can. $	U.K. £
Gloss	40.00	50.00	20.00

DA 130
Siamese Cat
Standing - Style Two

Beswick No.:	1897
Designer:	Albert Hallam
Height:	6 ½", 16.5 cm
Colour:	Cream and black (gloss)
Issued:	1990-1997

Description	U.S. $	Can. $	U.K. £
Gloss	55.00	65.00	30.00

DA 131
Black Cat

Beswick No.:	1897
Designer:	Albert Hallam
Height:	6 ½", 16.5 cm
Colour:	Black (gloss)
Issued:	1990-1994

Description	U.S. $	Can. $	U.K. £
Gloss	110.00	130.00	60.00

DA 132
Persian Cat
Standing

Beswick No.:	1898
Designer:	Albert Hallam
Height:	5", 12.7 cm
Colour:	See below (gloss)
Issued:	1990-1994

Colourways	U.S. $	Can. $	U.K. £
1. Ginger	60.00	75.00	30.00
2. Grey	60.00	75.00	30.00
3. White	60.00	75.00	30.00

*

DA 134
Desert Orchid
Style One

Model No.:	Unknown
Designer:	Graham Tongue
Height:	12" x 14", 30.5 x 35.5 cm
Colour:	Light grey
Issued:	1990 in a limited edition of 7,500

Description	U.S. $	Can. $	U.K. £
1. Ceramic base	725.00	875.00	400.00
2. Wooden base	725.00	875.00	400.00

*

DA 137
The Barn Owl
Style Three

Model No.:	Unknown
Designer:	Amanda Hughes-Lubeck
Height:	7 ½", 19.1 cm
Colour:	Browns and cream
Issued:	1990-1992
Series:	Wildlife Collection

Description	U.S. $	Can. $	U.K. £
Barn owl	175.00	200.00	100.00

DA 138
Kingfisher (on plinth)
Style Three

Model No.:	Unknown
Designer:	Warren Platt
Height:	8 ¾", 22.2 cm
Colour:	Blue and orange-red, cream and brown
Issued:	1990-1992
Series:	Nature Sculptures

Description	U.S. $	Can. $	U.K. £
Kingfisher	175.00	200.00	100.00

DA 139
Osprey (on plinth)

Model No.:	Unknown
Height:	7 ¾", 19.7 cm
Colour:	Browns and white
Issued:	1990-1992
Series:	Wildlife Collection

Description	U.S. $	Can. $	U.K. £
Osprey	175.00	200.00	100.00

*

DA 141
Cocker Spaniel
Seated - Style Two

Model No.:	Unknown
Designer:	Martyn C. R. Alcock
Height:	4 ¼", 10.8 cm
Colour:	See below (gloss and matt)
Issued:	1. Golden – 1990-1995
	2. Liver/white – 1990-1997

Colourways	U.S. $	Can. $	U.K. £
1. Golden	100.00	125.00	55.00
2. Liver/white	100.00	125.00	55.00

DA 142
Golden Retriever

Model No.:	D 142
Designer:	Amanda Hughes-Lubeck
Height:	5", 12.7 cm
Colour:	Golden brown (gloss and matt)
Issued:	1. Gloss – 1990-1999
	2. Matt – 1990-1997

Description	U.S. $	Can. $	U.K. £
1. Gloss	80.00	100.00	45.00
2. Matt	80.00	100.00	45.00

DA 143
Border Collie

Designer:	Amanda Hughes-Lubeck
Height:	4", 10.1 cm
Colour:	See below (gloss and matt)
Issued:	1. Black/white (gloss) – 1990-1999
	2. Black/white (matt) – 1990-1995
	3. Tan/black/white – 1990-1995

Colourways	U.S. $	Can. $	U.K. £
1. Black/white (gloss)	125.00	150.00	70.00
2. Black/white (matt)	125.00	150.00	70.00
3. Tan/black/white	125.00	150.00	70.00

DA 144
Kestrel (on plinth)
Style One

Model No.:	Unknown
Designer:	Graham Tongue
Height:	12 ¼", 31.1 cm
Colour:	Golden brown bird with black markings, pink bone china flowers
Issued:	1991 in a limited edition of 950
Series:	Artist's Signature Edition/Wildlife

Description	U.S. $	Can. $	U.K. £
Kestral	1,000.00	1,250.00	600.00

DA 145
Labrador, Standing - Style Two

Model No.:	D 145
Designer:	Warren Platt
Height:	5", 12.7 cm
Colour:	See below (gloss and matt)
Issued:	1. Black –1990-1999
	2. Chocolate – 1990-1996
	3. Golden – 1990-1999

Colourways	U.S. $	Can. $	U.K. £
1. Black	100.00	125.00	55.00
2. Chocolate	110.00	135.00	60.00
3. Golden	125.00	150.00	70.00

DA 148
Cat
Walking

Designer:	Alan Maslankowski
Height:	5 ½", 14.0 cm
Colour:	See below (gloss)
Issued:	1. Black with white – 1992-1995
	2. Ginger – 1997, special edition of 1,000
	3. White with black– 1992-1997

Colourways	U.S. $	Can. $	U.K. £
1. Black with white	65.00	80.00	35.00
2. Ginger	90.00	110.00	50.00
3. White with black	65.00	80.00	35.00

DA 149
Cat
Stalking

Model No.:	Unknown
Designer:	Alan Maslankowski
Height:	5 ½", 14.0 cm
Colour:	See below
Issued:	1. Grey – 1992-1998
	2. White – 1992-1999

Colourways	U.S. $	Can. $	U.K. £
1. Grey	55.00	65.00	30.00
2. White	55.00	65.00	30.00

DA 150
Panda

Designer:	Warren Platt
Height:	5 ½", 14.0 cm
Colour:	White
Issued:	Black and white panda, green-brown base
Issued:	1. 1991 in a limited edition of 2,500
	2. 1991-1992
Series:	1. Artist's Signature Edition
	2. Endangered Species

Description	U.S. $	Can. $	U.K. £
1. Artist's Edition	150.00	175.00	85.00
2. Endangered Species	150.00	175.00	85.00
*			

DA 154A
Spirit of Life (on wooden plinth)

Model No.:	Unknown
Designer:	Amanda Hughes-Lubeck
Height:	7 ½", 19.1 cm
Colour:	White (matt)
Issued:	1991-1997
Varieties:	DA 154B 'The Winner'
Series:	Spirited Horses

Description	U.S. $	Can. $	U.K. £
Spirit of Life	150.00	175.00	85.00

DA 154B
The Winner (on wooden plinth) - Style Two

Model No.:	Unknown
Designer:	Amanda Hughes-Lubeck
Height:	7 ½", 19.1 cm
Colour:	Brown with black mane and tail (gloss and matt)
Issued:	1991-1997
Varieties:	DA 154A 'The Spirit of Life'
Series:	Connoisseur Horses

Description	U.S. $	Can. $	U.K. £
1. Gloss	225.00	275.00	110.00
2. Matt	175.00	200.00	100.00

DA 155
Polar Bear (standing)
Style Two

Designer:	Amanda Hughes-Lubeck
Height:	4 ¾", 12.1 cm
Colour:	White, grey base
Issued:	1. 1991 in a limited edition of 2,500
	2. 1991-1992
Series:	1. Artist's Signature Edition
	2. Endangered Species

Description	U.S. $	Can. $	U.K. £
1. Artist's Edition	125.00	150.00	65.00
2. Endangered Species	125.00	150.00	65.00

DA 156
The Tawny Owl

Designer:	Graham Tongue
Height:	9 ¾", 24.8 cm
Colour:	Light and golden brown
Issued:	1. 1991 in a limited edition of 2,500
	2. 1991-1994
Series:	1. Artist's Signature Edition
	2. Connoisseur Birds

Description	U.S. $	Can. $	U.K. £
1. Artist's Edition	450.00	550.00	250.00
2. Connoisseur Birds	450.00	550.00	250.00
*			

DA 158
The Christmas Robin (on plinth)

Model No.:	Unknown
Designer:	Graham Tongue
Height:	5 ¼", 13.3 cm
Colour:	Red breast, brown feathers, green holly on snowy bough
Issued:	1990-1992

Description	U.S. $	Can. $	U.K. £
Christmas Robin	90.00	110.00	50.00

DA 159
African Elephant
Style Three

Designer:	Martyn C. R. Alcock
Height:	6", 15.2 cm
Colour:	Grey
Issued:	1. 1991 in a limited edition of 2,500
	2. 1991-1992
Series:	1. Artist's Signature Edition
	2. Endangered Species

Description	U.S. $	Can. $	U.K. £
1. Artist's Edition	150.00	175.00	85.00
2. Endangered Species	150.00	175.00	85.00

DA 161
Christmas Turkey

Model No.:	Unknown
Designer:	Graham Tongue
Height:	6 ¼", 15.9 cm
Colour:	White feathers, red head
Issued:	1990-1990
Varieties:	D 6449

Description	U.S. $	Can. $	U.K. £
Christmas turkey	125.00	150.00	70.00

DA 163A
Quarter Horse (not on plinth)

Model No.:	Unknown
Designer:	Graham Tongue
Height:	7 ½", 19.1 cm
Colour:	Brown (gloss)
Issued:	1991-1997
Series:	Nature Sculptures

Colourways	U.S. $	Can. $	U.K. £
Brown	150.00	185.00	85.00

DA 163B
Quarter Horse (on wooden plinth)

Model No.:	Unknown
Designer:	Graham Tongue
Height:	8 ½", 21.6 cm
Colour:	Bay (matt)
Issued:	1991-1997
Series:	Connoisseur Horses

Colourways	U.S. $	Can. $	U.K. £
Bay	175.00	225.00	100.00

DA 164
Welsh Mountain Pony
Style One

Model No.:	Unknown
Designer:	Amanda Hughes-Lubeck
Height:	6 ¼", 15.9 cm
Colour:	Dapple grey (gloss)
Issued:	1991-1997

Description	U.S. $	Can. $	U.K. £
Welsh mountain pony	150.00	175.00	85.00

DA 165
Poodle

Model No.:	Unknown
Designer:	Warren Platt
Height:	5 ½", 14.0 cm
Colour:	1. Black
	2. White
Issued:	1993-1993

Colourways	U.S. $	Can. $	U.K. £
1. Black	250.00	300.00	140.00
2. White	250.00	300.00	140.00

*

DA 168
Labrador and Pup

Model No.:	Unknown
Designer:	Warren Platt
Length:	7", 17.8 cm
Colour:	Golden brown (gloss)
Issued:	1992-1996
Series:	Dogs and Puppies

Description	U.S. $	Can. $	U.K. £
Labrador and pup	80.00	100.00	45.00

*

DA 172
Leaping Trout (on wooden plinth)

Model No.:	Unknown
Designer:	Graham Tongue
Height:	11", 27.9 cm
Colour:	Brown and cream trout on blue-grey base, yellow flowers, green reeds
Issued:	1994-1994
Series:	Connoisseur

Description	U.S. $	Can. $	U.K. £
Leaping trout	450.00	550.00	250.00

DA 173
Retriever and Pup

Model No.:	Unknown
Designer:	Warren Platt
Length:	6", 15.2 cm
Colour:	Golden brown (gloss)
Issued:	1992-1997
Series:	Dogs and Puppies

Description	U.S. $	Can. $	U.K. £
Retriever and pup	100.00	125.00	60.00

DA 174
Spaniel and Pup

Model No.:	Unknown
Designer:	Warren Platt
Length:	5 ½", 14.0 cm
Colour:	1. Golden (gloss)
	2. Liver and white (gloss)
Issued:	1992-1997
Series:	Dogs and Puppies

Colourways	U.S. $	Can. $	U.K. £
1. Golden	100.00	125.00	60.00
2. Liver and white	100.00	125.00	60.00

*

DA 176
Sheepdog and Pup

Model No.:	Unknown
Designer:	Warren Platt
Height:	4 ½", 11.4 cm
Colour:	Grey and white (gloss)
Issued:	1992-1997
Series:	Dogs and Puppies

Description	U.S. $	Can. $	U.K. £
Sheepdog and pup	90.00	110.00	50.00

*

DA 179
Black Bess

Model No.:	Unknown
Designer:	Graham Tongue
Height:	7 ¾", 19.7 cm
Colour:	Black (matt)
Issued:	1992-1997
Series:	Connoisseur Horses

Description	U.S. $	Can. $	U.K. £
Black Bess	225.00	275.00	125.00

*

DA 182
First Born (on wooden plinth)

Model No.:	A 182
Designer:	Amanda Hughes-Lubeck
Height:	7", 17.8 cm
Colour:	Chestnut mare and foal (matt)
Issued:	1992-1999
Series:	Connoisseur Horses

Description	U.S. $	Can. $	U.K. £
First Born	225.00	275.00	125.00

Note: This model is a combination of DA 180 and DA 181.

DA 183
Spirit of the Wild (on wooden plinth)

Model No.:	A 183		
Designer:	Warren Platt		
Height:	12", 30.5 cm		
Colour:	See below (matt)		
Issued:	1993-1999		
Series:	Spirited Horses		

Colourways	U.S. $	Can. $	U.K. £
1. Black	150.00	175.00	75.00
2. Brown	150.00	175.00	75.00
3. White	150.00	175.00	75.00

DA 184
Desert Orchid (on wooden plinth)
Style Two

Model No.:	A 184
Designer:	Warren Platt
Height:	7 ¾", 19.7 cm
Colour:	Light grey (matt)
Issued:	1994-1999
Series:	Connoisseur Horses

Description	U.S. $	Can. $	U.K. £
Desert Orchid	225.00	275.00	125.00

DA 185
Shetland Pony
Style Two

Model No.:	H 185
Designer:	Amanda Hughes-Lubeck
Height:	5 ¼", 13.3 cm
Colour:	Dapple grey (gloss)
Issued:	1992-1999

Description	U.S. $	Can. $	U.K. £
Shetland pony	100.00	125.00	55.00

DA 188
Mr. Frisk (on plinth)
Style One

Model No.:	Unknown
Designer:	Graham Tongue
Size:	12 ¼" x 14", 31.1 x 35.5 cm
Colour:	Chestnut (matt)
Issued:	1992 in a limited edition of 7,500
Series:	Connoisseur Horses

Description	U.S. $	Can. $	U.K. £
Mr. Frisk	725.00	900.00	400.00

*

DA 189
Vietnamese Pot-Bellied Pig

Model No.:	G 189	
Designer:	Amanda Hughes-Lubeck	
Length:	6", 15.2 cm	
Colour:	Dark brown (gloss)	
Issued:	1992-1999	
Series:	Connoisseur	

Description	U.S. $	Can. $	U.K. £
Vietnamese pot-bellied pig	60.00	70.00	30.00

DA 190
Mr. Frisk (on wooden plinth)
Style Two

Model No.:	Unknown	
Designer:	Warren Platt	
Height:	7 ½", 19.1 cm	
Colour:	Chestnut (matt)	
Issued:	1992-1997	
Series:	Connoisseur Horses	

Description	U.S. $	Can. $	U.K. £
Mr. Frisk	225.00	275.00	125.00

*

DA 193A
Horse of the Year 1992

Model No.:	A 193	
Designer:	Amanda Hughes-Lubeck	
Height:	8 ¼", 21.0 cm	
Colour:	Chestnut (matt)	
Issued:	1992-1992	
Varieties:	Also called 'My First Horse' DA 193B	

Description	U.S. $	Can. $	U.K. £
Horse of the Year	135.00	165.00	75.00

DA 193B
My First Horse (on wooden plinth)

Model No.:	A 193	
Designer:	Amanda Hughes-Lubeck	
Height:	8 ¼", 21.0 cm	
Colour:	Chestnut (gloss)	
Issued:	1994-1999	
Varieties:	Also called 'Horse of the Year 1992' DA 193A	

Description	U.S. $	Can. $	U.K. £
My First Horse	135.00	165.00	75.00

GLAZES - FLAMBÉ

English St. Bernard

Pekinese Ch. 'Biddee of Ifield'
(small)

Bloodhound

'Capricorn'
Mountain Goat

'The Leap'
Dolphin

GLAZES

Chicks (Two)

Drake, Preening

**Duckling
New born**

**Mallard Drake
Standing**

Cormorant on A Rock

GLAZES

**Monkeys
(Mother and Baby**

**Hare, Lying
Legs stretched behind (Small)**

Lop-Eared Rabbit

**Hare, Crouching
Style Three**

Rabbits

Polar Bear on Cube

GLAZES

Penguins

Fish (Shoal of Fish)

Dog of Fo

Rhinoceros

GLAZES

Airedale Terrier
Ch. 'Cotsford Topsail'
(medium)

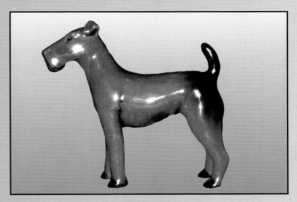

Fox Terrier
Standing, Style One

Frog
Style One, small

Pig Bowl

Emperor Penguin

Cat
Seated, Style One

'Sleepy Heads'
Two Cats

GLAZES

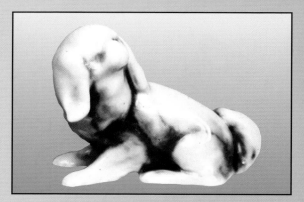

**Cavalier King Charles Spaniel
Style One, Chinese Jade**

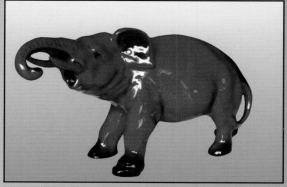

**Fighter Elephant
small**

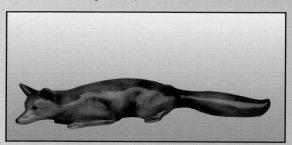

**Fox, Stalking
small**

Elephant, trunk down, curled

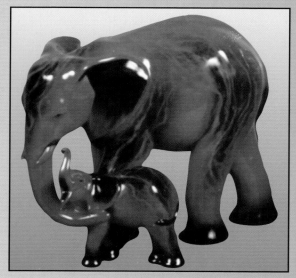

**'Motherhood'
Elephants**

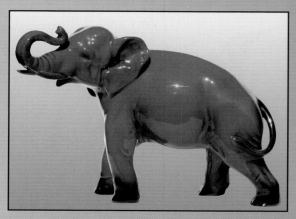

**Elephant, trunk in salute
Style One, small**

GLAZES

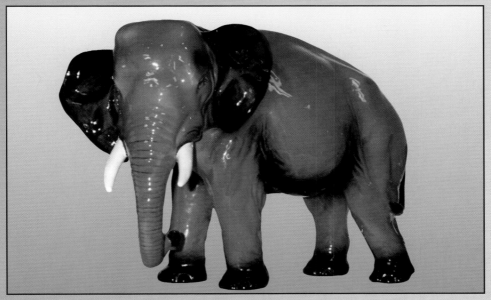

Elephant
Trunk down, curled
Flambé

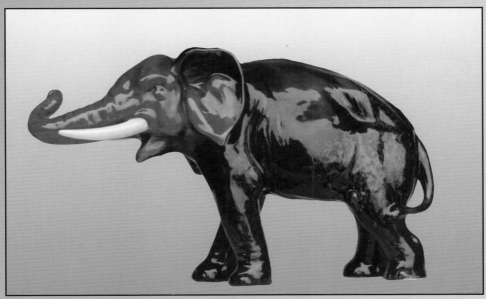

Elephant
Trunk stretching
Sung

GLAZES

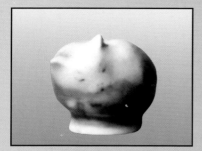

**Character Kitten
Curled, Style Two
Chinese Jade**

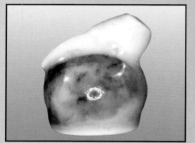

**Character Toucan With Hat
Style Six
Chinese Jade**

**Bulldog with Tam O'Shanter and Haversack
Titanian**

**Fighter Elephant
Small
Chinese Jade**

DA 194
Cat
Seated - Style Three

Model No.:	K194		
Designer:	Martyn C. R. Alcock		
Height:	3 ¾", 9.5 cm		
Colour:	See below (gloss)		
Issued:	1. Black/white – 1992-1999		
	2. Ginger – 1992-1997		

Colourways	U.S. $	Can. $	U.K. £
1. Black with white	40.00	50.00	20.00
2. Ginger	40.00	50.00	20.00

DA 195
Cat with Bandaged Paw

Model No.:	Unknown		
Designer:	Martyn C. R. Alcock		
Height:	3 ½", 8.9 cm		
Colour:	1. Grey		
	2. Ginger		
Issued:	1. 1992-1999		
	2. 1998		

Description	U.S. $	Can. $	U.K. £
1. Grey	50.00	60.00	25.00
2. Ginger	50.00	60.00	25.00

Note: Ginger colourway exclusive to Index Catalogue.

DA 196
Give Me A Home, Dog

Model No.:	Unknown		
Designer:	Martyn C. R. Alcock		
Height:	5 ¾", 14.6 cm		
Colour:	Brown and white (gloss)		
Issued:	1994-1997		

Description	U.S. $	Can. $	U.K. £
Give me a home, dog	80.00	100.00	45.00

DA 205
Kestrel
Style Two

Model No.:	Unknown		
Designer:	Graham Tongue		
Height:	10", 24.5 cm		
Colour:	Light and dark brown (matt)		
Issued:	1992 in a limited editon of 2,500		
Series:	Artist's Signature Edition		

Description	U.S. $	Can. $	U.K. £
Kestrel	225.00	275.00	125.00

*

*

DA 213
Vietnamese Pot-Bellied Piglet

Model No.:	G 213
Designer:	Warren Platt
Length:	3", 7.6 cm
Colour:	Grey (gloss)
Issued:	1993-1999

Description	U.S. $	Can. $	U.K. £
Pot-bellied piglet	35.00	40.00	20.00

DA 214
Mick the Miller (Greyhound) (on wooden base)

Model No.:	Unknown
Designer:	Graham Tongue
Height:	9 ½", 24.1 cm
Colour:	Pale brown and white (gloss)
Issued:	1993 in a limited edition of 7,500

Description	U.S. $	Can. $	U.K. £
Greyhound	150.00	175.00	85.00

DA 215
Tamworth Pig

Model No.:	G 215
Designer:	Amanda Hughes-Lubeck
Height:	6", 15.2 cm
Colour:	Brown (gloss)
Issued:	1994-1999

Description	U.S. $	Can. $	U.K. £
Tamworth pig	75.00	90.00	40.00

*

DA 218
'Red Rum'
Style Two

Model No.:	Unknown
Designer:	Graham Tongue
Height:	12", 30.5 cm
Colour:	Bay (matt)
Issued:	1993 in a limited edition of 7,500

Description	U.S. $	Can. $	U.K. £
1. Ceramic Base	725.00	875.00	400.00
2. Wooden plinth	725.00	875.00	400.00

*

DA 222
Bulldog
Seated - Style Six

Designer:	Warren Platt		
Height:	5", 12.7 cm		
Colour:	1. Fawn and white		
	2. White, tan patches over ears		
Issued:	1. 1996 in a special edition of 1,000		
	2. 1993-1999		

Colourways	U.S. $	Can. $	U.K. £
1. Fawn/white	120.00	150.00	65.00
2. White/tan patches	75.00	90.00	40.00

DA 223
Nigerian Pot-Bellied Pygmy Goat

Model No.:	G 223
Designer:	Amanda Hughes-Lubeck
Height:	5 ¼", 14.0 cm
Colour:	White with black patches (gloss)
Issued:	1993-1999

Description	U.S. $	Can. $	U.K. £
Pygmy goat	60.00	75.00	35.00

DA 224
Cancara - running

Model No.:	Unknown
Designer:	Warren Platt
Height:	7 ½", 19.1 cm
Colour:	Black (matt)
Issued:	1995-1997
Series:	Connoisseur

Description	U.S. $	Can. $	U.K. £
Cancara	325.00	400.00	175.00

DA 225
Spirit of Love, Horses (on wooden plinth)

Model No.:	Unknown
Designer:	Alan Maslankowski
Height:	6 ½", 16.5 cm
Colour:	Bay (matt)
Issued:	1994-1997
Series:	Spirited Horses

Description	U.S. $	Can. $	U.K. £
Spirit of Love	200.00	250.00	100.00

DA 226
'Red Rum'
Style Three

Model No.:	A 226
Designer:	Amanda Hughes-Lubeck
Height:	9", 22.9 cm
Colour:	Brown (matt)
Issued:	1995-1999

Description	U.S. $	Can. $	U.K. £
'Red Rum'	225.00	275.00	125.00

DA 227
'Arkle'
Style Two

Model No.:	Unknown
Designer:	Graham Tongue
Height:	12", 30.5 cm
Colour:	Bay (matt)
Issued:	1994 in a limited edition of 5,000

Description	U.S. $	Can. $	U.K. £
'Arkle'	725.00	900.00	400.00

DA 228
British Bulldog

Model No.:	Unknown
Designer:	Denise Andrews
Modeller:	Amanda Hughes-Lubeck
Size:	4 ½" x 5 ½", 11.3 x 14.0 cm
Colour:	1. Tan dog, white hat and jacket
	2. White dog, black hat and jacket
Issued:	Tan – 1994 in a limited edition of 1,000
	White – 1994 in a limited edition of 1,000

Colourways	U.S. $	Can. $	U.K. £
1. Tan dog	150.00	175.00	85.00
2. White dog	150.00	175.00	85.00

DA 229
Quiet Please, 'Cats'

Model No.:	K229
Designer:	Warren Platt
Height:	1 ¾", 4.4 cm
Colour:	See below
Issued:	1. 1998
	2. 1995-1999
Series:	Cute Cats

Colourways	U.S. $	Can. $	U.K. £
1. Ginger/white	45.00	55.00	25.00
2. Grey/white	45.00	55.00	25.00

Note: Ginger/white colourway exclusive to Index Catalogue.

DA 230
Gloucester Old Spot Pig

Model No.:	G230
Designer:	Amanda Hughes-Lubeck
Height:	3", 7.6 cm
Colour:	Pink with black markings (gloss)
Issued:	1995-1999

Description	U.S. $	Can. $	U.K. £
Pig	65.00	75.00	35.00

DA 231
Dinnertime

Model No.:	Unknown
Designer:	Warren Platt
Height:	2 ½", 6.3 cm
Colour:	See below
Issued:	1. 1995-1999
	2. 1998
Series:	Cute Cats

Colourways	U.S. $	Can. $	U.K. £
1. Black/white	45.00	55.00	25.00
2. Ginger	45.00	55.00	25.00

Note: Ginger colourway exclusive to Index Catalogue.

DA 232
New Toy

Model No.:	Unknown
Designer:	Amanda Hughes-Lubeck
Height:	2 ½", 6.3 cm
Colour:	Cream and white cat (gloss)
Issued:	1995-1999
Series:	Cute Cats

Description	U.S. $	Can. $	U.K. £
New toy	45.00	55.00	25.00

DA 233
In the News

Model No.:	Unknown
Designer:	Amanda Hughes-Lubeck
Height:	2 ½", 6.3 cm
Colour:	Cream and black striped cat (gloss)
Issued:	1995-1999
Series:	Cute Cats

Description	U.S. $	Can. $	U.K. £
In the news	45.00	55.00	25.00

DA 234
Cancara - rearing

Beswick No.:	3426
Designer:	Graham Tongue
Height:	16 ½", 41.9 cm
Colour:	Black (matt)
Issued:	1995-1999
Series:	Connoisseur

Description	U.S. $	Can. $	U.K. £
Cancara	550.00	650.00	300.00

Note: Previously released with a Beswick backstamp
to commemorate the centenary in 1994.   *

DA 236
The Flight of the Trakehner

Model No.:	Unknown
Designer:	Graham Tongue
Height:	15", 38.1 cm
Colour:	Brown (matt)
Issued:	1996 in a limited edition of 1,500

Description	U.S. $	Can. $	U.K. £
Trakehner	900.00	1,100.00	500.00

DA 237
'Peakstone Lady Margaret' (Shire horse)

Model No.:	Unknown
Designer:	Warren Platt
Height:	13", 33.0 cm
Colour:	Black, white feet, yellow ribbon, red rosette (matt)
Issued:	1996-1998

Description	U.S. $	Can. $	U.K. £
Shire horse	725.00	900.00	400.00

DA 238
Shire Horse
Style Two

Model No.:	Unknown
Designer:	Amanda Hughes-Lubeck
Height:	7", 17.8 cm
Colour:	Bay (matt)
Issued:	1996-1997

Description	U.S. $	Can. $	U.K. £
Shire horse	275.00	325.00	150.00

DA 239
Spirit of Tomorrow

Model No.:	Unknown
Designer:	Warren Platt
Height:	8", 20.3 cm
Colour:	1. Brown (matt)
	2. White (matt)
Issued:	1. 1996-1996
	2. 1996-1997

Colourways		U.S. $	Can. $	U.K. £
1.	Brown	125.00	150.00	65.00
2.	White	125.00	150.00	65.00

*

DA 243
The Lipizzaner

Model No.:	Unknown
Designer:	Shane Ridge
Height:	11", 28.0 cm
Colour:	Light grey (matt)
Issued:	1996 in a limited edition of 1,500
Series:	Connoisseur

Description	U.S. $	Can. $	U.K. £
Lipizzaner	725.00	900.00	400.00

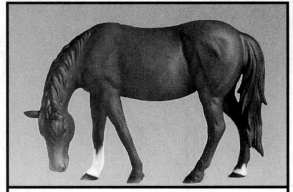

DA 244
New Forest Pony

Model No.:	A 244
Designer:	Shane Ridge
Height:	6", 15.0 cm
Colour:	Brown (matt)
Issued:	1997-1999

Description	U.S. $	Can. $	U.K. £
New Forest pony	150.00	175.00	75.00

DA 245
Milton

Model No.:	Unknown
Designer:	Martyn Alcock
Height:	12 ¼", 31.0 cm
Colour:	White (matt)
Issued:	1997 in a limited edition of 1,000
Series:	Connoisseur

Description	U.S. $	Can. $	U.K. £
Milton	725.00	900.00	400.00

*

DA 247
Welsh Mountain Pony
Style Two

Model No.: A 247
Designer: Graham Tongue
Height: 8 ¼", 21.0 cm
Colour: White, navy and red
Issued: 1998-1999
Series: Connoisseur

U.S. $225.00
Can. $275.00
U.K. £125.00

DA 248
The Bulldog Pups

Model No.: Unknown
Designer: Shane Ridge
Height: 3 ½", 8.9 cm
Colour: Cream, light brown (gloss)
Issued: 1997 in a limited edition
of 1,000

U.S. $ 90.00
Can. $110.00
U.K. £ 50.00

*

DA 250
Lammtarra

Model No.: A 250
Designer: Warren Platt
Height: 7 ¾", 19.5 cm
Colour: Chestnut (matt)
Issued: 1999-1999
Series: Connoisseur

U.S. $225.00
Can. $275.00
U.K. £125.00

*

DA 259
Palomino

Model No.: A 259
Designer: Shane Ridge
Height: 6 ¾", 17 cm
Colour: Palomino (gloss)
Issued: 1999-1999

U.S. $150.00
Can. $175.00
U.K. £ 75.00

DA 260
Hunter

Model No.: A 260
Designer: Graham Tongue
Height: 8", 20.3 cm
Colour: Grey (gloss)
Issued: 1999-1999

U.S. $150.00
Can. $175.00
U.K. £ 75.00

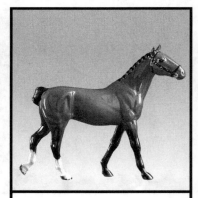

DA 261
Hackney Pony

Model No.: A 261
Designer: Martyn C. R. Alcock
Height: 6 ¾", 17.2 cm
Colour: Brown (gloss)
Issued: 1999-1999

U.S. $150.00
Can. $175.00
U.K. £ 75.00

RDA SERIES

RDA 1
Chihuahua

Height:	2 ½", 6.4 cm
Colour:	Brown and beige
Issued:	2004 to the present
Series:	Toy Dog Collection
U.S.	N/I
Can.	$80.00
U.K.	£25.00

RDA 2
Pug

Height:	2 ¾", 7.0 cm
Colour:	White and black dog; green mat; brown bowl
Issued:	2004 to the present
Series:	Toy Dog Collection
U.S.	N/I
Can.	$80.00
U.K.	£25.00

RDA 3
West Highland Terrier

Height:	2 ¾", 7.0 cm
Colour:	White dog; white rug with red and black stripes
Issued:	2004 to the present
Series:	Terrier Dog Collection
U.S.	N/I
Can.	$80.00
U.K.	£25.00

RDA 4
Jack Russell

Height:	3 ½", 8.9 cm
Colour:	White with brown patches
Issued:	2004 to the present
Series:	Terrier Dog Collection
U.S.	N/I
Can.	$80.00
U.K.	£25.00

RDA 5
STANDARD SCHNAUZER

Height:	4 ½", 11.9 cm
Colour:	Grey and white dog; beige bowl; brown base
Issued:	2004 to the present
Series:	Utility Dog Collection
U.S.	N/I
Can.	$95.00
U.K.	£30.00

RDA 6
CHOW CHOW

Height:	5 ½",14.0 cm
Colour:	Brown dog; grey base
Issued:	2004 to the present
Series:	Utility Dog Collection
U.S.	N/I
Can.	$95.00
U.K.	£30.00

RDA 7
DALMATIAN

Height:	5 ½", 14.0 cm
Colour:	White with black spots
Issued:	2004 to the present
Series:	Utility Dog Collection
U.S.	N/I
Can.	$95.00
U.K.	£30.00

RDA 8
DOBERMAN

Height:	6 ¼", 15.9 cm
Colour:	Black and brown
Issued:	2004 to the present
Series:	Working Dog Collection
U.S.	N/I
Can.	$95.00
U.K.	£30.00

RDA 9
Rough Collie

Height: 6", 15.0 cm
Colour: Beige and white
dog; green base
Issued: 2004 to the present
Series: Working Dog
Collection
U.S. N/I
Can. $95.00
U.K. £30.00

RDA 10
Corgi

Height: 3 ¼", 8.3 cm
Colour: Brown and white
dog; red and green
ball; blue and
maroon rug
Issued: 2004 to the present
Series: Working Dog
Collection
U.S. N/I
Can. $80.00
U.K. £30.00

RDA 11
Beagle

Height: 4", 10.1 cm
Colour: White, brown and
black
Issued: 2004 to the present
Series: Hound Dog
Collection
U.S. N/I
Can. $95.00
U.K. £30.00

RDA 12
Dachshund

Height: 2 ½", 6.4 cm
Colour: Brown and black
Issued: 2004 to the present
Series: Hound Dog
Collection
U.S. N/I
Can. $80.00
U.K. £25.00

Photograph not
available
at press time

RDA 13
Black Labrador

Height: 6", 15.0 cm
Colour: Black dog; green
base
Issued: 2004 to the present
Series: Gun Dog Collection
U.S. N/I
Can. $95.00
U.K. £30.00

RDA 14
Golden Retriever

Height: 5 ¼", 13.3 cm
Colour: Golden brown
Issued: 2004 to the present
Series: Gun Dog Collection
U.S. N/I
Can. N/I
U.K. £30.00

RDA 15
Pointer

Height: 6 ¾", 17.2 cm
Colour: White with brown
patches
Issued: 2004 to the present
Series: Gun Dog Collection
U.S. N/I
Can. $95.00
U.K. £30.00

RDA 16
Barn Owl

Height: 6 ¼", 15.9 cm
Colour: Brown, cream and
white
Issued: 2004 to the present
U.S. N/I
Can. N/I
U.K. N/A

RDA 17
British Shorthair

Height: 2", 5.0 cm
Colour: Dark grey cat;
           brown mat
Issued: 2004 to the present
Series: Cat Collection

U.S.   N/I
Can. $80.00
U.K.   £25.00

RDA 18
Maine Coon

Height: 3 ½", 8.9 cm
Colour: Brown and white
           cat; cream and gold
           rug; red ball
Issued: 2004 to the present
Series: Cat Collection

U.S.   N/I
Can. $80.00
U.K.   £25.00

RDA 19
Persian

Height: 3 ½", 8.9 cm
Colour: White cat; blue rug
           with white and red
           trim; red ball of
           wool
Issued: 2004 to the present
Series: Cat Collection

U.S.   N/I
Can. $80.00
U.K.   £25.00

RDA 20
Siamese

Height: 3 ½", 8.9 cm
Colour: Cream and black
           cat; gold rug
Issued: 2004 to the present
Series: Cat Collection

U.S.   N/I
Can. $80.00
U.K.   £25.00

RDA 26
Shire Horse

Height: 8 ¼", 21.0 cm
Colour: Dark brown and
           white
Issued: 2004 to the present

U.S.   N/I
Can.   N/I
U.K.   £65.00

Note: Pre-released to
           Sinclair's

RDA 31
Palomino

Height: 8 ¼", 21.0 cm
Colour: Golden brown horse
           with white mane and
           tail
Issued: 2004 to the present
Series: Horse and Pony
           Collection

U.S.   N/I
Can. $170.00
U.K.   £ 55.00

RDA 32
Appaloosa

Height: 8 ¼", 21.0 cm
Colour: White with black
           markings
Issued: 2004 to the present
Series: Horse and Pony
           Collection

U.S.   N/I
Can. $170.00
U.K.   £ 55.00

RDA 33
My First Horse

Height: 8", 20.3 cm
Colour: Brown
Issued: 2004 to the present
Series: Horse and Pony
           Collection

U.S.   N/I
Can. $170.00
U.K.   £ 55.00

RDA 34
My First Pony

Height:	4", 10.1 cm
Colour:	Brown with white mane and tail
Issued:	2004 to the present
Series:	Horse and Pony Collection
U.S.	N/I
Can.	$125.00
U.K.	£ 35.00

RDA 35
Appaloosa Foal

Height:	4", 10.1 cm
Colour:	White with black markings
Issued:	2004 to the present
Series:	Horse and Pony Collection
U.S.	N/I
Can.	$125.00
U.K.	£ 35.00

RDA 36
Golden Eagle

Height:	9 ¼", 23.5 cm
Colour:	Dark and light brown, yellow and green
Issued:	2004 to the present
Series:	Birds of Prey Collection
U.S.	N/I
Can.	$170.00
U.K.	£ 60.00

RDA 37
Barn Owl

Height:	6 ¼", 15.9 cm
Colour:	Brown and white bird, brown stand
Issued:	2004 to the present
Series:	Birds of Prey Collection
U.S.	N/I
Can.	$115.00
U.K.	£ 40.00

RDA 44
Abyssinian Cat and Kittens

Height:	2 ½", 6.4 cm
Colour:	Orangey-brown cats, yellow rug
Issued:	2004 to the present
U.S.	N/I
Can.	N/I
U.K.	£25.00

RDA 48
Cavalier King Charles

Height:	4 ¼", 10.8 cm
Colour:	Black and white dog; red cushion with yellow and blue braid; blue bowl; grey base
Issued:	2004 to the present
U.S.	N/I
Can.	N/I
U.K.	£25.00

RDA 51
Newfoundland

Height:	3 ½", 8.9 cm
Colour:	Black dog; brown bowl; white and red rug
Issued:	2004 to the present
U.S.	N/I
Can.	N/I
U.K.	£30.00

RDA 52
Scottish Terrier

Height:	3 ¼", 8.3 cm
Colour:	Black
Issued:	2004 to the present
U.S.	N/I
Can.	N/I
U.K.	£25.00

RDA 55
Clydesdale

Height:	7 ½", 19.1 cm
Colour:	Grey
Issued:	2004 to the present
Series:	Horse and Pony Collection
U.S.	N/I
Can.	N/I
U.K.	£59.00

RDA 56
Shetland Pony

Height:	6 ¼", 15.9 cm
Colour:	Dark brown
Issued:	2004 to the present
Series:	Horse and Pony Collection
U.S.	N/I
Can.	N/I
U.K.	£45.00

Photograph not
available
at press time

RDA 60
Cleveland Bay Foal

Height:	6", 15.0 cm
Colour:	Unknown
Issued:	2004 to the present
Series:	Horse and Pony Collection
U.S.	N/I
Can.	N/I
U.K.	£35.00

Photograph not
available
at press time

RDA 62
Cleveland Bay

Height:	8 ¼", 21.0 cm
Colour:	Unknown
Issued:	2004 to the present
Series:	Horse and Pony Collection
U.S.	N/I
Can.	N/I
U.K.	£55.00

RDA 67
Staffordshire Bull Terrier

Height:	5 ½", 14.0 cm
Colour:	Dark brown and white
Issued:	2004 to the present
U.S.	N/I
Can.	N/I
U.K.	£25.00

RDA 68
Yorkshire Terrier

Height:	1 ¾", 4.4 cm
Colour:	Brown, black and cream
Issued:	2004 to the present
U.S.	N/I
Can.	N/I
U.K.	£25.00

RDA 69
Border Collie

Height:	2 ½", 6.4 cm
Colour:	Black and white dog; brown fence
Issued:	2004 to the present
U.S.	N/I
Can.	N/I
U.K.	£30.00

RDA 73
Manx Cat

Height:	4", 10.1 cm
Colour:	Golden brown and white
Issued:	2004 to the present
U.S.	N/I
Can.	N/I
U.K.	N/A

RDA 85
Springer Spaniel

Height: 8 ¼", 21.0 cm
Colour: Brown and white
Issued: 2005 to the present
Series: Best of Breed
U.S.   N/I
Can.   N/I
U.K.   £30.00

RDA 86
Greyhound

Height: 8 ¾", 22.2 cm
Colour: White, brown and
          black
Issued: 2005 to the present
Series: Best of Breed
U.S.   N/I
Can.   N/I
U.K.   £30.00

RDA 87
German Shepherd

Height: 9 ¾", 24.7 cm
Colour: Black, tan, white
          and pink
Issued: 2005 to the present
Series: Best of Breed
U.S.   N/I
Can.   N/I
U.K.   £30.00

RDA 88
Border Collie

Height: 9 ¼", 23.5 cm
Colour: Black and white
Issued: 2005 to the present
Series: Best of Breed
U.S.   N/I
Can.   N/I
U.K.   £30.00

RDA 89
Golden Retriever

Height: 8 ¼", 21.0 cm
Colour: Golden brown
Issued: 2005 to the present
Series: Best of Breed
U.S.   N/I
Can.   N/I
U.K.   £30.00

RDA 90
West Highland Terrier

Height: 8 ¼", 21.0 cm
Colour: White
Issued: 2005 to the present
Series: Best of Breed
U.S.   N/I
Can.   N/I
U.K.   £30.00

RDA 91
Tawny Owl

Height: 4 ¾", 12.1 cm
Colour: Brown, tan, white,
          green and black
Issued: 2005 to the present
Series: Birds of Nature
          Collection
U.S.   N/I
Can.   N/I
U.K.   £25.00

RDA 92
Robin

Height: 4 ¾", 12.1 cm
Colour: Orange-red, brown,
          white, red and grey
Issued: 2005 to the present
Series: Birds of Nature
          Collection
U.S.   N/I
Can.   N/I
U.K.   £25.00

RDA 93
Zebra Finch

Height:	4 ¾", 12.1 cm
Colour:	Browns, greens, yellow, red and grey
Issued:	2005 to the present
Series:	Birds of Nature Collection
U.S.	N/I
Can.	N/I
U.K.	£25.00

RDA 94
Kingfisher

Height:	5", 12.7 cm
Colour:	Blue, red, brown, green and grey
Issued:	2005 to the present
Series:	Birds of Nature Collection
U.S.	N/I
Can.	N/I
U.K.	£25.00

RDA 95
Barn Owl

Height:	5", 12.7 cm
Colour:	White, very light brown, green and lilac
Issued:	2005 to the present
Series:	Birds of Nature Collection
U.S.	N/I
Can.	N/I
U.K.	£25.00

RDA 96
Wren

Height:	5 ½", 14.0 cm
Colour:	Golden brown, browns, orange, blue, yellow and green
Issued:	2005 to the present
Series:	Birds of Nature Collection
U.S.	N/I
Can.	N/I
U.K.	£25.00

ART IS LIFE

AIL 3
Wolves

Designer:	Alan Maslankowski
Height:	11 ¾", 29.5 cm
Colour:	White matt
Issued:	2000 in a limited edition of 1,500
Series:	Art Is Life
U.S.	$300.00
Can.	$350.00
U.K.	£165.00

AIL 4
Horses

Designer:	Alan Maslankowski
Height:	14", 35.5 cm
Colour:	White matt
Issued:	2000 in a limited edition of 1,500
Series:	Art Is Life
U.S.	$300.00
Can.	$350.00
U.K.	£165.00

AIL 5
Eagle

Designer:	Alan Maslankowski
Height:	16 ¼", 41.5 cm
Colour:	White matt
Issued:	2000 in a limited edition of 1,500
Series:	Art Is Life
U.S.	$300.00
Can.	$350.00
U.K.	£165.00

*

AIL 11
Lions

Designer:	Alan Maslankowski
Height:	7 ¼", 18.4 cm
Colour:	White matt
Issued:	2001 in a limited edition of 950
Series:	Art Is Life
U.S.	$350.00
Can.	$425.00
U.K.	£200.00

Note:	Limited edition of 15 coloured pieces auctioned 2004.

AIL 12
Bear

Designer:	Alan Maslankowski
Height:	12", 30.5 cm
Colour:	White matt
Issued:	2001 in a limited edition of 950
Series:	Art Is Life
U.S.	$350.00
Can.	$425.00
U.K.	£200.00

GLAZES

CHANG
CHINESE JADE
FLAMBÉ
MANDARIN
SUNG
TITANIAN
TREACLE

Photograph not
available
at press time

Bison
Style Two
Model No.: 1799
Designer: Joseph Ledger
Height: 5 ½", 14.0 cm
Size: Medium
Glaze: Flambé
Issued: c.1960

U.S.
Can. Very Rare
U.K.

Bison
Style Three
Model No.: 1847
Height: 3", 7.6 cm
Size: Small
Glaze: Flambé
Issued: c.1963

U.S.
Can. Very Rare
U.K.

Photograph not
available
at press time

Borzoi
Model No.: 261
Height: Unknown
Glaze: Flambé
Issued: c.1924

U.S.
Can. Very Rare
U.K.

Bull
Style One
Model No.: 612
Size: 7" x 10 ¾",
17.8 x 27.3 cm
Glaze: 1. Chinese Jade
2. Flambé
3. Sung
Issued: c.1928

U.S. $4,500.00
Can. $5,500.00
U.K. £2,500.00

Bull
Style Two
Model No.: Unknown
Designer: Eric Griffiths
Height: 10 ½", 26.7 cm
Glaze: Flambé
Issued: c.1927

U.S.
Can. Prototype
U.K.

Bulldog
Seated - Style One
Model No.: 38
Height: 4", 10.1 cm
Glaze: Flambé
Issued: 1912-1936

U.S. $1,750.00
Can. $2,100.00
U.K. £1,000.00

Bulldog
Seated - Style Two
Model No.: 120
Height: 3", 7.6 cm
Glaze: Flambé
Issued: c.1913

U.S. $1,750.00
Can. $2,100.00
U.K. £1,000.00

Butterfly
Model No.: 142A
Size: 2" x 4 ½",
5.1 x 11.4 cm
Glaze: Flambé
Issued: c.1912

U.S.
Can. Rare
U.K.

Cat
Seated - Style Two
Model No.:	2269
Designer:	A. Maslankowski
Height:	11 ½", 29.2 cm
Glaze:	Flambé
Issued:	1977-1996
U.S.	$800.00
Can.	$975.00
U.K.	£450.00

Chicks (three)
Model No.:	1163
Designer:	Charles Noke
Size:	2 ¼" x 3 ½",
	5.7 x 8.9 cm
Glaze:	Flambé
Issued:	c.1908
U.S.	$375.00
Can.	$450.00
U.K.	£200.00

Cockatoos
Model No.:	630
Designer:	Charles Noke
Height:	4 ½", 11.4 cm
Glaze:	Chinese Jade
Issued:	c.1929
U.S.	$2,000.00
Can.	$2,500.00
U.K.	£1,100.00

Cockerel Bowl
Model No.:	Unknown
Height:	3 ¼", 8.3 cm
Glaze:	Flambé with sterling silver rim
Issued:	Unknown
Varieties:	Cockerel Crouching HN 178, 180, 267
U.S.	
Can.	Rare
U.K.	

Cormorant on a Rock
Model No.:	22
Designer:	Harry Simeon
Height:	6", 15.0 cm
Glaze:	Flambé
Issued:	c.1930
U.S.	
Can.	Very Rare
U.K.	

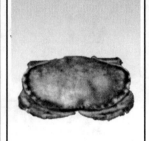

Crab
Model No.:	42
Size:	2" x 4 ½",
	5.1 x 11.4 cm
Glaze:	1. Crystalline
	2. Flambé
Issued:	c.1936
U.S.	
Can.	Very Rare
U.K.	

Dachshund, Begging
Model No.:	41
Height:	4", 10.1 cm
Glaze:	Flambé
Issued:	c.1912
U.S.	
Can.	Rare
U.K.	

Dachshund
Standing - Style One
Model No.:	36A
Size:	4 ½" x 6 ½",
	11.4 x 16.5 cm
Glaze:	Flambé
Issued:	c.1912
U.S.	$2,750.00
Can.	$3,250.00
U.K.	£1,500.00

Dog of Fo
Model No.: 2957
Designer: William K. Harper
Height: 5 ¼", 13.3 cm
Glaze: Flambé
Issued: 1982-1982
Series: RDICC

U.S.	$300.00
Can.	$350.00
U.K.	£175.00

Dragon
Style One
Model No.: 2085
Designer: John Bromley
Height: 7 ½", 19.0 cm
Glaze: Flambé
Issued: 1973-1996

U.S.	$ 800.00
Can.	$1,000.00
U.K.	£ 450.00

Elephant
Stylized
Model No.: 633
Height: 3", 7.6 cm
Glaze: Chinese Jade
Issued: c.1929

U.S.	
Can.	Extremely Rare
U.K.	

Elephant
Trunk down, curled - medium
Model No.: Unknown
Designer: Charles Noke
Height: 6 ½", 16.5 cm
Size: Medium
Glaze: Flambé
Issued: Unknown

U.S.	$ 900.00
Can.	$1,100.00
U.K.	£ 500.00

Elephant
Trunk stretching
Model No.: Unknown
Designer: Charles Noke
Size: 12" x 18", 30.5 x 45.7 cm
Glaze: 1. Flambé
2. Sung
Issued: c.1930

	Flambé	Sung
U.S.	$6,000.	7,500.
Can	$7,250.	9,000.
U.K.	£3,500.	4,200.

Fighter Elephant - small
Model No.: 624
Designer: Charles Noke
Height: 4", 10.1 cm
Size: Small
Glaze: 1. Chinese Jade
2. Flambé
Issued: c.1929

	Jade	Flambé
U.S.	$2,200.	1,500.
Can.	$2,600.	1,800.
U.K.	£1,200.	850.

Fish
Model No.: 625
Designer: Charles Noke
Height: 3 ½" x 5 ½", 8.9 x 14.0 cm
Glaze: Chinese Jade
Issued: c.1929

U.S.	
Can.	Rare
U.K.	

Fish (shoal of fish)
Model No.: 632
Height: 6 ½", 16.5 cm
Glaze: 1. Chinese Jade
2. Flambé
Issued: c.1929
Derivative: Lamp, Model No. L23

U.S.	
Can.	Rare
U.K.	

Fox
Seated - Style Two - medium
Model No.:	14A
Height:	5 ½", 14.0 cm
Size:	Medium
Glaze:	Flambé
Issued:	c.1912
U.S.	$ 900.00
Can.	$1,100.00
U.K.	£ 500.00

Photograph not
available
at press time

Fox Bowl
Model No.:	20
Size:	2 ½" x 12 ½",
	6.4 x 31.7 cm
Glaze:	Flambé
Issued:	c.1912-1936
U.S.	$2,200.00
Can.	$2,600.00
U.K.	£1,200.00

Frog
Style One - large
Model No.:	1162
Height:	Unknown
Size:	Large
Glaze:	Flambé
Issued:	c.1908-1936
U.S.	
Can.	Rare
U.K.	

Frog
Style One - medium
Model No.:	1162A
Height:	Unknown
Size:	Medium
Glaze:	Flambé
Issued:	c.1908-1936
U.S.	
Can.	Rare
U.K.	

Frog
Style One - small
Model No.:	1162B
Size:	1 ¼" x 3 ½",
	4.4 x 8.9 cm
Size:	Small
Glaze:	Flambé
Issued:	1908-1936
U.S.	
Can.	Rare
U.K.	

Gansu Fish
Model No.:	BA39
Designer:	A. Maslankowski
Height:	7 ¼", 18.4 cm
Colour:	Flambé
Issued:	2003 in a limited
	edition of 250
Series:	Burslem Artwares
U.S.	$1,400.00
Can.	$2,400.00
U.K.	£ 735.00

Note: A red, black and orange
colourway exists.

Photograph not
available
at press time

Hare
Standing - Style One
Model No.:	86
Height:	5 ¾", 14.6 cm
Glaze:	Flambé
Issued:	c.1912-14936
U.S.	
Can.	Rare
U.K.	

Hebei Goat
Model No.:	Ba 36
Designer:	A. Maslankowski
Height:	10 ¼", 26.0 cm
Glaze:	Flambé
Issued:	2002 in a limited
	edition of 250
Series:	1. Burslem
	Artwares
	2. Chinese Zodiac
U.S.	$1,645.00
Can.	$2,800.00
U.K.	£ 650.00

Photograph not available at press time

Horse

Model No.:	882
Height:	Unknown
Glaze:	Chinese Jade
Issued:	c.1934
Derivitive:	Lamp
U.S.	
Can.	Extremely Rare
U.K.	

Kitten Lying on Back

Model No.:	17
Size:	1 ½" x 2", 3.8 x 5.0 cm
Glaze:	Flambé
Issued:	Unknown
U.S.	
Can.	Rare
U.K.	

Leaping Salmon

Model No.:	666
Designer:	Charles Noke
Height:	12 ¼," 31.1 cm
Glaze:	See below
Issued:	1. Chinese Jade – c.1930
	2. Flambé – c.1940-1950

	Jade	Flambé
U.S.	$2,000.	1,250.
Can.	$2,500.	1,500.
U.K.	£1,200.	700.

Lion Lying

Model No.:	64
Size:	2 ½" x 7", 6.4 x 17.8 cm
Glaze:	Flambé
Issued:	c.1918-1936
U.S.	
Can.	Very Rare
U.K.	

Llama Style One

Model No.:	827
Height:	6", 15.2 cm
Glaze:	1. Chinese Jade
	2. Flambé
Issued:	c.1933
Derivitive:	Lamp
U.S.	
Can.	Very Rare
U.K.	

Lop-Eared Rabbit - Small

Model No.:	1165
Height:	2 ½", 6.4 cm
Glaze:	Flambé
Issued:	1913-1996
Varieties:	HN 1091A on fluted ashtray
	HN 1091B on plain ashtray
U.S.	$125.00
Can.	$150.00
U.K.	£ 70.00

Photograph not available at press time

Mouse Crouching

Model No.:	1164B
Height:	Unknown
Glaze:	Flambé
Issued:	c.1912
Varieties:	HN 1090B on Fluted Ashtray
	HN 1090A on Plain Ashtray
U.S.	
Can.	Rare
U.K.	

Photograph not available at press time

Mouse with a Nut

Model No.:	1164A
Designer:	Unknown
Height:	2 ¼", 5.7 cm
Glaze:	Flambé
Issued:	c.1912
U.S.	
Can.	Rare
U.K.	

Owl
Style Two
Model No.: 2249
Designer: A. Maslankowski
Height: 12", 30.5 cm
Glaze: Flambé
Issued: 1973-1996
U.S. $625.00
Can. $750.00
U.K. £350.00

Panther
Model No.: 111
Designer: Charles Noke
Size: 8 ½" x 9",
21.6 x 22.9 cm
Glaze: Flambé
Issued: c.1912
U.S.
Can. Very Rare
U.K.

Note: Model No.: 111 was
also used to produce
the Tiger Crouching
HN 225.

Parrot on Pillar
Model No.: 45
Height: 6 ½", 16.5 cm
Glaze: Flambé
Issued: c.1913-1936
U.S.
Can. Rare
U.K.

Peruvian Penguin on Rock -
small
Model No.: 1287
Height: 5", 12.7 cm
Size: Small
Glaze: Flambé
Issued: c.1925-1961
U.S. $1,000.00
Can. $1,200.00
U.K. £ 550.00

Pig
Seated
Model No.: Unknown
Height: 4 ¼", 10.8 cm
Glaze: Flambé
Issued: Unknown
U.S.
Can. Rare
U.K.

Pig
Standing
Model No.: 114
Size: 1 ¼" x 3 ¼",
3.1 x 8.3 cm
Glaze: Flambé
Issued: c.1912
U.S.
Can. Rare
U.K.

Pig Bowl
Style Two
Model No.: Unknown
Size: 1 ¾" x 3 ½",
4.4 x 8.9 cm
Glaze: Pink with Sterling
silver rim
Issued: c.1922
U.S. Only
Can. Two
U.K. Known

Pigs
Snoozing - Both Pigs With
Ears Down
Model No.: 62
Designer: Charles Noke
Size: 1 ¾" x 3 ¾",
4.4 x 9.5 cm
Glaze: Blue, black or
orange
Issued: 1912-1936
U.S.
Can. Rare
U.K.

**Pigs, Snoozing
One Pig With Ears Down, One
With Ears Up**
Model No.: 62
Size: 1 ¾" x 3 ¼",
4.4 x 8.3 cm
Glaze: Flambé
Issued: Unknown
U.S. $1,250.00
Can. $1,500.00
U.K. £ 600.00

Pigs at a Trough
Model No.: 81
Size: 2 ½" x 4",
6.4 x 10.1 cm
Glaze: Flambé
Issued: c.1931-1936
U.S. $2,500.00
Can. $3,000.00
U.K. £1,350.00

**Polar Bear and Cub on base -
small**
Model No.: 617
Designer: Charles Noke
Size: 8" x 10",
20.3 x 25.4 cm
Size: Small
Glaze: 1. Chang
2. Sung
Issued: c.1929
U.S.
Can. Extremely Rare
U.K.

Polar Bear on Dish
Model No.: 40
Height: 5", 12.7 cm
Glaze: Flambé
Issued: c.1912-1936
U.S. $1,500.00
Can. $1,800.00
U.K. £ 825.00

Polar Bears on Ice Floe
Model No.: 54
Height: 3 ½", 8.9 cm
Glaze: Flambé
Issued: c.1912-1936
U.S.
Can. Rare
U.K.

Quinghai Fu Dogs (Pair)
Model Nos.: BA 34, 35
Designer: A. Maslankowski
Height: 7 ¼", 18.4 cm
Glaze: Flambé
Issued: 2002 in a limited
edition of 250
Series: Lambethwares
U.S. $1,345.00
Can. $2,200.00
U.K. £ 750.00

**Rabbit
Crouching - Style One**
Model No.: 1165A
Height: 3 ½", 8.9 cm
Glaze: Flambé
Issued: c.1912-by 1946
U.S.
Can. Rare
U.K.

Photograph not
available
at press time

**Rabbit
Crouching - Style Two**
Model No.: 1165B
Height: 4", 10.1 cm
Glaze: Sung
Issued: c.1912-by 1946
U.S.
Can. Rare
U.K.

Rhinoceros
Lying
Model No.: 615
Designer: Leslie Harradine
Length: 9 ½", 24.1 cm
Glaze: Flambé
Issued: c.1973-1996
U.S. $1,100.00
Can. $1,300.00
U.K. £ 600.00

Shanxi Elephant
Model No.: BA42
Designer: A. Maslankowski
Height: 11 ½", 29.2 cm
Colour: Flambé
Issued: 2004 in a limited
        edition of 250
Series: Burslem Artwares
U.S. $1,955.00
Can. N/I
U.K. £1195.00

Shenlong Dragon
Model No.: BA 32
Designer: A. Maslankowski
Height: 14 ¾", 37.5 cm
Glaze: Flambé
Issued: 2002 in a limited
        edition of 250
Series: Burslem Artwares
U.S. $1,785.00
Can. $2,600.00
U.K. £1,000.00

Suzhou Monkey
Model No.: BA40
Designer: Martyn Alcock
Height: 8 ¾", 22.2 cm
Colour: Flambé
Issued: 2004 in a limited
        edition of 250
Series: 1. Burslem
           Artwares
        2. Chinese Zodiac
U.S. $875.00
Can. N/I
U.K. £520.00

Táng Horse
Model No.: BA 25
Designer: A. Maslankowski
Height: 10 ¼", 25.2 cm
Glaze: Sung
Issued: 2001 in a limited
        edition of 250
Series: 1 Burslem Artware
        2. Chinese Zodic
U.S. $2,000.00
Can. $2,500.00
U.K. £1,100.00

Note: Issued to celebrate
the Chinese Year of
the Horse, 2002.

Tiger on a Rock
Style Four
Designer: Fred Moore after
          Charles Noke
Length: 15 ¾", 40.0 cm
Size: Large
Glaze: Sung
Issued: c.1940s
U.S.
Can. Extremely Rare
U.K.

Tortoise - small
Model No.: 101A
Size: 1" x 3",
      2.5 x 7.6 cm
Size: Small
Glaze: See below
Issued: c.1912-by 1946

	Flambé	Sung
U.S.	$ 900.	1,250.
Can.	$1,100.	1,500.
U.K.	£ 500.	700.

Water Buffalo
Model No.: BA59
Designer: Martyn Alcock
Height: 7", 17.8 cm
Colour: Flambé
Issued: 2004 in a limited
        edition of 150
Series: Burslem Artwares
U.S. N/I
Can. $2,000.00
U.K. N/A

FROGS AND MOUSE CHESS SET

First modelled as a 'Mice' chess set in 1885 by George Tinworth a 'Frog and Mice' chess set, was issued in 2004 in a limited edition of 50, issue price £3,500.00

Designer: Unknown
Colour: Flambé
Issued: 2004 in a limited edition of 50

	Frog Rook	Frog Bishop	Frog Queen	Frog King	Frog Knight	Frog Pawn
Model No.:	BA 51	BA 49	BA 48	BA 47	BA 50	BA 52
Height:	3", 7.6 cm	3", 7.6 cm	3¾", 9.5 cm	3", 7.6 cm	3", 7.6 cm	2 ½", 6.4 cm

	Mouse Rook	Mouse Bishop	Mouse Queen	Mouse King	Mouse Knight	Mouse Pawn
Model No.:	BA 57	BA 55	BA 54	BA 53	BA 56	BA 58
Height:	3", 7.6 cm	3", 7.6 cm	4", 10.1 cm	4 ¼", 10.8 cm	3", 7.6 cm	2 ½", 6.4 cm

BOOKENDS
BROOCHES
WALL MOUNTS

CHAMPIONSHIP DOG BOOKENDS

The following medium size dog models were available by order as bookends. They were mounted on mahogany and sold by order for 21/10d to 22/- a pair. The bookends utilized the medium size (M/S) dogs in all known cases. The listing below is in alphabetical order cross-referenced with HN numbers for the medium size dogs in question.

Style	HN No.	Colour	Size	U.S. $	Price Can. $	U.K.
Bulldog	HN 1043	Dark brown and white	Medium	1,275.00	1,500.00	700.00
Cairn	HN 1034	Black and grey	Medium	750.00	900.00	425.00
Cocker Spaniel	HN 1109	Black and white	Medium	350.00	450.00	200.00
Cocker Spaniel with Pheasant	HN 1028	White and brown dog reddish brown pheasant	Medium	400.00	475.00	225.00
English Setter	HN 2621	Liver and white	Medium	4,000.00	5,000.00	2,250.00
Irish Setter	HN 1055	Reddish brown and black	Medium	400.00	500.00	225.00
Pekinese	HN 1012	Brown and black	Medium	300.00	360.00	170.00
Rough-haired Terrier	HN 1013	White, black and brown	Medium	700.00	850.00	400.00
Scottish Terrier	HN 1015	Black	Medium	700.00	850.00	400.00
Sealyham	HN 1031	White and brown	Medium	550.00	650.00	300.00

BROOCHES

Produced during the 1930s these china items had pin backs for use as jewellery brooches.

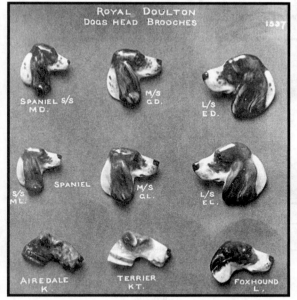

Dogs Head Brooches

Kingfisher Brooch

Butterfly Brooch

Style	Type	Colour	Size	Price U.S. $	Can. $	U.K. £
Dogs	Airedale	Dark brown and black	1"	850.00	1,000.00	475.00
	Cairn	Black and grey	1 ½"	850.00	1,000.00	475.00
	Chow	Golden brown	1"	850.00	1,000.00	475.00
	Cocker Spaniel	Liver and white	1"	750.00	900.00	425.00
			1 ½"	750.00	900.00	425.00
			2"	750.00	900.00	425.00
	Cocker Spaniel	Black and White	1"	750.00	900.00	425.00
			1 ½"	750.00	900.00	425.00
			2"	750.00	900.00	425.00
	Fox Terrier	White and dark brown	1"	850.00	1,000.00	475.00
	Foxhound	Brown and white	1"	850.00	1,000.00	475.00
	Greyhound	Dark brown and white	1 ¼"	1,200.00	1,450.00	675.00
	Pekinese	Brown and black	1"	1,000.00	1,200.00	550.00
	Pomeranian	Golden brown	1"	1,500.00	1,800.00	850.00
	Sealyham	White and brown	1 ½"	900.00	1,100.00	500.00
	Terrier	White and dark brown	1"	900.00	1,100.00	500.00
Misc.	Butterfly	Pink	N/A	1,000.00	1,200.00	550.00
		Peach	N/A	1,000.00	1,200.00	550.00
		Yellow/brown/blue	N/A	1,000.00	1,200.00	550.00
	Fox	Brown	N/A	1,000.00	1,200.00	550.00
	Kingfisher	Blue	1 ¼"	1,000.00	1,200.00	550.00
	Persian Cat	Cream with green eyes	1 ½"	1,200.00	1,450.00	650.00

* **N/A** - Not Available

WALL MOUNTS

In the 1930s Doulton produced a series of dogs' heads, plain and mounted on oval wooden panels as wall hangings. Similar heads were also mounted for bookends. Ten different models have been recorded, one in two colourways. The heads are numbered SK-21, to SK-31 but (possibly due to size) they show only the "K" and not "SK" resulting in possible confusion with the "K" series. Not all pieces have the Royal Doulton backstamp.

The original issue prices of the models were: Without plinths 5/-; With plinths 6/-; On bookends 8/- each. Prices are shown for a single bookend.

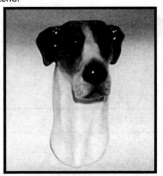

SK 25 Foxhound Plain	SK 31 Pekinese Mounted	804 Fox Mounted

Number	Style	Type	Colour	Size	U.S.$	Price Can. $	U.K. £
SK 21	English Setter	Plain	Black	3 ½"	850.00	1,000.00	475.00
		Mounted	and	8.9 cm	850.00	1,000.00	475.00
		Bookend	white		850.00	1,000.00	475.00
SK 22	Irish Setter	Plain	Reddish	3 ½"	850.00	1,000.00	475.00
		Mounted	brown and	8.9 cm	850.00	1,000.00	475.00
		Bookend	black		850.00	1,000.00	475.00
SK 23	Cocker Spaniel	Plain	Liver	4"	850.00	1,000.00	475.00
		Mounted	and	10.1 cm	850.00	1,000.00	475.00
		Bookend	white		850.00	1,000.00	475.00
SK 24	Cocker Spaniel	Plain	Black	4"	850.00	1,000.00	475.00
		Mounted		10.1 cm	850.00	1,000.00	475.00
		Bookend			850.00	1,000.00	475.00
SK 25	Foxhound	Plain	Brown	3"	850.00	1,000.00	475.00
		Mounted	and	7.6 cm	850.00	1,000.00	475.00
		Bookend	white		850.00	1,000.00	475.00
SK 26	Smooth Haired	Plain	White and	3"	1,000.00	1,200.00	550.00
	Fox Terrier	Mounted	dark	7.6 cm	1,000.00	1,200.00	550.00
		Bookend	brown		1,000.00	1,200.00	550.00
SK 27	Sealyham	Plain	White	3 ½"	900.00	1,100.00	500.00
		Mounted	and	8.9 cm	900.00	1,100.00	500.00
		Bookend	brown		900.00	1,100.00	500.00
SK 28	Airedale	Plain	Brown	3 ½"	1,000.00	1,200.00	550.00
		Mounted	and	8.9 cm	1,000.00	1,200.00	550.00
		Bookend	black		1,000.00	1,200.00	550.00
SK 29	Scottish Terrier	Plain	Black	3"	1,000.00	1,200.00	550.00
		Mounted		7.6 cm	1,000.00	1,200.00	550.00
		Bookend			1,000.00	1,200.00	550.00
SK 30	Cairn	Plain	Black	3 ½"	1,000.00	1,200.00	550.00
		Mounted	and	8.9 cm	1,000.00	1,200.00	550.00
		Bookend	grey		1,000.00	1,200.00	550.00
SK 31	Pekinese	Plain	Brown	4 ¾"	1,000.00	1,200.00	550.00
		Mounted	and	12.1 cm	1,000.00	1,200.00	550.00
		Bookend	black		1,000.00	1,200.00	550.00
804	Fox	Mounted	Reddish	3 ½"	1,000.00	1,200.00	550.00
			brown and	8.9 cm			
			white				

ADVERTISING ANIMALS

ERVAN LUCAS BOLS DISTILLERS
Bulldog

Type:	Liquor Container
Height:	6", 15.2 cm
Colour:	White with Union Jack - gloss
Issued:	1932
U.S.	$1,500.00
Can.	$1,800.00
U.K.	£ 850.00

ERVAN LUCAS BOLS DISTILLERS
Pekinese

Type:	Liquor Container
Height:	6", 15.2 cm
Colour:	Brown - gloss
Issued:	1940
U.S.	$2,250.00
Can.	$2,750.00
U.K.	£1,250.00

ERVAN LUCAS BOLS DISTILLERS
Salmon

Type:	Liquor Container
Height:	9 ½", 24.0 cm
Colour:	Silver-grey - gloss
Issued:	1940
U.S.	$550.00
Can.	$650.00
U.K.	£300.00

FINANCIAL TIMES
Partridge

Type:	Paperweight
Height:	2 ½", 6.4 cm
Colour:	Cream and brown - gloss
Issued:	1988 in a limited edition of 1,200
U.S.	$300.00
Can.	$350.00
U.K.	£165.00

GIROLAMA LUXARDO DISTILLERS
Bulldog

Type:	Liquor Container
Height:	11", 27.9 cm
Colour:	White - gloss
Issued:	1932
U.S.	$3,000.00
Can.	$3,600.00
U.K.	£1,600.00

Photograph not
available
at press time

GIROLAMA LUXARDO DISTILLERS
Bulldog

Type:	Anniversary
Height:	10 ½", 26.7 cm
Colour:	White - gloss
Issued:	1932
U.S.	$3,000.00
Can.	$3,600.00
U.K.	£1,600.00

Photograph not
available
at press time

GIROLAMA LUXARDO DISTILLERS
Polar Bear

Type:	Liquor Container
Height:	Unknown
Colour:	White - gloss
Issued:	1932
U.S.	$2,000.00
Can.	$2,500.00
U.K.	£1,100.00

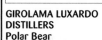

LOUIS WEARDEN & GUYLEE LTD.
Bulldog

Type:	Advertising
Height:	3", 7.6 cm
Colour:	White bulldog with Union Jack - gloss
Issued:	1932
U.S.	$1,350.00
Can.	$1,600.00
U.K.	£ 750.00

MATHEW GLOAG
Grouse

Type:	Flask
Designer:	David Lyttleton
Height:	9 ½", 24.0 cm
Colour:	Brown and red - matt
Issued:	1984-1987
U.S.	$150.00
Can.	$175.00
U.K.	£ 75.00

Note: Transferred from Beswick model no. 2798.

NATIONAL DISTILLERS CORP.
Old Crow

Type:	Liquor Container
Height:	12 ¾", 32.0 cm
Colour:	Black and white - gloss
Issued:	1954
U.S.	$225.00
Can.	$275.00
U.K.	£125.00

NATURAL BRANDY OF SOUTH AFRICA
Fish Eagle

Type:	Flask
Designer:	John G. Tongue
Height:	10 ½", 26.7 cm
Colour:	White, dark to light brown - gloss
Issued:	1984
U.S.	$175.00
Can.	$200.00
U.K.	£100.00

Note: Modification of Beswick model no. 2678, Fish Eagle facing front.

PENGUIN BOOKS
Penguin

Type:	Advertising
Height:	4 ½", 11.4 cm
Colour:	Black and white - gloss
Issued:	1987
U.S.	$75.00
Can.	$90.00
U.K.	£40.00

ROBERT PORTER & CO. LTD.
Bulldog

Type:	Advertising
Height:	6", 15.2 cm
Colour:	White, blue and brown - gloss
Issued:	1915
U.S.	$1,500.00
Can.	$1,800.00
U.K.	£ 850.00

ROYAL DOULTON ANGLING CLUB
Salmon

Type:	Presentation
Height:	9 ½", 24.0 cm
Colour:	Pale green and blue - gloss
Issued:	1985
U.S.	$450.00
Can.	$550.00
U.K.	£250.00

STAUFFER & SON CO.
Begging Dog

Type:	Advertising
Height:	8", 20.3 cm
Colour:	1. Black and white - gloss
	2. Tan and brown - gloss
Issued:	1929
U.S.	$ 900.00
Can.	$1,100.00
U.K.	£ 500.00

WHYTE & MACKAY DISTILLERS
Badger

Type:	Flask
Designer:	David Lyttleton
Height:	3", 7.6 cm
Colour:	Black and white - gloss
Issued:	1987-1991
U.S.	$30.00
Can.	$35.00
U.K.	£15.00

Note: Transferred from Beswick model no. 2687.

WHYTE & MACKAY DISTILLERS
Barn Owl

Type:	Flask
Designer:	Graham Tongue
Height:	6 ¾", 17.2 cm
Colour:	Tan-brown and white - gloss
Issued:	1987-2004
U.S.	$225.00
Can.	$275.00
U.K.	£125.00

Note: Transferred from Beswick model no. 2809.

WHYTE & MACKAY DISTILLERS
Buzzard

Type:	Flask
Designer:	Graham Tongue
Height:	6 ½", 16.5 cm
Colour:	Dark brown and grey - gloss
Issued:	1987-2004
U.S.	$135.00
Can.	$165.00
U.K.	£ 75.00

Note: Transferred from Beswick model no. 2640.

WHYTE & MACKAY DISTILLERS
Eagle

Type:	Flask
Designer:	Graham Tongue
Height:	4", 10.1 cm
Colour:	Brown - gloss
Issued:	1987-2004
U.S.	$30.00
Can.	$35.00
U.K.	£15.00

Note: Transferred from Beswick model no. 2104.

WHYTE & MACKAY DISTILLERS
Golden Eagle

Type:	Flask
Designer:	Graham Tongue
Height:	10 ½", 26.7 cm
Colour:	Light and dark brown - gloss
Issued:	1987-2004
U.S.	$135.00
Can.	$165.00
U.K.	£ 75.00

Note: Transferred from Beswick model no. 2678.

WHYTE & MACKAY DISTILLERS
Haggis

Type:	Flask
Designer:	J. Haywood
Remodelled:	Albert Hallam
Height:	2 ½", 6.4 cm
Colour:	Brown - gloss
Issued:	1987-1991
U.S.	$30.00
Can.	$35.00
U.K.	£15.00

Note: Transferred from beswick model no. 2350.

WHYTE & MACKAY DISTILLERS
Kestrel

Type:	Flask
Designer:	Graham Tongue
Height:	6 ½", 16.5 cm
Colour:	Dark grey and white - gloss
Issued:	1987-2004
U.S.	$100.00
Can.	$125.00
U.K.	£ 60.00

Note: Transferred from Beswick model no. 2639.

WHYTE & MACKAY DISTILLERS
Merlin

Type:	Flask
Designer:	Graham Tongue
Height:	6 ½", 16.5 cm
Colour:	Dark grey and white - gloss
Issued:	1987-2004
U.S.	$100.00
Can.	$125.00
U.K.	£ 60.00

Note: Transferred from Beswick model no. 2641.

WHYTE & MACKAY DISTILLERS
Nessie Flask

Type:	Flask
Designer:	Albert Hallam
Height:	3", 7.6 cm
Colour:	Grey-green - gloss
Issued:	1987-2004
U.S.	$30.00
Can.	$35.00
U.K.	£15.00

Note: Transferred from Beswick model no. 2051.

WHYTE & MACKAY DISTILLERS
Osprey

Type: Flask
Designer: David Lyttleton
Height: 7 ¾", 19.7 cm
Colour: Browns and white - gloss
Issued: 1987-2004
U.S. $125.00
Can. $150.00
U.K. £ 70.00

Note: Transferred from Beswick model no. 2583.

WHYTE & MACKAY DISTILLERS
Otter

Type: Flask
Designer: David Lyttleton
Height: 2 ¼", 5.7 cm
Colour: Grey and brown - gloss
Issued: 1987-1991
U.S. $30.00
Can. $35.00
U.K. £15.00

Note: Transferred from Beswick model no. 2686.

WHYTE & MACKAY DISTILLERS
Peregrine Falcon

Type: Flask
Designer: Graham Tongue
Height: 6 ½", 16.5 cm
Colour: Grey - gloss
Issued: 1979
U.S. $125.00
Can. $150.00
U.K. £ 70.00

Note: Transferred from Beswick model no. 2642.

WHYTE & MACKAY DISTILLERS
Seal

Type: Flask
Designer: Graham Tongue
Height: 3 ½", 8.9 cm
Colour: Grey - gloss
Issued: 1987-1991
U.S. $30.00
Can. $35.00
U.K. £15.00

Note: Transferred from Beswick model no. 2693.

WHYTE & MACKAY DISTILLERS
Short Eared Owl

Type: Flask
Designer: Graham Tongue
Height: 6 ¾", 17.2 cm
Colour: Dark and light brown - gloss
Issued: 1987-2004
U.S. $125.00
Can. $150.00
U.K. £ 70.00

Note: Transferred from Beswick model no. 2825.

WHYTE & MACKAY DISTILLERS
Snowy Owl

Type: Flask
Designer: Graham Tongue
Height: 6 ½", 16.5 cm
Colour: White - gloss
Issued: 1987
U.S. $135.00
Can. $160.00
U.K. £ 75.00

Note: Transferred from Beswick model no. 2826.

WHYTE & MACKAY DISTILLERS
Squirrel

Type: Flask
Designer: David Lyttleton
Height: 3 ½", 8.9 cm
Colour: Red-brown - gloss
Issued: 1987-1991
U.S. $30.00
Can. $35.00
U.K. £15.00

Note: Transferred from Beswick model no. 2636.

WHYTE & MACKAY DISTILLERS
Tawny Owl

Type: Flask
Designer: Graham Tongue
Height: 6 ¼", 15.9 cm
Colour: Brown - gloss
Issued: 1987-2004
U.S. $125.00
Can. $150.00
U.K. £ 70.00

Note: Transferred from Beswick model no. 2781.

Bluebird with Lupins, Style Two (HN 2543)

INDICES

ALPHABETICAL INDEX TO HN, K, D, DA AND RDA SERIES

ALPHABETICAL INDEX TO
STONEWARE SECTION

ALPHABETICAL INDEX TO
ROYAL ADDERLEY BIRD STUDIES

INDEX OF MODEL NUMBERS

MODEL NUMBERS PRE 1910

MODEL NUMBERS POST 1910

Pegasus (HN 3547)

INDEX OF BESWICK MODEL NUMBERS

The following Beswick Model Numbers were converted to DA (Doulton Animal) numbers and issued by Royal Doulton.

INDEX OF UNACCOUNTED MODEL NUMBERS

This index lists animal figure subjects by those model numbers assigned by Royal Doulton in their pattern books but subsequently were either not issued or issued but unrecorded.

Some of these model numbers may well exist as HN numbers but have not as yet been identified or cross-referenced with the HN system.

COLLECTING BY SERIES

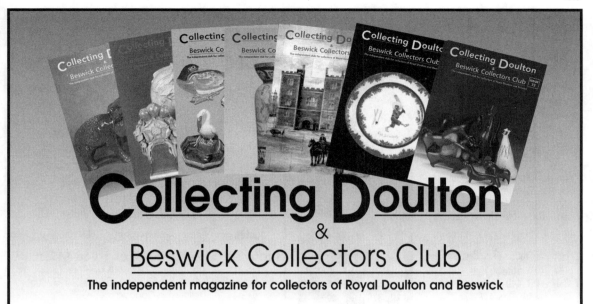

Collecting Doulton

&
Beswick Collectors Club

The independent magazine for collectors of Royal Doulton and Beswick

If you are a collector of Doulton or Beswick you cannot afford to be without this lively, authoritative and completely independent publication.

If you are a previous subscriber to Collecting Doulton, you may not know how much the magazine has improved over the past few months.

Published six times a year, Collecting Doulton contains articles by leading experts on the wide range of Doulton and Beswick ceramics, including:

- Latest auction results
- Your questions answered
- Collectors' profiles
- Free wants and for sale small ads

- Histories of artists, designers and wares
- Events diary
- News from around the world
- Book reviews

Amongst the subjects regularly covered are Lambeth wares, seriesware, figurines, character jugs, Bunnykins, Burslem wares, Doulton and Beswick animals, commemorative wares, advertising wares, new discoveries, rarities, Beatrix Potter etc etc... *Subscribe today*

Website: www.collectingdoulton.com • Email: barryjhill@hotmail.com

Please photocopy and mail

I wish to subscribe to Collecting Doulton magazine.
I enclose my cheque made out to Collecting Doulton Marketing for £21(UK) or £36 (overseas) for six issues.
Please start my subscription from issue No............/the current issue.
Mr/Mrs/Miss/Ms/Dr   First Name...
Surname ....
Address ....
....Town ....
Country ....Postcode ....
email ....
Please send to: Collecting Doulton Marketing, PO Box 310, Richmond, Surrey TW10 7FU England

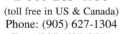

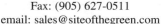

Royal Doulton Stores

DOULTON AND COMPANY STORES - UK

Doulton and Company is the new name for Royal Doulton on high street, offering the very best of our three brands plus selected collectables and giftware and homewares from a range of specialist brands.

Doulton and Company Dudley
Unit 52, Merry Hill,
Brierley Hill, Dudley
West Midlands
DY5 1SR

**Doulton and Company Outlet
Superstore Etruria**
Forge Lane, Etrura, Stoke-on-Trent
Staffordshire
ST1 5NN

Doulton and Company Hanley
The Potteries Centre
Hanley, Stoke-on-Trent
Staffordshire
ST1 1PS

Doulton and Company Hereford
19-21 Maylords Street,
Maylord Shopping Centre
Hereford, Herefordshire
HR1 2DS

Doulton and Company HOME
Central 12 Shopping Park
Southport
PR9 0TQ

Doulton and Company Swindon
McArthur Glen Designer Outlet
Great Western, Kemble Drive
Swindon, Wilts
SN2 2DY

LAWLEYS/CHINACAVES - UK

Lawleys Blackpool
Unit 37, Houndshill Shopping Centre,
Fylde, Blackpool
Lancashire
FY1 4HU

Lawleys Carlisle
63 Castle Street
Carlisle, Cumbria
CA3 8SL

Lawleys Chelmsford
42 High Chelmer
Chelmsford, Essex
CM1 1XU

**Lawleys Derby
Edwards**
71 St. Peters Street
Derby, Derbyshire
DE1 2AB

Lawleys Peterborough
7 Bridge Street
Peterborough, Cambridgeshire
PE1 1HJ

Lawleys Reading
21 Queen Victoria Street
Reading, Berkshire
RG1 1SY

Lawleys Torquay
38 Fleet Street
Torquay, Devon
TQ2 5DJ

Chinacave Llandudno
94 Mostyn Street
Llandudno, Gwynedd
LL30 2SB

Chinacave Macclesfield
Unit 1, 25 Castle Street Mall
Macclesfield, Cheshire
SK11 6AF

FACTORY SHOPS AND OUTLETS - UK

Factory Shop Burslem
Nile Street, Burslem
Stoke-on-Trent, Staffordshire
ST6 2AJ

Factory Shop Fenton
Disribution Centre, Victoria Road
Fenton, Stoke-on-Trent
Staffordshire, ST4 2PJ

Factory Shop Regent
Regent Works, Lawley Street
Longton, Stoke-on-Trent
Staffordshire, ST3 1LZ

Factory Shop Stourbridge
Crystal Glass Centre, Churton House
Audnam, Stourbridge
West Midlands, DY8 4AJ

Factory Outlet Bridgend
Unit 66, Welsh Designer Outlet
Village, Bridgend, Shropshire
CF32 9SU

*FOR YOUR NEAREST ROYAL
DOULTON DEPARTMENT, PLEASE
CALL ROYAL DOULTON CONSUMER
ENQUIRIES ON 01782 404041*

Factory Outlet Colne
Boundary Mill Stores, Burnley Road
Colne, Lancashire
BB8 8LS

Factory Outlet Dover
De Bradelei Wharf
Cambridge Road
Dover, Kent, CT17 9BY

**Factory Outlet
Ellesmere Port**
Unit 106, Cheshire Oaks
Kinsey Road, Ellesmere Port
Cheshire, L65 9LA

Visit our website at:

ROYAL DOULTON www.royaldoulton.com

Royal Doulton Stores

ROYAL DOULTON STORES – CANADA

Calgary
Market Mall
C2 - 3625 Shaganappi Trail
NW, Calgary, AB T3A 0E2

Cookstown
Cookstown Manufacturers
Outlet, RR1, Cookstown,
ON L0L 1L0

Dartmouth
Micmac Mall, 21 Micmac
Dartmouth, NS B3A 4K7

Edmonton
West Edmonton Mall
8882 - 170th Street
Edmonton, AB T5T 3J7

Fredericton
Regent Mall
1381 Regent Street,
Fredericton, NB
E3C 1A2

London
White Oaks Mall
1105 Wellington Road
London, ON
N6E 1V4

Markham
Markville Shopping Centre
5000 Highway #7
Markham, ON
L3R 4M9

Pickering
Pickering Town Centre
1355 Kingston Road
Pickering, ON
L1V 1B8

Surrey
Guildford Town Centre
Surrey, BC
V3R 7C1

Toronto
Fairview Mall
1800 Sheppard Avenue East
Willowdale, ON
M2J 5A7

Vaughan
Vaughan Mills
Royal Doulton Home
1 Bass Pro Mills Drive
Vaughan, On
L4K 5W4

Waterloo
St. Jacobs Factory Outlet
Mall, 25 Benjamin Road
Waterloo, ON N2V 2G8

Winnipeg
Polo Park Shopping Centre
1485 Portage Ave.
Winnipeg, MA
R3G 0W4

ROYAL DOULTON STORES – UNITED STATES

**Belz Factory Outlet World
(Mall 1)**
Orlando Shopping Center|
Space #47-A
5401 West Oak Ridge Road
Orlando, Florida 32819

Burlington
Prime Outlets – Burlington
288 Fashion Way, Store #5
Burlington, WA 98233

Calhoun
Prime Outlets - Colhoun
455 Belwood Rd., Suite 20
Calhoun, GA 30701

Camarillo
Camarillo Premium Outlets
740 Ventura Blvd,   Suite
530
Camarillo, CA 93010

Central Valley
Woodbury Common
Premium Outlets
161 Marigold Court
Central Valley, NY 10917

Ellenton
Gulf Coast Factory Store
5501 Factory Shops Blvd.
Ellenton, Fl 34222

Estero
Miromar Outlets
10801 Corkscrew Rd.
Suite 366, Estero, Fl 33928

Flemington
Liberty Village
Premium Outlets
34 Liberty Village
Flemington, NJ08822

Gilroy
Premium Outlets – Gilroy
681 Leavesley Road
Suite C290
Gilroy, CA 95020

Jeffersonville
Ohio Factory Shops
8150 Factory Shops Blvd.
Jeffersonville, OH 43128

Kittery
Kittery Outlet Center
Route 1
Kittery, ME 03904-2505

Las Vegas
Belz Factory Outlet World
7400 Las Vegas Blvd.
South Suite 244
Las Vegas, NV 89123

Pigeon Forge
Belz Factory Outlet
2655 Teaster Lane
Suite 26
Pigeon Forge TN 37683

Prince William
Potomac Mills
2700 Potomac Mills Circle
Suite 976
Prince William, VA 22192

San Marcos
Tanger Factory Outlet Centre
4015 Interstate 35 South
Suite 402
San Marcos, TX 78666

St. Augustine
Belz Factory Outlet World
500 Belz Outlet Blvd
Suite 80
St. Augustine, Fl 32084

Vacaville
Factory Stores at Vacaville
336 Nut Tree Rd.
Vacaville CA 95687

Visit our website at:
www.royaldoulton.com

ROYAL DOULTON